Workers in Hard Times

**THE WORKING CLASS
IN AMERICAN HISTORY**

Editorial Advisors
James R. Barrett
Julie Greene
William P. Jones
Alice Kessler-Harris
Nelson Lichtenstein

*A list of books in the series appears
at the end of this book.*

Workers in Hard Times

A Long View of Economic Crises

Edited by
Leon Fink,
Joseph A. McCartin,
and Joan Sangster

UNIVERSITY OF ILLINOIS PRESS
Urbana, Chicago, and Springfield

"Transformative Power: Lessons from the Greek Crisis and Beyond"
by Hilary Wainwright was previously published in *Socialist Register
2013* and has been reprinted with permission of the Merlin Press Ltd.
© Merlin Press Ltd. www.merlinpress.co.uk.

First Illinois paperback, 2020
© 2014 by the Board of Trustees
of the University of Illinois
All rights reserved
1 2 3 4 5 C P 5 4 3 2 1
∞ This book is printed on acid-free paper.

The Library of Congress cataloged the cloth edition as follows:
Workers in hard times : a long view of economic crises /
edited by Leon Fink, Joseph A. McCartin, and Joan Sangster.
pages cm. — (The working class in American history)
Includes bibliographical references and index.
ISBN 978-0-252-03817-4 (cloth : alk. paper)
ISBN 978-0-252-09597-9 (ebook)
1. Working class—Case studies.
2. Business cycles—Case studies.
3. Economic policy—Case studies.
I. Fink, Leon, 1948– II. McCartin, Joseph Anthony.
III. Sangster, Joan, 1952–
HD4854.W597   2014
331.09—dc23   2013034370

Paperback ISBN 978-0-252-08512-3

We dedicate this book
to the memory
of David Montgomery:
scholar, teacher, friend.

Contents

Introduction 1

Part I. Depressions and Working-Class Lives

1. Marching under Flags Black and Red:
   Toronto's Dispossessed in the Age of Industry 19
   Gaetan Heroux and Bryan D. Palmer

2. Working People's Responses to Past Depressions 45
   David Montgomery

3. Soviet Workers and Stalinist Terror:
   The Crisis of Industrialization 60
   Wendy Goldman

Part II. Economic Dislocation as Political Crisis

4. The Labor of Capitalism: Industrial Revolution
   and the Transformation of the Global
   Cotton-Growing Countryside 83
   Sven Beckert

5. The Ordeal of Eugene Debs: The Panic of 1893,
   the Pullman Strike, and the Origins
   of the Progressive Movement 99
   Scott Reynolds Nelson

Part III. Social-Welfare Struggles from the Liberal to the Neoliberal State

6. Workers' Social-Wage Struggles during the Great Depression and the Era of Neoliberalism: International Comparisons   113
    Alvin Finkel

7. Politics and Policies in the 1970s and Early Twenty-first Century: The Linked Recessions   141
    Judith Stein

8. Neoliberalism at Work in the Antipodean Welfare State in the Late Twentieth Century: Collusion, Collaboration, and Resistance   161
    Melanie Nolan

Part IV. Workers and the Shakeup of the New World Order

9. Want amidst Plenty: The Oil Boom and the Working Class in Newfoundland and Labrador, 1992–2010   187
    Sean Cadigan

10. Whose Hard Times? Explaining Autoworkers Strike Waves in Recent-Day China   213
    Lu Zhang

11. Transformative Power: Lessons from the Greek Crisis and Beyond   243
    Hilary Wainwright

12. How Workers and the Government Have Dealt with Economic Crisis and Industrial Decline: 1929 and 2007   263
    Edward Montgomery

Contributors   289

Index   293

Workers in Hard Times

Introduction

Across the industrialized world, urgent questions have been raised and in some cases reopened by recent events. The financial crisis that rocked the global economy and led to a steep downturn in 2008 has caused mass suffering and taken a severe toll on working people and their collective organized strength. The accompanying loss of popular confidence in governments and financial institutions has triggered protest movements against austerity measures in Greece and Spain, and against the depredations of the "one percent"—as identified by the Occupy Wall Street movement—in the United States.

As the world economy struggles to cope with the last effects of the Great Recession amid growing inequality and stagnating incomes for the many, the impact of the economic crisis on workers has moved steadily toward the center of public and scholarly discourse. This volume puts the present economic crisis and its impact on workers in historical perspective, situating recent developments in the context of previous economic crises that have marked the industrial era. For, while much as been written about the origins and impact of the present crisis, most of it treats that crisis in historical isolation, and most of it treats workers as mere casualties or as an afterthought, if at all.

The volume is premised on the notion that the historical contextualization of the present economic crisis demands an approach that is both transnational and cross-disciplinary, and one that takes the experiences of working people seriously. Thus, the essays included here, which (but for one) were first presented at a conference at Georgetown University in September 2011, sponsored by the journal *Labor: Studies in Working-Class History of the Americas* and Georgetown's Kalmanovitz Initiative for Labor and the Working Poor, address the history of economic crises in North America, Europe, Asia, and Australasia, and draw on scholarship in history and political economy. These essays push us toward a rethinking of the relationship between capital and labor, the waged and unwaged, the employed and jobless. They reposition thinking about economic crises in transnational perspective and consider how states, ranging from capitalist to communist, struggled and failed to cope with past economic crises, with consequences that were often devastating for workers. Yet the essays in this volume do not cast workers and their movements as mere victims of economic calamity and restructuring. They suggest various ways in which workers' agency was expressed during periods of disempowering change, including this most recent period.

Putting the recent economic crisis in historical perspective, these essays also suggest its distinctiveness from past crises by highlighting the degree to which this crisis has emerged from a particular historical moment in the history of global capitalism, a moment shaped by the framework of neoliberalism. The contextualization helps make clear that the present economic restructuring, more than simply a deep downturn in the business cycle, might best be understood as a moment in the restructuring of a global regime of capital accumulation and labor distribution that is likely to have profound, enduring consequences for ordinary people the world over.

Toward a Long View of Economic Crises

The essays in this volume push us toward the long view. Long before debates about the necessity of state-sponsored unemployment insurance, or economists' theories of "long waves" of capitalist development, workers were well acquainted with the experience of economic crisis. Severe downturns in the economy were filtered through daily life as degraded work, less work, no work, making do through the household economy, intensified work, informal labor, bartering, forced public labor, charity, relocating, and, at the extreme end of the spectrum, illness and starvation. Across the globe, this array of responses to crisis remains central to the lives of the working class, reminding us of what Bryan Palmer and Gaetan Heroux in their contribution to this volume call the "continuum" of waged and unwaged labor that characterizes the ongoing process of capitalist proletarianization, dispossession, and exploitation.

In the industrialized nations that are the focus of this book, economic crises were apparent long before industrialization, hitting rural producers and self-employed artisans in debilitating ways. Still, the increased importance of a market economy in which wage earning was central, and the eventual (if very uneven) triumph of industrial capitalism, meant that economic crises had increasingly visible, concentrated effects on the working class, simply because more people were dependent on the wage system for survival. Indeed, before the post–World War II period, some argue, unsteady rather than steady work characterized the majority of working-class families in many countries: when an American working man reached the age of seventy in 1921, argues the American historian Alexander Keyssar in his study of unemployment, he would already have "lived through six downturns in the economy."[1]

Over time, one can point to changes in state, employers', and workers' views of economic crises, particularly how these actors thought they should be handled. In terms of one of the most visible manifestations of crisis, job loss, nineteenth-century notions of self-help, voluntarism, and the primacy of private charity gave way, by the mid-twentieth century, to more state intervention, professional and expert assessments of employment, combinations of private and public relief, unemployment-insurance plans, and internal union protections. This is not to suggest a whiggish history in which crisis is increasingly managed well. State aid for the jobless, for example, did not become an inalienable entitlement for the working class; in recent decades, hard-won economic supports have been removed, as nineteenth-century notions of voluntarism and self-help have reappeared in new, neoliberal forms. Moreover, these very broad changes were experienced differently according to race and gender, and they varied considerably across region and nation. Distinct national political cultures and path dependencies marked out diverse experiences of unemployment and welfare, as indicated in essays by Alvin Finkel and Melanie Nolan in this volume.

How working people coped with economic downturns also altered over time; their strategies for survival were framed by the economic, social, cultural, and political context in which they lived, by the categories of colonialism, race, ethnicity, gender, and occupation. In late nineteenth-century America, some laborers mobilized in unruly crowds to demand work and wages from local politicians, but in the craft American Federation of Labor unions, mass unemployment encouraged an even more exclusive and restrictive business unionism, as leaders viewed the "chronic insecurity" of the unskilled as a threat and a "blight" to be avoided in *their* union.[2] During the Great Depression, some Canadian homemakers with families accepted the inevitable fate of economic crisis and redoubled their efforts to survive by doing without, mending, moving, taking in work, and many other strategies of domestic economy. In the same country, even the same city, more politicized, left-wing women demanded an end to capitalism, marched in the streets, and called, at the very least, for food for their children and fully funded unemployment insurance provided by the state.[3]

Documenting working-class interpretations of, and responses to, economic crises, both on and off the job, has been a central part of labor history, particularly since the advent of New Left and new social-history paradigms in the 1970s, which put an emphasis on the categories of experience, working-class life and culture, and politics and resistance. From the 1970s to more recent writing, the material environment, cultural meanings, and political responses to economic crisis—ranging from joblessness to intensified work, from increases in women's reproductive labor to consolidation of union "seniority" (i.e., security for *some* in the face of crisis)—have been explored by labor historians. This work has engaged with theory and placed workers within the broader context of capitalist crises, but many labor historians nonetheless placed more accent on workers' experiences than on abstract analyses of what a crisis actually *is*, why crises emerge, and why they have been endemic to industrial, monopoly, and now neoliberal capitalism. Labor historians have also been satisfied with fairly expansive and flexible, as opposed to mathematical and economistic, definitions of crisis, since they were acquainted with the variable effects of economic downturns on different sectors of the working class.

They are not alone: recent political commentators suggest that economists' precise definition of a recession as a "decline in the rate of growth for two economic quarters," or even a depression, a much longer and deeper downturn, do not adequately reflect the actual experiences of working-class families. William Peterson argues that American families have in fact been going through a "silent depression" since 1973, if we measure their real income and labor productivity—and the former in particular shows loss of purchasing power, growing inequality, and social distress.[4] Such critics may not locate themselves in a Marxist tradition, but they are nonetheless cynical toward what they see as "globalization for the capitalist class / deepening inequality for the working class." Neither team A (Keynesians) or team B (monetarists), argues Robin Hahnel, understand that capitalism needs to be "fundamentally redirected" to represent the interests of workers.[5]

In labor history accounts, working-class experience was never fully divorced from the macroeconomic landscape; however, economists and social scientists, whether neoclassical, Marxist, Keynesian, or monetarist (or variations, hybrids, and offshoots of those), have tended to engage more deeply with the concept and causes of economic crisis, though obviously, from different perspectives. Drawing on Marx's analogy in the first volume of *Capital* to the many spheres or "floors" of capitalist society, the political economist Giovanni Arrighi, for example, invites us to move from the surface area, the "bottom floor" where labor is expended and exploited and where "all is visible," to the upper floors, the scene of the "hidden abode of production," where the "secret of profit making" is revealed, where those possessing economic power interact with those with political power. These are "complementary projects," he notes, but—to paraphrase him simplistically—it is difficult to be on two floors at once.[6] Socialists might respond that both floors need to be analyzed, since labor and capital are inseparable conceptually, and since a consciousness of one's exploited position in the bottom floor may only emerge when the extraction of surplus value at the upper floor is apprehended. However, Arrighi's proposition is an apt reflection of the way in which scholarly literature has evolved; labor historians have tended to concentrate more on the bottom floor, political economists on the top one.

"Why do economic crises emerge and how do they differ?" is a question political economists have asked since the emergence of the dismal science itself. A long line of thinkers whose writing became the foundation of mainstream economics analyzed both limited financial crises—in which financial institutions suddenly lose their assets or value—and broader economic crises leading to recessions and depressions, which may or may not, according to the theory propounded, have been stimulated initially by financial crises. These writers may see crises as a repeated theme in the historic unfolding of capitalism, but they do not tend to see them as evidence of the inherent contradictions of capitalism, as Marx and later Marxists do. Ideas about crises, however, have not remained fixed in absolute theoretical boxes. John Stuart Mill wrote about the tendency of the rate of profit to fall over time, an idea that, though significantly altered, was important to later Marxist theorizing. The Soviet economist Nikolai Kondratieff developed a theory about "long waves" of capitalist development over periods of up to fifty years, and even if this idea was Marxist in its genealogy,[7] it was taken up by other economists, though they tended to use price and money movements as economic benchmarks, while Marxists focused on production and commodities.[8] Kondratieff paid a high price for this theory, which did not appeal to Stalin; his ideas led to exile and death within the USSR.

Many mainstream economic historians have explored the underlying tendencies and also the specific empirical causes, events, and policies that have led to crises, and for some scholars, this has produced theories that postulate what the "soft spots" of instability within capitalism are and how they exhibit continuities, or change, over time. Looking at the history of manias, panics, and crises, Charles Kindleberger suggests that crises often come after innovations that cause "displacements" in the investment system, and his theory, he indicates, builds on the earlier work of the American economist Harold Minsky, whose "financial instability hypothesis" explored credit, debt, and leverage. Minsky, resurrected more recently, drew on a variety of classical and Keynesian ideas; he explored the way in which the financial system oscillates between strength and vulnerability, with stability leading to rising leverage and larger risk taking, which can then become fertile ground for instability and crisis.

Minsky also appears in Paul Krugman's recent discussion of depression and crisis.[9] Analyzing the 1997 Asian economic crisis, Krugman combines a list of factors into an understandable explanation, detailing the existing points of economic vulnerability: the "vicious circle" of loss of confidence; plunging currency and financial bank and company failures; the process of transborder contagion; and the lack of experience dealing with such a crisis.[10] But for mainstream economists like Krugman, crisis does not inherently doom capitalism: it can still be managed and reformed. Indeed, he is dismissive of anyone who still thinks socialism has any relevance today.[11]

Crisis is recognized by these writers as an often-reappearing part of capitalism, though there are significant differences and debates, even within mainstream economics, on its origins and solutions. In John Kenneth Galbraith's comparison of two crises, those triggered by the stock market "convulsions" of 1929 and 1987, he points to similar economic causes: recent tax deductions for the wealthy, changes in corporate finance, speculative market buildups, and especially "a vested interest in euphoria"[12] that all led to internal contradictions and an eventual crash, no matter what the specific precipitating factor. For an economist like Galbraith, the market was not perfect, infallible, and self-correcting, and he understood that the effects of crises were "tragic"[13] for many working people, a recognition that went along with his critique of the affluent society. His analysis of the crash and the Great Depression differs from that of the monetarist Milton Friedman, who emphasizes faulty monetary policies on the part of the Federal Reserve after the crash and bank panics as the cause of the prolonged and severe depression.

After World War II, the paradigm shift that occurred in the wake of Keynes's writing opened up new analyses, not only of the causes of crisis, but also new strategies for reigniting economies, by addressing the collapse of demand that characterized depressions. His "central dictum," echoed by Krugman, is "the boom, not the slump, is the time for austerity."[14] In the post–World War II period, those like Galbraith, who favored Keynesian and other interventionist approaches believed in either or both social investment and regulation by the state as a means of heading off and assuaging crises. While such thinking was influential in political circles for decades, the monetarist counterrevolution led, by the 1980s, to arguments that the market was self-correcting, even if setbacks and crises occurred. For those who accepted this idea, the notion that workers might be those suffering through such self-corrections was seemingly not a major concern.

The influence of monetarist discourse, given its increasing rootedness in academe and think tanks and its appeal to conservative governments and media owned largely by private enterprise, has been considerable. If wealth did not trickle down during the Reagan-Thatcher period, the ideology that capitalism was the origin of all progress, that there was "no alternative," and that state intervention would only worsen an economic crisis did. Even those expounding the need for some regulation as a means of dealing with economic crises exalt the "good" of competitive capitalism. In Robert Barbera's recent *The Cost of Capitalism*, written after the 2008 market meltdown, we do not get a critique of the costs of capitalism—inequality, exploitation, homelessness, and the despoliation of the earth—but rather a call to make capitalism live up to its "true potential." While he admits that capitalism has both "virtues and flaws," he believes that "free market risk" is one of its chief virtues. He simply sees the need to balance "free market risk" with policies that rein in its "excesses" to save "the best system" around.[15] Barbera, interestingly, also adopted Minsky's ideas about how financial crises emerge but rejected Minsky's solution to the crisis, namely "social investment" by the state. The latter, an essentially liberal idea, is now labeled by Barbera and others as "left wing," indicating the extent to which the spectrum of debate has narrowed over the past two decades as the tenets of neoliberalism became mainstream orthodoxy.[16]

In response to these developments, what might a twenty-first-century Marxian analysis of crises look like? Marx's writing offered a paradigm shift from mainstream economic versions of crisis, and his thought continues to shape current political economy, though there is no single Marxist interpretation: debates within Marxism are as wide-ranging as those between Marxists and anti-Marxists. The notion that economic crises are inherent to the capitalist mode of production, emerging from the internal contradictions in the system, though shaped also by exogenous factors, lies at the heart of most Marxist explanations. Marx's argument that the tendency of the rate of profit to fall over time is another key element, though in more orthodox interpretations, the concept is the primary driving force behind crisis,[17] while other Marxists, such as Ernest Mandel, note that Marx saw this as a "tendency" that elicited "countertendencies," and further, that this tendency takes shape in different historical ways—thus echoing Marx's own methodological emphasis on dialectical investigation in which the empirical informs the abstract, and vice versa.[18]

Inevitably, according to Marx, the drive for increased production and accumulation, and the changing ratio of constant to variable capital—the latter representing living labor power—results in pressure for more consumption and a higher rate of surplus value and exploitation, leading to contradictions that undermine the equilibrium of the system. Crises did not foretell the end of capitalism, but they did reveal its irrationalities and contradictions. Marx also allowed (however unhappily for socialists) that capitalism is very adaptable. Capital, he suggested, does not necessarily act as a monolith; even as a "reshaping" of the system after a crisis might leave some capitalists by the wayside, still others will benefit; and what may be needed to save the system as a whole may not serve the interests of some capitalists.[19] There is "no crisis so deep," suggests Alexander Callinicos in a paraphrasing of Marx, "that the capitalist class cannot recover from it, provided the working class is prepared to pay the price in unemployment, falling living standards, deteriorating working conditions"—words that have resonance in our own time.[20]

Marxists like Ernest Mandel have theorized capitalism as a system that is characterized by "long waves" that are, in essence, part and parcel of the accumulation process. What is important is that these long waves are shaped by explainable economic factors and social relations; they are not simply arbitrary, or the result of one event, policy, or the influence of one "personality." They can be explained by the dynamic internal to capitalism, along with "exogenous environmental changes and their mediation through socio-political developments, which include the balance of class forces, wars, and so on."[21] Long waves and crises thus always need to be historically situated, and economic rationalizations for them understood in a materialist rather than idealist vein; ideological explanation tends to follow economic shifts rather than vice versa. Thus, postwar capital's acceptance of Keynesian policies reflected an understanding that these would not "upset the apple cart"[22] of profits, while the counterrevolution against Keynesianism in the 1970s emerged not simply because inflation was suddenly recognized as a problem, but rather because monetarism reflected a key shift in capitalist class strategies as it strove to repair the rate of profit. The result was questions and challenges to key elements of the earlier Keynesian compromise, including its (fragile) entitlements for workers, such as social security and wage increases.[23]

Those writing in a Marxist tradition may share an approach that is historical and materialist, as well as certain basic assumptions about contradictions within capitalism, but their analyses can be quite different in orientation and emphasis. David Harvey's oeuvre, for instance, advanced our understanding of the global and spatial organization of capitalism and its relationship to crisis. Exploring the limits of capital, his unraveling of capitalist crisis starts with a "first cut" explanation, which examines unstable contradictions in "commodity production and exchange,"[24] while a "second cut" of the explanation goes on to investigate the financial and monetary aspects of crisis, including (but not limited to) speculative crises, since these may occur on a "semi-autonomous" basis. Even if they occur on their own account, he adds, they are still the "surface froth upon much deeper currents making for disequilibrium" in the system.[25] Finally, a "third cut" explanation adds the "geography of uneven development" into the mix. Harvey's work on the spatial and global nature of capitalism suggests a complex understanding of crisis that eschews a determinist reading of Marx while still accepting an element of determination. The circulation of capital across the globe, he shows, often reflects the search for a "spatial fix," as capital searches for ways of alleviating disequilibrium or crisis in one area by searching out new forms of labor, land, and profit in another.

The importance of understanding capitalist crisis has not been limited to political economists looking at the "capital" side of labor-capital social relations. In their writing on segmented work, David M. Gordon, Richard Edwards, and Michael Reich argue that crises are an inherent part of the world system of accumulation, since capitalism must continue to expand, but in the process of doing so, it runs into "walls of its own making which limit its existing structures."[26] Like Mandel, they too argue that crises do not only emerge from "crashes" but also out of periods of prosperity, as the 1973–74 downturn did, leading to a realignment of class forces and even reconfiguration within the capitalist class itself. Capitalist accumulation may be an uneven process, but it is explainable: there is a "social structure" of accumulation, a multidimensional set of environmental and social factors that shape how accumulation occurs and thus also shape the long swings, the booms and busts of the economy. Their conclusion, that the resolution of any crisis is shaped not only by the power and objectives of capitalism but also by workers and other economic actors, is an important recognition that class is not simply an inert structure but also a process of reciprocal social relations.

The call to examine historical specificity and the array of class forces within times of crisis is repeated in recent political-economy theorizing on the crisis in profitability that has unfolded since the mid-1970s, including those exploring intensified global financialization. Leo Panitch and Sam Gindin, for instance, caution that we should not see a "neverending" crisis since the 1970s (as they suggest Robert Brenner does), since this ignores the way in which the capitalist system changed over these years, including experiencing "another technological revolution." In other words, if we see crisis as the new normal, we cannot really understand the precise contradictions of each conjuncture. Even more important, they "bring the working classes back in," cautioning that capitalism can only be understood when the whole array of class forces, including class struggle (or the lack of it), is taken into account. If crises cannot be avoided by capitalism, they can be managed, and a key factor in this process is whether working people and organized labor can mobilize, or whether their weakness—as in the last decades—has played a role in capitalism's success. They caution that if we do not take the working class into account as a potential force, we may join the triumphalist "end of history" determinists: "[C]risis does not just lead capitalism to unravel on its own . . . our theories of crisis must be politicized to integrate the responses of both states and class actors, including the working class."[27]

The explosion of writing in international political economy over the last few decades reflects academic efforts to come to terms with world capitalism since the unraveling of the postwar boom. Significant theoretical differences exist between schools of international political economy, but there is some common understanding that capitalism needs to be analyzed *as* a world process, in which trade and markets, the circulation of commodities (including labor), as well as power and imperialism, both formal and informal, are all critical elements.

Some writing, however, continues to emphasize the significant role of states, and in particular the American state, in the making of global capitalism.[28] Writing on globalization has built on a long line of world-history thinkers like Immanuel Wallerstein and Fernand Braudel: Braudel's "world historical analysis" of systemic cycles of accumulation, Arrighi notes, was used as a building block for his recent analysis of the hegemonic blocs of capitalist expansion of Genoa, Holland, and Britain over centuries, a study that explores how capital sought out flexibility, choice, expansion, and profit through the world economy.[29]

Mainstream and Marxist economists alike have analyzed crisis in relation to the global nature of capitalism, through different theoretical lenses and with different political objectives. Influential Marxist scholars of development, such as Andre Gunder Frank and Samir Amin, with their focus on development and underdevelopment, centers and peripheries, north and south, indicated how booms and crises are experienced differently in the First and Third Worlds. Indeed, Amin warns emphatically that it is a mistake to confuse capitalist expansion with "development," while Frank argues that the postwar boom was wrongly assumed to be a "universal" phenomenon: capitalism has always been uneven, "spatially and sectorally," and what was a boom in the West did not "serve the Third World well."[30]

Studies of world capitalism have thus shown the nearsightedness of economic analyses that presume the "West is the rest"; the causes, nature, and experience of economic crises may affect global regions quite differently, leading to different theoretical perspectives in their analysis. Even before the downturn in the mid-1970s, Frank was pointing to signs of impending capitalist crisis; he then took some delight in puncturing the overstated optimism of the mainstream doyen of economics, Paul Samuelson, who noted in 1972 that "the business cycle had been so well analyzed and counteracted as to have practically gone out of existence."[31] The boom in the West, Frank suggested, led to a collective forgetting of inherent features of capitalism, including the tendency for the rate of profit to decline. That Frank's pessimistic prediction more accurately described the following decades than Samuelson's can hardly be cause for celebration, since the impact of 1970s stagflation on workers' lives was quite negative. Short time, no time, intensified unpaid and paid work, unemployment, ill health: these were, and are, the very real consequences of crisis for workers. The challenge for historians of labor is to be cognizant of the political economy debates that help us explain crisis without losing sight of the human lives and the costs for workers and their communities. Finding an intellectual space that encompasses the bottom and top floor of capitalism may be a difficult enterprise, but it is one worth pursuing.

Rethinking Workers' Agency
in an Era of Global Transformation

A second characteristic of the essays gathered in this volume is that they view workers as more than victims of economic crisis. They take workers, their organizations, and their struggles seriously. And yet the way in which they treat working-class agency also indicates important changes in the field of labor history across the past half-century.

The emerging New Labor History in the 1960s and 1970s frankly celebrated working-class subjectivity, sweeping aside the economistic behaviorism of labor economists like John R. Commons and Selig Perlman, who had first shaped the field in North America. The generation of historians who came of age with the New Labor History set out to correct a historical record that tended, in the influential words of E. P. Thompson, "to obscure the agency of working people, the degree to which they contributed, by conscious efforts, to the making of history."[32] During the 1970s and the early 1980s, led by the work of David Montgomery, Herbert Gutman, and their students, a raft of books and articles recovered aspects of working-class resistance to capitalist values or management's control of the workplace, whether expressed on the shop floor or in the realm of culture.[33]

By the mid-1980s the infatuation with working-class agency was tempered by worries, at least in U.S. circles, over the lack of synthesis in a field that was producing an abundance of craft and community studies but no compelling master narrative, and by the growing sense that social historians were giving short shrift to questions of politics and political power. More structural-minded historians such as David Brody or Melvyn Dubofsky urged labor historians to return to institutional questions surrounding the history of collective bargaining, the function of law, and state power. Their approach drew strength from historical sociologists such as Theda Skocpol, who sought to "bring the state back in" to the realm of scholars' concerns,[34] a call that had some resonance with labor historians in countries such as Canada, where political economy had long maintained a strong, parallel presence, or Australia, where the influential role of governing labor parties and highly developed state structures of labor regulation made the state an inevitable focus of debate.

A confluence of intellectual and historical developments made it more difficult to write meaningfully about working-class agency in the years since 1980. The accelerating globalization of the world economy, resurgent conservatism (including working-class conservatism), the erosion of union power, and the decline of collective action made the historical agency of common people less visible than it had been in the tumultuous 1960s or strike-prone early 1970s. New fields of scholarship further complicated the effort to identify or recover, much less celebrate, working-class agency. Poststructuralist theories, a shift from social to cultural history, and the attendant accent on representation and discourse resulted in challenges to the very categories of agency and experience that had underpinned earlier studies of working-class life. Historians of gender, race, and whiteness helped us understand the extent to which working-class agency was always refracted through prisms of race or gender privilege.[35] Historians of the new conservatism showed that workers' agency could be expressed in defense of individual freedom or capitalist values as readily as it was expressed in defense of a distinctly working-class interest,[36] while analyses of corporate and state assaults on workers' legal and economic entitlements revealed how ideologically successful they often were, dampening working-class and trade-union resistance. And historians of capitalism began to move away from the experiences or consciousness of workers as they sought to understand capitalism's development over what Fernand Braudel called the "longue durée."[37]

It seemed to some that the triumph of the neoliberal paradigm by the end of the twentieth century marked not only "the end of history" but also the end of any meaningful discussion of working-class agency in history. Yet this has not been the case. The economic instability of the last decade has given rise to new evidence of workers' agency, whether expressed in the protests of workers on the streets of Madrid or Athens; the upheavals of the Arab Spring, in which workers and their organizations played a major role; emerging organizations of excluded or "precarious" workers; or the growing backlash against financial power embodied by phenomena like the Occupy movement. The Great Recession has again forced us to reconsider the contours of working-class agency.

The essays in this volume come to terms with working-class agency during hard times in different ways and with varying levels of attention to the question. Yet they share one general characteristic in common. They do not seek to uncritically recover and celebrate working-class agency, as one early strand of the New Labor History once did; they search for a balance between agency and determination, between an appreciation of the impact that workers' struggles have had on history, on the one hand, and a clear understanding of the larger forces that have limited working-class responses, especially in periods of crisis and transformation, on the other hand. Some essays in this volume see a greater degree of agency in their working-class subjects than others, but all grapple in one fashion or another with how to strike the right balance between what workers have done and what has been done to them. In this respect, the essays gathered here help mark how much the field of labor history has changed over the last forty years. Thus these essays have been influenced not only by the shadow of the Great Recession but also by the historical and intellectual developments of recent decades.

Organization of the Volume

The volume is organized in four parts. Part I focuses on the effects of economic depression on workers' lives. In a close look at turn-of-the-twentieth century Toronto, Gaetan Heroux and Bryan D. Palmer offer an account of mass distress that considers how the poor, waged and unwaged, were subjected to state-based regimes of disciple and how they struggled to fight back. In the last essay he completed before his death, David Montgomery sketches out a broad overview of economic panics and workers' responses to them in the United States from Jacksonian times to the Great Depression. In the third contribution, Wendy Goldman reconceptualizes the Depression-era Soviet experience, using Marx's concept of primitive accumulation, with its emphasis on dispossession, proletarianization, and violence.

Part II highlights the relationship between economic upheaval and political crisis. As the two essays included here indicate, however, the influence can move in either direction. Scott Reynolds Nelson focuses on the worst crisis of the nineteenth century to show how the panic of 1893 led to the Pullman strike, the radicalization of Eugene Debs, and the origins of the progressive movement. Sven Beckert begins with the worldwide crisis of cotton production touched off by the American Civil War, emancipation, and the subsequent frantic search for alternatives, including coolie and sharecropping labor systems.

Part III shifts the focus to the relations of working people and state services: in particular, how have national welfare systems (as buttressed by labor movements) forded the stream of economic crisis? Alvin Finkel provides a sweeping reinterpretation of workers' wage struggles across the West from the Great Depression through the rise of neoliberalism in the 1970s. The latter moment is the point of takeoff for two other essays: Judith Stein concentrates on the default of U.S. governmental stewardship over the industrial economy during the 1970s, while Melanie Nolan emphasizes how coincident attacks on workers' welfare in Australia were met by a progressive counterresponse.

Part IV connects historical analysis to the contemporary crisis unleashed by the global Great Recession in four distinct settings. Sean Cadigan describes a new, highly gendered economy of boom and bust, haves and have-nots, in the Canadian Maritimes. Lu Zhang trains her sights on the continuing tug-of-war between Chinese state managers, eager to replace permanent workers with a cheaper, contingent labor force, and autoworkers, who sense their leverage within a world market and an ideological system formally committed to worker rights. Hilary Wainwright's essay offers a transnational, historical, and comparative look at the political mobilization of the European working classes against austerity and inequality. She examines the recent example of Syriza, a radical left coalition that emerged in opposition to neoliberal attempts to impose a crushing austerity on the Greek population, comparing this experiment to earlier political efforts mounted by the left wing of the British Labour party in London in the early 1980s, and by the Brazilian Porto Alegre movement, closely identified with the Brazilian Workers party, from 1989 to 2004.

The volume concludes with an essay by the economist Edward Montgomery contrasting the U.S. government's response to the Great Recession to that of the Great Depression. Like his father, David Montgomery, the younger Montgomery takes a long view of events. His examination of recent economic trends leads Montgomery to sobering conclusions about what the post–Great Recession world holds in store for workers. Ironically, the vision Edward Montgomery sketches of the likely future that seems to be taking shape for American workers resembles in some ways the picture of working-class insecurity that the elder Montgomery found in the nineteenth century. In the current fiscal crises touched off by the Great Recession, we witness worldwide struggles over the defense of a social wage fought for over a century by popular movements across the West. Perhaps it is not surprising that it is in Europe, where labor and its associated political parties had gone furthest in regulating capitalist markets, that the contemporary clashes are fiercest and most explicit. Even within Europe, the recent neoliberal crisis and workers' responses have taken on different forms, made complex by center-periphery relations among European states, the design of the Economic and Monetary Union, and the permeation of neoliberalism into former Soviet-bloc states. The ideological power of capital and some states to construct the crisis as one of "hard-working" nations versus "spend-thrifty"[38] ones is being challenged in the streets by those suffering the crisis on a daily basis, and their responses will be conditioned by their own actions and labor-movement history as well as the macroeconomic relations of capitalism, precisely the dual dynamics featured in many of the essays in this volume.

The essays in this volume do not offer up easy solutions for the present, but they do indicate the approaches and perspectives necessary to analyze current crises. Taken together, they emphasize the necessity of historicizing our present problems, balancing context and specificity, structure and human agency. Indeed, they make clear that cogent historical thinking is crucial to understanding the problems with which workers the world over are grappling today.

Notes

1. Alexander Keyssar, *Out of Work: The First Century of Unemployment in Massachusetts* (Cambridge: Cambridge University Press, 1986), 47.

2. Ibid., 218.

3. Denyse Baillargeon, *Making Do: Women, Family, and Home in Montreal during the Great Depression* (Waterloo, Ont.: Wilfrid Laurier University Press, 1999); Joan Sang-

ster, *Dreams of Equality: Women on the Canadian Left, 1920s–1950s* (Toronto: Oxford University Press, 1989).

4. Wallace C. Peterson, *Silent Depression: The Fate of the American Dream* (New York: W. W. Norton and Co., 1994), 30–34.

5. Robin Hahnel, *Panic Rules: Everything You Need to Know about the Global Economy* (Cambridge, Mass.: South End Press, 1999), 5.

6. Giovanni Arrighi, *The Long Twentieth Century: Money, Power, and the Origin of Our Times* (London: Verso, 1994), 25.

7. Mandel noted that the theory originated with Karl Kautsky, Leon Trotsky, and Charlie Van Gelderen. Ernest Mandel, *Long Waves of Capitalist Development* (Cambridge: Cambridge University Press, 1980), 1.

8. Ibid., 8.

9. Paul Krugman, *End This Depression Now!* (New York: W. W. Norton, 2012), 42–43.

10. Paul Krugman, *The Return of Depression Economics and the Crisis of 2008* (New York: W. W. Norton, 2009), 90–91.

11. "But who can now use the words of socialism with a straight face?" (ibid., 14).

12. John Kenneth Galbraith, *The Great Crash of 1929* (Boston: Houghton Mifflin Co, 1988), xii.

13. Ibid., xii–xv.

14. Krugman, *End This Depression*, xi.

15. Robert Barbera, *The Cost of Capitalism: Understanding Market Mayhem and Stabilizing Our Economic Future* (New York: McGraw Hill, 2009), 5.

16. Ibid., 9.

17. Murray Smith, *Global Capitalism in Crisis: Karl Marx and the Decay of the Profit System* (Halifax: Fernwood, 2010).

18. Mandel, *Long Waves*, 10–11. David Harvey maintains that Marx was "infuriatingly ambivalent" in his writings on this issue: "Marx also stated that overproduction does not call forth a constant fall in profit but periodic over production. . . . and that Adam Smith's argument that the fall in the rate of profit from an overabundance of capital is not correct. The transitory overabundance of capital, overproduction, and crises are something different. Permanent crises do not exist." David Harvey, *The Limits to Capital* (Oxford: Basil Blackwell, 1982), 191.

19. Ernest Mandel, *The Second Slump*, trans. Jon Rothschild (London: Verso, 1980), 178.

20. Alex Callincos, *The Revolutionary Ideas of Marx* (London: Bookmarks, 1987), 139.

21. Mandel, *Long Waves*, 97.

22. Ibid., 99.

23. Ibid., 98–99.

24. Harvey, *Limits to Capital*, 192.

25. Ibid., 325.

26. David M. Gordon, Richard Edwards, and Michael Reich, *Segmented Work, Divided Workers: The Historical Transformation of Labor in the United States* (Cambridge: Cambridge University Press, 1982), 29.

27. Leo Panitch and Sam Gindin, "Finance and the American Empire," in *American Empire and the Political Economy of Global Finance,* ed. Leo Panitch and Martijn Konigs (London: Palgrave, 2008), 43.

28. Leo Panitch and Sam Gindin, *The Making of Global Capitalism* (London: Verso, 2012).

29. Arrighi, *Long Twentieth Century,* xi.

30. Andre Gunder Frank, *Crisis in the World Economy* (New York: Homes and Meier, 1980), 12.

31. Ibid., 21.

32. E. P. Thompson, *The Making of the English Working Class* (New York: Pantheon Books, 1963), 12.

33. Herbert Gutman, *Work, Culture, and Society in Industrializing America, 1815–1919* (New York: Knopf, 1976); David Montgomery, *Workers' Control in America: Essays in the History of Work, Technology, and Labor Struggles* (New York: Cambridge University Press, 1979).

34. Tony Judt, "A Clown in Regal Purple: Social History and the Historians," *History Workshop Journal* 7 (1979): 66–96; Melvyn Dubofsky, "The 'New' Labor History: Achievements and Failures," *Reviews in American History* 5 (June 1977): 249–54; Melvyn Dubofsky, *The State and Labor in Modern America* (Chapel Hill: University of North Carolina Press, 1994); David Brody, "The Old Labor History and the New," *Labor History* 20 (Winter 1979): 511–26; David Brody, "Reconciling the Old Labor History and the New," *Pacific Historical Review* 62 (February 1993): 1–18; David Brody, *Workers in Industrial America* (New York: Oxford University Press, 1980).

35. The literature on these subjects is too deep to adequately summarize in a footnote. Among the representative works are Alice Kessler-Harris, *In Pursuit of Equity: Women, Men, and the Quest for Economic Citizenship in Twentieth-Century America* (New York: Oxford University Press, 2003); Bruce Nelson, *Divided We Stand: American Workers and the Struggle for Black Equality* (Princeton, N.J.: Princeton University Press, 1991); and David Roediger, *The Wages of Whiteness: Race and the Making of the American Working Class* (New York: Verso, 1991).

36. Jennifer Luff, *Commonsense Anti-Communism: Labor and Civil Liberties between the World Wars* (Chapel Hill: University of North Carolina Press, 2012); Elizabeth Tandy Shermer, "Counter-Organizing in the Sunbelt: Right-to-Work Campaigns and Anti-Union Conservatism, 1943–1958," *Pacific Historical Review* 78 (February 2009): 81–118.

37. Fernand Braudel, "Histoire et sciences sociales: La longue durée," in *Écrits sur l'histoire* (Paris: Flammarion, 1969), 41–83.

38. Ingo Schmidt, "European Capitalism: Varieties of Crisis," *Alternate Routes: A Journal of Critical Social Research* 22 (2010): 71–86.

PART I

Depressions and Working-Class Lives

1

Marching under Flags Black and Red

Toronto's Dispossessed in the Age of Industry

GAETAN HEROUX
AND BRYAN D. PALMER

Introduction: Capitalism as Crisis

When capitalism is understood not merely as a political economy of development, advance, and progress but also as a social order of destruction, how we view workers necessarily changes. For capitalism is not merely a regime of accumulation giving rise to a complex amalgam of contradictory impulses and episodic clashes of antagonistic interests. It has historically also been fundamentally about crisis, as is abundantly evident in the history of the present.[1]

This insight framed Marx's oeuvre, the 1873 afterword to the second German edition of *Capital: A Critical Analysis of Capitalist Production* declaring: "The contradictions inherent in the movement of capitalist society impress themselves upon the practical bourgeois most strikingly in the changes of the periodic cycle, through which modern industry runs, and whose crowning point is the universal crisis. That crisis is once again approaching, although as yet but in its preliminary stage; and by the universality of its theatre and the intensity of its action it will drum dialectics even into the heads of the mushroom upstarts."[2] More clearly than any other thinker of his time, Marx understood that capitalism's logic and dynamic was premised on an internal reciprocity in which profit's preservation built on destructiveness. "The growing incompatibility between the productive development of society and its hitherto existing relations of production expresses itself in bitter contradictions, crises, spasms," Marx wrote in the *Grundrisse,* concluding, "The violent destruction of capital not by relations external to it, but rather as a condition of its self-preservation, is the most striking form in which advice is given it to be gone and to give room to a higher state of social production." Harnessing capitalism's far-reaching capacities to develop production and advance civilization was socialism's purpose, the intention being to tame its equally far-reaching tendencies to destroy output and generate and exacerbate debilitating conflicts.[3]

Appreciating capitalism *as* crisis and accumulation *as* destruction entails looking at labor differently, more dialectically. Michael Denning has recently advocated reconceptualizing life under capitalism in ways that "decentre wage labour" and replace a "fetishism of the wage" and the "employment contract" with attention to "dispossession and expropriation." Marx, after all, did not invent the term "proletarian" but adapted it from its common usage in antiquity, when, within the Roman Empire, the word designated the uncertain social stratum, divorced from property and without regular access to wages, reproducing recklessly. J. C. L. Simonde de Sismondi drew on this understanding in an 1819 work of political economy that chronicled the "threat to public order" posed by a "miserable and suffering population," dependant as it was on public charity. "[T]hose who had no property," Sismondi wrote, "were called to have children: *ad prolem generandum.*" Max Weber commented similarly: "As early as the sixteenth century the proletarianizing of the rural population created such an army of unemployed that England had to deal with the problem of poor relief." Three centuries later, across the Atlantic, transient common laborers were being described in a discourse seemingly impervious to change: "a dangerous class, inadequately fed, clothed, and housed, they threaten the health of the community." As Denning concludes, "Unemployment precedes employment, and the informal economy precedes the formal, both historically and conceptually. We must insist that 'proletarian' is not a synonym for 'wage labourer' but for dispossession, expropriation, and radical dependence on the market."[4]

Although Denning captures the fundamental importance of wagelessness, all the more so within a context of capitalism *as crisis,* his dichotomization of wageless life and waged labor is myopic. It nearsightedly clarifies the importance of dispossession while obscuring the extent to which this fundamental feature of proletarianization is meaningless outside of the existence of the (often distant) wage as both an enduring if universally unpleasant end and a decisive means of survival within modern capitalist relations. David Montgomery captures the connectedness of being waged and unwaged in his rich discussion of common laborers: "Whether they were working flat out, sleeping behind a furnace or inside a boxcar, getting 'quitting mad,' enjoying the conviviality of the saloon, or being thrown back into the ranks of the unemployed . . . one thing was clear: For common laborers, work was the biblical curse. It was unavoidable, undependable, and unrewarding. But they had urgent need for money."[5] Wagelessness and waged employment are not oppositions, then, but gradations on a spectrum traversing desire and necessity that encompasses many possibilities for the proletarianized masses.

Unemployed Protests under the Black Flag, 1873–96

By the time Toronto had embarked on its Age of Industry in the 1870s and 1880s, major enterprises employed almost thirteen thousand workers in a population of roughly eighty-five thousand. Decades of socioeconomic differentiation and dislocation had served as the primitive accumulation that fueled the Queen City's material development. Economic crises, devastating in their human toll, punctuated the 1830s, the 1850s, and the 1870s, and would close the century in the 1890s. Pauper immigration, health epidemics, and the emergence of class conflict all struck daggers of fear in the bosom of emerging bourgeois society.[6] Beginning in the 1830s, a set of carceral institutions, the most prominent of which was the House of Industry, were established, criminalizing the poor and marking them with the stigma of dependency.[7] As much as the boundaries separating the "rough" and the "respectable" within working-class Toronto were often fluid, with individuals passing through highly porous separations, these distinctions were nonetheless socially constructed in the ideology of the times and often reinforced materially. "Unemployment" emerged as a derogatory designation.[8]

Toronto's nineteenth-century industrial-capitalist revolution spawned the unmistakable growth of workers' organizations, political mobilizations, and protests, including strikes, fully 122 of a national total of 425 fought over the course of the 1880s being waged in Toronto. Labor newspapers like the *Ontario Workman* and the *Palladium of Labor* anchored themselves in Toronto, just as the Nine-Hour League and the Canadian Labor Union in the 1870s and the Knights of Labor and the Trades and Labor Congress of Canada played significant roles in the now bustling capital of Canadian manufacturing, which boasted a population approaching two hundred thousand by the end of the nineteenth century. This was the unmistakable expression of a working-class presence that, however much it was accommodated to the logic of capitalist class relations and the disciplines of the wage, did indeed challenge the hegemony of employers and their often servile state.[9]

Entrenched ideologies of British Poor Law discourse proved remarkably resilient in nineteenth-century Canada. The "undeserving poor" were to be subject to the laws of "less eligibility," stipulating that relief would only be made available to those among the wageless who *would* work for their aid, which could only be dispensed in ways that made it even less attractive than what could be secured by the worst-paid unskilled labor. Toronto's *Globe* made all of this abundantly clear in an 1877 manifesto-like declaration on the wageless: "[W]e do not advocate a system which could leave them to starve, but we do say that if they are ever to be taught economical and saving habits, they must understand that the public have no idea of making them entirely comfortable in the midst of their improvidence and dissipation. If they wish to secure that they must work for it and save and plan. Such comfort is not to be had by loafing around the tavern door, or fleeing to charity at every pinch."[10]

A floating mass of workless males generated intensified panic as the depression of 1873 deepened into 1877–78. Masses of migrant laborers, ostensibly traveling to secure elusive waged employment, became the scourge of small towns and large cities alike. Welcomed with the lockup and public derision in the press, tramps were criminalized and vilified, socially constructed as thieves and denigrated as "pests," "voracious monsters," and "outrageously impertinent," an "irrepressible stampede" deserving of "a well-aimed dose of buckshot rubbed in well with salt-petre." In Lindsay, Ontario, roughly ninety miles from Toronto, the local *Canadian Post* carried over one hundred news items relating to tramps in the 1874–78 years. Tramps were depicted as an outcast stratum rarely interested in finding employment, poor because they were "work-shy and degenerate." Many, riding the rails, were en route to Toronto, where police stations in 1877 and 1878 reported sheltering over 1,200 "waifs" annually.[11]

If the 1880s saw the economy struggle out of its 1870s doldrums, the recovery was anything but robust, and the migratory wageless continued to unsettle respectable society. Toronto's newspapers competed against one another, pushing the denunciations of the "loafing aristocracy" to new extremes, calling for the expulsion of tramps from the city, judicious use of the lash against those for whom work was an aversion, and vigilant police monitoring of peripatetic vagrants given to "murders, burglaries, incendiaries, and highway robberies." A little "hard labour," suggested the *Globe*, would do this "dissipated" and "shiftless" element good, since the House of Industry had supposedly become increasingly lax in enforcing earlier expectations than those seeking accommodations for the night or outdoor relief of established, but faltering, households would chop wood for their food and lodging or charitable reliance on coal, food, or other necessities. Some called for a more rigorous "labour test," suggesting that stone-breaking establish a new standard for deservedness. The House of Industry concentrated instead on establishing an expanded wayfarer's lodge in 1884–85, where large numbers of indigent men could be put up for the night in a "casual" ward, their bodies soaked in a hot bath, their heads doused in vermin-killing liquid solution, and their clothes fumigated, "cleansed and classified" in the vernacular of poor-relief officialdom. But the growing number of habitual tramps furnished with temporary board and lodging by the de facto Poor House in the mid-1880s necessitated adoption of a modified labor test, if only to deter the ostensibly shiftless and physically weak from staying in the expanded casual ward of the refuge too long. Making inmates saw a quarter-cord of wood, a job that took the able-bodied and reasonably dexterous approximately three hours, before they were allowed to lunch on a watery bowl of soup and a hunk of stale bread had its effect. Those checking into the wayfarer's lodge declined from totals of 730 in 1886 to 548 in 1889.

The worsening economic climate of the depressed 1890s saw an expanded need for the House of Industry's relief, however, and the casual ward was opened for the summer as well as winter months. The number of "casuals" staying at the enlarged lodge thus soared, climbing to highs of 1,700 in 1891 and 1,500 in 1895 and 1897, rarely falling below 1,200. The average contingent sleeping at the House per night never dipped below sixty between 1890 and 1897, when a high of one hundred was reached (a comparable figure for the 1880–85 years had been roughly twenty-six). In 1891, 832 casuals stayed in the wayfarer's lodge of Toronto's House of Industry for two or three nights, while 415 put up in the poor house for more than three days; twenty-four hardcore recidivists spent more than one hundred nights in the refuge.[12] Increased use of the House of Industry's relief facilities and provisions drew a backlash. Rev. Arthur H. Baldwin, rector of Toronto's All Saints church and one of the House of Industry's most outspoken trustees, provided advance notice that Toronto's premier institution of poor relief was not interested in coddling itinerant idlers. "It seems a great pity," he pontificated, "that these people should be allowed to go in and dwell [in the casual ward] and do nothing but cut a little wood, as we insist upon their doing."[13] A new labor regime was clearly in the offing.

"Until the vagrant is offered some alternative that even he will recognize as more unpleasant and disagreeable than work," claimed the Board of the House of Industry in 1891–92, "the tramp trouble will never be cured." Cutting wood wasn't cutting it: relatively few refused this labor test. Between 1891 and 1895, according to James Pitsula's calculations from the *Annual Reports of the House of Industry*, 29,652 requests of the indigent to cut wood were complied with, while a bare 432 refusals were registered. In 1896, the House of Industry abandoned wood-cutting, replacing it with the more onerous discipline of stone-breaking. Almost immediately the new regime met with resistance: only 792 completed the required task of stone-breaking, compared to 1,202 who balked at undertaking the new labor test. As indicated by the vagrancy convictions of John Curry and Thomas Wilson in January 1896, those who refused stone-breaking assignments at the House of Industry were soon subject to confinement. Magistrate Denison sentenced this duo, who said that they preferred jail to the new labor test, to a three month-term in the refuge of their choice. One month later, upping the ante, City Alderman Jolliffe introduced a motion making it mandatory for all able-bodied applicants for relief in Toronto applying for outdoor assistance to break a yard of stone in return for their coal subsidy, doubling the amount of work required to receive winter fuel. "The stonepile," as Pitsula concludes, had become "an emblem for the work ethic."[14]

An offensive against the tramps was clearly being waged in the name of morality and the disciplining power of relief.[15] This class war was not waged one-sidedly. Not only was stone-breaking unpopular, but it occasioned organized protests by the poor. The rush of refusals in 1896 could not have happened without discussions and deliberations on the part of the wageless. Consequences of their recalcitrance were quite severe. For the single unemployed men, the tramps, of whom 65 to 75 percent came from outside Toronto,[16] refusal to break stone left them homeless, without viable means of support and sustenance, possibly confined to a cell. Family men seeking outdoor relief in the form of food and fuel put themselves and their wives and children at risk with their oppositional stands. And yet not only did casuals and those domestic providers in need bolt from stone-breaking, some of the indigent gathered outside of City Hall to protest against Jolliffe's motion. An unidentified spokesman, described as "a strong hulk fellow," spoke for his wageless counterparts: "And they calls that charity, do they? Got to crack a heap o' stones for what yer get. Ain't no charity in that es' I can see."[17]

The rebellion of stone-breaking refusal in the 1890s was, to be sure, a minor event, but it signaled a shift in the activities of the workless, which had taken a more organized and collective turn in the depression of 1873–77 and its immediate aftermath. With industrialists acknowledging that "fifty percent of the manufacturing population of the country are out of work," and fledgling newspapers of the organized working class addressing unemployment and its evils, it was but a short step to deputations of the jobless marching in demand of some kind of redress.[18] Ottawa became a center of this 1870s agitation, a natural enough development given Parliament's proximity and the possibility of federal politicians voting funds for expanded public works.[19] Over the course of the winter of 1879–80, Ottawa newspapers bristled with accounts of petitions, marches, torchlit processions, and other gatherings of hundreds of "unemployed workingmen." Editorials chastened those who were described as looking "needy and seemed determined to get work or fight," claiming that the government could not be expected to provide for them. Canada was not a land of "State Socialism."[20]

To be sure, the unemployed protests of 1873–80 were seldom unambiguous stands of unity expressing a solidarity of the waged and the wageless. Racism kept workers divided, and native-born Canadians and English-speaking immigrants resented deeply the suggestion that they could cure the disease of wagelessness by moving west to take advantage of the booming resource and railway frontier. The unemployed of 1880 protested the unfairness of suggesting that mechanics in Canada's capital "leave the city" of Ottawa when they had contributed so much to "building it up." They buttressed this legitimate argument with angry statements far less salutary: "It was nonsense to ask residents of the city to go away west and live with Indians and half-breeds, and to work upon the railway in British Columbia, competing with Chinese cheap labour."[21]

Nonetheless, the trajectory of laboring experience in the 1880s *was* towards a more inclusive sense of the collectivity of class experience, the common interests of skilled and unskilled, and, as a consequence, the importance of addressing not only the struggles of the waged but also the plight of the wageless, which demanded, as the Knights of Labor promoted with its understanding of "one big union" of all workers, organization. Labor-reform intellectuals of the 1880s, such as Toronto's Phillips Thompson, were acutely aware of the ongoing nature of capitalist crisis, of acquisitive individualism feeding on the contributions of labor and the despoliation of the working class. "Capitalism has created a monster which threatens to destroy the classes, if not the system, that gave it life," Thompson wrote. "The number of men and women who cannot get work on any terms implies a far larger class whose pay has become a mere pittance." Thompson's *The Politics of Labor* (1886) sought to break down the separations of the skilled and unskilled and eradicate, to some degree, the barriers to working-class solidarity erected by gendered and racialized prejudice, not to mention craft exclusion. "Where is the advantage of cheapness of production to the army of the unemployed and half-employed, or to those whose labor has been so cheapened by competition that their purchasing power is correspondingly lessened?" he asked. The half-employed, the cheapeningly employed, and the unemployed—for Thompson this was the army that would march against capital, the beginning of a union of the dispossessed.[22]

As this union struggled, against all odds, to realize itself in the 1880s, evidence of how the lives of the waged and the wageless shaded into one another surfaced in many quarters. Toronto workers surveyed by the Bureau of Industries at the end of the decade averaged only forty-four weeks of employment a year, if they happened to find work six days a week. This was in the best of times. For many workers, being out of work for a goodly part of every year was the norm. Testimony before the Royal Commission on the Relations of Labor and Capital in the late 1880s, from employers and workers, made it abundantly clear that few industrial establishments, building projects, and transportation endeavors paid workers for more than eight to ten months annually. The Toronto House of Industry accommodated tramps, to be sure, but to the extent that the migratory wageless who depended on its shelter and subsistence fare can be classified occupationally, skilled workers were not far behind unskilled laborers in lining up for relief. Toronto printers claimed that 30 percent of their number was without work in the 1890s. "I am not alone in my trouble," declared one Toronto unemployed father of six in 1891. "There are two hundred members of the union to which I belong in the same position as myself." If the organization of the wageless was not dramatic in this period, it had nonetheless surfaced and made particular kinds of statements. At one of the 1880 Ottawa demonstrations of the unemployed, a black flag was unfurled. Those responsible thought that they "would be clubbed by the Police and shot down like dogs." As a fitting symbol, the anarchist banner signified for the angry workers who marched under it the possibility of death—the wages of the war on the dispossessed. But if those out of work understood that their own demise by starvation might well be imminent, they shook their defiant fists in the face of authority and vowed "death to the government" that they claimed was responsible for their destitution.[23]

In February 1891, two Toronto procession protests of three hundred to one thousand wageless also marched under the black flag, this one emblazoned with the words "Work or Bread." "There are many others hungry," declared one of the unemployed, most being reluctant to admit that they had appealed to "the charities" for the first time in their lives. The crowd, which convened in anger, grew progressively more agitated as Mayor Clarke told the protesters that no more public-works projects could be funded. Threatening disorder, one man shouted, "Necessity knows no law," and claimed that his need was for immediate work to feed a "dependant family." Many of those demonstrating were craft "breadwinners"—building tradesmen, transportation workers, printers—and there was noticeable discontent that such domestic providers were not privileged over the single unemployed in the granting of work on municipal sewer-construction jobs.[24] This kind of division mirrored the House of Industry's labeling of "casuals" and recipients of outdoor relief. It suggested the ways in which divisions among the waged and the wageless might survive the breaking down of the material walls keeping these two linked halves of proletarianization apart. Nonetheless, a new page had been turned in the late nineteenth century, as workers began to address the experience of dispossession as one in which long-separated working-class contingents congealed. This organized protest, however, also hinted at the decisive role that left politics would play in future mobilizations of what had now come to be referred to as "the unemployed."

The black flag that flew at demonstrations of the wageless in the late nineteenth century proclaimed the presence of the left among the jobless. Memories of this haunted Toronto's community of relief professionals for some time. In 1908, Superintendant Arthur Laughlan of Toronto's House of Industry explained how it had come to pass that the labor test of breaking stone, so exemplary in its disciplining capacities, had been charitably reduced from two yards to half a yard, which still constituted a crate weighing over six hundred pounds:

[W]e were the victims of considerable imposition during the depression about 14 years ago, when the unemployed were carrying the black flag.... We then decided to establish a stone-yard, and before we would give relief each able-bodied man had to break two yards of stone. This innovation was pronounced a success, and the applications for relief began to fall off at a rapid rate, until we had very few families to talk of. We found, however, that two yards of stone was too much for a man to break, and at my suggestion the Board reduced it to one yard. It was afterwards reduced to half, and today they only have to break a quarter of a yard.

The labor test of "cracking the stone," it turns out, was born under the black flag.[25]

Crisis and Escalating Protest in the Pre–World War I Era

The left would fly other flags, including those of "deepest red" that were associated with the arrival of socialism and communism in the 1890–1925 years. And among some in this often fissiparous and differentiated left, antagonism to the wageless as little more than capitalism's refuse would surface in denunciations of the poor as parasites. In Lindsay, Ontario, echoes of the earlier 1870s tramp panic could be heard in a Socialist Party of Canada publication, *Gems of Socialism* (1916), which declared confidently, "The tramp and the millionaire are brothers under the skin. They both live without labor, or rather, live on the labor of others." This was but the most jaundiced side of a more inclusive left response to the jobless. "Revolts of the unemployed" erupted across Canada in the opening decades of the twentieth century, fueled as often as not by the crisis-nature of capitalism. With the revolutionary left's involvement in and support of these uprisings, a more expansive understanding of the complex reciprocity that joined the employed and the out-of-work under capitalism emerged.[26]

Toronto had helped nurture the Canadian socialist left in the 1880s and 1890s, becoming a haven for bohemian radicalism and dissident thought. It was a center of the Canadian Socialist League, the first indigenous and popularly based socialist organization in the country, founded in 1899. The long capitalist crisis of 1873–96 had convinced many Toronto radicals, nascent socialists, and developing Marxists that chronic unemployment, among other afflictions plaguing the working class, could only be resolved by a root-and-branch alteration of the entire capitalist system. Many such critics were Christian socialists, and they found themselves locking horns with more conservative, churched voices in the eclectic Social Problems Conferences that often addressed issues of poverty in the 1890s. As early as 1889, such radical types had clashed in the Toronto Labour Council with one of Canada's leading public intellectuals, Goldwin Smith, who had a penchant for denouncing William Morris, John Ruskin, the British Fabians, and other "poverty destroyers." As this broad left coalesced, it articulated increasingly radical views on how capitalism, recurring economic crises, mechanization of industry, and concentration of wealth and ownership of the productive forces were widening the domain of wagelessness.[27]

During the period 1900–1925, Toronto was transformed. The largest manufacturing center in Ontario, the heartland of Canada's regionalized industrial-capitalist development, the city grew by leaps and bounds. Fed by a massive influx of immigrants, Toronto's population soared, increasing 75 percent between 1901 and 1911, when it surpassed 375,000. Annexation gobbled up new physical territory, which was needed for developing industries and working-class suburbs. Capital invested in manufacturing increased by 618 percent between 1900 and 1921, while the gross value of production, indexed at 100 in 1900, climbed to 148 in 1905, 255 in 1910, and 847 in 1919. Changes in the lives of working-class people living in Toronto abounded. White-collar jobs expanded as the offices and financial institutions facilitating the new economic order proliferated. Work opportunities for women, who now had employment alternatives to domestic service and sweated work in the garment trades, increased significantly. But for all the change experienced by Toronto's expanding working class, the continuity in capitalism as crisis was perhaps most decisive. Boom years were never long enough; bust inevitably followed. Panics and acute depressions occurred in 1907–8, 1911–15, and again in the postwar climate of 1919–21. Wagelessness, for a time, became the lot of "all but a relatively small number of wage earners."[28]

The left perspective on capitalism, crisis, and unemployment may not have resonated that well in Toronto's boom years of expansion (1896–1906) that followed on the heels of the final ending of the long, late nineteenth-century economic malaise. Claims were made that the Trades and Labor Congress of Canada had grown from a membership of eight thousand in 1900 to one hundred thousand in 1914, and much of this affiliation would have been in often conservative, craft-conscious, job-protecting American Federation of Labor (AFL) unions. These bodies, with little use for the wageless, numbered only sixteen in Toronto in the 1880s but totaled 106 by 1902. No other city came close to rivaling this AFL presence. When the voice of the unemployed was heard early in the century, it sometimes spoke in the idiom of the rights of the skilled to be protected from competition in the labor market.[29]

In December 1903, a "meeting of the unemployed of the city of Toronto," undoubtedly spurred to action by the prospects of winter's oncoming layoffs, adopted a resolution deploring the misrepresentation of industrial conditions in Canada and the resulting "encouragement of indiscriminate immigration." By 1907–8, however, with the economy slowed to a snail's pace and the ranks of the out-of-work reaching crisis proportions, Toronto was forced to open a Civic Bureau to register the names of those in need of work in January 1908. Three thousand promptly signed up, those three hundred fortunate enough to secure work at snow removal receiving two dollars daily for a maximum three-day stint. The next December, winter again threatening, another Free Employment Bureau was opened, and within three months 5,500 jobless workers had registered. City of Toronto disbursements for the House of Industry's usual outdoor relief jumped from an average of around ten thousand dollars annually in 1904–7 to over twenty-six thousand dollars in the depressed years 1908–9. At the height of the 1908 economic crisis, 240 so-called tramps were being sheltered in Toronto's House of Industry, with fully ninety of them forced to sleep on concrete floors for want of beds. Those who refused to "crack the stone" for such accommodations faced the increased possibility of criminal charges and incarceration. Vagrancy arrests, never above 975 in any two-year period between 1901 and 1906, ballooned to over eight hundred annually in 1908–10. In this climate, when the wageless were driven to destitution and marked out for a variety of coercions, the left critique of capitalist crisis undoubtedly registered more forcefully with Toronto's dispossessed.[30]

Organized protests reflected this. March 1908 saw one thousand unemployed converge on Toronto's City Hall, demanding work. Rebuffed by the mayor, who stated clearly that temporary employment would never be provided solely as a means of relief, the wageless retreated. Nine months later they were back in force, a contingent of socialists at their head. The January 1909 wageless rebellion in Toronto was led by the well-known agitators Ernest Drury and Wilfred Gribble. More militant than their 1908 predecessors, one thousand unemployed surrounded City Hall and spilled over into an adjacent street, blocking the road. Drury had barely begun to address the crowd when the police intervened, forcing the unemployed protest to reassemble in Bayside Park, a kilometer distant from the downtown core. Ankle-deep in mud, the wageless listened to a parade of revolutionaries, whose speeches scaled the heights of political denunciation of capitalism as well as addressing more immediate prosaic demands. There was talk of the forcible seizure of property to provide for the poor. The Socialist Party of Canada soap-boxer Wilfred Gribble told those assembled, "It goes hard with me to have to stand here in three or four inches of mud when we want to hold a meeting. You men built these great buildings . . . you built these railways, you built the big halls in this city, but when you want to meet you can't have one of them." A petition was soon placed with the City's Board of Control, demanding a hall at which the unemployed could assemble.[31]

A few days later, the wageless again convened at City Hall, their mood described as "dangerous." Albert Hill climbed atop a wagon to address the large throng, which had once more spilled over into the streets, prompting the police to disperse the gathering. He pointed out, as had Gribble earlier, that while the "big guns and important people" received warm welcomes at the municipal seat of power, the unemployed could not find a place to meet. Making their way to

Bayside Park, the body promptly appointed a committee of twelve to return to City Hall and demand access to St. Andrew's Hall as a place where the out-of-work could gather. Five hundred demonstrators trailed the delegation and, upon arrival at the seat of municipal power, swarmed the front and side entrances, seeking out the top-floor meeting rooms of the Board of Control. Told to depart by the police, the unemployed offered no resistance but determined to return.[32]

As several hundred of the unemployed milled about City Hall the next day, their movements watched closely by the police, Drury led a delegation into the building, where the Board of Control was addressed. It was beseeched to let out St. Andrew's Hall for regular meetings of the unemployed to urge upon civic officials the necessity of providing the wageless with work. Mayor Oliver remarked that Drury had led "every unemployed deputation" that had crossed his threshold over the course of the last year and a half. As Drury detailed the suffering of those unable to find paid employment, he was told by the mayor that the House of Industry was always available to the destitute, which drew heckles from the crowd. Controller Geary demanded to know if the protesters were socialists. Three of the contingent acknowledged that they were indeed advocates of a radical overhaul of capitalist institutions. This unleashed a flurry of concern that St. Andrew's Hall would be used to "preach a doctrine of discontent."[33]

Over the next few days, the nascent unemployed movement enlisted the support of sympathetic reverends, preeminent among them Dr. G. S. Eby of the College Street People's church, a.k.a. the Church of the Revolution. The travails of the outdoor relief system were now being complained about by religious figures and elected municipal officials, who questioned the long delays experienced by destitute families applying for emergency aid from the House of Industry. Meanwhile, an organized group of eighty-five refused the labor test at the Poor House two days running in what was obviously a direct-action protest, albeit one that left the single unemployed casuals homeless in the dead of winter.[34] Over one thousand unemployed gathered at St. Andrew's Hall on January 21, 1909, to hear a rousing social-gospel address from the Reverend Dr. Eby. "The day has come when men are tired of talking of hell and heaven," Eby thundered. "There are multitudes of people in the churches whom want to bring heaven to earth." Drury proved more provocative in his speech. Urging the wageless to refuse the symbolism and the substance of the discipline of "cracking the stone," he railed against the quality of the House of Industry's provisions, urging relief recipients to refuse stone-breaking and steal what provisions they could from the Poor House pantry. "I wouldn't give a pig the provisions I got there," he snorted in derision.[35]

Out of this initial St. Andrew's Hall meeting came an extraordinary set of recommendations, quite unlike anything before articulated by those seeking relief. The six demands generated out of the unemployed mobilization of

January 1909 stood as an unambiguous indictment of decades of Toronto's treatment of the dispossessed, governed as it was by routines of labor tests and procedures of "cleansing and classifying." They also united the interests of the casual single unemployed men who stayed overnight in the House of Industry, recipients of indoor relief, and resident families drawing on outdoor dispensations. The wageless, whatever their station, wanted the abolition of the civic-relief department; "running baths" for workmen; daily fare composed of more than cheap servings of adulterated soup and hard bread; provision of adequate winter clothing; investigation of the bread depots so that there was monitoring of their activities and assurances that distressed families would not suffer; and, finally and most strikingly, control of the distribution of relief, taking it out of the hands of the Associated Charities of Toronto and vesting it in a committee of the unemployed. Not yet ready to demand the abolition of "cracking the stone," the socialist-led wageless had, in 1909, nonetheless mobilized their ranks, broadened their struggle, and crystallized a fundamental challenge to their dispossession.[36]

With Mayor Oliver making threatening noises that troublemaking advocates of the right of the wageless to control the relief system could be deported, a letter to the editor of the *Toronto Star* bemoaned the "Brutal Treatment of the Unemployed." It hinted at the way in which resistance to "cracking the stone" had unleashed an ideological counterassault of property and propriety, described as "savage":

> [W]hen a man goes to a place like the House of Industry, it is plain that he is half starved already. There he gets bread and some warm water called tea, at night, and in the morning. Most likely he will not get a bed the first three nights, but will sleep on a floor, with hardly any room to turn. When he gets up in the morning, after what little sleep he had been able to get, he is required to break a lot of stones. The quantity of stones to be broken will take a man used to it three hours, but a man not used to that kind of work will take from four to six hours. Six hours hard work for a bit of dry bread and a rest on the floor. And we sing "Britons Never Shall Be Slaves." Let the people of Toronto reflect a little on the conditions in this city and cease casting slurs upon those who are for the time being in bad circumstances.

The letter, signed simply "Out of Work," was a reflection of what the dispossessed were up against in their daily struggle to survive, as well as in their organized effort to resist.[37]

A year later, in February 1910, seven members of the non-stone-breaking brotherhood refused the House of Industry labor test and found themselves before Magistrate Ellis, charged with vagrancy. Amidst growing animosity to the Ontario workless flooding into Toronto from parts unknown, turning the city into an "Eldorado of the tramp fraternity," the men became scapegoats in an age-old ideological assault on the "undeserving poor." Unimpressed with the lot before him, the magistrate sentenced the group to jail terms of from thirty days to three months, promising them "a chance to do real work." Meanwhile, the House of Industry, pleading economies, doubled the quantity of stone it required from all casuals receiving bread, water, and a place to lay their heads.[38]

The criminalization of the dispossessed proceeded apace as the crisis of worklessness deepened in 1911–12 and plummeted even further in a severe 1913–15 depression. National in scope, the economic downturn generated what one historian has termed a "Canadian unemployed revolt," in which the prod to action often came from the Industrial Workers of the World on the prairies or the Social Democratic Party in Ontario. Toronto's wageless were hit particularly hard. The municipal relief system sagged under the pressures of more and more applications for aid. In the winter of 1914–15 more than five thousand families, representing in excess of twenty-five thousand people, were applying for relief to the beleaguered House of Industry. Long queues of men, "two and three deep, lined up outside the . . . building waiting for shelter for the night." One official commented that he "had never before seen anything like it." The usual recourse to a series of start-up/close-down Civic Employment Bureaus did little to ease the situation. Maladministered and overwhelmed by applications, such ad hoc agencies competed with corrupt private employment enterprises and managed, for the most part, only to secure temporary work, in limited amounts, for the growing army of the unemployed. Calls for "able-bodied vagrants" to be "made to work for their living until they have acquired the habit of self-support" continued to be heard. Ontario's Commission on Unemployment reported:

> The vagrant thrives on Soup Kitchens, Houses of Industry, Salvation Army Shelters and similar institutions maintained for the purpose of rendering temporary assistance to a worthier class. . . . Men are coming into Toronto from the mining camps and smaller places, spending their money in drink, and complaining of not being able to get work. A lot of them don't want it and wouldn't take it if they had a chance. This class of men augment the already too numerous criminal class.

Decimating the trade unions, whose numbers in Ontario dropped 25 percent, and straining the disciplinary order of relief to the breakpoint, the crisis of 1913–14 left the waged and the wageless in the same sinking boat of capitalist crisis.

In September 1914, six hundred delegates to the Toronto Trades and Labor Council gathered in an effort to compile information on the unemployment crisis. They set up a committee system with captains appointed for each ward, tasked to assemble complete statistical returns on the dimensions of joblessness in the city. A labor-movement-funded Trades Industrial Toy Association was set up to give work to unemployed mechanics in the manufacture of children's playthings. Joseph T. Marks, his *Industrial Banner*, something of a beachhead of Toronto trade-union laborite radicalism, spearheaded a Provincial Publicity Campaign on Unemployment, but his efforts apparently led to little. The situation for working women was particularly dire, as they were often driven to accept "situations in the country, glad to be able to rely thereby upon board and lodging at least." Contemporary claims were made that the unemployment crisis of 1913–14 was the most severe in the history of the Dominion of Canada, with routine reports in the *Labour Gazette* detailing the worsening conditions in Toronto.[39]

Toronto's wageless thus faced an uphill battle in the crisis of 1911–15. Many refused the labor discipline of "cracking the stone." "I'd lay down on the street and die before I'd go to the House of Industry or any such place. The jail's the place for me," stated one malcontent hauled into the courts. He was sentenced to four months. In February 1915, casuals spending nights in the wayfarer's lodge ward of the House of Industry were again refusing to break stone for their keep. George Bust and Nick Melasel were charged with vagrancy for their insubordinate behavior. Described as sullen, his court testimony defiant and unrepentant, Bust got as good as he gave. Stands of combativeness before constituted authority had a way of being repaid in kind. "I think you need looking after," concluded his Worship Squire Ellis. "It'll be $20 and costs or 90 days." Other shelters, too, faced similar resistance to the labor test. At the Fred Victor Mission, which housed upwards of seventy homeless people a night, the unemployed organized a protest against what they considered "unfair practice." The Mission was of the view that the agitation was the work of socialists.[40]

World War I ended the particular 1911–15 capitalist crisis. Wartime production eased wagelessness. This happened, for the most part, in the aftermath of military enlistment, be it coerced or voluntary. The pressures put on the relief order by the sheer numbers of unemployed requiring assistance and the increasing and challenging resistance to relief discipline, often orchestrated by left agitators, lessened. One measure of this is revealed in the statistics of the poor's utilization of police jail cells as lodging. In 1915, Toronto reports indicated that over 10,500 people had been sheltered at various police stations across the city. One year later, in 1916, with the war drive and its recruitment campaigns in full swing, less than 375 had availed themselves of the jail's beds. The Canadian Patriotic Fund, privately financed and administered, provided the families of unemployed men who enlisted a "reasonable standard of comfort," and tens of thousands of single men joined the armed forces to extricate themselves from wagelessness. Roughly six hundred thousand served in the Canadian Expeditionary Force, with 250,000 joining between June 1915 and May 1916. Sixty thousand families benefited from the Patriotic Fund's largesse, which totalled almost forty million dollars in the 1914–19 years. The unemployed had been vanquished, as it were, with capitalism finding something of a resolution to its economic and political crises in the breakout of hostilities in Europe. Inducements to patriotic duty were everywhere and often overrode understandings of the class solidarities of the waged and the wageless. In a January 1915 fundraising entertainment at Massey Hall, organized by the Toronto District Labor Council on behalf of the jobless, the message of fighting against wagelessness was drowned out in dutiful renditions of "The Death of Nelson" and "We'll Never Let the Old Flag Down," the evening being capped off by a recitation of "The Empire Flag," with the address delivered by a speaker wrapped in the Union Jack.[41] No black flags flew at this unemployed rally.

Preparing the Offensive of the Outcasts: The Red Flag Unfurled, 1918–25

War ended. Capitalist crisis continued. But the 1914–18 years had mobilized the state to harness the productive enterprise and energy of the nation, refining a new apparatus of the regulatory state, and in doing so it galvanized initiatives in monitoring and addressing unemployment. By war's end, amidst the winding down of specialized industrial pursuits and the return of veterans, it was feared that unemployment nationally would swell to 250,000 in 1918 alone. Labor was in a combative mood, having tasted the possibilities of full employment during wartime, providing waged and wageless to the battlefront lines, domestically and in the European theater. Class-based criticism of war and the conscription of labor, but not wealth, was commonplace. Tensions were exacerbated by a growing left-wing presence in the unions and among the unorganized and unwaged working class. Talk of the revolution in Soviet Russia and ideas of production for use not for profit grew more menacing. The coalition government leader Sir Robert Borden was warned by one high-ranking advisor in 1918: "People are not . . . in a normal condition. There is less respect for law and authority than we probably have ever had in the country. If . . . Canada faces acute conditions of unemployment without any adequate programme to meet the situation, no one can foresee just what might happen." Setting up the Employment Service of Canada, a national network of labor exchanges funded and run by the joint efforts of provincial and federal governments, was one component of the state response. Unemployment-insurance systems were studied, drawing a surprisingly strong consensus of favorable opinion among government officials, mainstream trade-union leaders, and progressive employers. But the political will to implement such a system evaporated in the Red Scare climate of 1919. Clamping down on working-class militancy, suppressing a 1919 general-strike wave, deporting "alien" radicals, and using state trials of socialist agitators to establish decisively that the red flag, Soviets, and workers' control of production would not become part of the Canadian way of life trumped a forceful state program that would decisively address unemployment in new ways.[42]

Toronto had contributed more recruits to the Canadian war effort than any other city. It would see the return of more soldiers, all of them looking for work, as well. No city, however, had been harder hit than Toronto in the closure of wartime's munitions industries. Amidst the labor revolt of 1919, there was a push not only for sympathetic and general strikes but for a cash bonus to be paid to World War I veterans. One commentator described the proposed two-thousand-dollar gratuity as "one grand solution for virtually all the troubles due to unrest, unemployment, discontent and Bolshevism." Many Toronto veterans agreed and rallied on the legislative grounds at Queen's Park to demand action. There was, however, to be no bonus granted in 1919. Instead, out-of-work veterans were advised to head to the hinterland. A Back to the Land movement, said many employers and not a few farmers, would allow rural producers to "get labour more cheaply." At this the Toronto Great War Veteran's Association took considerable umbrage, arguing that those who had served overseas for four years had not been separated from loved ones and served their country only to be told they could "take employment mucking in the bush," far from the family hearth.[43] Toronto-headquartered Frontier College put a novel spin on the idea that movement to the country could alleviate unemployment, suggesting that municipalities purchase homesteads and employ the jobless in clearing 160 acres and building a house and barn on each improved lot, which could then be sold for a profit.[44]

The crisis of wagelessness that afflicted veterans and nonsoldiers alike deepened until, in the fall of 1920, the economy took another turn for the worse, plunging into depression. Toronto employers reduced working time in order to stave off mass layoffs, but such band-aid solutions were of little help. Veterans who had managed to secure work now lost their jobs, with estimates that one in five able-bodied ex-soldiers had been forced into wagelessness. As national unemployment rates soared to over 10 percent, encompassing 214,000 jobless individuals, the situation in Toronto taxed the public employment bureaus to the break point. More than three thousand of those registered with the bureaus, which favored veterans, were "unplaced"; at the height of the crisis, in the winter of 1921, the number skyrocketed to fifteen thousand. Federal payments to the municipality of Toronto for the emergency relief of the unemployed over the course of December 1920 to April 1921 totalled $134,128, or almost 40 percent of the total distributed across the country. Toronto police cells, a home to so many destitute in 1915 but largely empty of these patrons in 1916, began to fill again. By 1925, a record 16,500 people were housed in city jails, many of them ex-servicemen who had joined the army of the unemployed.[45]

At the Toronto House of Industry the litany of complaint and register of inadequacy rose. A nurse who regularly visited homes of the Toronto indigent saw children going hungry and concluded that it was "impossible for human beings to live at all on what the city supplies." The plight of the workless, claimed these critics, was reminiscent of the "Dark Ages."[46] Such charges and allegations were met with the usual arsenal of denial. Officially constituted and often church-affiliated Neighbourhood Workers' Associations and the superintendant at the House of Industry continued age-old claims that "[e]veryone should know that no man needs to sleep in the parks or walk the streets in Toronto. There is shelter for him. When we encourage begging on the street—which is against the law in the first place—you are encouraging something at the same time that is most deadly for the man."[47]

When frustrated jobless veterans sought relief in paying their rent, which was owing and thus leaving them fearful of eviction, they found themselves "chasing around from one place to another . . . for . . . three weeks," unable to find any agency to lend them a hand. Seeking only loans that they committed to pay back, the ex-servicemen formed a delegation and went to City Hall to seek out Mayor Maguire. Finance Commissioner Ross curtly dismissed the group. "Anybody who thinks that we are going to liquidate his arrears of rent is in error." The former soldiers who decided to organize a Toronto-to-Ottawa trek in protest of inaction on unemployment fared no better. They hoofed it the 220 miles to the nation's capital, only to be sent back emptyhanded on the train.[48] Liberal reformers like Bryce Stewart looked disdainfully on the tendencies of those in power to pass the buck of unemployment to the next generation. "If we wait long enough," he wrote in 1921, "the bread lines and out-of-work doles will cease, unemployment will be gone, men and women will rise out of dull inaction and find joy again in the work of head and hands." Then, all would be forgotten: "The present time will be referred to as the 'hard times of 1920–1921,' an unfortunate experience to be forgotten if possible." But Bryce had seen it all before, having written on the 1913–15 crisis, and he was convinced that "the divine right of unpreparedness" was not going to stave off the next, inevitable downturn: "Men will pursue their usual ways and in 1925, or 26 or 27 or some other year, the dark ogre of unemployment will again thrust his long arm into the factories and mines and shops and offices, tear the workers from their tasks, bank the fires, hang out the 'No Help Wanted' signs and shut the doors against them."[49]

Even as the economy resuscitated somewhat in the years after 1921, the 1920s hardly saw unemployment extinguished. Between 1922 and 1929, the annual average unemployment rate was 11 percent, and 30 percent of all workers found themselves wageless at some point in the year, usually for around eighteen weeks.[50] By 1925, the presence of beggars on city streets and the ongoing influx of the wageless into Toronto from other municipalities precipitated yet another round of ideological and material attacks on the poor. Toronto's chief medical officer, Dr. Charles Hastings, campaigned to rid the city of beggars, whom he considered a variant of the age-old "undeserving poor." Known as an aggressive advocate of improved public health and an enemy of slum conditions, Hastings was also capable of sounding the tocsin of vigilance against the vagrants. He suggested that Toronto civic officials publicize "through the local papers and the Canadian press generally" their intention next winter to terminate "relief to non-residents, or anyone unable to prove their residence, and that, in addition to this, citizens of Toronto be urged not to give promiscuously to men soliciting help at private houses, or to those accosting individuals on the streets, but that they be asked to refer all such persons to the House of Industry, where their case can be properly investigated and where those deserving will receive the necessary food and shelter." Hastings's harangue occurred at a time when George Hamilton, of a government employment bureau, noted that every day between 1,500 and 2,500 men were applying for jobs of any kind. For every hundred, there was work for one. Malnutrition and exposure incapacitated many of those seeking labor, 75 percent of whom, according to one representative of the unemployed, Frank Fleming, were veterans.

Moderate in his views, Fleming still stressed that for all its efforts to relieve the poor, the House of Industry was not able to keep up with the rising pressures on its resources. Hundreds of the unemployed spent their nights huddled in "cold box cars and [on] cement floors." The vast majority of the unemployed were genuinely wanting, Fleming insisted, and they were actively looking for work and should receive sympathy from Toronto residents. "Misery and suffering," Fleming claimed, were widespread. If there was indeed unrest among these poor folk, he suggested, it was the work of "Reds" and "Communists," who were prodding the army of the unemployed to vocalize its discontents and mobilize its ranks.[51]

The red flag had apparently been unfurled among the wageless. The Workers Party of Canada, born amidst the post–World War I downturn, had from its inception been active in forming "large and militant" Unemployed Associations in Toronto and Hamilton. Capitalism was assailed as the cause of the crisis of wagelessness, and among these advocates of a Soviet Canada the demand among the jobless was for "work or full maintenance." Communists considered unemployment central to the class struggle, on a par with wage reductions and the open shop as an issue around which revolutionaries organized and cultivated resistance. "Moscow Jack" MacDonald, a Toronto pattern maker who would emerge in the 1920s as one of Canadian communism's mass leaders, toured the country in the hard winter of 1921, speaking to fellow militants on the scourge of unemployment. Nonetheless, the communist presence in Canadian working-class circles, be they waged or wageless, was weak, subject to the red-baiting of the mainstream press as well as employers, not to mention a contingent of dyed-in-the-wool reactionaries ensconced in conservative corners of trade-union officialdom. Since 1919, this layer of the labor bureaucracy had taken direct aim at revolutionaries in the workers' movement. Two Toronto District Labor Council figures, W. J. Hevey and Arthur O'Leary, were representative of this trend, launching a newspaper, the *Labor Leader,* as a strident voice of the most entrepreneurial wing of business unionism. It railed against IWWism, One Big Unionism, and Bolshevism; the wageless found little in the way of support within its pages. As the economic downturn of the early 1920s sapped the strength of the waged and threw more and more of the wageless into the trough of material despondency, conservatizing tendencies could thus be discerned within the Toronto dispossessed. Tim Buck, a Toronto machinist and perennial communist candidate for the presidency of the Trades and Labor Congress of Canada, polled 25 percent of the delegates at the 1923–24 annual convention. Thereafter it was downhill, and as the capitalist crisis of the early 1920s abated in 1925–26, the workless, their numbers declining, had a brief reprieve. The red flag, flying listlessly over the thinning ranks of the unemployed, readied itself for the next capitalist crisis. It would not be long in coming. A reinvigorated offensive of the outcasts would soon break out in the Great Depression of the 1930s. The reception of the red flag, unfurled in the agitations of the wageless in the 1900–1925 years, would prove unprecedented.[52]

Notes

1. For an introduction to modern capitalist crises, see Ernest Mandel, *The Second Slump: A Marxist Analysis of Recession in the Seventies* (London: New Left Books, 1978); and for different approaches to the ongoing nature of crises, reaching destructively into our own times, see Robert Brenner, *The Economics of Global Turbulence: The Advanced Capitalist Economies from Long Boom to Long Downturn, 1945–2005* (New York: Verso, 2006); Murray E. G. Smith, *Global Capitalism in Crisis: Karl Marx and the Decay of the Profit System* (Halifax: Fernwood, 2010); Greg Albo, Sam Gindin, and Leo Panitch, *In and Out of Crisis: The Global Financial Meltdown and Left Alternatives* (Oakland, Calif.: PM Press, 2010).

2. Karl Marx, *Capital: A Critical Analysis of Capitalist Production,* vol. 1 (Moscow: Foreign Languages Publishing House, n.d.), 20.

3. Karl Marx, *Grundrisse: Foundations of the Critique of Political Economy (Rough Draft)* (Harmondsworth, U.K.: Penguin, 1973), 749–50; Karl Marx, "The Future Results of the British Rule in India," in *Surveys from Exile: Political Writings,* vol. 2 (Harmondsworth, U.K.: Penguin, 1973), 324–25.

4. Michael Denning, "Wageless Life," *New Left Review* 66 (November–December 2010): 79–81; J. C. L. Simonde de Sismondi qtd. in Gareth Stedman Jones, *An End to*

Poverty? A Historical Debate (London: Profile Books, 2004), 151; Max Weber qtd. in G. E. M. de Ste. Croix, *The Class Struggle in the Ancient Greek World* (London: Duckworth, 1981), 262; Edith Abbott, "The Wages of Unskilled Labor in the United States," *Journal of Political Economy* 13 (June 1905): 324; and Catharina Lis and Hugo Soly, "Policing the Early Modern Proletariat, 1450–1850," in *Proletarianization and Family History*, ed. David Levine (Orlando, Fla.: Academic Press, 1984), 163–228.

5. David Montgomery, *The Fall of the House of Labor: The Workplace, the State, and American Labor Activism, 1865–1925* (New York: Cambridge University Press, 1987), 91. See also Peter Way, *Common Labor: Workers and the Digging of North American Canals, 1780–1860* (Baltimore: Johns Hopkins University Press, 1993); Andrea Graziosi, "Common Laborers, Unskilled Workers, 1880–1915," *Labor History* 22 (Fall 1981): 512–44.

6. For an introduction only to Toronto in the 1830–90 years, see Albert Schrauwers, "The Gentlemanly Order and the Politics of Production in the Transition to Capitalism in Upper Canada," *Labour/Le Travail* 65 (Spring 2010): 9–46; Lisa Chilton, "Managing Migrants: Toronto, 1820–1880," *Canadian Historical Review* 92 (June 2011): 231–62; Stephen A. Speisman, "Munificent Parsons and Municipal Parsimony: Voluntary vs. Public Poor Relief in Nineteenth-Century Toronto," *Ontario History* 65 (March 1973): 32–46; Gregory S. Kealey, *Toronto Workers Respond to Industrial Capitalism, 1867–1892* (Toronto: University of Toronto Press, 1980).

7. See, for instance, Albert Schrauwers, *"Union Is Strength": W. L. Mackenzie, the Children of Peace, and the Emergence of Joint Stock Democracy in Upper Canada* (Toronto: University of Toronto Press, 2009), esp. 56–65; and for a useful general statement, see Michael B. Katz, "The Origins of the Institutional State," *Marxist Perspectives* 4 (Winter 1978): 6–23. We offer an extended discussion of this early history in Bryan D. Palmer and Gaetan Heroux, "'Cracking the Stone': The Long History of the Toronto Dispossessed," *Labour/Le Travail* 69 (Spring 2012): 9–62.

8. See, for instance, Peter Baskerville and Eric W. Sager, *Unwilling Idlers: The Urban Unemployed and Their Families in Late Victorian Canada* (Toronto: University of Toronto Press, 1998). For statements on unemployment's recognition in the nineteenth century, see also John Garraty, *Unemployment in History: Economic Thought and Public Policy* (New York: Harper and Row, 1978), esp. 4, 109–28; and Alexander Keyssar, *Out of Work: The First Century of Unemployment in Massachusetts* (New York: Cambridge University Press, 1986).

9. Kealey, *Toronto Workers Respond to Industrial Capitalism*; Bryan D. Palmer, "Labour Protest and Organization in Nineteenth-Century Canada, 1820–1890," *Labour/Le Travail* 20 (Fall 1987): 73; Gregory S. Kealey and Bryan D. Palmer, *Dreaming of What Might Be: The Knights of Labor in Ontario, 1880–1900* (Cambridge: Cambridge University Press, 1982).

10. "Help but Not Pauperize," *Daily Globe*, 26 January 1877, qtd. in *The Workingman in Nineteenth-Century Canada*, ed. Michael Cross (Toronto: Oxford University Press, 1974), 197.

11. Richard Anderson, "'The Irrepressible Stampede': Tramps in Ontario, 1870–1880," *Ontario History* 84 (March 1992): 33–56. This period saw repeated concern expressed

by trustees of the House of Industry that other Ontario municipalities were dumping their poor on Toronto, especially in the depths of winter. *Report of the House of Industry, City of Toronto, 1877* (Toronto: Henry Rowsell, 1878), 3; *Report of the House of Industry, City of Toronto, 1879* (Toronto: Henry Roswell, 1880), 6.

12. James M. Pitsula, "The Treatment of Tramps in Late Nineteenth-Century Toronto," Canadian Historical Association, *Historical Papers* (1980): 116–32; "The Support of the Poor," *Canada Presbyterian,* 7 January 1881; "Tramps and Waifs," *Toronto Globe,* 22 March 1887. One part of the inner history of wood cutting as a labor test involved the Board of the House of Industry subcontracting the delivery of cord wood and the transportation of cut wood sold to clients of the Rogers Coal Company. The owner of this enterprise, Elias Rogers, was involved in a price-fixing ring in the coal industry in the late 1880s. See J. M. S. Careless, *Toronto to 1918: An Illustrated History* (Toronto: James Lorimer, 1984), 143.

13. *Report of the Commissioners appointed to Enquire into the Prison and Reformatory System of Ontario, 1891* (Toronto: Warwick and Sons, 1892), 682–85. See also the comments on "work tests" in *All Saints Church Parish Magazine* 5 (December 1895): 138.

14. *Fifty-Fifth Annual Report of the House of Industry, City of Toronto, 1891–1892* (Toronto: Henry Rowsell, 1893); *Report of the Commissioners Appointed to Enquire into the Prison and Reformatory System of Ontario, 1891*; Pitsula, "Treatment of Tramps in Late Nineteenth-Century Toronto," 131–32; "Talking of the Law," *Toronto Evening Star,* 10 January 1896; "House of Industry Still in a Bad Way Financially," *Toronto Evening Star,* 19 February 1896; *Report of the Commissioners Appointed to Enquire into Prison and Reformatory System in the Province of Ontario, 1891,* 684.

15. "The Labor Test," *Toronto Evening Star,* 16 May 1896; Thomas Conant, *Upper Canada Sketches* (Toronto: William Briggs, 1898), 195.

16. Pitsula, "Treatment of Tramps in Late Nineteenth-Century Toronto," 130.

17. "Around a Stove. Daily Gathering of Queer People at City Hall. Men out of Employment and Those Seeking Charity. How They View Officials and How Officials View Them," *Toronto Evening Star,* 22 February 1896. See also "Stone Test Scares Them. Tramps Object to Work for Food and Lodging," *Toronto Evening Star,* 21 December 1897.

18. B. Rosamund qtd. in Steven Langdon, "The Emergence of the Canadian Working Class Movement, 1845–1875," part 2, *Journal of Canadian Studies* 8 (August 1973): 21. For relevant discussions in the Toronto-based *Ontario Workman,* see "Number and Condition of the Unemployed," 18 December 1873; "The Unemployed," 5 February 1874.

19. Debi Wells, "'The Hardest Lines of the Sternest School': Working-Class Ottawa in the Depression of the 1870s" (M.A. thesis, Carleton University, 1982). Much of the discussion of unemployed demonstrations in this thesis is summarized in Baskerville and Sager, *Unwilling Idlers,* 30–33. For political context, see Bernard Ostry, "Conservatives, Liberals, and Labour in the 1870s," *Canadian Historical Review* 61 (June 1960): 93–127, and for 1878 Quebec City public-works protests demanding "work and bread," see Jean Philip Mathieu, "'C'est le people qui est maître; nous sommes les maîtres a Québec': La grève des ouvriers des travaux publics, juin 1878," *Labour/Le Travail* 70 (Fall 2012): 133–58.

20. See, for instance, *Ottawa Herald,* 23 February 1880; *Ottawa Daily Free Press,* 23 February 1880, among dozens of other newspaper accounts that might be cited.

21. Qtd. in Wells, "'Hardest Lines of the Sternest School,'" 98, and in Baskerville and Sager, *Unwilling Idlers,* 33. Note the wider discussion in David Goutor, *Guarding the Gates: The Canadian Labour Movement and Immigration, 1872–1934* (Vancouver: University of British Columbia Press, 2007).

22. Phillips Thompson, *The Politics of Labor* (New York: Belford, Clarke, 1887), 186–88; Russell Hann, "Brainworkers and the Knights of Labor: E. E. Sheppard, Phillips Thompson, and the Toronto *News*, 1883–1887," in *Essays in Canadian Working-Class History,* ed. Gregory S. Kealey and Peter Warrian (Toronto: McClelland and Stewart, 1976), 35–57.

23. Bettina Bradbury, "The Home as Workplace," in *Labouring Lives: Work and Workers in Nineteenth-Century Ontario,* ed. Paul Craven (Toronto: University of Toronto Press, 1995), 417. For a small sampling of the testimony, see Greg Kealey, ed., *Canada Investigates Industrialism: The Royal Commission on the Relations of Labor and Capital, 1889* (Toronto: University of Toronto Press, 1973); Charles Lipton, *The Trade Union Movement of Canada, 1827–1959* (Toronto: NC Press, 1973), 90; *Ottawa Free Press,* 27 February 1880; Wells, "Hardest Lines of the Sternest School," 95; Baskerville and Sager, *Unwilling Idlers,* 33 and 40 (quoting the *Toronto Globe,* 21 February 1891).

24. The *Globe's* 19 February 1891 image of a black-flag "Work or Bread" demonstration adorns the cover of Baskerville and Sager, *Unwilling Idlers,* where the event of 11 February 1894 is discussed (39–40), citing and quoting "Work or Bread," *Toronto Globe,* 12 February 1891; *Toronto Globe,* 13 February 1891; and *Labor Advocate,* 20 February 1891 and 27 February 1891. See also Lipton, *Trade Union Movement of Canada,* 90; Russell G. Hann, Gregory S. Kealey, Linda Kealey, and Peter Warrian, *Primary Sources in Canadian Working Class History* (Kitchener: Ont.: Dumont, 1973), 9–10.

25. "Need Not Hunger If They'll Work. Superintendant Laughlan of House of Industry Willingly Feeds the Industrious. He Has a Work Test—It's Work. . . . Soup, Fuel and Grocery Orders Result," *Toronto Daily Star,* 28 January 1908. On the amount of stone that had to be broken and its weight, see Dennis Guest, *The Emergence of Social Security in Canada* (Vancouver: University of British Columbia Press, 1980), 37. The unemployed who carried the black flag in Toronto's 1891 protest did so a mere five years after eight anarchists were tried and convicted after an 1886 clash in Chicago's Haymarket Square. Five of these men were sentenced to death; one committed suicide in his cell, four went to the gallows, and three more were imprisoned until their sentences were commuted in the 1890s. The Haymarket story is told in two important studies: Paul Avrich, *The Haymarket Tragedy* (Princeton, N.J.: Princeton University Press, 1986); James Green, *Death in the Haymarket: The Story of Chicago, the First Labor Movement, and the Bombing that Divided Gilded Age America* (New York: Pantheon, 2007). Phillips Thompson recorded his sense of the climate surrounding this first North American Red Scare, condemning "the hideous brutality which found in the death sentence of the . . . convicted Anarchists a subject for ghoulish rejoicing and heartless jests." Thompson, *Politics of Labor,* 167.

26. Ian McKay, *Reasoning Otherwise: Leftists and the People's Enlightenment in Canada, 1890–1920* (Toronto: Between the Lines, 2008), 208–11.

27. Gene Homel, "'Fading Beams of the Nineteenth Century': Radicalism and Early Socialism in Canada's 1890s," *Labour/Le Travailleur* 5 (Spring 1980): 7–32; Colin McKay, *For a Working-Class Culture in Canada: A Selection of Colin McKay's Writings on Sociology and Political Economy, 1897–1939*, ed. Ian McKay (St. John's: Canadian Committee on Labour History, 1996), esp. 34–39, 47–52.

28. Michael J. Piva. *The Condition of the Working Class in Toronto, 1900–1921* (Ottawa: University of Ottawa Press, 1979); Leonard C. Marsh, "The Problem of Seasonal Unemployment: A Quantitative and Comparative Survey of Seasonal Fluctuations in Canadian Employment" (M.A. thesis, McGill University, 1933), 134–35. For women workers, see Leonard C. Marsh, *Canadians In and Out of Work: A Survey of Economic Classes and Their Relation to the Labour Market* (Oxford: Oxford University Press, 1940), 273–79.

29. Robert H. Babcock, *Gompers in Canada: A Study of American Continentalism before the First World War* (Toronto: University of Toronto Press, 1974), esp. 44, 53; Palmer, "Labour Protest and Organization in Nineteenth-Century Canada," 82.

30. Martin Robin, *Radical Politics and Canadian Labour* (Kingston: Queen's University Industrial Relations Centre, 1968), 117; Piva, *Condition of the Working Class in Toronto*, 69, 71–74; *Labour Gazette* 4 (July 1903-June 1904): 614; *Labour Gazette* 8 (July 1907-June 1908): 962–63; "Toronto Free Employment Bureau," *Labour Gazette* 9 (July 1908-June 1909): 1343; "Need Not Hunger if They'll Work," *Toronto Daily Star*, 28 January 1908.

31. *Toronto Globe*, 17 March 1908, qtd. in Piva, *Condition of the Working Class in Toronto*, 74; "Hot Talk in Muddy Park. Orators of the Soap-Box Order Harangue a Crowd on the Waterfront. And Talk of Taking Forcible Possession of Contents of Warehouse," *Toronto Daily Star*, 5 January 1909.

32. "Ugly Temper of Idle Men. The Unemployed Gatherered Swiftly This Morning into Army at City Hall. Blocked Street but Had to Move On," *Toronto Daily Star*, 13 January 1909.

33. "To Get Work for Idle Men. Heard Deputation Today. The Speaker Dropped the Violent Tone When They Entered City Hall. A Large Force of Police on Hand to Guard against Any Disturbance," *Toronto Daily Star*, 14 January 1909.

34. "Stuck a Pin in Ald. J. J. Graham," *Toronto Daily Star*, 18 January 1909.

35. "A Preacher to the Unemployed. Rev. Dr. Eby Roused the Crowd to Very High Pitch of Enthusiasm. Then Speaker Got Hot and Proceeded to Abuse the Civic Authorities in Angry Terms," *Toronto Daily Star*, 21 January 1909. On the social gospel, see Richard Allen, *The Social Passion: Religion and Social Reform in Canada, 1914–1928* (Toronto: University of Toronto Press, 1973). McKay, *Reasoning Otherwise*, 472, refers to Eby's 1909 Church of the Revolution, noting its connection to the Social Democratic party and the encouragement of early socialist feminism.

36. "A Preacher to the Unemployed," *Toronto Daily Star*, 15 February 1909.

37. "Brutal Treatment of the Unemployed," *Toronto Daily Star*, 15 February 1909.

38. "Vagrants Sent Where They'll Have to Work. House of Industry Too Easy for Them and They Go to Prison—Early," *Toronto Daily Star*, 8 February 1910; "More Stone Breaking. Casuals at House of Industry Must Crack Double Quantity," *Toronto Daily Star*, 25 January 1910; "Toronto a Mecca of Tired Tramps. Tramps Flock Here, and the

Associated Charities Want Steps Taken to Keep Them Working. Also Asks that Province Make a Grant to the House of Industry," *Toronto Daily Star,* 21 December 1910.

39. The above paragraphs draw on many sources. Piva, *Condition of the Working Class in Toronto,* 75–86, presents a good summary of the Toronto situation, and provides the quote from Ontario, *Report of the Ontario Commission on Unemployment* (Toronto, 1916), 77–78, 201–2. Note, as well, McKay, *Reasoning Otherwise,* 209; James Naylor, *The New Democracy: Challenging the Social Order in Industrial Ontario, 1914–1925* (Toronto: University of Toronto Press, 1991), 18–19, 80; Baskerville and Sager, *Unwilling Idlers,* 176–84; *Labour Gazette* 15 (July 1914-June 1915), 464–65, 666–67; *Eighty-Fourth Annual Report of the House of Industry, City of Toronto, 1920–1921* (Toronto: Henry Rowsell, 1921), 7, 10; "100,000 Jobless: The Forgotten Depressions of 1908–1916," in *The Canadian Worker in the Twentieth Century,* ed. Irving Abella and David Millar (Toronto: Oxford University Press, 1978), 73–76; James Struthers, *No Fault of Their Own: Unemployment and the Canadian Welfare State* (Toronto: University of Toronto Press, 1983), 12–16; Bryce Stewart, "Unemployment and Organization of the Labour Market," American Academy of Political and Social Science, "Social and Economic Conditions in the Dominion of Canada," *The Annals* 107 (May 1923): 286–93.

40. "Preferred the Jail to Any Other Place. Aged Vagrant Insisted on Being Sent across the Don, and He Was Obliged," *Toronto Daily Star,* 18 December 1912; "Refused to Work, but Took Meals—Jailed. George Bust Was Defiant in Police Court—Received a Lesson. Couldn't Find Work. Wouldn't Crack Stone at the House of Industry for His Breakfast," *Toronto Daily Star,* 5 February 1915; Cary Fagan, *The Fred Victor Mission Story: From Charity to Social Justice* (Winfield, B.C.: Wood Lake Books, 1993), 62.

41. *Annual Report of the Chief Constable of the City of Toronto, 1915* (Toronto: Cardwell Co., 1916), 20; *The Canadian Patriotic Fund: A Record of its Activities from 1914 to 1919,* ed. Phillip Morris, qtd. in Struthers, *No Fault of Their Own,* 14; Desmond Morton and Glenn Wright, *Winning the Second Battle: Canadian Veterans and the Return to Civilian Life, 1915–1930* (Toronto: University of Toronto Press, 1987), ix, 24; Naylor, *New Democracy,* 23.

42. Struthers, *No Fault of Their Own,* 14–27; *Report of the Ontario Commission on Unemployment* (Toronto, 1916); Udo Sauter, "The Origins of the Employment Service of Canada," *Labour/Le Travail* 6 (Autumn 1980): 89–112; Morton and Wright, *Winning the Second Battle,* 108. On the climate of this era, see Gregory S. Kealey, "1919: The Labor Revolt," *Labour/Le Travail* 13 (Spring 1984): 11–44; McKay, *Reasoning Otherwise,* 417–530; Reinhold Kramer and Tom Mitchell, *When the State Trembled: How A. J. Andres and the Citizens' Committee Broke the Winnipeg General Strike* (Toronto: University of Toronto Press, 2010); and Craig Heron, ed., *The Workers' Revolt in Canada, 1917–1925* (Toronto: University of Toronto Press, 1998).

43. Morton and Wright, *Winning the Second Battle,* 124–29; Struthers, *No Fault of Their Own,* 28.

44. "Work of the Frontier College, Toronto: Proposal for Reduction of Unemployment," *Labour Gazette* 21 (1921): 1289.

45. G. D. Robertson to Walter Rollo, 15 December 1921, in *Labour Gazette* 21 (1921): 46; Morton and Wright, *Winning the Second Battle,* 142; Struthers, *No Fault of Their*

Own, 29; Piva, *Condition of the Working Class in Toronto*, 83–84; "Emergency Relief for Unemployed in Canada," *Labour Gazette* 21 (1921): 999; *Annual Report of the Chief Constable of the City of Toronto, 1925* (Toronto: United Press Limited, 1926), 24; Marsh, *Canadians In and Out of Work*, 257–70.

46. "Can't Keep Wolf from Door with Doles from City. Families Would Starve If They Had to Depend on Civic Help Alone. Tales of Sufferers. Work of Other Institutions Hampered by Parsimony of the City," *Toronto Daily Star*, 27 August 1921.

47. "No Man Needs to Beg on Streets Though Destitute in Toronto. Your Response to Appeal of Furtive Individuals Is Likely to Be Tribute to the Professional 'Pan-Handler,'" *Toronto Daily Star*, 14 January 1922.

48. "Where to Get Relief, Many Still in Doubt," *Toronto Daily Star*, 7 February 1922; *Report of the Commissioner of the Ontario Provincial Police, 1922*, qtd. in Morton and Wright, *Winning the Second Battle*, 142.

49. Bryce Stewart, "The Problem of Unemployment," *Social Welfare* (March 1921): 170, qtd. in Struthers, *No Fault of Their Own*, 43.

50. Struthers, *No Fault of Their Own*, 4.

51. On Hastings, see Piva's repeated accounts of his aggressiveness as a public-health official in Piva, *Condition of the Working Class in Toronto*; "Is Appointed to Study Single Man's Problem. Dr. Hastings Also Warns Non-Residents Not to Expect Aid during Winter," *Toronto Daily Star*, 17 September 1925; "Women Pledge to Help Unemployed Men," *Toronto Daily Star*, 3 February 1925.

52. Naylor, *New Democracy*, 118–21, 248; Walter Rodney, *Soldiers of the International: A History of the Communist Party of Canada, 1919–1929* (Toronto: University of Toronto Press, 1968), 47–48; Bryan D. Palmer, *Working-Class Experience: Rethinking the History of Canadian Labour, 1800–1991* (Toronto: McLelland and Stewart, 1992), 227. On early Canadian communism, see Ian Angus, *Canadian Bolsheviks: The Early Years of the Communist Party of Canada* (Victoria: Trafford, 2004).

2

Working People's Responses to Past Depressions

DAVID MONTGOMERY

Since the founding of the Republic, working men and women have been all too familiar with alternating periods of boom times and hard times, with seasonal unemployment, with marked differences in availability of jobs among various parts of the country, and with general depressions abruptly precipitated by overproduction of wares or by bank panics. Not all downturns struck with the same severity. The crisis of the early 1840s pitched nine state governments into default (primarily in the rapidly expanding cotton kingdom), while the depression that began in 1873 sent ten state governments into default over the ensuing eleven years. The sharp collapse between the spring of 1907 and the spring of 1908 so crippled the economy that for many months more immigrants left the United States for their homelands or other countries than disembarked here, while the depressions of 1873–79, 1893–98, and 1929–40 set the stage for fundamental restructuring of industrial, agricultural, and political life.[1]

Vigorous economic expansion between the mid-1820s and the crisis of 1837 (augmented by rising tariffs and by chronic surpluses in federal budgets) stimulated massive sales and transportation of slaves from the Southeast to the booming Cotton Belt. They also attracted a swelling tide of immigration from Europe and migration of rural women to seek wages in port cities and in scattered mill towns. These boom years gave rise to numerous strikes and to the formation of effective trade unions, especially in the thriving ports of Philadelphia and New York. Representatives of fifty occupations in Philadelphia, ranging from dock laborers, handloom weavers, and suburban factory operatives at the poorer end of the income scale to bookbinders, cabinet makers, and butchers at the upper end, contributed monthly dues to citywide delegate bodies (called the Trades' Union) to help finance each other's strikes and the city's famous general strike for a ten-hour day in 1835.² Prominent leaders of the Trades' Unions in both cities became heavily involved in municipal politics.

The depression that had gripped much of the nation by the summer of 1837 crushed most unions, emptied their formerly lucrative treasuries, and left little possibility of successful strikes. As one prominent Philadelphian confided to his diary in 1842:

> The streets seem deserted, the largest houses are shut up and to rent, there is no business, there is no money, no confidence & little hope, property is sold every day by the sheriff at a 4th of the estimated value of a few years ago, nobody can pay debts, the miseries of poverty are felt by both rich & poor.[3]

By the mid-1840s, however, a renewal of capital inflows from Europe, resurgence of canal and railroad construction, conquest of half the previous territory of Mexico, and a flood of German, Irish, and other immigrants opened the way to almost three decades of rather steady increases in per capita output—to be sure, punctuated by half a dozen relatively brief recessions and a severe manufacturing downturn between 1857 and 1861, not to mention a civil war. The 1850s represented a nodal point in this transformation. The iron ship, the telegraph, railroad trunk lines, gold rushes, and enactment by several states of general incorporation laws lent a modern flavor to the era. Most noteworthy, at some point between the census of 1850 and that of 1860, the number of people over ten years of age who were counted as wage laborers (in the United States, which was still dominated by agricultural landowners) came to surpass the number of those counted as slaves.[4] The subsequent destruction of slavery by the Civil War enabled the census of 1870 to classify as wage earners more than half of the men and women then listed as "gainfully employed."[5]

In the autumn of 1873, the overinvestment in railroad expansion led the banking house of Jay Cooke to collapse—the bank whose sales of 5-20 bonds to both small investors and large financial institutions from the earliest days of the Civil War onward had decisively funded the Union war effort and earned Cooke the reputation of the financier who rallied ordinary people to save the imperiled Union. Prices and wages fell to historically unprecedented levels after Cooke's failure, devastating the standards once upheld by even the strongest unions, like those of Pennsylvania's anthracite miners and New England's shoe workers, and ultimately in July 1877 unleashing a wave of strikes that swept along the country's major railroad lines from Maryland to California and prompting President Hayes to proclaim a state of insurrection and dispatch troops from the South and the West to put down strike activity.[6]

By the spring of 1879 the economy had resumed its expansion, vigorously until 1882 and sporadically thereafter, with rising manufacturing and agricultural output producing intense business competition, falling prices, many business failures, and (usually ineffective) efforts by competing businesses to bolster prices by means of trusts and pools. Most important for the working class, the level of immigration had soared as soon as the economy recovered from the 1870s depression, bringing 2,855,000 newcomers to the United States between 1880 and 1885.

Germans came to dominate working-class life in Detroit, St. Louis, Chicago, and elsewhere in the Old Midwest. Because most immigrants were of working age, the labor force grew much faster than the total population. The number of female wage earners also rose sharply, while their most common occupations gradually changed, first from domestic service to factory work, and then at the turn of the century to office and sales work. Simultaneously, farm families were more likely to intensify their own toil than to hire additional hands. Many farmers, black and white, either worked seasonally in manufacturing, lumber, or transportation or gave up farming altogether and often moved step by step to town. In brief, the key to industrial growth in the late nineteenth century was more people devoting more of their lives to working harder than ever before.[7]

Alexander Keyssar's study of unemployment in Massachusetts during the last half of the nineteenth century concluded that occasional joblessness had become a commonplace experience for these wage earners, and that textile-manufacturing communities suffered the most severe fluctuations in levels of employment. For most people, however, three or four months without a reliable job simply led them to move someplace else. A city like Boston provided more varied opportunities for picking up at least some casual job, though as cities became more congested it became increasingly difficult for inhabitants to feed themselves with gardens, livestock, or orchards. Credit from local grocers was often the most likely form of relief, though many employers were known to cut wages rather than lay people off (at least keeping their more skilled workmen). Moreover, by the early 1880s trade-union benefit funds and loans from fraternal organizations sustained many of the better-paid craftsmen, and union traveling cards helped many get established in more promising locations. One consequence of these practices was a growing spread between the earning levels of people in skilled trades and those of laborers and machine operatives (wider than the differentials then found in Europe). This divergence set the stage for a major assault on the high pay scales during and after the 1890s.[8] For most families, however, three or four months without a reliable job simply led them to rely for survival on women's ingenuity and/or moving someplace else.[9]

From the 1850s onward, the questions of who should aid the jobless poor and which impoverished women and men deserved any aid at all became increasingly controversial issues. A commissioner of the New York State Board of Charities declared in the 1870s: "The policy of the law should be to treat as criminal those who levy upon the public for support while able to earn their own living."[10] According to an influential 1880s treatise on law, because no one was required by law to be a productive citizen, the criminal offense was becoming a "public burden."[11] Reformers of public charities sought to privatize poor relief and apply their own strict standards to the determination of who among the poor was truly deserving and who was simply shiftless and pretending to be in need. By the 1870s, the Association for Improving the Condition of the Poor had come to lead the crusade to privatize and systematize the distribution of alms. Their efforts had a special impact on poor women. One must add, however, that urban society in this country then spawned such a variety of religious, fraternal, trade-union, and other institutions offering some assistance, not to mention local customs that induced working men to patronize stores and bars run by widows, as to limit the effectiveness of the association.[12]

It also became increasingly common during periods of high unemployment for urban workers to demand that municipal governments create work projects that would provide some income to the unemployed—especially to men. In turn, the marked increase in voter-participation rates after about 1840 prompted urban political leaders to pay increasing attention to working-class voters. Moreover, many recent immigrants brought with them experience of Europe's revolutions of 1848—and especially of the emergency workshops then established in response to workers' demands in Paris.[13]

Western European workers, especially in the Rhineland, had also momentarily been granted the right to hold their meetings in city halls. It was not astonishing, therefore, that New York's Board of Aldermen granted the trade delegates and social reformers who formed New York's Industrial Congress in 1850 permission to conduct their meetings in the Supreme Court room of City Hall. Delegates assembled there demanded regular use of the meeting rooms, the creation of public baths, a reading room for public use, and a labor exchange, where workers could meet potential employers.[14]

By 1852, however, Tammany Hall had secured control of the Industrial Congresses, inducing delegates from trade unions to exclude politicians, land reformers, and representatives of cooperatives from their assemblies. Nevertheless, the severe unemployment that afflicted New York during the antebellum recession of 1857–59 prompted Mayor Fernando Wood to institute widespread public-works projects, among them improving Central Park.

To be sure, Wood was a most unusual mayor. He is most famous for his proposal that New York City secede from the union in 1861 and become a neutral free city.[15] During the latter half of the century, however, working people around the land often appealed to municipal authorities for work relief, when jobs had disappeared from the private sector. Those in New Albany and Evansville, Indiana, had some success with their towns' Know-Nothing administrations in the 1850s, as did the black members of the Knights of Labor in Richmond in the 1870s and the immigrants mobilized by Social Revolutionaries facing Mayor Carter Harrison's regime in Chicago during the 1880s. As mines and mills failed around Denver in the early 1890s, the city's Trades and Labor Assembly established Camp Relief, which provided clothing and shelter in a tent colony governed by its own inhabitants, and the Maverick Restaurant, which fed 550 people a day.[16]

Mayor William Shelton of New Haven, Connecticut, in 1877 had summed up the argument that the city government should be the employer of last resort:

> [H]umanity should prompt a liberal provision for giving [jobless residents] a partial employment until our industries assume their normal condition, as the condition of the laboring classes is a sad one. The distribution of labor should be general among those out of employment. To keep a set of men continually at work, to the exclusion of others equally worthy at a time like this, is morally wrong; a change should be made every week, and no favoritism shown, except to those in great need.[17]

By no means did all local political leaders share Shelton's view. Boss Tweed's regime in New York had borrowed heavily from European banks and poured the funds so obtained into the development of mid-Manhattan, and also into Catholic and other charities to aid the poor. In the early 1870s the foreign banks called in their loans, while a mobilization of the propertied electorate, and Protestants irate over Catholic influence, overthrew Tweed's government. Its successors in City Hall pared public expenditures to the bone, even during the protracted depression that struck the country in 1873, while the city's larger factories began to leave Manhattan for more spacious surroundings and lower rents.[18] When jobless workers gathered in Tompkins Square in 1874 to demand work from the city, they were brutally assaulted by municipal police.[19]

The hardened lines of ideological confrontation had already been evident in the division between advocates and foes of other efforts of working people to improve the accessibility and terms of employment. During a national economic slump in the immediate aftermath of the Civil War, state legislatures in Illinois, Missouri, California, Wisconsin (in 1867), and Pennsylvania (in 1868) enacted laws making eight hours "a legal day's work," though a major strike in Chicago starting May 1, 1867, and aiming to force the state's employers actually to close after eight working hours ended without success. In the same year, the legislature of Massachusetts rejected bills to shorten the hours for women and children, though in 1874 it did outlaw the employment of women for more than ten hours a day, and thus forced a general reduction of work hours in the state's large textile industry.

In the South, plantation areas experienced considerable turmoil over the terms of work during the summer of 1867, while black dock workers in Mobile and Charleston engaged in strikes, and some southern branches of the Union

League encouraged freedmen to boycott conservative planters, seize crops if they were defrauded, slow down work, and squat on planters' land.[20] But even the gatherings of the Union Leagues in the South soon became centers of stormy controversy. When black delegates to the League conference in Richmond demanded confiscation and partition of plantations, they were shouted down by the white delegates. Most prominent black elected officials also opposed confiscation and advised assembled freedmen to rely on hard work, frugality, and steady habits to improve their lives. Nevertheless, one black laborer at the Richmond League meeting who spoke passionately in favor of confiscation of estates was greeted with thunderous applause from his colleagues.[21]

During the same postwar year, the *New York World* had warned its readers of the perils awaiting the nation if political leaders endorsed the legislative demands of working people. The columnist wrote: "When the government, that is, the taxing power, represents the poverty of the community, and not its property, there will be a constant tendency to rob property of its rights." This was true, he added, whether the poor were black or white. They will have government "squandering prodigality," becoming "wasteful and corrupt."[22] Later, in 1892, a learned commentary on criminal law written by Joel Bishop made the point clear: "There is, in just principle, nothing which a government has more clearly the right to do than to compel the lazy to work; and there is nothing more absolutely beyond its jurisdiction than to fix the price of labor."[23]

In contrast, workers' remedies for unemployment focused on mutual assistance and on their influence on local and state governments. The platforms and declarations of principles adopted by most international unions and by the Knights of Labor stressed the ways workers should behave toward each other: solidarity, brotherhood, and sisterhood.[24] Between the founding of the National Labor Union in 1867 and the demise of its successor, the Industrial Congress, in 1874, labor's legislative demands on the federal government focused on the freedom to form trade unions, on the creation of a national ("greenback") currency that would provide entrepreneurs and farmers with higher prices and ready access to loan capital, on attempts to protect the Homestead Act against large land grants to corporations, and on a legal eight-hour day for federal employees.[25] The eight-hour standard was actually made federal law in 1868 and was even strengthened during President Grant's reelection campaign in 1872, but it was rendered toothless by subsequent Supreme Court decisions.

During the spasmodic economic growth of the 1880s, however, labor advocates, often in tandem with Farmers' Alliances, did develop a growing list of demands for action by Washington, among them the creation of a bureau of labor statistics, postal savings banks, and public ownership of railroads and of coal, iron, gold, and other mines.[26] It was, however, the response of Coxey's Army and other mobilizations of the unemployed during the catastrophic depression that followed the crisis of 1893 that formulated and popularized demands for federal action aimed directly at revitalizing the economy and generating jobs. Jacob Coxey was a prosperous businessman whose thinking was rooted in the post–Civil War greenback movement. When Coxey announced his plan in April 1894 for a march on Washington to arrive on May 1, he specifically endorsed bills introduced by Senator W. A. Peffer of Kansas for the printing of five hundred million dollars in legal-tender notes to fund the building of roads by workers, who were to be paid not less than $1.50 for an eight-hour day. Coxey also called for states and localities to deposit non-interest-bearing bonds with the U.S. treasury to finance the building of "their own markethouses, public libraries, museums, enginehouses, schoolhouses, and public halls, where people can come and discuss all questions that interest them . . . own and build their own electric light plants, water works, street railroads, and other public improvements that . . . promote the advancement of the whole people."[27]

The famous march set out from Massilon, Ohio, on Easter Sunday, 1894, and crossed Pennsylvania and Maryland preceded by an African American flag bearer and usually with 150 to 200 men participating, regularly inspired by sermons about Jesus's works "viewed from the purely humanitarian standpoint." In some communities, like Beaver Falls, Pennsylvania, local inhabitants greeted them warmly, while in others, like Allegheny City and Hagerstown, they were met with hostility. Kaufman's department store in Pittsburgh welcomed the marchers with a contribution of three hundred pairs of shoes and three hundred vests. In Frederick, Maryland, the sheriff kept them under surveillance, only to be denounced by local citizens, who contributed generously to the marchers. In the steel towns of the Monongahela Valley, which had lately been shaken by the Homestead strike, the friendly reception was tumultuous.[28]

Other marchers set out from Seattle, Denver, Birmingham, Grand Rapids, and elsewhere. The ranks of some of them swelled at times to more than two thousand, and some marchers in Butte and Council Bluffs seized trains, rousing the ire of Attorney General Richard Olney. National Guard units were called out eight times against various groups of marchers. Some California marchers crossed Arizona on trains its members had commandeered. The Knights of Labor in Chicago endorsed the jobless army (though the city council barred approaching members from the city).[29] Coxey's Army did reach Washington by May 1, but Coxey and other leaders were not permitted to address Congress, and they were arrested when they tried to speak on the capitol lawn. Nevertheless, several congressmen did introduce "Coxey bills" for federal public works. None passed.[30] But the legacy of marching on Washington for jobs and public assistance survived to become a regular feature of subsequent depressions.

The stormy decade of the 1890s is best remembered by historians of labor for the titanic union battles such as the Homestead strike, the Pullman boycott, and the huge strikes of coal miners in the Midwest and in southern Colorado, which were spread from pit to pit by strikers' marches, the total shutdowns of textile mills in Lawrence and Fall River, the frequency with which immigrants in the lowest pay grades joined strikers from the most skilled ranks, and the solidarity exhibited between black and white New Orleans dockers in 1892. Time and again, the courts enjoined such solidarity, making this a critical epoch in the development of labor law, while federal or state authorities mobilized their armed forces to enforce such rulings.[31]

By the 1890s, the United States added more value to its national income by manufacturing than did any other nation in the world. It also exported unequaled quantities of agricultural products. By 1900, a handful of countries in Western Europe and North America accounted for some 80 percent of the manufactured goods of the world.[32] Those countries in turn had partitioned most of the rest of the world into colonies and spheres of influence. They poured resources into the development of naval power, like the Great White Fleet that President Theodore Roosevelt was to send around the world and the Japanese flotilla that crushed Russia's Pacific power in 1904. Subsidies provided by rival European powers to their respective merchant and passenger fleets made it possible for immigrants to sail to the Western Hemisphere at fares far cheaper than immigrants from Asia had to pay, forcing the Asians into resurgent forms of indentured servitude.[33] Military confrontations, like the Anglo-French standoff in the Sudan, Italian invasions of Ethiopia and later of Libya, German seizure of Shandong from China, and the destruction of the Spanish Empire by the United States, all contributed to making fear of pending world war the primary concern of the Socialist International as the new century dawned.[34]

The depression of the 1890s deserves close comparison with our own times. The decline of sales began in mining and commercial agriculture, the major shippers for the vast railway network. The railroads' loss of revenues precipitated the failure of the giant British banking house Baring Brothers, which in turn provoked British investors to unload U.S. stocks and the New York Stock Exchange to collapse. By the end of 1893, 491 American banks and over fifteen thousand other commercial institutions had failed. Gold was drained out of the U.S. treasury at an unprecedented rate, receipts from the highly protective tariff shriveled, and the huge Civil War pensions enacted by the previous Republican administration and Congress commandeered more than 40 percent of federal expenditures.[35] President Grover Cleveland stood like Horatio at the bridge, prepared to sacrifice his presidency and his party's control of Washington and to endure in secret a painful operation so that he might slash government expenditures, pare down the tariff, fight off incessant opposition efforts to remonetize silver, and save the gold standard--to him and to his admirers, the ultimate emblem of Euro-American civilization and bulwark of unfettered global commerce. By early 1895, when the rapid flow of gold out of Washington threatened the federal government with default, only the intervention of a consortium of banks assembled by J. P. Morgan saved the government—the last time in history the private sector rescued the public sector. As Cleveland's resolve made starkly evident, pegging national currencies to gold imposed a tight discipline on the "free market" of every industrialized country. Gunboats and marines were soon to be deployed to impose similar budgetary discipline on less-developed countries (or, to use the language of Theodore Roosevelt, those who were less "civilized").[36] Cleveland's determination shaped his negative responses to all measures intended to expand the currency, to the Pullman boycott, and to Coxey's Army.

The economic crisis also opened the way to effective consolidation of the country's business structure. During the decade 1895–1905, most of the major corporations that were to dominate the U.S. economy until the 1970s were created. One thinks of U.S. Steel, Westinghouse, General Electric, International Harvester, Armour, and Standard Oil (all soon to be joined by General Motors), whose eternal life we older folks long took for granted. Unsuccessful strikes in steel, meat packing, and farm equipment had left large-scale industry overwhelmingly nonunion by 1910.[37]

The consolidation and revitalization of industrial capitalism at the turn of the century was international in scope. The French economist Leon Dupriez calculated that the average annual change in physical output per capita for advanced industrial countries as a group between 1895 and 1913 was double what it had been between 1880 and 1894. The United States, which had already emerged during the 1880s as the world's leading industrial producer, increased its output even more than its leading rivals, England, Germany, and France. Although most manufacturing and construction firms remained relatively small and privately owned as the twentieth century dawned, the average worker in manufacturing now worked for one of the new giant enterprises. By 1909, fully 62.2 percent of all wage earners in manufacturing were employed by only 4.8 percent of the firms.[38] As *Iron Age* reported in 1912, "millions of dollars in specifications for ... special and semi-special machinery, and the newest types of high-power, high-speed and standard tools" reshaped production processes, with the result, according to the 1910 Census of Manufactures, that the value added per worker had grown by more than 40 percent, whereas the number of wage earners in American manufacturing had risen 37 percent between 1899 and 1909.[39]

The framework of business life that emerged from the depression of the 1890s lasted with important modifications in federal relief measures, in labor law, and in social insurance until the 1970s. It also reshaped working-class life, the labor movement, and workers' responses to depressions for the next three-quarters of a century.

Space will not allow us to discuss the growing popularity after the 1890s of social ownership of industry and of the numerous municipal-reform movements, the appeal of direct action (around the world after Russia's 1905 revolution), both through the IWW and outside of it, or Americans' part in the transnational Great Upheaval of strikes dominated by unskilled workers between 1910 and the recession of 1913, or the wartime and postwar upsurge of labor unions in the economy's dominant corporations. In the prosperous months of these decades, workers not only launched spectacular strikes but also simply quit their jobs in astonishing numbers (Ford suffered a quit rate of 415 percent in 1912–13). Big companies undertook major efforts to retain their experienced employees, with growing success during the 1920s. The median quit rate in manufacturing fell to 30 percent by 1929, and less than 15 percent in 1936–37.[40]

The New Deal experience was a remarkable example of American Exceptionalism. The depression pushed most European and South American governments to the right—either to durable conservative coalitions (Britain) or to outright dictatorships. The moment of Popular Front influence (France, Belgium, Spain) proved brief. As Daniel Rodgers has observed:

> The institution of new social insurance systems came virtually to a halt in the early 1930s. Canadian Conservatives pushed through an unemployment insurance act on the New Deal example in 1935, only to be voted out of office and watch their Liberal successors nullify the measure in the courts. The Swedish unemployment benefits act of 1934 was a belated, subsidarist measure. New Zealand's Social Security Act of 1938 eschewed insurance principles altogether. Only in the United States was there a major push forward in social insurance during the Depression decade.[41]

In addition to the innovations enacted by federal and state governments, working men and women often intervened on their own initiative to secure and improve their own livelihoods—sometimes successfully, sometimes not. Let us look briefly at some such actions undertaken during the second round of the Great Depression, 1937–39. The union movement, though crushed in most basic industries during the earlier depression years of 1920–22, had revived vigorously, aided by the New Deal. Its total membership by 1940 would surpass that of 1920, its previous record high. But it was also evident that an upward leap in worker productivity had lifted output per worker by 1935–36 above the previous high of 1928, even though the level of unemployment remained high, especially for older, youthful, and nonwhite men and women. Then, late in 1937, a sharp downturn in orders for capital goods encouraged many companies large and small to revive their anti-union policies, while also contributing to the sharp rightward turn of the electorate in 1938. Many workers concluded that capital had gone on strike against the New Deal, and many advocated a planned economy. But it also challenged millions of workers to use their new unions to voice immediate answers to the resurgence of unemployment.[42]

The Steel Workers Organizing Committee found its employed membership literally cut in half in the final months of 1937, as did the important St. Louis district of the United Electrical Workers. Both unions fought successfully to arrange for laid-off members to be instated immediately on relief rolls, without going through welfare agencies. In major industrial centers like Pittsburgh and Tarentum, union officers and activists won the power to manage local relief rolls directly. Other local unions fought for and won the power to place unemployed members directly onto the rolls of the Works Progress Administration (WPA). When a newly conservative Congress in 1939 terminated all nonmanual WPA relief work, required a loyalty oath of all WPA employees, and prescribed a one-month dismissal of everyone who had been on WPA rosters for more than a year and a half, CIO locals in Minnesota and the famous Trotskyist-led local of the Teamsters threw their support behind a strike by WPA members—one of the strongest of many WPA strikes across the country. The unemployed refused to go to work![43]

Moreover, it was during and after the 1930s that the principle that seniority should govern layoffs and promotions was elevated from an occasional union or company practice to a basic tenet of working-class morality. Some building trades and other unions with effective hiring halls fixed quotas of workers older than fifty-five whom contractors had to retain during any reduction of force. The aim was to prevent a threatened elimination of older workers from trades whose unions had rarely interfered with employers' decisions to fire individual workers, so long as the dismissal was not for union activity, and any replacement was a union member paid union scale. At the other extreme, major locals of the United Electrical Workers, like that at Westinghouse in East Pittsburgh, fought for an unqualified seniority principle even before the union had been certified, but they were so staggered by the numbers of people dismissed in 1937 that they changed their demand to a general reduction of weekly hours and no layoffs. But when the short time they had won dragged on for month after month, the local shifted to a complex plan calling for a reduction of weekly hours to thirty-six in any affected division, followed by dismissing anyone with less than a year's seniority, followed by further stair-step reductions if needed, and finally by department negotiations if things got even worse than that. Control of layoffs and recall according to seniority was far better than leaving all choices up to the management, but it was hardly a cure for unemployment.[44]

Our own time calls for still more imaginative responses. Manufacturing and agriculture have yielded place to public employment, service work, and clerical jobs as the dominant sources of employment. Stimulus efforts introduced by one major country risk disrupting those undertaken by competitors. In the United

States, profits and subsidies accumulated by companies are far more likely to be invested in labor-saving equipment than in employment of more people. Most important, figures released by the United Nations in the late 1990s revealed that 78 percent of all manufacturing employees in the world are now employed outside of the industrial powers that had dominated the world economy before 1970. Both government measures and workers' collective efforts to restore declining incomes must now take an international shape.[45]

Notes

Unfortunately, David Montgomery passed away before he was able to submit a final version of his paper for this volume. Joseph McCartin edited his original contribution with assistance from Edward Montgomery, and in a few instances they added details to footnotes whose citations were incomplete at the time of Professor Montgomery's death.

1. Carmen M. Reinhart, "This Time Is Different Chartbook: Country Histories on Debt, Default, and Financial Crises," Working Paper 15815, National Bureau of Economic Research, Cambridge, Mass., March 2010, accessed 5 June 2013, http://www.nber.org/papers/w15815.

2. David Montgomery, "The Shuttle and the Cross: Weavers and Artisans in the Kensington Riots of 1844," *Journal of Social History* 5 (Spring 1972): 411–46; Bruce Laurie, *Working People of Philadelphia, 1800–1850* (Philadelphia: Temple University Press, 1980); Sean Wilentz, *Chants Democratic: New York City and the Rise of the American Working Class, 1788–1850* (New York: Oxford University Press, 1984); Christine Stansell, *City of Women: Sex and Class in New York, 1789–1860* (New York: Knopf, 1986).

3. Stephen G. Fisher, *A Philadelphia Perspective: The Diary of Sidney George Fisher Covering the Years 1834–1871*, ed. Nicholas B. Wainwright (Philadelphia: Historical Society of Pennsylvania, 1967), 134–35.

4. David Montgomery, *Citizen Worker: The Experience of Workers in the United States with Democracy and the Free Market during the Nineteenth Century* (New York: Cambridge University Press, 1993), 13, n.1; Joseph G. Baldwin, *Flush Times of Alabama and Mississippi: A Series of Sketches*, 2d ed. (New York: D. Appleton and Co., 1854).

5. David M. Gordon, Richard Edwards, and Michael Reich, *Segmented Work, Divided Workers: The Historical Transformation of Labor in the United States* (New York: Cambridge University Press, 1982).

6. J. A. Dacus, *Annals of the Great Strikes in the United States* (Chicago: L. T. Palmer and Co., 1877); Philip S. Foner, *Great Labor Uprising of 1877* (New York: Monad Press, 1977); Michael J. Perman, *Road to Redemption: Southern Politics, 1869–1879* (Chapel Hill: University of North Carolina Press, 1984).

7. David Montgomery, *Fall of the House of Labor: The Workplace, the State, and American Labor Activism, 1865–1925* (New York: Cambridge University Press, 1987), 46–57; Alice Kessler-Harris, *Out to Work: A History of America's Wage-Earning Women in the United States* (New York: Oxford University Press, 1982); John Mack Faragher, *Sugar Creek: Life on the Illinois Prairie* (New Haven, Conn.: Yale University Press, 1986); Tera R.

Hunter, *To 'Joy My Freedom: Southern Black Women's Lives and Labors after the Civil War* (Cambridge, Mass.: Harvard University Press, 1997); Estelle Feinstein, *Stamford in the Gilded Age* (Stamford, Conn.: Stamford Historical Society, 1974); Jacqueline Dowd Hall, *Like a Family: The Making of a Southern Cotton Mill World* (Chapel Hill: University of North Carolina Press, 1987).

8. Alexander Keyssar, *Out of Work: The First Century of Unemployment in Massachusetts* (New York: Cambridge University Press, 1983), chaps. 3 and 5; David Montgomery and Marcel van der Linden, eds., *August Sartorius von Waltershausen: The Workers' Movement in the United States, 1879–1885* (New York: Cambridge University Press, 1998); Shelton Stromquist, *A Generation of Boomers: The Pattern of Railroad Labor Conflict in Nineteenth-Century America* (Urbana: University of Illinois Press, 1987); Peter Bischoff, "D'un atelier de moulage à un autre: les migrations des mouleursoriginaires des Forges du Saint-Maurice et la segmentation du marché du travail nord-américain, 1851–1884," *Labour/Le Travail* 40 (Fall 1997): 21–73.

9. S. J. Kleinberg, *The Shadow of the Mills: Working-Class Families in Pittsburgh, 1870–1907* (Pittsburgh: University of Pittsburgh Press, 1989).

10. Qtd. in Amy Dru Stanley, *Bondage to Contract: Wage Labor, Marriage, and the Market in the Age of Slave Emancipation* (New York: Cambridge University Press, 1998), 104.

11. Ibid., 106.

12. Kleinberg, *Shadow of the Mills*; Montgomery and Van der Linden, *Sartorius von Waltershausen.*

13. On voter turnout, see Paul Kleppner, *The Third Electoral System, 1853–1892: Parties, Voters, and Political Cultures* (Chapel Hill: University of North Carolina Press, 1979). On Paris workshops and Rhineland uprisings, see P. H. Noyes, *Organization and Revolution: Working-Class Associations in the German Revolutions of 1848–1849* (Princeton, N.J.: Princeton University Press, 1966).

14. Wilentz, *Chants Democratic*; Carl Frederick Wittke, *The Utopian Communist: A Biography of Wilhelm Weitling, Nineteenth-Century Reformer* (Baton Rouge: Louisiana State University Press, 1950).

15. Iver Bernstein, *New York Draft Riots: Their Significance for American Society and Politics in the Age of the Civil War* (New York: Oxford University Press, 1990).

16. Peter J. Rachleff, *Black Labor in the South: Richmond, Virginia, 1865–1890* (Philadelphia: Temple University Press, 1984), 161–62; Todd DePastino, *Citizen Hobo: How a Century of Homelessness Shaped America* (Chicago: University of Chicago Press, 2003); Carlos C. Closson Jr., "The Unemployed in American Cities," *Quarterly Journal of Economics* 8 (January 1894): 168–217, 257–58.

17. Mayor's Address, *City Year Book for the City of New Haven, 1877* (New Haven: City of New Haven, 1877), 23.

18. Montgomery, *Citizen Worker*, 141–43; Bernstein, *New York Draft Riots.*

19. David Montgomery, *Beyond Equality: Labor and the Radical Republicans, 1862–1872* (Urbana: University of Illinois Press, 1981), 320–31: Herbert Gutman, "The Failure of the Movement by the Unemployed for Public Works in 1873," *Political Science Quarterly* 80 (1965): 254–76.

20. Heather Cox Richardson, *Death of Reconstruction: Race, Labor, and Politics in the Post–Civil War North, 1865–1901* (Cambridge, Mass.: Harvard University Press, 2001), 37–56; Michael W. Fitzgerald, "Union League Movement in Alabama and Mississippi: Politics and Agricultural Change in the Deep South during Reconstruction" (Ph.D. dissertation, University of California–Los Angeles, 1986).

21. Richardson, *Death of Reconstruction*, 55.

22. Qtd. in ibid., 59.

23. Joel Bishop, *New Commentaries on the Criminal Law*, vol. 1 (Chicago: T. H. Flood, 1892), 273–74.

24. See, for example, George McNeill, *Labor Movement: The Problem of To-day* (Boston: A. M. Bridgman and Co., 1887), 483–96.

25. Andrew Cameron, editorial, *Workingman's Advocate*, 25 March 1865.

26. See, for example, "Nine Things Needed," *John Swinton's Paper*, 14 October 1883.

27. Henry Vincent, *Story of the Commonweal* (Chicago: W. B. Conkey Co., 1894), 52–53; Carlos A. Schwantes, *Coxey's Army: An American Odyssey* (Lincoln: University of Nebraska Press, 1965).

28. Vincent, *Story of the Commonweal*, 69–105 (quotation on 69). See also DePastino, *Citizen Hobo*.

29. Vincent, *Story of the Commonweal*, 174, 181.

30. Montgomery, *Citizen Worker*, 156–57.

31. Christopher L. Tomlins, *The State and the Unions: Labor Relations, Law, and the Organized Labor Movement in America, 1880–1960* (New York: Cambridge University Press, 1985); William E. Forbath, *Law and the Shaping of the American Labor Movement* (Cambridge, Mass.: Harvard University Press, 1991).

32. By way of contrast, in 1800, 33 percent of the world's manufacturing output had been fabricated in China (roughly the same as Europe including Britain) and almost 20 percent in India. Mike Davis, *Late Victorian Holocausts: El Niño Famines and the Making of the Third World* (New York: Verso, 2001), 294.

33. David Northrup, *Indentured Labor in the Age of Imperialism, 1834–1922* (New York: Cambridge University Press, 1995), 8–9, 156–61; Stanley Engerman, "Servants to Slaves to Servants: Contract Labour and European Expansion," in *Colonialism and Migration: Indentured Labour before and after Slavery*, ed. P. C. Emmer (Dordrecht, Neth.: M. Nijhoff, 1986), 263–94.

34. David Montgomery, "Workers' Movements in the United States Confront Imperialism: The Progressive Era Experience," *Journal of the Gilded Age and Progressive Era* 7 (January 2008): 7–42.

35. On veterans' pensions, see Theda Skocpol, *Protecting Soldiers and Mothers: The Political Origins of Social Policy in the United States* (Cambridge, Mass.: Harvard University Press, 1992). On the simultaneous extensive but unsuccessful campaign for reparations for former slaves, see Mary Frances Berry, *My Face Is Black Is True: Callie House and the Struggle for Ex-Slave Reparations* (New York: Alfred A. Knopf, 2005).

36. Horace Samuel Merrill, *Bourbon Leader: Grover Cleveland and the Democratic Party* (Boston: Little Brown, 1957); Nick Salvatore, *Eugene V. Debs: Citizen and Socialist* (Urbana: University of Illinois Press, 1982); John Sproat, *"The Best Men": Liberal Reform-*

ers in the Gilded Age (NewYork: Oxford University Press, 1968), 170–203; Theodore Roosevelt, "Fourth Annual Message . . . December 6, 1904," in *A Compilation of the Messages and Papers of the Presidents,* vol. 15 (New York: Bureau of National Literature, 1914), 7053–54; Lloyd C. Gardner, Walter F. LaFeber, and Thomas J. McCormick, *Creation of the American Empire* (Chicago: Rand McNally, 1976).

37. James Livingston, *Origins of the Federal Reserve System: Money, Class, and Corporate Capitalism, 1890–1913* (Ithaca, N.Y.: Cornell University Press, 1986), 83–99.

38. Ibid., 56–57. See also Daniel Nelson, *Managers and Workers: Origins of the New Factory System in the United States, 1880–1920* (Madison: University of Wisconsin Press, 1975), 3–10. Compare that figure with 1995, when only 19 percent of the country's workers were employed by firms with more than five hundred employees.

39. Gordon, Edwards, and Reich, *Segmented Work,* 103; Nelson, *Managers and Workers,* 9; *Iron Age* 89 (18 April 1912): 1004.

40. David Montgomery and Ronald Schatz, "Facing Layoffs," in *Workers' Control in America: Studies in the History of Work, Technology, and Labor Struggles,* ed. David Montgomery (New York: Cambridge University Press, 1979), 140.

41. Daniel T. Rodgers, *Atlantic Crossings: Social Politics in a Progressive Age* (Cambridge, Mass.: Harvard University Press, 1998), 435.

42. Walter Licht, *Getting Work, Philadelphia, 1840–1950* (Cambridge, Mass.: Harvard University Press, 1982).

43. Montgomery and Schatz, "Facing Layoffs," 144–47.

44. Ibid., 146–51.

45. Catherine Rampell, "Companies Spend on Equipment, Not Workers," *New York Times,* 10 June 2011, A1. For a provocative proposal for stimulus on an international basis, which was devised by Germany's Free Trade Unions (Social Democratic) shortly before Hitler stamped it out, see Wladimir Woytinsky, "International Measures to Create Employment: A Remedy for the Depression," *International Labour Review* 25.1 (January 1932): 1–22 (quotations on 20 and 21). The article was brought to my attention by Jeremy Brecher.

3

Soviet Workers and Stalinist Terror
The Crisis of Industrialization

WENDY GOLDMAN

As capitalism scours the globe, leaving no remote rural corner untouched, it is worth noting that its dynamic destruction began almost half a millennium ago. A systemic transformation that began in England in the sixteenth century continues to uproot peasantries, fuel new industrial revolutions, and remake classes and markets today. In the Soviet Union, many of these vast changes, which spanned about four hundred years in the West, were telescoped into a mere decade. In the 1930s, the world's first socialist state embarked on an economic program aimed at avoiding the inequality, poverty, and urban slums created by capitalism. While millions of people in the United States and Europe were standing in bread lines, Soviet citizens enjoyed full employment, free education, and rapid upward mobility. Workers all over the world looked hopefully to a new model that promised to transcend the anarchic boom-and-bust cycles of capitalism.

Yet Soviet leaders, faced with the challenge of developing an overwhelmingly peasant country, confronted the same need for investment capital that drove the bourgeoisie. In 1929, they adopted the first Five-Year Plan, an ambitious program of industrialization financed by capital extracted from the labor of peasants and workers. The ensuing decade encompassed a dizzying succession of upheavals: industrialization, collectivization, reorientation of the trade unions, state control of the food supply, urbanization, passportization, and the Great Terror. The peasantry was dispossessed as a class of small holders, state and collective farms replaced the household as the primary units of production, the *kulaks* were exiled, and millions of people migrated to towns with nothing to sell but their labor power. The government entered a long, protracted struggle with peasants and workers over production and consumption, a struggle that Marx never imagined under socialism. The state assumed the role of the capitalist in appropriating surplus, and although it was ploughed back into development, neither peasants nor workers fully acquiesced to the sacrifices required. The resulting social crisis badly shook the Communist Party and led to mass repressions of alleged "class enemies" and former oppositionists by the decade's end.

In *Capital*, Marx advanced the idea of primitive accumulation, a process that characterized the transition from feudalism to capitalism. For Marx, what distinguished capitalism from earlier forms of wealth accumulation through trade was the dispossession of the peasantry, an agricultural population set free with nothing to sell but its labor power: "The so-called primitive accumulation, therefore, is nothing else than the historical process of divorcing the producer from the means of production." This central element of capitalism—dispossession and the creation of waged labor—set other great historical changes in motion. It destroyed rural domestic industry and created vast national and international markets for goods. The small property of the many became the great property of the few, and individual landowners took over the commons. New, harsh legislation criminalized vagabondage. The newly dispossessed were forced to work through an array of laws, punishments, and institutions, including whipping, workhouses, forced indentures, slavery, branding, and execution. The history of this expropriation, according to Marx, was violent and painful, "written in the annals of mankind in letters of blood and fire."[1]

Soviet historians have carefully studied the decade of the 1930s. Yet each wrenching episode of transformation—collectivization, industrialization, the Great Terror—was of such magnitude that it has largely been studied in isolation from the others. This essay is an attempt to reconceptualize the decade as a whole by using Marx's concept of primitive accumulation and emphasis on dispossession, proletarianization, and violence. It has but one distant precedent: the last theoretician to apply Marx's concept to Soviet development was Evgeny Preobrazhensky, an Old Bolshevik and member of the left opposition. Preobrazhensky recognized that capitalist and socialist accumulation might share certain painful social and economic features. In the early 1920s, he posited that workers and peasants might be subjected to a brief period of "hyper exploitation," in which the state would extract a high level of surplus value to pump back into socialist industrial development. At the time Preobrazhensky developed his idea, however, he had little inkling of how much disruption and suffering this "hyper exploitation" would entail. In fact, Preobrazhensky, who was executed in 1937 at the height of the terror, had no way of knowing that his theory would turn him into one of the many political victims of the very processes he sought to understand.

The Tussle over Grain

On the eve of the great industrialization drive in 1929, Stalin wrote to V. I. Molotov, a Politburo member and trusted supporter, "The grain procurements have gone well. Stick to a firm policy.... If we can beat this grain thing, then we will prevail in everything, both in domestic and foreign policies."[2] In this short message, Stalin summed up the key to Soviet economic development: the ability to extract enough surplus grain from the peasantry to quell urban discontent and accumulate capital through export. Soviet leaders were keenly aware that the peasantry's sale of grain at prices favorable to the state was critical to industrialization. Over the next decade, the accumulation of capital through agricultural and industrial production became a driving force within the regime, locking the state in a struggle with its two largest social classes, workers and peasants. The Party itself was profoundly split over this struggle, and Stalin believed that the very fate of socialism depended on the outcome. The responses of workers and peasants varied, but each consistently sought to bend state policy to their own interests. The state aimed to maximize surplus for investment, while workers and peasants tried to retain it in order to improve the painful conditions of life.

The problem of trade between city and countryside had bedeviled the Bolsheviks since the revolution in 1917. Forced to requisition grain to feed the Red Army and the starving cities during the Civil War, the Bolsheviks had lost considerable peasant support by 1920. In many areas, peasants openly rebelled against requisitions despite their support for the land program of the Reds.[3] The New Economic Policy (NEP), adopted in 1921, aimed to repair relations with the peasants by allowing them to sell grain on the private market over and above a tax imposed by the state. Under the Bolshevik slogan "Land to the Tiller," the peasants received the land of the nobles, which they promptly divided among themselves on the basis of family size. In accordance with the age-old traditions of the *mir*, the peasants divided the land according to a socialist labor principle, but each household marketed its own grain. The "socialist" traditions of the Russian peasantry that so captivated Marx in his later years were limited to the land; they did not extend to its fruits. Peasants were fiercely attached to the market, and wealthier peasants avidly sought to obtain the best price through a variety of strategies, including withholding grain until later in the season when prices began to rise. Although NEP proved successful in rebuilding the shattered economy and the state's relationship with the peasantry, it also committed the state to annual negotiations with the peasants over grain prices and deliveries, which in turn affected the availability of food in the towns.

The middle and prosperous peasants (*seredniaki* and *kulaki*) thrived under NEP, but many workers were angered by the fluctuations in the cost and supply of food and the power of small businessmen. The Workers' Opposition, representing this perspective within the Bolshevik party, sarcastically deemed NEP the "New Exploitation of the Proletariat." The Workers' Opposition understood that the revolution had not entirely eliminated classes, or their clashing interests, and they noted that the Party found itself in the unenviable role of mediator: "The Party finds itself in a difficult position regarding control over the Soviet state. It is forced to adapt itself to three economically hostile groups: workers demand a rapid advance toward communism, the peasantry, with its petty-bourgeois proclivities, demands the freedom of trade, and they are supported by the ranks of officialdom."[4]

Throughout the 1920s, these conflicting interests were expressed politically through various oppositions within the Party, and economically through state pricing of industrial and agricultural goods (a recurring problem that Trotsky called "the scissors crisis"). The left opposition, representing the interests of industrial workers, pushed a program of rapid development of heavy industry to be financed by lower state procurement prices for grain. The mainstream of the Party (and later, the right opposition), reflecting the interests of the peasants, advocated a slower tempo of development based on investment in light industry and higher prices for grain. The Party, and its various fractions and tendencies, thus reflected the competing interests of the two largest classes in Soviet society.

The conflict came to a head with the end of the reconstruction period in 1926–27. NEP was increasingly ineffective as a policy for capital accumulation and further industrial development. Shortfalls in grain procurement in 1926 and again in 1927 resulted in urban riots, bread lines, and protests, placing heavy pressure on party leaders to protect their working-class base and resolve the impasse with the peasantry. Stalin and his supporters embarked on an ambitious program of industrialization. Breaking with the slower tempo of economic development of the 1920s, they chose to invest in heavy industry, gain firm control of the grain supply, and herd peasants into collective farms. The centuries-old traditions and practices of peasant agriculture were uprooted. Collective farms forcibly supplanted individual, extended, patrilocal households. These policies rapidly produced unintended consequences and massive social upheaval. Peasants slaughtered their livestock in protest, food supplies plummeted, and prices spiraled out of control. Amid widespread resistance, 1.8 million peasants were branded as kulaks and sent into exile.[5]

The dispossession and exile of the kulaks paralleled the earlier dispossession of poorer peasants in the English and Irish countryside in the transition to capitalism. In the Soviet Union, entire families were deported under terrible conditions. Dumped in special settlements in forests and wastelands, people died from starvation, illness, and cold. Moreover, between 6 and 26 percent of the exiles were not in fact kulaks but victims of mistakes made by overzealous local activists.[6] Thousands of people attempted to escape from these impoverished settlements. Itinerant, embittered, and hunted, they crisscrossed the country, concealing their former identities in a search for work and housing. Like the dispossessed, who took to the roads in England in the eighteenth century, and former peasants living in vast urban Third World slums today, the Soviet kulaks tried to make new lives under harsh laws that sought to control movement and fix their labor in place.[7]

Criminalizing Vagabondage

By the early 1930s, millions of Soviet villagers had left the countryside in search of work. Between 1929 and 1932, about 10.8 million people entered the waged labor force, almost doubling the number of workers and employees from 11.9 million in 1929 to 22.6 million in 1933.[8] The Soviet economy, in contrast to the depression prevailing in the capitalist West, was booming. People found jobs easily, although housing did not keep pace. Waves of people poured into the cities and receded. Labor turnover was high, record keeping, time clocks, and attendance were still rudimentary, and foremen frequently had no idea who worked in their shops.[9]

In 1932, Soviet leaders reinstituted the internal passport, a document that was first introduced by Peter the Great in 1724, reviled by revolutionaries everywhere, and abolished by the Bolsheviks in 1918. In an attempt to control the flood of people into the cities and maintain urban stability, the state established mandatory passports for all urban inhabitants.[10] The passport system, first applied to large cities and industrial centers, eventually encompassed wide areas around Moscow and Leningrad, all population centers near the western border, and additional towns, regions, workers' settlements, and construction sites. Every citizen sixteen years and older, living permanently in towns, new construction sites, and workers' settlements, or employed in transport and on state farms had to register for a passport, their only valid proof of identity. Children were listed on the passports of their parents, orphans with their institution, and soldiers with the military. Citizens were required to carry their passports at all times. Anyone found without a passport was liable to a large fine or criminal prosecution. In order to take a job, receive urban housing, or move from one area to another, a citizen had to register with the militia and present a passport. Although the state eventually found many uses for the passport system, the primary impetus for its revival originated in the state's need to stop the influx of peasants to the cities, control sources of new labor, slow labor turnover, purge the towns of criminals and vagabonds, and promote new forms of labor discipline. Peasants did not need to register unless they intended to move to an urban area, but they could not move without a passport. After passportization slowed the entrance of peasant migrants into the overcrowded, overstrained towns, urban women became the only source of incoming new industrial labor during the second Five-Year Plan (1933–37).[11]

The decree on passports fixed the waged population and narrowed opportunities for the peasantry, the unwaged, and the itinerant. Officials used the passport system to remove dispossessed kulaks, private traders, former NEPmen, *lishentsy* (people deprived of voting rights), and *byvshie liudi* (former nobles, industrialists, tsarist officials, etc.) from the cities. These people, frequently deprived of jobs because of their social backgrounds, joined with freewheeling criminals and homeless street children to support a shadowy and often illegal private market that traded in shortage at the expense of the state.

The passport decree was also used to purge industry of those who came from "suspect" backgrounds. In February 1933, the Commissariat of Labor instructed the unions, labor departments, and local soviets that all workers who did not receive passports were to be fired within ten days. Factory directors were encouraged to comb their personnel records to ensure that former kulaks, traders, small-business owners, or lishentsy were not "masquerading" as workers. Moreover, those who were fired were to be marked so that future employment would be impossible.[12] For those who successfully concealed their pasts, the passport became a ticket to a new life. Yet a passport not only concealed the bearer's past; it also ensured his or her silence. Any worker who participated in a work stoppage or protest immediately ran the risk of a background check.[13]

Sacrifice and Hardship

Collectivization precipitated a crisis that party leaders never anticipated. Peasants refused to enter the collective farms and slaughtered their livestock in protest. Dairy and meat products disappeared, along with manure for future harvests. In 1932–33, famine killed between five and eight million people, mostly in the countryside. In the cities, too, food supplies plummeted and prices spiraled out of control. The unforeseen food shortages immediately created a sharp drop in living standards. Real wages fell about 50 percent among industrial workers during the first Five-Year Plan and continued to fall until 1934. They made a slow recovery between 1935 and 1938, yet even in 1937, real wages were only 66 percent of their 1928 level. According to one historian, living standards could not have dropped further without causing "a complete disintegration of economic life." The Soviet economy was in crisis.[14]

The fall in real wages pushed urban women into the labor force. A single wage earner could no longer support a family, and the addition of women's wages allowed the family to preserve a basic standard of living. Women's entrance into the labor force, an unintended consequence of inflation and the food crisis, had great and unexpected benefits for the state. It helped to offset losses in the standard of living and to defuse workers' protests. The hire of women already lodged in the towns also assured the state considerable savings on housing and municipal services. Most important, inflation and the fall in real wages allowed the state to employ two workers for the price of one. Whereas a man's wages once sufficed to cover the basic costs of rearing a family, beginning in 1929, a family needed at least two wage earners to maintain itself. The state realized the output of two workers for the price of one, plowing "profit" or surplus value back into industrialization. Planners did not intentionally create inflation, but from the state's perspective, a better strategy could scarcely have been designed to lower real wages, to attract women into the workforce, and to squeeze desperately needed capital from the labor of the working class.

In an effort to manage the crisis and guarantee affordable food to the cities, the state moved to control the food supply, replacing a lively private market with a closed network of workers' cooperative stores. But the new state distribution system was not yet equal to the task. In Ivanovo, a textile region, workers' brigades, empowered to check prices and provisions in 1932, discovered that the stores had received only 13 percent of the consumer goods allotted by plan. Workers fled the textile factories because there was nothing to eat. Fights over food broke out in the canteens, and the militia was called in to restore order. Hungry peat-bog cutters tried to beat up the heads of the party committee and the union in Teikovo.[15] Everywhere, shortages spawned black markets. Retail clerks raised prices illegally and pocketed the difference. They took bread off the shelves and resold it at high profits in the private market to hungry workers, itinerant peasants, criminals, and *byvshie* liudi desperate for bread. Widespread pilfering further reduced the small number of products available for sale.[16]

Living conditions in the cities and new industrial settlements were harsh. A. Abolin, a Central Council of Trade Unions (VTsSPS) secretary, visited the Petrovskii iron and steel plant in Dnepropetrovsk in 1933 at the height of the famine. His horrifying report prompted the Central Committee to recall the heads of the regional party and factory committees to Moscow. In many respects, the Petrovskii plant was typical of new and expanding industrial enterprises. It employed 28,500 workers, 40 percent of whom had worked there for less than a year. In one nearby settlement of thirty thousand people, the outdoor toilets were broken and boarded up. People relieved themselves outside on the ground, creating vast "Egyptian pyramids" of waste. The dormitories had no kitchens, no water during the day, and only occasional water at night. The canteens were vastly overburdened. One canteen, equipped to serve 150 people, routinely served four thousand. Meals were three to six hours late, and lines of two to three hundred people stretched out the door. Workers often left without eating because they had to return to work. Most of the canteens had no silverware.[17]

Abolin discovered that thirty-one people had died in the plant's hospital from starvation and exposure, and 123 more were suffering from malnutrition. Rank-and-file party members suffered along with other workers. Those ill from malnutrition were not only new migrants but also included the head of a party cell, party members, and older skilled workers with long seniority. Some of the starving had lost their ration cards; others were sending money home to the village. One woman was scrimping on food in an attempt to buy a warm coat. The unheated dormitories had no blankets, and workers slept in their clothing. Abolin moved quickly to rectify the worst conditions, creating a brigade to visit malnourished workers, but chaotic records and labor turnover stymied his best efforts to locate people and provide assistance.[18]

The doctor of the plant's hospital noted that the Petrovskii plant was inundated with starving peasants, desperate for food. His malnourished patients called themselves "collective farmers," but in his opinion, they must have been "dekulakized peasants" and homeless teenagers because they lacked documents or passports. By day, they waited patiently near the factory for unskilled day labor, hoping eventually to be hired into permanent jobs. At night, "masses of people" broke into the hot shops and canteens to sleep on the floors and tables. Homeless and poorly clad, constantly dodging the militia, they gradually "became exhausted and fell into the hospital." The doctor had already buried a number of them.[19] The Petrovskii plant, located at the epicenter of the 1933 famine, served as a magnet for starving peasants, but its overall conditions did not differ substantially from those of construction sites and factories in other parts of the country. An older way of life had been uprooted, but new systems of agricultural and industrial production, distribution, and provisioning had yet to take its place.

Workers' Moods and Protests

Before the opening of the Russian archives in the early 1990s, historians knew little about actual conditions and less about workers' protests. Newspapers and other published sources printed nothing at the time to indicate that workers were discontented with the policies of the state, and government reports on protests were kept in secret, specially classified archival holdings. By 1929, the Party had transformed the unions into "levers of production" aimed at mobilizing workers to meet output targets of the first Five-Year Plan, and workers had few official or public outlets for their grievances. Once-secret archival documents now reveal considerable dissatisfaction with party policies. Workers bypassed the unions and expressed their dissatisfaction with wages, shortages, and conditions through a variety of individual strategies, including complaints, quitting, passive resistance, and collective protests, including disruption of meetings, slow-downs, walkouts, strikes, and riots.[20]

Under the impact of hardship and hunger, the new working class splintered politically. Many workers remained strong supporters of the Party and its policies, maintaining a high level of enthusiasm for the development of the country. Young workers in particular benefited greatly from new opportunities for education, skilling, and upward mobility. Yet food shortages, poor living conditions, disorganized distribution networks, and strained services also eroded support for party policies. Many workers questioned how much they should be expected to sacrifice to finance industrial development. When an older worker in Moscow's Kauchuk rubber factory was transferred to a new job in 1934, his wages dropped to 120 rubles a month. He marched into the union office, removed his hat, and told the local organizer, "I want to thank you as a representative of Soviet power. After thirty-five years of work, I am guaranteed starvation."[21] Many workers also questioned whether the Party's commitment to heavy industry would ever improve consumption. Apprentices in the Izhora machine-building works in Leningrad province wrote a letter to the Central Council of Unions in 1933 complaining that the dormitories had no toilets and no firewood or coal for heat. They joked bitterly, "At the end of the second Five-Year Plan, we will eat tractors."[22]

Collectivization, the 1932–33 famine and dekulakization left many former peasants with bitter memories. Now workers, they retained close ties with their native villages, returned regularly to visit, and observed the poverty of their relatives on the new collective farms first-hand. The news they brought back from the villages to the factories contradicted the glowing accounts of agricultural success in the newspapers. In the barracks of Factory No. 45, about forty workers became involved in a heated discussion about collectivization. A worker lying on his bed sarcastically asked a young, recent migrant, "Tell me Vania, did you have to leave the countryside because of famine or because of your prosperous life?" "Of course, because of famine," Vania replied. "And tell me please," the worker continued, "where is the grain of the *muzhik*?" "Taken away by the state," Vania said. "And where are the cattle, the cows, and the horses?" "They took the cows," Vania answered simply. "The horses died of hunger because there was nothing to feed them." A cleaning woman, overhearing the conversation, intervened and declared that Soviet power had freed her and her mother from poverty. The worker sneered, "Only to you they gave a life."[23]

For many, the optimism of union and party officials rang increasingly false. Tired of listening to long speeches, one worker in *Elektrosila*, a Leningrad electrical-engineering plant, asked sarcastically, "How long will the communists torture people with their 'correct' policies?" And a painter in a railroad car factory exclaimed, "A good state would be one without communists because they only promise to better the position of the workers. When will we finally see this improvement? The first Five-Year Plan is already ended, and where are their promises?"[24] These comments, collected by party informants in the factories, were not representative of the views of all workers. But the hardships of daily life took a terrible toll. And while few workers advocated a return to the prerevolutionary order, shortage, hunger, and difficult conditions eroded support for the Party within the class that had initially brought it to power.

Support for party policies tended to be weakest among poorer workers: those in light industry, outside major cities, and in unskilled jobs. To provide incentive, the Party had created elaborate hierarchies of consumption and privilege differentiating workers by type of industry, region, and skill level.[25] The differentials among breadwinners also affected their families. Dependents of workers in heavy industry, for example, received larger rations than those in light industry. The policies aimed to encourage workers to better their skills, but they also fomented resentment against those with greater privileges. Workers in light industry could find neither justice nor logic in the differentials for family members. An older garment worker called the daily one-hundred-gram bread ration his wife received "slow death."[26] Workers outside Moscow were angry that the capitol was better provisioned than other regions.[27] And many were furious at the higher salaries, access to closed stores, and special food packets commanded by officials. One construction worker asked, "Why do we workers not have the right to buy things in the stores for engineering and technical personnel? We also need food."[28] Some workers spoke in favor of wage leveling, a policy followed in the 1920s but rejected in 1931. Others were even more critical, maintaining that a new elite was being created at the expense of their labor.[29]

Organized collective action was strongest among workers in undercapitalized, ailing, low-paid light industry. Textile workers, a group with a long history of labor organizing dating back to the 1880s, mounted the largest, most coordinated and sustained protests. In April 1932, over sixteen thousand textile workers participated in a wave of strikes in the Ivanovo region.[30] When the state lowered ration norms for children in December, the textile factories again erupted in protests. In several meetings, communist workers sided with their workmates against official policy, a stance that opened them to disciplinary action and even expulsion from the Party. One party member declared, to strong applause, "The Party is split now, and it is not listening to the voice of the people. They only feed the officials."[31]

Textile workers launched the strongest protests, but they were not alone. Workers in heavy industry also took action, launching short strikes in the Nikopol iron and steel works, in Moscow's Krasnyi Fakel machine-building works, in Leningrad's Krasnyi Putilov machine-building works, in the Donbas mines, on the docks in Leningrad, Arkhangelsk, and Odessa, and in the Sormovo shipyard. Young workers were frequently the most militant, and even shock workers and party activists, the Party's main base of support, took leading roles. Workers in

Liudinovo's locomotive factory in Kaluzhskaia province called for a strike in 1932 after their rations were cut. About half the workers were new migrants, many still bitter about collectivization. Former Mensheviks and Socialist Revolutionaries were also active in the factory, offering a political critique of Bolshevik policies. On Mayday, someone scrawled an appeal on the wall in one shop: "Workers, Restore Power to the Soviets!" a slogan popular in 1917 but subsequently rendered subversive by the preeminence of the Party. Following the great organizing traditions of the 1905 and 1917 revolutions, the workers sent an appeal to their comrades in a neighboring glass factory to join them. The district party committee quickly commandeered and distributed two boxcars of bread. These measures were successful in ending the strike, although they only temporarily alleviated the food shortage.[32]

Throughout the 1930s, protests were concentrated in the first, and most tumultuous, half of the decade. They tended to be short, spontaneous, and easily defused, rarely spreading beyond a single shop or factory. It is perhaps a measure of how strongly workers supported socialism that the fierce social tensions of industrialization did not produce more sustained protest. The Party and the unions tried to remedy the most egregious situations through arbitration and emergency food deliveries, but workers' needs were fundamentally at odds with the rapid tempo of capital accumulation, investment in heavy industry, and high production targets, the very cornerstones of party policy. Emergency aid was effective in quelling protest, but it did not create lasting change. Workers lacked independent organizations to represent their interests, and the absence of large-scale protest was hardly a sign of satisfaction. Material hardship and mistrust eroded the close connection party leaders once had with their working-class base.

Doubt in the Party

The strains of industrialization not only undermined workers' confidence in party policies but promoted wavering among the Party's own rank-and-file members. Working-class party members, facing the same hardships as their fellow workers, found it increasingly difficult to support the Party's policies. Among the workers suffering from malnutrition in the Petrovskii iron and steel works, for example, were the secretary of the local party cell and other party members.[33] After the state initiated a campaign of national bonds to raise money for industrialization, many communist workers refused to organize fellow workers to subscribe at the expense of already meager paychecks. One report noted that their mood "was about the same as the mood of the workers." Some even defied party discipline and spoke out against the bonds. A communist lathe operator in a machine shop in Briansk announced at a meeting,

"What is this bond subscription for? Why do we need a second Five-Year Plan when we haven't gotten anything from the first?"[34] The disillusionment among working-class party members resonated at every level of the Party.

In the 1920s, numerous groupings had formed within the Party. Scarcely an issue emerged that did not engender passionate debate. By 1927, Stalin and his supporters had gained the support of the majority to outmaneuver the left opposition. L. D. Trotsky was expelled from the Party and eventually exiled abroad, and G. E. Zinoviev and L. B. Kamenev were removed from their posts. Their supporters were silenced; some abandoned protest, while others were expelled or exiled. With the adoption of the first Five-Year Plan, however, many former left oppositionists recanted and rejoined the Party. Enthusiastic about the adoption of the first Five-Year Plan and eager to work in industry, many were appointed to prominent posts. At the same time, other party members, including N. I. Bukharin, A. I. Rykov, and M. P. Tomskii, who had once been firmly in the majority, now opposed the new policy of rapid industrialization, forced grain requisitioning, and collectivization. Branded as "right deviationists," by 1929, this group, too, was isolated within the Party and expelled.

After the purge of the rightists, small oppositional groups from both the left and right revived again in 1932 in protest against Stalin's agricultural and industrial policies. Several former leftists, now occupying leading industrial posts, met with Trotsky and his son in Berlin. M. N. Riutin, a "rightist" expelled in 1930, organized a small group around a 194-page manifesto, known as the "Riutin Platform," that circulated in various cities. The "Riutin group" too was soon isolated, expelled, and arrested. Of all these groups, only the Trotskyists had a base of support among workers. Yet even the Trotskyists were hesitant to mobilize disaffected workers and peasants. Although they supported their grievances, they were appalled by the bitter "anti-Soviet," even antisocialist views of many recent peasant migrants. Reluctant to ally with such people, they were increasingly isolated from any potential base.[35]

By 1934, no active, organized opposition to Stalin's policies from either the left or the right remained. Open debate ceased to exist, although former oppositionists of both left and right retained supporters in prominent posts throughout the Party and the government. At the January 1933 Central Committee Plenum, one delegate noted that party and state organizations were filled with discontented critics, harping on Stalin's mistakes. Even the Council of People's Commissars (Sovnarkom), the highest governmental body, seethed with criticism. "If you want repulsive anecdotes about the work of the Party," he said, "sit in the Sovnarkom dining room."[36] Former oppositionists continued to meet informally, exchange news, and discuss politics. Some had assumed high posts, while others remained in the factories; some were in exile, and others had rejoined the Party. Yet in every city and institution, they remained: a scattering of politically sophisticated comrades with proud revolutionary histories, long memories, and deep reservations about Stalin and his policies.

Terror and Mass Repression

Against this broad background of massive social upheaval and political discontent, only a small trigger was needed to ignite mass repression. On December 1, 1934, L. V. Nikolaev, a distraught former party member, slipped into Leningrad party headquarters and shot S. M. Kirov, the head of the Leningrad party organization. Within twenty-four hours of the murder, the state passed emergency measures abrogating civil rights and establishing extra judicial trials for those suspected of "terrorism." Nikolaev and a small group of associates were tried immediately and shot. Over the next two years, the growing campaign against "terrorism" broadened into a full-scale "terror," as the investigation of the murder widened to encompass former Zinovievites, Trotskyists, rightists, anyone with associational or familial ties to those arrested, and entire social and national groups. Each new wave of arrests led to interrogations and fresh confessions, which in turn led to more arrests. The repression reached its height in 1937–38, when approximately 2.5 million people were arrested for political and nonpolitical crimes. The NKVD was responsible for the majority of these arrests, seizing 1,605,259 people in total, of whom 1,372,382 were accused of counterrevolutionary offenses. Out of the total number arrested, 1,344,923 were convicted, and about 683,000 executed.[37] Among the more prominent victims were former oppositionists, party and military leaders, industrial managers, and cultural figures. Yet the victims also included an even larger share of the dispossessed and disenfranchised and various national groups, arrested under the "mass and national operations." These people, targeted en masse, included former kulaks, priests, criminals, and various nationalities suspected of potential disloyalty in the event of war.

Most historians have focused on the terror as a discrete political episode, triggered by the Kirov murder and disconnected from the larger social crisis of industrialization. The Kirov murder alone, however, is insufficient to explain the repressions of the mid and late 1930s. Indeed, Stalin and his supporters responded so strongly to the murder precisely because of their larger fears concerning the social stability of the country. With fascism ascendant and a two-front war looming with Japan in the east and Germany in the west, they feared that former oppositionists would ally with those elements of the population discontented by industrialization and collectivization. In the absence of this larger fear, the Kirov murder would have, in all likelihood, led to little more than a limited investigation, the conviction of Nikolaev, and a brief period of national mourning. Yet Stalin and other party leaders were soon convinced that the murder was part of a vast conspiracy involving former oppositionists and "masked enemies" throughout industry, the Party, the military, and other institutions. By 1936, the leadership had come to believe that supporters of Trotsky and Zinoviev had formed a "united center" in 1932 aimed at assassination and terror.[38] According to this narrative, Trotsky sent this "united center" instructions from abroad to murder Kirov, Stalin, and other party leaders, organize terrorist cells in the army, and seize power in event of war. Ongoing investigations set off a chain of arrests in the Comintern, and German communists, who had earlier escaped Hitler and settled in the Soviet Union, were accused of terrorism and spying on behalf of the Gestapo.[39] In 1936, the state charged Zinoviev, Kamenev, and fourteen others with Kirov's murder, as well as the attempted murders of Stalin and other party leaders.[40] The charges, which also included foreign espionage, fascist contacts, and terrorist conspiracies, resulted in the first Moscow show trial.[41] The defendants, many of whom had long revolutionary histories, all declined the assistance of counsel; their confessions and mutual denunciations constituted the main evidence. Found guilty of organizing a terrorist center, murdering Kirov, and attempting to murder Stalin and other Soviet leaders, they were shot the day after the trial ended.[42] The party officially admitted in 1991 that the confessions, extracted under torture and duress, were false.[43]

The trial transcript was useless as a record of the defendants' actual activities or beliefs. Yet viewed as an imaginative script, conceived, written, and directed by the Stalinist leadership, it provided considerable insight into their deepest anxieties and fears. Domestic upheaval, hidden oppositionists, and the foreign threat were the trial's major themes. Both A. Ia. Vyshinskii, the prosecutor, and the defendants referred repeatedly to the social discontent created by the upheavals of the first Five-Year Plan. Kamenev testified, for example, that in 1932 he was confident that the country's "insuperable difficulties, the state of crisis of its economy, [and] the collapse of the economic policy of the party leadership" would expose the mistakes of Stalin's policies.[44] The confessions, stripped of their falsified activities, contained hard truths: the Party had barely survived the economic crisis of the early 1930s, peasants and workers were embittered by collectivization and the drop in living standards, and many former oppositionists retained strong misgivings about Stalin. Repelled by his policies, they remained within the Party, outwardly professing loyalty while inwardly maintaining their reservations.

Workers followed the trial attentively. It was broadcast live in many factories, and the newspapers reprinted the verbatim proceedings. The Party held mass meetings with thousands of workers to explain the charges, presenting the state's response as a necessary antiterrorist measure. Workers responded with an outpouring of support for the state.[45] In fall 1936, several months after the trial ended, an explosion in a coal mine in Kemerovo killed a number of workers. The

NKVD quickly arrested a group of engineers, managers, and former Trotskyists. In a widely reported trial, the group was found guilty of wrecking industry and trying to assassinate Soviet leaders. The Kemerovo trial was followed in January 1937 by a second Moscow show trial of prominent party leaders, who were accused of wrecking in the Kemerovo mines, the chemical industry, and on the railroads. Both trials, as reported in the national press, encouraged the public, and workers in particular, to interpret the problems of Soviet industry as the calculated work of "wreckers." The trials deflected blame away from the state and onto managers and former oppositionists, inviting workers to couch their complaints about safety, housing, work conditions, and food shortages in the new language of "wrecking."[46]

By early 1937, the mood in the factories, and in the country more generally, had shifted decisively. The shocking and highly publicized confessions of the defendants in the Kemerovo and 1937 Moscow show trials, coupled with the growing threat of war, convinced many Soviet citizens that their country was besieged by foreign and domestic enemies. Newspapers emphasized that ordinary people had reason to be alarmed. Hidden wreckers, linked to fascist powers, aimed to overthrow socialism, kill Stalin and other leaders, and murder workers in factories, in mines, and on the railroads.[47] Allegations of wrecking spread quickly throughout all branches of the economy, offering a handy excuse for any breakdown, shortage, accident, or failure. What began as antiterrorist measures by the state in response to an assassination rapidly became a full-blown terror.

Less than a month after the January 1937 trial ended, the Central Committee Plenum met from February 22 to March 7, 1937.[48] Party leaders focused on several important issues, including the alleged treason of former rightists and industrial wrecking, but they also introduced a new campaign for secret ballot, multi-candidate elections in the unions, the soviets, and the Party itself.[49] The new democracy campaigns encouraged rank-and-file party members and workers to criticize their leaders. By inviting the "little people" to purge officialdom, party leaders hoped to expose those former oppositionists of both right and left who were protected by high-level officials and to gain support from below for the ongoing repressions. Democracy and terror, far from being contradictory, went hand in hand.[50] A new Soviet Constitution had recently been adopted, introducing an electoral system that extended voting rights to all citizens, including former nobles, white guards, priests, kulaks, and other groups previously excluded from the political process (*lishentsy*). Urban votes would no longer be weighted more heavily than rural votes; all would be counted equal. Most important, elections were to be genuine contests between individual candidates rather than rote endorsement of lists, and voting was to occur by secret rather than open ballot.[51]

Regional party leaders were deeply anxious about the outcome of the elections. A gallows humor, based in dread that the Party would not fare well in real elections, pervaded the Plenum. When I. D. Kabakov, head of the Sverdlovsk regional committee, dully intoned, "Never have the masses of people been such active creators of socialist development and socialist society as after the acceptance of the Constitution," A. I. Mikoian quipped to nervous laughter, "Yeah, there is going to be a big bang."[52] Various regional leaders voiced concern that the Party had little contact with people in isolated rural areas, impoverished urban neighborhoods, new workers' settlements, and enclaves of exiled kulaks. R. I. Eikhe, the head of the Siberian and Western Siberian regional committees and the Novosibirsk city committee, referred to the "unkempt desolate villages and similar areas in the towns" inhabited by embittered peasants, impoverished "former people," criminals, prostitutes, *besprizorniki* (homeless children), and other poor and desperate castoffs of industrialization. He noted that large numbers of exiled kulaks hated the government and "would slander and provoke during the elections."[53] Throughout days of discussion, various regional party leaders offered a grim view of the country in the wake of collectivization and industrialization.[54] They doubted the support of new workers, former kulaks, white-collar employees, exiles, small craftsmen, collective farmers, workers in smaller factories, and the urban and rural poor. Ultimately, these doubts proved too dangerous to test. Secret-ballot, multi-candidate elections were held for the unions and the Party, but not for the government. In December 1937, the population went to the polls, but only to endorse a list of candidates chosen by the Party.[55]

Following the Plenum, regional leaders began lobbying the Politburo to initiate limited mass arrests of those groups considered to be a threat to Soviet security. The orders that followed were patterned on the mass sweeps launched after the passport decree at the end of 1932. Once again, regional NKVD departments were instructed to make mass arrests and send their victims for extrajudicial sentencing. This time, however, quotas were set for every region for arrest, exile, and execution of various groups. In July 1937, the Politburo issued Order 00447, which set target numbers for the imprisonment and execution of recidivist criminals, village clergy, religious activists, former kulaks, *lishentsy* (nobles, industrialists, and others deprived of voting rights), and other "hostile elements." This was followed by Order 00485, which led to the mass roundup of Polish nationals, and Order 00486, which mandated the arrest of the wives of men convicted of counterrevolutionary crimes. Additional orders targeted alleged spies from Germany, Romania, Finland, Latvia, and other countries. Many of the victims of these national operations were Communist and left-wing refugees from fascist regimes.[56]

"Letters of Blood and Fire"?

The process of accumulation in the Soviet Union shared certain similarities with that of capitalism. Under both systems, the dispossession of the peasantry and the creation of the proletariat provoked great resistance. The labor of workers and peasants created the surplus that fueled industrialization, and the struggles over appropriation shaped both groups' relationships to the appropriators. A body of law aimed at eliminating itinerancy, fixing both the rural and urban populations in place, and criminalizing vagabondage and beggary developed in response to the chaos of dispossession and the mobility of labor. And massive violence accompanied the transformation under both systems.

In the Soviet Union, the terror and mass repressions of the late 1930s can be seen as a final spasm of violence in a decade ruled by upheaval, social dislocation, hardship, and discontent. The need to accumulate capital placed a heavy burden on workers and peasants. Food shortages, decline in real wages, rural famine, and painful living conditions all eroded social support for the Party's policies. Stalin and party leaders were keenly aware of the growing lack of support in factories, cities strained by new migrants, rural villages reeling from collectivization, regions of exile and rapid industrialization, and small provincial towns. The widespread discontent in turn encouraged doubts and oppositional sentiments at every level of the Party, from local cells to the Politburo. The Kirov murder served as a catalyst, provoking investigations, arrests, and coerced confessions that convinced the leadership that "masked enemies" and embittered social groups posed a real threat. The ensuing trials were not only an attack on former oppositionists but also an attempt to mobilize waning popular support around the Stalinist leadership and its policies. Soviet leaders were not paranoid. They understood that the Party's social base had been shaken by the economic crisis of the early 1930s and that its ranks were riddled with hidden doubters. Terrified that former oppositionists might mobilize discontented workers and peasants in event of war, the leadership moved to eliminate all potential political and social threats. After Kirov's murder, repression spread outward, first targeting former oppositionists and then widening to engulf those social groups that had suffered most in collectivization and industrialization. The Party rode a wild horse in its frantic drive toward industrialization, and its unrestrained use of spurs, bit, curb, and whip helped define what we know as "Stalinism," or the first socialist variant of primitive accumulation.

Notes

1. Karl Marx, *Capital: A Critique of Political Economy*, vol. 1, trans. Samuel Moore and Edward Aveling (London: Lawrence and Wishart, 2003), 669, 668.

2. Lars Lih, Oleg Naumov, and Oleg Khlevniuk, eds., *Stalin's Letters to Molotov* (New Haven, Conn.: Yale University Press, 1996), 169.

3. Orlando Figes, *Peasant Russia, Civil War: The Volga Countryside in Revolution, 1917-1921* (Oxford: Oxford University Press, 1989); Donald Raleigh, *Revolution on the Volga: 1917 in Saratov* (Ithaca, N.Y.: Cornell University Press, 1986); and Donald Raleigh, *Experiencing Russia's Civil War: Politics, Society, and Revolutionary Culture in Saratov, 1917-1922* (Princeton, N.J.: Princeton University Press, 2002).

4. Ronald Suny, *The Structure of Soviet History: Essays and Documents* (New York: Oxford University Press, 2003), 106; Barbara Allen, "Worker, Trade Unionist, Revolutionary: A Political Biography of Alexander Shliapnikov, 1905-22" (Ph.D. dissertation, Indiana University, 2001).

5. Lynne Viola, *The Unknown Gulag: The Lost World of Stalin's Special Settlements* (New York: Oxford University Press, 2007), 196.

6. Ibid., 63, 87. See also Viola's descriptions of the misery and high death rates within the special settlements. In the northern territory, where conditions were especially harsh, over twenty-one thousand people died in the first year after resettlement.

7. On urban slums today, see Mike Davis, *Planet of Slums* (London: Verso, 2006).

8. *Trud v SSSR: Statisticheskii spravochnik* (Moscow: TsUNKhU Gosplana, 1936), 25; Wendy Z. Goldman, *Women at the Gates: Gender and Industry in Stalin's Russia* (New York: Cambridge University Press, 2002), 89.

9. For a fuller discussion of conditions during the early 1930s, see Goldman, *Women at the Gates*, chap. 8.

10. "Ob Ustanovlenii Edinoi Pasportnoi Sistemy po Soiuzu SSR i Obiazatel'noi Propiski Pasportov," *Sobranie zakonov i rasporiazhenii* (Moscow: Gosudarstvennoe Izdatel'stvo, 1934), 821-23. Historians have interpreted the state's motivation in various ways. See Wendy Goldman, "The Internal Soviet Passport: Workers and Free Movement," in *Extending the Borders of Russian History*, ed. Marsha Siefert (Budapest: Central European University Press, 2002), 315-31; Mervyn Matthews, *The Passport Society: Controlling Movement in Russia and the USSR* (Boulder, Colo.: Westview Press, 1993); Paul Hagenloh, *Stalin's Police: Public Order and Mass Repression in the USSR, 1926-1941* (Baltimore: Johns Hopkins University Press, 2009), 89-146; David Shearer, *Policing Stalin's Socialism: Repression and Social Order in the Soviet Union, 1924-53* (New Haven, Conn.: Yale University Press, 2009), 181-218, 243-84.

11. Between 1929 and 1935, women constituted a significant and unprecedented source of waged labor: 37 percent of all newly hired waged workers and 50 percent of those entering industry were women. A significant percentage of these women came from working-class families: initially over one-third. *Trud v SSSR*, my calculations based on figures on pp. 10, 25, and 91. Data on class background based on workers entering industry in 1931.

12. Gosudarstvennyi Arkhiv Rossiskoi Federatsii (hereafter GARF), fond 5515, opis' 33, delo 54, ll. 3-10.

13. GARF, f. 5515, o. 33, d. 55, ll.78, 219-20, 128, 125.

14. Solomon Shwarz, *Labor in the Soviet Union* (New York: Praeger, 1951), 139-64; Janet Chapman, *Real Wages in Soviet Russia since 1928* (Cambridge, Mass.: Harvard

University Press, 1963); R. W. Davies, *The Soviet Economy in Turmoil, 1929-1930* (Cambridge, Mass.: Harvard University Press, 1989), 304-9; R. W. Davies, *Crisis and Progress in the Soviet Economy, 1931-33* (London: Macmillan, 1996), 459, 176-82, 234-43; Eugene Zaleski, *Planning for Economic Growth in the Soviet Union, 1918-1932* (Chapel Hill: University of North Carolina Press, 1971), 392; Goldman, *Women at the Gates,* 76-82.

15. GARF, f. 5451, o. 43, d. 12, pp. 185, 182, 181. See also Jeffrey Rossman, *Worker Resistance under Stalin: Class and Revolution on the Shop Floor* (Cambridge, Mass.: Harvard University Press, 2005); Donald Filtzer, *Soviet Workers and Stalinist Industrialization: The Formation of Modern Soviet Production Relations, 1928-1941* (London: Pluto Press, 1986); Wendy Z. Goldman, *Terror and Democracy in the Age of Stalin: The Social Dynamics of Repression* (New York: Cambridge University Press, 2007), 11-51; and Goldman, *Women at the Gates,* 70-88.

16. GARF, f. 5451. o. 43, d. 12, ll. 127, 126. On food crisis, see also Davies, *Crisis and Progress in the Soviet Economy,* 195-96.

17. GARF, f. 5451, o. 43, d. 30, ll. 118-13.

18. GARF, f. 5451, o. 43, d. 30, ll. 112-108.

19. GARF, f. 5451, o. 43, d. 30, ll. 107-103, 199-101.

20. On labor turnover and workers' protests, see Filtzer, *Soviet Workers and Stalinist Industrialization,* 51-53, 81-90. Filtzer provided the first overview of labor protest.

21. GARF, f. 5451, o. 43, d. 67, l. 252.

22. GARF, f. 5515, o. 33, d. 50, l. 115 ob.

23. GARF, f. 5515, o. 33, d. 50, l. 115.

24. GARF, f. 5451, o. 43, d. 27, l. 11.

25. Joseph V. Stalin, *The New Russian Policy* (New York: Stratford Press, 1931); Filtzer, *Soviet Workers and Stalinist Industrialization,* 102-7; Davies, *Crisis and Progress,* 65-76.

26. GARF, f. 5451, o. 43, d. 30, l. 131.

27. GARF, f. 5451, o. 43, d. 13, l. 16.

28. GARF, f. 5515, o. 33, d. 50, l. 114.

29. GARF, f. 5451, o. 43, d. 13, l. 21.

30. Jeffrey Rossman, "The Teikovo Cotton Workers' Strike of April 1932: Class, Gender, and Identity Politics in Stalin's Russia," *Russian Review* 56 (January 1997): 44-69. Only sporadic reports of strikes are contained in the VTsSPS previously classified opis' (f. 5451, o. 43). It is possible that the severe labor disturbances that Rossman documented in Ivanovo occurred in other places as well. Davies, *Crisis and Progress,* 188-92.

31. GARF, f. 5451, o. 43, d. 13, l. 17.

32. GARF, f. 5451, o. 43, d. 12, ll. 67-66.

33. GARF, f. 5451, o. 43, d. 30, l.112.

34. GARF, f. 5451, o. 43, d. 12, l. 112.

35. Aleksei Gusev, "The 'Bolshevik-Leninist' Opposition and the Working Class, 1928-29," in *A Dream Deferred: New Studies in Russian and Soviet Labour History,* ed. Donald Filtzer, Wendy Z. Goldman, Gijs Kessler, and Simon Pirani (Bern: Peter Lang, 2008), 153-69.

36. "Stalin i Krizis Proletarskoi Diktatury: Platforma 'Soiuza Marksistov-Lenintsev' (Gruppa Riutina)," in *Reabilitatsiia politicheskie protsessy 30–50-x godov*, ed. I. V. Kurilov, N. N. Mikhailov, and V. P. Naumov (Moscow: Izdatel'stvo Politicheskoi Literatury, 1991), 334–442. See also J. Arch Getty and Oleg V. Naumov, *The Road to Terror: Stalin and the Self-Destruction of the Bolsheviks, 1932–1939* (New Haven, Conn.: Yale University Press, 1999), 52–54; Davies, *Crisis and Progress*, 245–46, 328.

37. Some of the people convicted may have been arrested before 1937. J. Arch Getty, Gábor Rittersporn, and Viktor Zemskov, "Victims of the Soviet Penal System in the Pre-War Years: A First Approach on the Basis of Archival Evidence," *American Historical Review* 98.4 (October 1993): 1022–24. According to data from the Tsentral'nyi Arkhiv Federal'noi Sluzhby Bezopasnosti Rossiiskoi Federatsii, f. 80s., o. 1, d. 80, and cited by V. N. Khaustov, V. P. Naumov, and N. S. Plotnikova, eds., *Lubianka: Stalin i glavnoe upravlenie gosbezopasnosti NKVD, 1937–8. Dokumenty* (Moscow: Izdatel'stvo 'Materik,' 2004): 659–60, the NKVD arrested 1,575,259 people in 1937–38.

38. "O Tak Nazyvaemom 'Antisovetskom Ob"edinennom Trotskistsko-Zinov'evskom Tsentr,'" "Zakrytoe pis'mo TsK VKP (b). Uroki sobytii, sviazannykh s zlodeiskim ubiitstvom tov. Kirova," *Izvestiia TsK KPSS* 8 (1989): 82–84, 95–100.

39. "Zakrytoe Pis'moTsK VKP (b). O Terroristicheskoi Deiatel'nosti Trotskistsko-Zinov'evskogo Kontrrevoliutsionnogo Bloka," *Izvestiia TsK KPSS* 8 (1989): 100–15; William Chase, *Enemies within the Gates: The Comintern and Stalinist Repression* (New Haven, Conn.: Yale University Press, 2001), 146–77.

40. "Zakrytoe Pis'moTsK VKP (b). O Terroristicheskoi Deiatel'nosti Trotskistsko-Zinov'evskogo Kontrrevoliutsionnogo Bloka," 100–15.

41. The defendants were G. E. Zinoviev, L. B. Kamenev, G. E. Evdokimov, I. N. Smirnov, I. P. Bakayev, V. A. Ter-Vaganyan, S. V. Mrachkovsky, E. A. Dreitser, E. S. Holtzman, I. I. Reingold, R. V. Pickel, V. P. Olberg. K. B. Berman-Yurin, Fritz David (I. I. Kruglyansky), M. Lurye, and N. Lurye.

42. *The Case of the Trotskyite-Zinovievite Terrorist Center: Report of Court Proceedings* (Moscow: People's Commissariat of Justice USSR, 1936): 55–56, 65, 68, 71–72, 178–80, 117 (hereafter *Report of Court Proceedings*); "O Tak Nazyvaemom 'Antisovetskom Ob"edinennom Trotskistsko-Zinov'evskom Tsentr,'" 78–81.

43. "O Tak Nazyvaemom 'Antisovetskom Ob"edinennom Trotskistsko-Zinov'evskom Tsentr,'" 78.

44. *Report of Court Proceedings*, 119.

45. For workers' responses to the trial, see Wendy Z. Goldman, "Terror in the Factories," in *A Dream Deferred: New Studies in Russian and Soviet Labour History*, ed. Donald Filtzer, Wendy Z. Goldman, Gijs Kessler, and Simon Pirani (Bern: Peter Lang, 2008), 193–218.

46. "Soderzhanie Prigovora," *Trud*, 23 November 1936, 2.

47. "Trotskistskie Shpiony, Diversanty, Izmenniki Rodiny," *Kirovets*, 22 January 1937, 4; "Sdelat' Vse Vyvody iz Protsessa," *Kirovets*, 3 February 1937, 2.

48. The full stenographic report was published in *Voprosy Istorii* in installments between 1992 and 1995. Getty and Naumov provide a long excerpt in English dealing

mainly with the cases of Bukharin and Rykov (*Road to Terror,* 364–419). Many historians consider this Plenum a turning point in the development of the terror, "a signal for a new wave of mass repression." See "Materialy Fevral'sko-Martovskogo Plenuma," *Voprosy istorii* 2–3 (1992): 3; J. Arch Getty, "The Politics of Repression Revisited," in *Stalinist Terror: New Perspectives,* ed. J. Arch Getty and Roberta Manning (New York: Cambridge University Press, 1993), 40–63; O. V. Khlevniuk, *1937-i: Stalin, NKVD i sovetskoe obshchestvo* (Moscow: Respublika, 1992), 72–153. Roy Medvedev, *Let History Judge: The Origins and Consequences of Stalinism* (New York: Columbia University Press, 1989): 364–68, contains an accurate description of the Bukharin and Rykov cases; Chase, *Enemies within the Gates,* 221–28, describes the effect of the Plenum on the Comintern.

49. "Materialy Fevral'sko-Martovskogo Plenuma," *Voprosy istorii* 11–12 (1995): 20, 14–15.

50. See Goldman, *Terror and Democracy in the Age of Stalin,* 109–61.

51. J. Arch Getty, "State and Society under Stalin: Constitutions and Elections in the 1930s," *Slavic Review* 50.1 (Spring 1999): 18–35.

52. "Materialy Fevral'sko-Martovskogo Plenuma," *Voprosy istorii* 6 (1993): 27.

53. Ibid., 5–6.

54. See, for example, the speech of S. V. Kosior, secretary of the Ukrainian Central Committee, "Materialy Fevral'sko-Martovskogo Plenuma," *Voprosy istorii* 6 (1993): 6–9.

55. Getty, "State and Society under Stalin."

56. "Zapiska N.I. Frinovskogo v PolitbiuroTsK VKP (b) s Prilozheniem Operativnogo Prikaz NVKD SSSR No. 00447," in Khaustov, Naumov, and Plotnikova, *Lubianka,* 273–81. On mass and national operations, see J. Arch Getty, "'Excesses Are Not Permitted': Mass Terror and Stalinist Governance in the Late 1930s," *Russian Review* 61 (January 2002): 113–38; Paul R. Gregory, *Terror by Quota: State Security from Lenin to Stalin, an Archival Study* (New Haven, Conn.: Yale University Press, 2009); Hagenloh, *Stalin's Police,* 227–87; Oleg Khlevniuk, "The Objectives of the Great Terror, 1937–1938," in *Soviet History, 1917–1953: Essays in Honor of R.W. Davies,* ed. J. M. Cooper, Maureen Perrie, and E. A Rees (New York, St. Martin's Press, 1995), 83–104; Barry McLoughlin, "Mass Operations of the NKVD, 1937–9: A Survey," Nikita Firsov and Arsenii Roginskii, "The 'Polish Operation' of the NKVD, 1937–8," and David Shearer, "Social Disorder, Mass Repression, and the NKVD during the 1930s," in *Stalin's Terror: High Politics and Mass Repression in the Soviet Union,* ed. Barry McLoughlin and Kevin McDermott (Houndmills, Basingstoke, Hampshire: Palgrave Macmillan, 2004), 118–52, 153–70, 85–117; Shearer, *Policing Stalin's Socialism,* 320–70; A. Iu. Vatlin, *Terror raionnogo masshtaba: "massovye operatsii" NKVD v Kuntsevskom raione Moskovskoi oblasti, 1937–8* (Moscow: Rosspen, 2004).

PART II

Economic Dislocation as Political Crisis

4

The Labor of Capitalism
Industrial Revolution and the Transformation of the Global Cotton-Growing Countryside

SVEN BECKERT

A new specter is haunting labor historians: transnational labor history. Wherever we encounter labor history today, it is often pursuing the history of labor across national boundaries.[1] In these stories, workers migrate, capital swooshes around the globe, techniques for organizing work are telegraphed to and from distant labor markets, even working-class political ideologies and institutions transcend boundaries. The story of capitalism itself is now told as one that is fundamentally global. An Indian historian writing in Singapore studies Indian sugar workers on Mauritius, and an African historian describes the links that connect the larger story of labor in Africa to that of the Atlantic and Indian Ocean slave trade.[2] New centers for the study of labor have emerged in India, South Africa, Mexico, and elsewhere; new kinds of workers such as sharecroppers appear more frequently in our histories; and the connections between the unfolding of global capitalism and different labor regimes move to center stage.[3] Altogether, this is the most significant departure in the study of labor during the past thirty years. It has generated new interest in the study of work and workers and promises to restore labor's place at the heart of our accounts of the human past—a place it deserves by any metric of the human experience.

In retrospect, it is not surprising that the paradigmatic labor history of the 1970s and 1980s ran out of steam. As accounts of the "making" of this or that working class accumulated, the story became predictable, even if the details were new.[4] Nearly all of these accounts shared a focus on local, regional, or—at most—national working classes. Few questioned that the proper container for working-class history was the nation-state. To a degree, of course, that made sense. The political project of workers, their unions, and their parties throughout the twentieth century was focused on capturing power at the local, state, and national levels. To write the history of labor, historians tried to account for how particular groups of workers gained the inclination, ability, and power to shape political institutions. While acknowledging that this choice was informed by the politics of labor in strong nation-states and Fordist production regimes, we can see in retrospect that this narrow perspective had two fundamental flaws: For one, it radically underemphasized the transnational character of capitalism, ignoring ironically one of the most basic insights that nineteenth-century theorists of capitalism had developed. And, secondly, its attempts to produce a "useful history" of how movements gained and lost political influence turned out to be politically useless in contending with the radical spatial rearrangement of the world's political economy during the past thirty years or so.

A third weakness has been documented brilliantly by Marcel van der Linden: primary subjects of the New Labor History of the 1970s and 1980s were workers in the industrial core.[5] The quintessential characters in these tales were the steelworkers of Bochum, the shoe workers of Lynn, Massachusetts, the miners of Carmaux and Ashio, or the weavers of Bradford.[6] While they had much that set them apart from one another, they had one crucial thing in common: they were wage workers who were free in the classic Marxian sense. We have reconstructed their histories in painstaking detail, producing in the process some of the best historical writing of the period. Simultaneously, however, we lost sight of the fact that most workers labored not in industry but in agriculture, in rural settings, not in cities. We pushed onto the margins of the discipline most accounts of labor different from the classical wage-labor model, such as slavery studies, women's domestic production, and studies of sharecroppers or indentured workers. And, most crucially, we largely ignored the fact that capitalism radically recast the nature of work not only in Western Europe and the United States but also as profoundly in Asia, Africa, and the Americas. Compounding this omission, those who looked found that the changes in the hinterland of industry seemed to go contrary to the plot lines we were spinning about the workers of the world.

Once we broaden our perspective to a global view of labor history, we see the vast labor done outside of North America and Europe, cities and factories. We also note that much of that labor does not correspond to the images we drew when considering Bochum, Lynn, Carmaux, Ashio, or Bradford. Moreover, by any measure we cannot deny that this labor was not marginal but central to the history of the grand narrative of the rise of capitalism that many of us hope to uncover. Indeed, viewed afresh, the quintessential worker of early nineteenth-century capitalism might better be cast as a slave working on a cotton plantation in the Americas. Fifty years later, in the 1880s, the lead role could be assumed by sharecroppers in India, Egypt, or the American South, whose daily toil was as much at the center of capitalism's onward march as the weavers, iron puddlers, and shoemakers of lore. By the twentieth century,

Congolese peasants working at gunpoint on railroad-construction sites were just as essential to the global capitalist economy as the new army of white-collar workers staffing the offices of giant corporations in Germany, the United States, France, Japan, or England.[7]

• • •

That labor under capitalism includes a great diversity of labor regimes becomes immediately obvious even if we only look at one area of the world. The story of economic development and industrial revolution in the United States, for example, was in fundamental ways linked to the story of African labor, as the economy of the United States gained its place within the global division of labor in the first six decades of the nineteenth century principally because of its export of agricultural commodities, agricultural commodities grown by enslaved Africans and their descendants on the plantations of the American South. But even North America's industrial history—the mills of Massachusetts and the metal shops of Rhode Island (which all drew on wage labor)—depended on the labor of Africans who grew the cotton that fed the newfangled machines spinning yarn and who used the agricultural implements that these northern manufacturers produced.

Once we open our view to such connections, we immediately see that even in particular national contexts, but even more so in a global context, labor systems as they emerged in the nineteenth century were not only diverse but also tightly linked to one another. It is thus not just the diversity of labor regimes that needs to be noted and investigated; we need to tackle the more interesting question of how they were related to one another. After all, the diversity of labor systems as such was nothing specific to the modern world—to the contrary, such diversity had been a feature of human history for several millennia. What was new, however, was that in the course of the eighteenth and nineteenth centuries, this diversity was increasingly linked. And, just as importantly, it was not only linked by Smithian global trade, in which comparative advantage left the conditions of production—at least potentially—largely untouched, but by capital and states and the relations of power embedded within both. The two master processes of the modern era—the social and geographic spread of capitalism along with the formation of nation-states—created in fact new kinds of links between diverse forms of labor and in the process transformed them.

The diversity of labor regimes cannot be understood without paying close attention to these connections. But this emphasis on connections itself also suggests a common logic at work that would create an increasing similarity of outcomes. This was clearly not the case. We are thus facing a puzzle: how are we to explain the diversity of labor systems in different parts of the world in the face of what might seem like the universal logic of capital and state power? This is the core question faced by labor historians committed to global perspectives. And answers to this question will allow us to understand much better the emergence of particular labor regimes in a wide range of places—from nineteenth-century cotton plantations in the United States to the factories of Alsace.

Any such answers must be informed by two observations. For one, and most generally, we need to acknowledge that capitalism is not a static system but a system essentially characterized by permanent and revolutionary transformation, a system in which crisis, including the crisis of particular labor regimes, is a recurrent feature. Second, we need to be cognizant of the fact that just at the moment when states and capitalists linked labor regimes in various parts of the world to one another and transformed them in the process, the spatial distribution of power around both was increasingly distributed in radically unequal ways. While in the eighteenth century capital was still spread widely and relatively equally across vast spaces (at least in comparison to later centuries), state power had become radically concentrated in one very small area of the world—namely western and northern Europe—and that unequal distribution of state power would result in the nineteenth century in a radical unequal distribution of capital as well. The links created between various labor regimes in various parts of the world were now forged by very few unusually powerful and rich individuals located in only a few regions of the world. And it was at this intersection of concentrated capital and concentrated state power that labor regimes became increasingly linked to one another—and it was at this intersection that we find the reasons for their diversity.

• • •

This new global story of labor—its diversity and its interconnection—can be glimpsed from many different perspectives. One particularly promising vantage point, I will argue, is a commodity history of cotton. By focusing on a commodity, I can trace how labor regimes in various parts of the world were interrelated and how the expansion of capitalism sparked different, often seemingly contradictory changes, such as the simultaneous expansion of both wage labor and slavery. This perspective shows empirically how different forms of labor evolved under capitalism, replacing the singular trajectory of an industrial working class with a model sensitive to the emergence of particular labor regimes in particular places at particular times due to the structure of labor supply and demand, work patterns, the balance of social power in particular locales, and, especially, the state.

Focusing on an agricultural commodity with manufactured end products is an especially promising way to study global labor under capitalism. After all, throughout much of human history, most labor was deployed for the growing, harvesting, and processing of food and fiber. Accelerating economic change in eighteenth-century and especially in nineteenth-century Europe transformed the way foods and fibers were produced, as hungry urban-dwelling mouths and machines in Europe consumed ever-greater quantities from the fields of Asia, Africa, and the Americas. As a result, an unprecedented demand for labor emerged in the global South. European imperial statesmen and capitalists led the campaign to mobilize the needed labor frequently by recourse to force, especially in the Americas, which they transformed in the eighteenth and nineteenth centuries into Europe's most significant source of imported food and fiber. As a result, slavery spread rapidly throughout the Americas, powered by millions of deported Africans. These slaves grew sugar, coffee, tobacco, indigo, rice, and eventually also cotton for European markets. Coerced labor was not marginal but essential to the development of European capitalism and a crucial factor in Europe's "Great Divergence."[8] How to mobilize labor in ever-greater areas of the world was a prime preoccupation of metropolitan capitalists and the leaders of expansive European nation-states.

・ ・ ・

Cotton was of particular importance to the economic development of Europe. The global cotton industry had come late to Europe, but once it arrived, it flourished there like nowhere before in history.[9] As is well known, the cotton mills sparked an industrial revolution in England. As is less-well understood, it generated significant changes in areas remote from Europe itself. First, it vanquished domestic manufacturing in much of the world. Secondly, and more importantly for our purposes, it led to huge demands for imported fiber: as basically no cotton grew in Europe, the cotton-manufacturing industry depended for its supply of raw materials entirely on places outside of Europe. At first, in the early eighteenth century, cotton was mostly bought from local merchants in the port cities of the Ottoman Empire, but once demand exploded, that supply was insufficient, not least because European capital had only limited ability to recast the Ottoman countryside under a still formidable independent state. In response, European capitalists opened up new areas of production, at first in the West Indies and then in Brazil, experimenting with combinations of depopulated land and slave labor. By the late eighteenth century, this innovative cotton-producing complex moved to the United States, which became rapidly the world's most important producer of cotton for world markets. Unlike other parts of the world, the United States had practically unlimited supplies of depopulated territories and an existing, large population of enslaved Africans increasingly superfluous to the declining tobacco plantations of Virginia and elsewhere.

・ ・ ・

Slavery was an essential ingredient (along with conquered lands) for the production of ever-increasing quantities of raw cotton at ever lower prices for European factories. By the early nineteenth century, slave-grown cotton dominated global markets, and with it slavery had been woven into the very foundation of Europe's Industrial Revolution. Indeed, when the British economist J. T. Danson considered in 1857 the "[c]onnection between American Slavery and the British Cotton Manufacture," he concluded that "there is not, and never has been, any considerable source of supply for cotton, excepting the East-Indies, which is not obviously and exclusively maintained by slave-labour."[10] The growing, trading, and manufacturing of cotton was fabulously profitable to European manufacturers, Atlantic merchants, and some of the most important international financiers of the nineteenth century—from the Barings to the Rothschilds. Cotton profits fueled Europe's economic takeoff.

To the shock and horror of these cotton capitalists, this slave-powered cotton-producing system erupted into crisis by the 1860s. With the outbreak of Civil War on the North American continent, future supplies of slave-grown cotton for the factories of Europe were threatened. Indeed, when shots were fired on Fort Sumter in April 1861, some of the central production and trade relations in the world disintegrated in rapid order, illuminating brilliantly the underlying foundations of the global cotton industry and capitalism more broadly. Without slave-grown cotton pouring out of the ports of the U.S. South, in fact, Europe's most important industry came to a standstill.[11]

This crisis inaugurated among European statesmen and capitalists a frantic search for new sources of cotton and for new forms of labor to produce all that white gold.[12] After all, in the war's wake, nearly four million slaves gained their freedom in the world's leading cotton-producing nation. Merchants and manufacturers understandably feared that that the disruption of the "deep relationship between slavery and cotton production" might "destroy one of the essential conditions of the mass production" of cotton textiles.[13] By exploding global confidence in the structure of one of the world's most important industries, the war encouraged a new regime of bureaucrats and industrialists in cotton-consuming countries to secure supplies of the "white gold" not from slaves but from sharecroppers, tenants, and peasants. And by removing several million bales of cotton from global markets between 1861 and 1865, the war forced manufacturers to find new sources for their crucial raw material, catapulting in the decades after Appomattox large areas of the world into the global economy. New forms of labor, the growing encasement of capital and capitalists within imperial nation-states, and the rapid spatial expansion of capitalist social relations were the building blocks of a new political economy that dominated global affairs until the First World War half a century later. Indeed, the unimaginably long and destructive American struggle, the world's first "raw materials crisis," was midwife to the emergence of new global networks of labor, capital, and state power.[14]

• • •

By 1865, slavery had ceased to be an essential component of the empire of cotton. With slavery abolished in the world's most important cotton-growing areas, the question of how to secure cotton without slavery gained urgency in the offices of European statesmen and capitalists. Pessimism prevailed, reflecting the experiences of cotton capitalists in prior decades experimenting with nominally free labor to grow cotton elsewhere in the world. At prevailing antebellum world-market prices, few cultivators in India, Brazil, Africa, or, for that matter, the American South had produced very much cotton for European markets—despite the best efforts of some manufacturers. These peasants had spun cotton themselves or sold it to nearby spinners, but not to Liverpool or Le Havre merchants. That was why "until very recently," according to the *Liverpool Mercury,* "cotton has been the grand product of slave labour."[15]

Moreover, the experience of emancipation in the Caribbean, in St. Domingue above all, taught merchants and manufacturers to doubt the cash-crop-production abilities of former slaves. It was widely known in cotton circles throughout the world, for example, that upon emancipation in British Guyana, once an important cotton-growing region, freedpeople had moved into subsistence farming, "with evil consequences."[16] As early as 1841, Herman Merivale had observed that it was difficult to compel "the negroes to perform hired labour while they have their own provision grounds, and other resources, at their disposal."[17] Looking at other emancipations in other parts of the world, cotton capitalists and imperial statesmen observed that freedpeople wanted to control their own land and labor and, if given an opportunity, focus on subsistence agriculture, to the detriment of producing cotton for export.[18] It was believed in cotton-growing circles that this move into subsistence agriculture was the more likely, as "*in the tropics Nature has given man the benefit, or the curse, of a perpetual poor law, a prodigality of food which of itself established a minimum of wages.*"[19] Freedpeople's retreat into subsistence agriculture, envisioned by so many former slaves as a true foundation for their newfound freedom, was the nightmare of cotton merchants and manufacturers the world over.[20]

Capitalists and imperial bureaucrats worked zealously to counteract the threat that emancipation posed to the well-being of the world's cotton industry. In articles and books, speeches and letters, they belabored the question of whether and where cotton could be grown by nonslave labor. The Massachusetts cotton manufacturer Edward Atkinson, for example, contributed to this debate in 1861 with his *Cheap Cotton by Free Labor.* The British colonial official W. H. Holmes followed suit a year later with *Free Cotton: How and Where to Grow It,* and an anonymous French author added his voice the same year with *Les Blancs et les Noirs en Amérique et le Coton dans les deux Mondes.*[21]

Most importantly, cotton capitalists and imperial statesmen had learned during the years of the U.S. Civil War that labor, not land, constrained the production of cotton. Members of the Manchester Cotton Supply Association, the world's leading experts on such matters, observed that three things were necessary for successful cotton cultivation: "soil and climate fit for the growth of cotton"—and labor. They understood that land and climate of a "quality equal and in many cases superior to that" of America was available in many different parts of the globe. But these experts on global cotton found that "only two regions" possessed "the very first requisite, which was labor": West Africa and India.[22] The dearth of labor was by far the greatest concern when it came to imagining the empire of cotton without slaves.[23]

But how should this labor be mobilized? During the American Civil War and its immediate aftermath, the efforts of cotton interests focused squarely on accessing labor in regions that formerly had not grown significant amounts of cotton for European markets. As the president of the Cotton Supply Association put it, "[W]e are now opening up the interior."[24] This strategy had a long history; since the 1820s, for example, largely unsuccessful efforts had been afoot to enable the production of greater amounts of cotton for British markets in India. The Civil War, however, focused the energies of capitalists and statesmen in unprecedented ways. Indeed, even these short-term efforts during the crisis resulted in a sustained increase in cotton production in India, Brazil, Egypt, and Central Asia. As *The Economist* remarked, "For five years we have been laying widely and deeply the foundations of a vast future trade with these fertile tropical countries."[25] Aided by dramatic advances in transportation and communications technology, European capital and arms rapidly expanded capitalist social relations in the global hinterland and sparked a sharp surge of global economic integration, resulting in a long-lasting commercialization of regions that before 1861 had remained remote from world markets. The *Revue des Deux Mondes*, in fact, observed this intimate connection between "[t]he emancipation of the enslaved races and the regeneration of the people of the East."[26]

• • •

This rapid geographic expansion of the worldwide web of cotton production was limited by the necessity of finding new ways to motivate nominally free rural cultivators to grow the white gold and move it to market. While until 1861 American slavery had answered the question as to how to extract labor for cotton production, during the war it had become obvious that slaves would never again produce much cotton for world markets, even in regions in which slavery persisted, such as in Brazil and Africa.[27] A new system of labor thus had to be invented. Antebellum experiences suggested that this would be difficult, since non-slave cotton had arrived only in small quantities in the ports of Liverpool,

Bremen, and LeHavre. Rural cultivators in control of their labor and land usually had resisted growing cotton for world markets at prices competitive with slave-grown cotton. Cotton merchants did not succeed in extracting sufficient amounts of cotton from precapitalist producers at what they considered to be reasonable prices—not in India nor in Africa, Egypt, or, for that matter, the upcountry of the southern United States. Moreover, efforts by cotton planters to rely on wage workers failed, as cultivators the world over refused to work for wages on cotton plantations.[28] As the political scientist Timothy Mitchell has wondered presciently, how could rulers make peasants grow crops that "they could not eat, or process to serve local needs?"[29]

How, then, would global labor be mobilized in an age of freedom? How could, as the French observer M. J. Mathieu asked already in 1861, "black workers be disciplined and stimulated?"[30] Throughout the empire of cotton, bureaucrats and capitalists agonized over the question of whether "the negroe [sic] will from now on be a good worker."[31] In a long and programmatic article, *The Economist* greeted the end of the U.S. Civil War with an extended deliberation on the issue. They argued that "[t]here is probably no one point of politics which involves economic results so wide or so permanent as the relation between the white and the dark races of the world." For the authors, it was clear that "[i]t is probably the destiny, it is even now the function, it is certainly the interest of the European, and more particularly of the English family of mankind, to guide and urge and control the industrial enterprises of all Asia, of all Africa, and of those portions of America settled by African, Asiatic, or hybrid races. Those enterprises are very large indeed." To affect such control,

> [t]he one necessity essential to the development of these new sources of prosperity is the arrangement of some industrial system under which very large bodies of dark labourers will work willingly under a very few European supervisors. It is not only individual labour which is required, but organized labour, labour so scientifically arranged that the maximum of result shall be obtained at a minimum of cost, that immense sudden efforts, such as are required in tunnel cutting, cotton picking and many other operations, shall be possible without strikes or quarrels, and that, above all, there shall be no unnatural addition to the price of labour in the shape of bribes to the workmen to obey orders naturally repulsive to their prejudices.

To be sure, *The Economist* argued that "[a]ll these ends were secured, it must freely be acknowledged, by slavery. For the mere execution of great works cheaply no organization could be equal to that which placed the skilled European at the top, and made him despotic master of the half-skilled black or copper-coloured labourer below. The slaves obtained only food, could not strike, and were not liable to those accidental temptations to desert work which so frequently impede great operations both in India and Egypt. The relation was almost as perfect as that of brain and hand." But slavery had also, according to *The Economist*, "moral and social consequences which are not beneficial." And for that reason, "A new organization . . . therefore must be commenced, and the only one as yet found to work effectively is . . . one based upon perfect freedom and mutual self-interest. Half slavery . . . does not work. . . . If, however, complete freedom is to be the principle adopted, it is clear that the dark races must in some way or other be induced to obey white men willingly."[32]

But how would "the dark races . . . be induced to obey white men willingly"? To some, it was contract labor that might return manpower to cotton plantations. Thousands upon thousands of contract laborers already populated sugar plantations in various parts of the world, and it was only logical to think that that system could be expanded to cotton growing as well. In 1862, for example, a group of cotton manufacturers from Senones in the Vosges appealed to Napoleon III to bring Chinese workers to Algeria to grow cotton there.[33] The (British) Cotton Supply Association hoped that sending Indian and Chinese "coolies" to Queensland, Australia, would allow that part of the world to grow cotton.[34] "As with regards to coolies," observed the *Cotton Supply Reporter*, "we have made our columns accessible on the subject to all, and we have stated our own conviction that we shall surely have them here, and that cotton will be grown by their means."[35] And indeed, a few Indian and Chinese indentured workers eventually came to produce cotton. But by and large, coolie labor was to play no significant role, probably because labor needs were too vast to allow for the rapid import of indentured workers in sufficient numbers and because labor patterns of cotton plantations were different from heavily capitalized sugar plantations, requiring different forms of labor mobilization.

In the shadow of this failure, an entirely different system of labor control began to show promise: cotton would be grown by cultivators on their own or rented land with family labor and, crucially, unprecedented injections of metropolitan capital. Sharecropping, crop liens, and powerful local merchants in control of capital characterized the countryside in which they lived.[36] New forms of private property in land and a new "rule of law" spread to these global hinterlands to make the debts and contracts at the heart of this system truly binding. These cotton farmers, the world over, were deeply enmeshed in debt, vulnerable to world market fluctuations, generally poor, subject to newly created vagrancy statutes and labor contracts designed to keep them on the land, and politically marginalized. To serve these debts and, in many regions of the world, to pay taxes to increasingly cash-hungry colonial governments, peasants were forced to grow cash crops. In the process, they were often subject to extra-economic coercion. These were the people who would grow ever-larger amounts of cotton in the new empire of cotton, from India to Central Asia, and from Egypt to the United States.[37]

In this global process of the commodification of cotton-growing labor, states played an exceedingly important role. In some parts of the world, such as in western Anatolia and Central Asia, rising central governments pressured formerly nomadic people to settle and grow cotton. In the southern United States, when efforts failed to make former slaves into ill-paid wage workers laboring in gangs, sharecropping emerged as a social compromise, giving cultivators a modicum of control over their labor power, while keeping them landless. This system was buttressed by a wide variety of vagrancy, debt, and labor laws passed by legislatures recently "redeemed" by planters' representatives. In a small number of other places, wage labor came to dominate, such as in northern Mexico, where powerful landlords recruited migrant workers, drawing on the state for expansion of transportation and irrigation infrastructures and labor control. Indeed, throughout the world, governments captured new territories on which cotton could be grown, changed property laws to allow for the infusion of European capital into the global countryside, built transportation infrastructures that allowed for the removal of cotton to world markets, used the coercive powers of the state to subdue workers' collective action and keep people attached to the land, and regulated the cotton trade to the benefit of European merchants. Indeed, nearly all European states engaged in this vast effort to secure the labor power for the growing of cotton.

Ideologically, of course, it remained difficult in an age of liberalism to justify such measures by reference to the laws of supply and demand. However, eventually statesmen and capitalists found a way. Yet the desperate attempt to secure cotton along with the desire to undercut the market power of American planters resulted in widespread calls for state support. It was for that reason that even *The Economist*, the world's leading visionary of the benefits of free trade and laissez-faire capitalism, eventually endorsed state involvement in securing cotton, especially from India. It was hard to justify these steps in terms of the laws of supply and demand, but eventually *The Economist*, and with it many others, found a way: "The answer, at least a great part of the answer is, that there appears to exist in many important parts of Indian society very peculiar difficulties, which to some extent impede and counteract the action of the primary motives upon which political economy depends for its efficacy." In India, they continued, "The primitive prerequisites of common political economy ... are not satisfied. You have a good-demanding Englishman, but, in plain English, not a good-supplying Indian." For that reason, "[t]here is no relaxation of the rules of political economy in the interference of Government in a state of facts like this. Government does not interfere to prevent the effect and operation of 'supply and demand,' but to create that operation to ensure that effect.... There is no greater anomaly in recommending an unusual policy for a State destitute of the ordinary economical capacities, than in recommending an unusual method of education for a child both blind and deaf."[38]

Yet this reconstruction of cotton-growing labor regimes involved not only the actions of states, merchants, landowners, and capitalists. Rural cultivators themselves often shaped this project. The outcome of their struggles was different from one region of the world to another, even though the broad contours of the emerging labor system in cotton growing were similar. Nowhere in the world were workers reenslaved. At the same time, the desire of many rural cultivators, especially in the southern United States, to turn themselves into landowning farmers who would be able to prioritize subsistence production also failed. Instead, a system of sharecropping and tenant farming evolved in which cotton growers owned themselves and, sometimes, their tools and, drawing on metropolitan capital, grew cotton for world markets. In some parts of the world, petty commodity production became dominant, especially in western Africa, but significant increases in export proved difficult to accomplish. This led to ever-greater regulation of markets by colonial powers and escalating coercion of farmers. In the Belgian Congo, for example, cotton production for export was forced upon small cultivators, as was the case in German Togo.[39] Much more typically and pacifically, sharecropping arrangements emerged, as in the U.S. South, India, and Central Asia. These sharecropping arrangements had a tendency to shade into wage labor, and they did so increasingly as the nineteenth century came to a close. And in some parts of the world, such as northern Mexico, where the distribution of political power was such that landowners and capitalists could act unilaterally or populations were migratory, wage-labor arrangements emerged.

Despite the variety of these labor regimes, cotton cultivators everywhere faced essentially similar challenges of labor in the global age: market fluctuations, state coercion, inescapable debt and contract regimes, and political marginalization. These were the people who would grow ever-larger amounts of cotton, from India to Central Asia, from Egypt to the United States, and the new labor regimes in which they found themselves symbolized one of the most significant changes of the nineteenth century.[40]

• • •

The last third of the nineteenth century thus witnessed a dramatic recasting of cotton-growing labor regimes. Metropolitan industry—expanding, dynamic, and exceedingly important for domestic employment and capital accumulation—continued to draw upon labor from the global periphery. Yet if they once had drawn decisively on slave labor, by the 1870s and beyond, sharecroppers, tenants, and owner-occupiers produced the vast majority of the world's cotton—

mobilized by decisive state action and the infusion of European capital into the global countryside. The world's cotton industry thus continued to rest on a vast array of different labor regimes, as the commodification of labor continued along a spectrum of possibilities. These possibilities expanded simultaneously—and it would be wrong to assert that the forms of labor to be found in the cotton industry's manufacturing centers should be taken as the "true work of capitalism." Instead, capitalist expansion continued to rest on a variety of forms of labor mobilization. While the conditions of proletarianization in Europe rested decisively on the commodification of agricultural labor in the global periphery, European proletarianization resulted just as much in the often violent spread of capitalist social relations in the global countryside. Not only did different forms of labor coexist under the conditions of global capitalist expansion, they depended on one another for their very existence. The crisis of one labor regime begot the emergence of another, as the social and geographic expansion of capitalism led to a state of permanent revolution.

Despite the constant reinventions that were at the core of capitalism's transformative powers, this diversity of labor regimes can be made sense of if we understand the links between them as well as the local conditions that the seemingly universal logic of capital and state power encountered. To understand both the connections and the local conditions, however, it is not sufficient to focus only on labor itself—indeed, the global history of the bourgeoisie and the global political economy of an increasingly dominating capitalism need to be just as much at the heart of this project.

Notes

1. I want to acknowledge the support of the Weatherhead Center for International Affairs at Harvard University for supporting some of the research on which this article is based. This is the translation of an article orginally published in *Le Mouvement Social*. "La main-d'œuvre du capitalisme: Révolution industrielle et transformation des campagnes cotonnières dans le monde," *Le Mouvement Social* 241 (2012): 151–65.

2. See Amit Mishra, "Indian Labour Diaspora: Issues and Experiences," *Journal of Mauritian Studies* 10 (October 2004): 110–29; Ibrahima Thioub, "L'esclavage et les traites en Afrique occidentale: entre mémoires et histoires," in Petit précis de remise à niveau sur l'histoire africaine à l'usage du président Sarkozy, ed. Adam Bâ Konaré (Paris: La Découverte, 2008), 201–13; and Ibrahima Thioub, "L'histoire vue d'Afrique: Enjeux et perspectives," *L'Afrique de Sarkozy: Un déni d'histoire,* ed. Jean-Pierre Chrétien, Pierre Boilley, Achille Mbembe, and Ibrahima Thioub (Paris: Karthala, 2008), 155–80.

3. Marcel van der Linden, *Workers of the World: Essays toward a Global Labor History* (Boston: Brill, 2008).

4. Some of the best examples of this work include Roy Rosenzweig, *Eight Hours for What We Will: Workers and Leisure in an Industrial City, 1870–1920* (New York: Cambridge University Press, 1983); Hartmut Zwahr, *Zur Konstituierung des Proletariats als*

Klasse: Strukturuntersuchung über das Leipziger Proletatiat während der industriellen Revolution (Berlin: Akademie-Verlag, 1978); Alan Dawley, *Class and Community: The Industrial Revolution in Lynn* (Cambridge, Mass.: Harvard University Press, 1976); Mary Blewett, *Men, Women, and Work: Class, Gender, and Protest in the New England Shoe Industry, 1780–1910* (Urbana: University of Illinois Press, 1988); Sven Beckert, "Migration, Ethnicity, and Working-Class Formation: Passaic, New Jersey, 1889–1926," in *People in Transit: German Migrations in Comparative Perspective, 1820–1930*, ed. Dirk Hoerder (New York: Cambridge University Press, 1995), 347–77.

5. Marcel van der Linden, *Workers of the World: Essays toward a Global Labor History* (Boston: Brill, 2008).

6. Alan Dawley, *Class and Community: The Industrial Revolution in Lynn, Massachusetts* (Cambridge, Mass.: Harvard University Press, 1976); Rolande Trempé, *Les mineurs de Carmaux 1848–1914* (Paris: Editions Ouvrières, 1971); Kazuo Nimura, *The Ashio Riot of 1907* (Durham, N.C.: Duke University Press, 1997); Theodore Koditschek, *Class Formation and Urban-Industrial Society, Bradford, 1750–1850* (Cambridge: Cambridge University Press, 1990).

7. See, among others, Laxman Satya, *Cotton and Famine in Berar, 1850–1900* (New Delhi: Manohar, 1997); Sven Beckert, "Emancipation and Empire: Reconstructing the Worldwide Web of Cotton Production in the Age of the American Civil War," *American Historical Review* 5 (2004): 1405–38; Julia Seibert, "Travail Libre ou Travail Forcé?—Die 'Arbeiterfrage' im belgischen Kongo 1908–1930," *Journal of Modern European History* 7.1 (2009): 93–108.

8. Kenneth Pomeranz, *The Great Divergence: China, Europe, and the Making of the Modern World Economy* (Princeton, N.J.: Princeton University Press, 2000).

9. For this history, see Sven Beckert, *The Empire of Cotton: A Global History* (New York: Knopf, 2014). To understand the contemporary world of cotton, see especially Erik Orsenna, *Voyage aux pays du coton: Petit précis de mondialisation* (Paris: Fayard, 2006).

10. J. T. Danson, "On the Existing Connection between American Slavery and the British Cotton Manufacture," in *Journal of the Statistical Society of London* 20 (March 1857): 7. For a similar argument, see also Elisée Reclus, "Le Coton et la Crise Américaine," *Revue des Deux Mondes* 32 (1862): 176, 187. Arguments about the connection between capitalism and slavery can also be found in Philip McMichael, "Slavery in Capitalism: The Rise and Demise of the U.S. Ante-Bellum Cotton Culture," in *Theory and Society* 20 (June 1991): 321–49; Joseph Inikori, *Africans and the Industrial Revolution in England: A Study in International Trade and Economic Development* (New York: Cambridge University Press, 2003); and Eric Williams, *Capitalism and Slavery* (Chapel Hill: University of North Carolina Press, 1994).

11. Beckert, "Emancipation and Empire."

12. *Merchants' Magazine and Commercial Review* 45 (June 1861): 675.

13. *Bremer Handelsblatt* (1862): 335.

14. Allen Isaacman and Richard Roberts, "Cotton, Colonialism, and Social History in Sub-Saharan Africa: Introduction," in *Cotton, Colonialism, and Social History in Sub-Saharan Africa*, ed. Allen Isaacman and Richard Roberts (Portsmouth: Heinemann, 1995), 7.

15. *Liverpool Mercury,* 22 September 1863, 7.

16. W. H. Holmes, *Free Cotton: How and Where to Grow It* (London: Chapman and Hall, 1862), 18.

17. Herman Merivale, *Lectures on Colonization and Colonies, Delivered before the University of Oxford in 1839, 1840, and 1841* (London: Humphrey Milford, 1928), 315.

18. Holmes, *Free Cotton,* 22.

19. "The Economic Value of Justice to the Dark Races," *The Economist* 1163 (9 December 1865): 1487.

20. *Cotton Supply Reporter,* 16 December 1861, 722.

21. Holmes, Free Cotton; Edward Atkinson, *Cheap Cotton by Free Labor: By a Cotton Manufacturer* (Boston: A. Williams and Co., 1861); *Les Blancs et les Noirs en Amérique et le Coton dans les deux Mondes, par L'auteur de La Paix en Europe par l'Alliance Anglo-Francaise* (Paris: Dentu, 1862).

22. In the "west of Africa, though there was labor, the people were savage." "Protocol of the Annual Meeting of the Manchester Cotton Supply Association," 11 June 1861, in *Liverpool Mercury,* 12 June 1861, 3. As the superintendent of the Cotton Gin factory in the Dharwar Collectorate reported in May 1862, "[A]lthough the cultivation of native cotton is capable of extension to an enormous degree, yet the amount of labour available is barely sufficient to clean the quantity now produced." Qtd. in *Times of India,* 12 February 1863, 3.

23. August Etienne, *Die Baumwollzucht im Wirtschaftsprogram der deutschen Übersee-Politik* (Berlin: Verlag von Hermann Paetel, 1902), 28. The theme of labor shortage was also an important subject in discussions on the expansion of Indian cotton production during the U.S. Civil War. See, for example, *Times of India,* 18 October 1861, 3; *Times of India,* 27 February 1863, 6; *Zeitfragen,* 1 May 1911, 1.

24. *Cotton Supply Reporter,* 15 June 1861, 530.

25. Supplement to *The Economist,* Commercial History and Review of 1865 (10 March 1866): 3.

26. Reclus, "Le Coton et la Crise Américaine," 208.

27. Luiz Cordelio Barbosa, "Cotton in Nineteenth-Century Brazil: Dependency and Development" (Ph.D. dissertation, University of Washington, 1989), 170.

28. Kolonial-Wirtschaftliches Komitee, "Deutsch-koloniale Baumwoll-Unternehmungen, Bericht XI" (Spring 1909), 28, in 8224, R 1001, Bundesarchiv Berlin, Berlin, Germany; Thaddeus Sunseri, "Die *Baumwollfrage*: Cotton Colonialism in German East Africa," *Central European History* 34 (2001): 46, 48. Peasant resistance against colonial cotton projects in a very different context is also described in Allen Isaacman, "'Cotton is the Mother of Poverty': Peasant Resistance to Forced Cotton Production in Mozambique, 1938–1961," *International Journal of African Historical Studies* 13 (1980): 581–615; Kolonial-Wirtschaftliches Komitee, "Verhandlungen der Baumwoll-Kommission des Kolonial-Wirtschaftlichen Komitees vom 25. April 1912," 169; Eric Foner, *Reconstruction: America's Unfinished Revolution, 1863–1877* (New York: Harper and Row, 1988); J. E. Horn, *La Crise Cotonnière et les Textiles Indignes* (Paris: Dentu, 1863), 15.

29. Timothy Mitchell, "Principles True in Every Country," in *Rule of Experts: Egypt, Techno-politics, Modernity* (Berkeley: University of California Press, 2002), 6.

30. M. J. Mathieu, "Quel mode employer pour discipliner et stimuler les travailleurs negres?" in *De La Culture du Coton Dans la Guyane Française* (Epinal: Alexis Cabasse, 1861), 25.

31. *Bremer Handelsblatt,* 14 October 1865, 372.

32. *The Economist* 1163 (9 December 1865), 1488.

33. "Pétition a Sa Majesté L'Empereur Napoléon III au Sujet de la Culture du coton en Algérie, Senones, February 13, 1862," in *F/80/737, Fonds Ministériels,* Archives d'outre Mer, Aix-en-Provence, France.

34. *Cotton Supply Reporter,* 15 June 1861, 530.

35. *Cotton Supply Reporter,* 1 July 1861, 554.

36. See Herbert S. Klein and Stanley L. Engerman, "The Transition from Slave to Free Labor: Notes on a Comparative Economic Model," in *Between Slavery and Free Labor: The Spanish-Speaking Caribbean in the Nineteenth Century,* ed. Manuel Moreno Fraginals, Frank Moya Pons, and Stanley L. Engerman (Baltimore: Johns Hopkins University Press, 1985), 255–70.

37. This was a different system of labor than the one that emerged in the global sugar industry after emancipation. There, indentured workers took on a prominent role. The difference is probably related to the fact that sugar production is much more capital-intensive than the growing of cotton and, moreover, because there are efficiencies of scale in sugar that do not exist in cotton. For the effects of emancipation on sugar, see especially Rebecca J. Scott, *Slave Emancipation in Cuba: The Transition to Free Labor, 1860–1899* (Princeton, N.J.: Princeton University Press, 1985); David Northrup, *Indentured Labor in the Age of Imperialism, 1834–1922* (New York: Cambridge University Press, 1995); Frederick Cooper, Thomas C. Holt, and Rebecca Scott, *Beyond Slavery: Explorations of Race, Labor, and Citizenship in Postemancipation Societies* (Chapel Hill: University of North Carolina Press, 2000).

38. *The Economist* 20 (4 October 1862): 1093–94.

39. For cotton in Africa, including its long history before European conquest, see Marie Phliponeau, *Coton et Islam, Fil d'une histoire africaine* (Algiers: Casbah Editions, 2009); "From Tuskegee to Togo: The Problem of Freedom in the Empire of Cotton," *Journal of American History* 92 (September 2005): 498–526.

40. For an account of this transition with regard to cotton, see Beckert, "Emancipation and Empire."

5

The Ordeal of Eugene Debs

The Panic of 1893, the Pullman Strike, and the Origins of the Progressive Movement

SCOTT REYNOLDS NELSON

The American panic of 1893 had origins in—of all places—the fiscal policy of the U.S. Congress. No grand conflict between workers or owners started it; no fear of a growing socialist movement extended it. Yet within a year, the 1893 panic ushered in one of the most famous labor conflicts in American history. The American Railway Union's support for workers locked out of the Pullman Palace Car Company became a titanic general strike centered in Chicago. What began as international doubt about the dollar's convertibility into gold became by 1894 a test of Eugene Debs's new American Railway Union, then an abortive strike, then a collapse of the traditional two-party system. This story is often told differently by political scientists, labor historians, and scholars of socialism, the South, or the transition from the Gilded Age to the Progressive era. This essay will attempt to put some of those histories and historiographies together.

While the previous financial panics of the eighteenth and nineteenth centuries derived from serious problems with assets, whether cotton-based bonds, state bonds, or railroad securities, the 1893 panic started in Congress.[1] Prior to the panic, Congress had faced almost thirty years of party conflict around the issues of the Civil War. After the war concluded, the Democratic and Republican parties sharply divided on sectional and ethnocultural lines. Veterans' organizations enjoined their members to "vote as they shot," and in large measure they did. Though the postwar South saw black workers and farmers choosing Republicans, the collapse of Reconstruction in the South led the southern white majority of workers, farmers, and shop-owners overwhelmingly into the Democratic party.[2] While the gradual disfranchisement of black voters in the South assured a "Solid South" for a hundred years, the issues in the South would change drastically in 1893. In the North, some one in twenty workers joined craft unions during the Civil War. Many—like Eugene Debs—were Democrats in the first few decades after the Civil War. That too would change in 1893.[3] Workers not in trade unions continued to vote along the ethnocultural lines that divided them, assuring that neither party would be a workers' party. Confessional Christians like the Irish and Italian Catholics more often voted with organized workers for the Democratic party. Protestants, including English, German, and Swedish immigrants and their children, generally voted Republican. The Protestant majority in the North combined with veteran Republican voting to assure that northern states voted reliably Republican. Democrats were competitive in only a few northern states with large numbers of skilled workers: New York, Indiana, and Ohio. These were also, not coincidentally, the home states of nearly all the late nineteenth-century presidential candidates of both parties. It should not be surprising that Debs would also come from one of these competitive battleground states.[4]

A Congress riven by regional and ethnocultural blocs proved incapable of any sustained action for workers, though working people (if we include independent farmers and farm hands) were certainly the American majority. Party conflict traded on different issues that affected workers, but neither party fully represented them. Republican support for a national state and publicly subsidized railroads trumped attempts to insure the rights of black voters in the South. Democrats defeated these attempts again and again in Congress by the use of parliamentary procedure. Democratic attempts to shrink tariffs or trim federal expenditures failed repeatedly as Republicans used the same tactics of blocking quorums and filibustering. The roughly even balance of Democrats and Republicans in Congress assured that neither party would simultaneously gain the two houses of Congress and the presidency after Reconstruction ended.[5]

A fateful change came in 1889, when Republicans took the House, Senate, and the presidency. Before 1889, when opponents of a bill sought to quash it they simply refused to answer the roll call required before the vote. By sitting in their seats and refusing to answer, they prevented the quorum necessary to vote on a bill. New house rules passed by Republican speaker Thomas Reed prevented this: congressional opponents in their seats would be noted by the Clerk and counted as "present" against their will. When Democratic congressmen in the House discovered that the clerk counted them as present on a test vote, it provoked three days of chaos in House chambers. Democrats vilified the speaker as "Czar" Reed. After the dust had cleared and the Democrats lost, Congress became suddenly and surprisingly efficient. The House more than quadrupled its legislative output in 1890, passing 611 bills and admitting the Dakotas, Montana, Washington, and Idaho into the Union. Most significantly, it nearly doubled U.S. tariffs on imported goods while eliminating the tariff on raw sugar and passing a two-cent-per-pound bounty for sugar produced at home.[6]

Sugar was no small thing to the United States. Since the Civil War, the tariff on imports provided roughly two hundred million dollars a year in U.S. revenue. The single largest source of tariff revenue was the sugar duty. Sugar, especially white sugar, was crucial to the American canning industry, the fastest-growing American export industry in the Gilded Age. When Congress removed the tariff on sugar and paid a bounty for local sugar, it put a 25 percent dent in federal revenue. This, combined with a scheme to purchase fifty million dollars worth of silver, caused federal gold holdings to drop precipitously. By 1893 the U.S. treasury's gold reserves dropped below one hundred million dollars. That fateful drop prompted international investors to question whether the U.S. government could pay all its obligations in gold. Hundreds of foreign lenders cashed in U.S. state, federal, and railroad bonds, leading to a run on the U.S. dollar. The run on the dollar caused the panic of 1893.

• • •

Eugene Victor Debs was a working-class intellectual born in the hog-killing town of Terre Haute, Indiana. His father, the outcast son of Alsatian intellectuals, had named him after the renegade French novelists Eugene Sue and Victor Hugo. A renegade himself, Eugene dropped out of school in 1870, at age fourteen, to seek work in railway shops. A sign painter first, he soon became a locomotive fireman. When the Panic of 1873 struck Terre Haute, he had traveled west, finding work briefly as a fireman in St. Louis and finally returning home to office work at a wholesale grocery house. Though his career on the footboards had ended in 1874, in 1875 he sought to join the Brotherhood of Locomotive Firemen (BLF) and pay dues as an affiliated member. The Brotherhood, a secret fraternal order and life-insurance society, rarely took on unaffiliated members, but Debs gained the admiration of the Terre Haute organizer. Debs became the local secretary of the order and then rose through its ranks as an editor of its monthly magazine.[7]

Debs regretted never finishing high school and became a lifelong autodidact. For years he taught himself literature and science through private reading. As he continued to work in the Terre Haute grocery warehouse, he took business courses at night. These principles of edification and self-improvement had initially attracted him to the editing of the *Locomotive Firemen's Magazine*. Previously the magazine—costing a dollar a year—had been an adjunct to the order, a simple account of the actions of locals and members. By the 1880s Debs turned the magazine into a social-networking and organizing tool that proved vital to the growth of the order.

Distributing the magazine was uniquely easy for firemen. Because conductors and engineers accorded a fireman the right to free travel on railway cars, it was possible for a tramp fireman to earn a small commission from the union by selling subscriptions to other firemen, and thus geographically expanding the membership base. Indeed, "locomotive fireman" was a broad category. A fireman promoted to engineer moved from the left side of the train to the right. Having crossed to the other side, an engineer was usually eligible to leave the BLF and join the Brotherhood of Locomotive Engineers, a smaller and less active order in the 1880s. But if an engineer continued to pay his BLF dues, he remained in good standing as a fireman and thus entitled to death benefits and the right to vote in the local meetings. A current magazine under the arm became an informal calling card to discreetly demonstrate membership in the secret order.

Debs drastically changed what was inside the magazine under the traveling fireman's arm. Beginning in 1880, his magazine grandly promised to explain the fundamentals of science and civilization to firemen. The first issue explained the relationship between mathematics, algebra, calculus, and chemistry. It promised that the union promoted the slow and steady march of civilization. Just as coral was built over millions of decades by dying water bugs, and pyramids rose from the labor of hundreds of years (according to Debs's editorial), so the common brotherhood of men that the union promoted would slowly bring civilization toward a cooperative moral order.

As the dead water bugs and pyramids suggest, death was discussed on every page of every issue of the *Locomotive Firemen's Magazine.* The connection between death and the railroad brotherhoods in the late nineteenth and early twentieth centuries should not be surprising. The order's foremost calling, after all, was to provide death benefits to widows and children of members of perhaps the single most dangerous profession of the century. The first article in Debs's 1880 issue described the plight of a widow who believed her husband's claim that he was a paid-up member, only to discover that a tragic accident had killed him the next day. By not paying his dues, the widow and children received nothing but a one-time charity payment from a few members who fondly remembered him. After his burial, the family was penniless.

Anton Rosenthal, a historian of Ecuadorian and Rhodesian labor history, has called the railroad brotherhoods in those two countries a "death cult," and this in many ways captures the imaginative vocabulary of railroad-brotherhood publications in the late nineteenth century. Rosenthal translates a famous quotation from a railway brakeman, conductor, and organizer describing railway workers' obsession with death and tragedy: "Death always spoke in the ear of the railroad worker. The squeaking wheels never ceased their music, the wheels that also carried future victims."[8]

It was a peculiar combination in Debs's magazine: the regular discussion of the death of workers, and its ambition to instruct workers in physical chemistry, botany, classical rhetoric, and the history of religions. Debs the autodidact became Debs the instructor in scientific universals. The other brotherhood magazines frequently cribbed from scientific magazines of the day, but none had the audacity to blend familiar stories of union meetings and railway relief offices with descriptions of the role of foreign consuls, schematics of explosive air guns, and speculation on the ancient origin of coined money.[9] By the middle of the 1880s, the British Locomotive and Engineers Brotherhood took notice of this successful American strategy of organization-by-magazine and introduced their own *Monthly Journal* in 1888.[10]

Debs's joining of day-to-day union business with transcendent issues of science and political economy struck the other American brotherhoods as well. In 1886, a jealous letter to the editor in the Brotherhood of Locomotive Engineers' magazine complemented the peculiar "attractive ability" of Debs's magazine: the firemen's magazine clearly drew in members. But at the same time, the engineer resented Debs's printed criticism of a speech by the chief of the engineers. "This article," wrote engineer J. E. Phelan, "must have been written some night when [Debs] sat up late reading Henry George . . . and his feet getting cold and digestion impaired he allowed forbearance a negative and assumed an attitude of labor in its abstract and imaginary sense." What Phelan failed to understand was that Debs's "abstract and imaginary sense" of labor as a movement that spanned centuries may have been the very source of the appeal of the firemen's magazine. Debs the social networker understood that the most bedraggled fireman would scan the magazine for family news of the brothers he knew in St. Louis or Denver or Knoxville but then be intrigued by stories that linked his own experience with that of mountain explorers, the Jews in Pharoanic Egypt, Muskogee Indians expelled by General Jackson, and "women who work."[11]

By 1892, Debs the intellectual severed his connection to the Brotherhood of Locomotive Firemen precisely because of the expansiveness of his vision of unionism. A series of internecine conflicts between the brotherhoods had led to some spectacular failures. The worst conflict was the 1888 Chicago, Burlington, and Quincy strike in which the Knights of Labor actively recruited strikebreakers against the Engineers in retaliation for the Engineers having previously broken a strike by the Knights.[12] The brotherhoods tried to create a Supreme Council in the aftermath of that strike, but it collapsed in 1892 when the other unions ignored a switchmen's strike in Buffalo. "Organized labor appealed to organized labor for support in a just cause," wrote Debs in the aftermath of the 1892 strike. The other unions provided only "oceans of sympathetic drool."[13]

• • •

By January 1892, a railway owners' organization called the General Managers' Association (GMA) began operations, uniting under a single banner the twenty-four railroads that converged in the city of Chicago. The city stood at the natural meeting point of the Great Lakes and the Mississippi River: nature made it a watershed; the railroads made it the nerve center for the nation's coast-to-coast transportation.[14] The GMA quickly established rules for, in the words of one investigator, "switching, car service, loading and unloading cars, weights of live stock," and other matters. But the GMA also established what it called a "Chicago scale" for the pay of switchmen and other employees. The GMA directly communicated its demands to unions and established agencies to bring replacement workers "to come to Chicago in case of necessity."[15]

Debs and a council composed of former Grand Masters of the Railway Firemen, Conductors, and Carmen responded to the GMA by organizing to form their own consolidated agency, the American Railway Union, in February 1893. This first meeting took place a few months before a plunge in the international market for American bonds precipitated the 1893 depression. It was a depression that had little to do with labor and much to do with sugar and gold, yet Debs's union would be at the center of the post-depression conflict. The new organization would be opened to all white men, including engine wipers and sign painters. It would be an industrial union modeled in part on the Knights of Labor, but without the Knights' willingness to accept black union locals. Debs in 1892 was still a staunch Indiana Democrat, committed to the ideology that drove the old party system from 1865 to 1893. He shared with Indiana Democrats all the racial antipathy to black men that the Democracy entailed. While Debs was proud of the Union army for breaking slavery in the South, he saw no place for black men in his grand plan of union. Debs's views on race and class would change drastically in the two years that followed.[16]

In the spring of 1894, before the members had met to write a constitution, the newly formed American Railway Union (ARU) quickly won two victories by the use of binding arbitration. On the Union Pacific, then under receivership because of the depression, the court heard testimony from Debs and others and then required the company to settle with ARU representatives. On the Great Northern Railway, railroad president James J. Hill confidently believed that he could crush the new union with outside arbitration as he had a year earlier in a conflict with two of the railroad brotherhoods. In May 1894 he agreed to arbitration with the ARU under the auspices of the St. Paul Chamber of Commerce. Too late, Hill discovered that the influential flour baron George Pillsbury—with thousands of sacks of flour rotting in railway cars outside of his mills—was inclined to seek an instant settlement. On the first day of their interviews, the chamber cut the ARU's demands only slightly and then ordered the railway to resume operation. After these two successes, the ARU gained members at the rate of two thousand a day.[17]

Members of the Firemen's Brotherhood complained that Debs's new union was simply a correspondence union and no different from the subscription service that he had created when he built up his magazine. In May 1894 they complained that the ARU still lacked a constitution and had only two requirements for membership: that a man be a railway worker and sign the union's roll. The locomotive fireman William Crane compared this ARU mobilization to a "patent medicine" drive and complained that this lax method of entry caused the union to unknowingly recruit anyone, including "Mexicans, dagoes, and Negroes," men who would quickly abandon the union. With dues of less than two dollars a year, Crane predicted that the ARU would quickly fail when put to the test in a strike.[18] That test came in Pullman, Illinois.

Days after the financial panic in 1893, George Pullman cut piece rates for 4,500 men and women who manufactured and repaired Pullman cars, in some cases cutting piece rates by more than 50 percent. He did not, however, lower the rent for company-owned tenements and cottages in the company-owned town of Pullman, Illinois. Because Pullman ran a few miles of track in Pullman, disgruntled carpenters and painters tried to join the American Railway Union but were initially rebuffed. When Pullman refused to meet with a grievance committee on May 9, 1894, and then fired the grievance committee on May 10, the local craft unions voted to strike. On May 11 Pullman locked all employees out. Then Pullman refused to meet with the nearby Chicago Civic Federation or the common council of Chicago, both of whom had offered to arbitrate. The ARU sought to galvanize support for the Pullman workers in neighboring Chicago, drawing financial and food pledges from the mayor, the *Chicago Daily News,* and the city's many other trade unions.[19]

As Chicagoans marveled at Pullman's unwillingness to discuss the lockout, the ARU convened its first annual meeting in Chicago between June 9 and 26. Delegates—moved by the testimony of men and women overworked, underpaid, and expelled by Pullman—overruled Debs's warnings about bringing fired workers from a manufacturing plant into a new union of railway workers. The members allowed the locked-out Pullman workers to join the ARU and then voted to boycott Pullman cars on all associated railways on June 26, 1894.[20]

• • •

News of the sympathy strike spread even faster than the ARU itself, as nonaffiliated and even nonunionized railway workers refused to carry Pullman cars. The five major eastern trunk lines had competing hubs in Chicago. All five saw a drop in traffic. West of Chicago, ARU members in Montana and California stopped nearly all traffic between Chicago and the West Coast.[21]

In the last days of June, the Democratic President Cleveland's Attorney General Richard Olney, still acting as counsel for the Chicago, Burlington, and Quincy Railroad, ordered mail cars attached to Pullman cars. It was a bald attempt to justify the use of federal troops to stop the Chicago strike. These federal troops were selected and appointed directly by the GMA; the mayor of Chicago and the governor of Illinois both opposed their arrival. They came to Chicago on July 3, inflaming the city's population. In the first days of July, pitched night battles broke out between supporters of the strike and federal troops on the hundreds of square acres of railroad property in Chicago. Four buildings were consumed by fire in the Chicago Exposition. The federal troops blamed the strikers; the mayor blamed the federal troops for covertly starting the fire themselves. By the third of July there were thirty thousand federal, state, and local troops in the city of Chicago.[22] The members of the ARU were enjoined by a federal court to stop the strike and then jailed for contempt when they proved unable to stop it. It made Debs a martyr to workers around the country.

An appalled Texas governor who had traveled to Chicago to visit the Columbian Exposition saw the conflict first-hand. He declared the strike peaceful and the president's calling of troops both disorderly and a violation of states' rights. "This strike is but the preliminary of terrible times in this country," he declared when he returned to Texas. "Unless a change is made those fourteen-story buildings in Chicago will be bespattered with blood, brains, hair, hides, livers, and lights, and the horrors of the French revolution will be repeated two-fold."[23] Likewise the Chicago reformer Jane Addams recalled, "There had been nothing in my experience [before 1894] to reveal that distinct cleavage of society, which a general strike at least momentarily affords. . . . [D]uring all those dark days . . . the growth of class bitterness was most obvious." She admired Pullman and knew his workers well but was shocked to discover the growing gulf between her upper-class friends and Chicago's workers as the strike progressed through June and July.[24]

Democrats in control of the House and Senate were mostly appalled by the actions of Olney but nonetheless supported the president's calling in troops. They sensed that public opinion in rural areas served by the railroads had turned strongly against the strikers, and newspapers as far away as Texas and Florida suggest this. Though Republicans in Congress had largely caused the depression by emptying the treasury in 1890, they reveled in the crisis that a nationwide railroad strike had bequeathed to the Democrats.

Pennsylvania's Republican congressman (and songwriter!) Marriott Brosius predicted a Republican "avalanche" in the November 1894 election as workers left the Democratic party. Republicans circulated a campaign pamphlet titled *What Congress Has Done*; all the pages were blank. Voters defected from the Democratic party. Some workers broke toward the Populist party, particularly when Debs was considered as a candidate. Others joined him in the Socialist party. But many workers—to the dismay of Populists, Socialists, and AFL Democrats—became Republicans. In the words of a song that Brosius composed, anger at a Democratic Congress would bring the avalanche:

Another day of crashing banks, of mills a-shutting down
From rock-ribbed old New England to Kansas prairies brown;
For idle men in cities, and idle men in farms,
More reinforcements of idle men in empty-handed swarms;
[. . .]
Courage, honest son of labor, vainly hustling for a job.
(Perchance with vacant stomach, weary brain, and empty fob);
Though the actors are disgusting, and the drama long and tame,
Yet the powers that be are moving, and we'll get there just the same.
In this dreary land of Grover, neither milk nor honey flows;
Party chose revel only where the promised "clover" grows;
And 'tis hard lines for the toiler where no factory spindle hums,
But there's hope a little later
When
The
Big
Storm
Comes
[. . .]
But the voters will be heard from ere this devil's work is done,
With an avalanche of ballots that will startle Washington;
November's blasts will chill their souls, from Congressmen to bums,
And they'll hustle for the cellars
When
The
Big
Storm
Comes.[25]

Eighteen ninety-four was and still is the largest shift in congressional power in American history. Before the midterm election, the Democrats had majorities in both houses of Congress. With the 1894 election Democrats lost 125 seats in the House, most along the railway corridor from Chicago to New York. Workers angry at a Democratic president for the injunction became Republicans. At the same time, farmers angry at Democratic governors in Illinois for *supporting* the strikers also voted Republican. In a bitter irony for Democrats, those for and against the Debs strike voted down Democrats in the 1894 upheaval. Hundreds of thousands of other workers left both parties to become Socialists.

If the depression of 1893 and the general strike of 1894 caused Democrats to lose traction among northern workers, Gompers and the AFL spent the next dozen years trying to reel them back in, with little result. For organized workers who stayed within the two-party system, ethnocultural lines continued to organize them.[26]

In 1894, Democrats also lost traction among farmers in the South. The Populist movement grew more quickly in the South after 1894 than before. A fusion between Populists and Republicans in late July 1894 put a Republican-Populist governor in North Carolina. This threat led southern Democrats like Pitchfork Ben Tillman to embrace a more direct and violent opposition to black voting.[27] The lynching movement in the South reached its peak around the time of the 1894 election, as the overheated rhetoric of the southern Democratic party justified terrifying violence against individual black men.

Eugene Debs the writer and intellectual helped build an intellectual movement among firemen, and then among railway workers, that called attention to the consolidation of political power in the General Managers Association. As the depression of 1893 and a run on the dollar brought financial crisis, a railway strike galvanized the nation and cracked apart the Second Party System. Democrats and Republicans quickly reorganized; Republicans won a substantial and irrevocable victory in the House that would last until the next financial depression. Defectors from the two parties joined a Populist movement that peaked in 1896 and a socialist movement that peaked in the 1910s. Their calls for federal regulation of railroads, a flexible currency, a system of postal banks, an eight-hour day, a forty-hour week, and national pension plans were ridiculed by both parties as the utopian visions of those who allowed themselves, in the words of Debs's critic, "an attitude of labor in its abstract and imaginary sense."

In the end, the energy of those third-party movements was adopted piecemeal by both parties under the label of Progressivism and the New Deal. Eugene Debs, the American labor movement's most effective master of social networking, might have been pleased by the final reckoning. The dying water bugs of the American Railway Union had crusted over to form the coral reef that became the American welfare state, just as Debs had unknowingly predicted in 1880.

Notes

1. Scott Reynolds Nelson, *A Nation of Deadbeats: An Uncommon History of America's Financial Disasters* (New York: Alfred A. Knopf, 2012).

2. Eric Foner, *Reconstruction: America's Unfinished Revolution* (New York: Harper and Row, 1988); Scott Reynolds Nelson, *Iron Confederacies: Southern Railways, Klan Violence, and Reconstruction* (Chapel Hill: University of North Carolina Press, 1999).

3. Not all trade-union members were Democrats, of course. See David Montgomery, *Beyond Equality: Labor and the Radical Republicans, 1862–1872* (Urbana: University of Illinois Press, 1981); Julie Greene, *Pure and Simple Politics: The American Federation of Labor and Political Activism, 1881–1917* (New York: Cambridge University Press, 1998).

4. Ira Katznelson, *City Trenches: Urban Politics and the Patterning of Class in the United States* (Chicago: University of Chicago Press, 1982); Robert Kelley, *The Cultural Pattern in American Politics: The First Century* (New York: Alfred A. Knopf, 1979); Mark W.

Summers, *The Gilded Age: Or a Hazard of New Functions* (New York: Prentice Hall, 1997).

5. Summers, *Gilded Age.*

6. Robert Remini, *The House: The History of the House of Representatives* (New York: Harper Perennial, 2007).

7. Ray Ginger, *The Bending Cross: A Biography of Eugene Victor Debs* (New Brunswick, N.J.: Rutgers University Press, 1949).

8. Anton Benjamin Rosenthal, "Controlling the Line: Worker Strategies and Transport Capital on the Railroads of Ecuador, Zambia, and Zimbabwe, 1916–1950" (Ph.D. dissertation, University of Minnesota, 1990), chap. 7 (quotation on 285).

9. See the lead and secondary articles in *Locomotive Firemen's Magazine* 10 (1886) between January and May.

10. See the cover article in *Locomotive Engineers and Firemen's Monthly Journal* 1 (February 1888): 1–2.

11. "Correspondence," *Locomotive Engineer's Monthly Journal* 20 (April 1886): 225–26; "Frontier Reminiscences," *Locomotive Engineer's Monthly Journal* 10 (September 1886): 527–29; Ida A. Harper, "Woman's Work," *Locomitive Engineer's Monthly Journal* 8 (June 1884): 350–51.

12. Ginger, *Bending Cross,* 70.

13. "Farewell 1892," *Locomotive Firemen's Magazine* 16 (December 1892): 1061.

14. William J. Cronon, *Nature's Metropolis: Chicago and the Great West* (New York: W. W. Norton, 1992).

15. U.S. Senate, *Report on the Chicago Strike of June–July, 1894 by the United States Strike Commission . . .,* 53d Cong., 3d Sess., Senate Executive Document 7 (Washington, D.C.: Government Printing Office, 1895), xxvii–xxix, 242–43.

16. Nick Salvatore, *Eugene Debs: Citizen and Socialist* (Urbana: University of Illinois Press, 1982), 72–75, 102–8, 114–18.

17. Ibid., 120–25.

18. William D. Crane, "The Old Dispensation," *Locomotive Firemen's Magazine* (June 1894): 606–7.

19. U.S. Senate, *Report on the Chicago Strike,* xxxii–xxxix; Jeremy Brecher, *Strike!* (Boston: South End Press, 1972), 79–91; Salvatore, *Eugene Debs,* 127–28.

20. Salvatore, *Eugene Debs,* 128–29; Brecher, *Strike!* 80–81.

21. Richard White, *Railroaded: The Transcontinentals and the Making of Modern America* (New York: W. W. Norton, 2011), 430–47.

22. U.S. Senate, *Report on the Chicago Strike,* xlii–xliv; White, *Railroaded,* 440–43.

23. *Dallas Morning News,* 1 August 1894.

24. Jane Addams, *Twenty Years at Hull-House* (New York: Macmillan, 1911), 214.

25. *Congressional Record,* 53d Cong., 1st Sess. (August 13, 1894), app., 1351.

26. Greene, *Pure and Simple Politics;* Michael Kazin, *A Godly Hero: The Life of William Jennings Bryan* (New York: Knopf, 2006), 155–61.

27. C. Vann Woodward, *Tom Watson, Agrarian Rebel* (New York: Macmillan, 1938); Stephen Kantrowitz, *Ben Tillman and the Reconstruction of White Supremacy* (Chapel Hill: University of North Carolina Press, 2000).

PART III

Social-Welfare Struggles from the Liberal to the Neoliberal State

6

Workers' Social-Wage Struggles during the Great Depression and the Era of Neoliberalism
International Comparisons

ALVIN FINKEL

The early working-class movements scorned notions of a "social wage" provided by state programs, extolling equal wages for all workers, though Karl Marx argued that such abstract equality ignored the special needs of individuals and households.[1] The organized-labor and socialist movements disdained early bourgeois proposals for social insurance because these were actuarially based, relying on forced savings of individuals rather than redistribution of wealth. When Bismarck copied Napoleon III's contributory pension fund (1850) and accident-insurance (1868) plans in Germany in 1883, adding a sickness-insurance plan for the poorest groups of blue-collar workers that covered medical costs and a partial payment of wages during lost workdays,[2] German Social Democrat leaders responded scornfully that they were no substitute for decent wages and guarantees of work. Socialists in Britain and France contemptuously concurred.[3] But rank-and-file workers supported programs that might spare them from the hardships of Poor Law and private charity when unemployment or illness struck. So socialist parties relented and became the chief promoters of a wide expansion of social insurance.[4] Generally, they advocated redistributive programs that embody a notion of social wages rather than forced savings.[5]

This essay traces and compares workers' and especially workers' organizations' responses in North America, South America, Europe, and Australia during the Great Depression and the crisis of capital accumulation that has been more or less steady since 1975. It suggests that the extent to which the organized working class has been willing and able to defend prior social gains during times of crisis depends upon the degree of organization and militancy present within the working class before the crisis begins. In countries where class collaboration is deeply embedded in the ideology of the trade-union and labor political leadership, the response of the organized working class to economic crisis has paralleled that of capital: "national" sacrifice is required, and that means the workers giving up some social gains along with making wage sacrifices. In others, especially where the workers' movements have been unable or unwilling to integrate closely with capital at a political level, or where labor has a political dominance to which capital has partly accommodated, the working-class movement has made improved social wages its central demand, and made the continued existence of private capital dependent on its accommodating that demand.

Origins of Social Wages

Before the Great Depression, many countries introduced programs of limited social protection for Bismarckian reasons, only to see them expand under working-class pressures.[6] In Germany, by 1925, about twenty-one million workers, or two thirds of the work force, were enrolled in old-age pension and disability plans, as well as health-insurance plans, that the state had mandated.[7] The Social Democratic party used its participation in the early postwar governments to support the creation of Ambulatorien, outpatient clinics funded by health insurance that provided everything from physician and dental care to spectacles, infant gymnastics, and holiday camps.[8]

In France, the government's limited social interventions before World War I were precipitated by natalist concerns about fertility and infant mortality and targeted mothers and young women. The Roussel Law in 1874 legislated state-financed maternal pensions and work leaves, along with child-health programs, though this early welfare legislation needs to be seen in the context of what Mary Lynn Stewart calls the "social patriarchy" embodied in the sex-specific labor legislation that characterized French labor policies before the 1920s.[9] Pressures from labor and the left parties built up mini–welfare states at the local level after World War I, which in turn produced an impetus for national action. In 1928, France passed a social-insurance bill providing health, maternity, death, and seniors' pensions benefits to about a third of the population, mostly the poorest sections who had no private coverage.[10] Former charity hospitals came increasingly under the control of municipalities, and medical services were increasingly viewed as a social right.[11]

The French trade-union movement from 1922 to 1936 was bitterly divided between the Socialist-leaning Confédération générale du travail (CGT) and the Communist-led Confédération générale du travail unitaire (CGTU). The CGTU regarded social-welfare programs as a bourgeois deception. By contrast, the CGT were major proponents of universal social programs; they also pushed for social insurance to be administered by the unions, as much as possible, though that yielded only minor victories in the interwar period.[12]

If early Communists in France mistrusted the welfare state, so, for different reasons, did the leaders of the American Federation of Labor (AFL). They regarded protection of male workers as unmanly. Manly men would join trade unions to fight for their rights, not look to the state to defend their interests. The main social programs implemented in the United States before the 1930s were poorly funded maternal and child-health programs.[13]

But in the United Kingdom a Liberal government, fearing the rising Labour party, funded by the trade unions, made decisive moves to establish a Bismarckian welfare state. They introduced a means-tested old-age pension in 1908 for destitute people over seventy. Then in 1911, prepaid health insurance, guaranteed old-age pensions, and unemployment insurance for two million workers in engineering and the building and construction trades were introduced in one sweeping bill, which included some state funding for programs that were mainly to be paid for by workers and employers. The schemes created by the bill to administer each program were meant to be actuarially sound, including the employment-insurance fund, which assumed that the rate of unemployment would never rise above 4.6 percent. The extension of National Insurance Act coverage to all industrial workers in 1920 proved inevitable because of trade-union and Labour party pressures, but also almost immediately demonstrated that the funds were not actuarially sound.[14]

On another continent, Australia and New Zealand moved earlier than Britain to provide rudimentary social insurance. In the six colonies that became Australia in 1901, the rise of the trade-union movement and its entry into politics in the 1890s produced pressure for state programs for workers in financial distress because of health, employment, or age reasons. Union campaigns for old-age pensions led to two state victories before the commonwealth acted in 1908. Health insurance was also implemented that year.[15]

In Latin America, the extent of social-welfare programs before 1930 varied, mainly dependent on the strength of the organized working class and their political parties. In dominantly agricultural countries such as Bolivia, where a Spanish-descended elite continued its control over the mainly Indigenous campesinos, no social-insurance programs were instituted to mollify the militancy of the tin miners, or the anarchist and socialist parties. The elite even resisted public education because they feared the Native majority ever questioning its subordinate status.[16] By contrast, Chilean blue-collar workers won a package of social-insurance programs in 1924. Union and left party pressures accounted for the changes in Chile, but in Uruguay, a bourgeois urban party, attempting to differentiate itself from the principal rural party and hoping to incorporate workers into its plans, led the effort to implement forced-savings programs.[17] But informal employment has always loomed large in Latin American employment, insuring that employment-related social programs excluded the most precarious workers; indeed, during recessions, many of the workers in the formal economy lost their jobs and ended up in the informal sector, where they enjoyed no social protections.[18]

Depression Responses

When the Depression struck and the actuarial calculations underpinning social-insurance programs proved farcical, labor responded initially with stunned disbelief. Suddenly hard-won social benefits were presented by capital and its states as amenable to cuts to protect profits and to save the state from either increasing debt or implementing new taxation. The dominant labor groups in most countries had focused on building laborite or socialist parties, which in turn had become part of the parliamentary edifice and were accustomed to making compromises with the bourgeois and aristocratic parties. So it was natural that the nonrevolutionary trade-union movement and the labor-oriented parties were pulled in two directions at once: wanting to continue to defend and extend programs that gave workers a guaranteed social wage, and wanting to cooperate with bourgeois forces to protect their legitimacy in the existing order. The Communists had no desire to compromise with bourgeois forces or even with the social democrats. In 1928, they had adopted the Comintern's Third Period thesis that capitalism was headed for collapse and that workers, if they had a revolutionary leadership, would overthrow the capitalist system and replace it with Soviet-style socialism. But the sectarian politics of the Third Period mostly isolated the Communists.[19] In any case, defense of existing programs that benefited the working class and demands for their extension was part of Third Period politics, though the goal was mainly to demonstrate that capitalism would not accommodate workers' needs.[20] When the Comintern/Profintern line shifted towards Popular Fronts among trade unionists and leftist political parties, with revolutionary politics temporarily shelved, an emphasis on state programs of direct benefit to workers became a hallmark of Communist politics.

Perhaps the most striking example of a labor movement that had become too incorporated into class-collaborationist strategies to mount much defense of its social-policy achievements was Australia's. The fledgling labor movement in that country, responding to a string of defeats in strikes from 1890 to 1894, agreed in the early 1900s to largely surrender the strike weapon in favor of compulsory state-run arbitration. That system made it relatively easy to organize workers who wanted the opportunity to have their wage demands heard. But the downplaying of the strike weapon shaped a conservative trade-union movement whose conservatism was reinforced by craft organization largely trumping industrial organization. The labor movement also spawned state labor parties and then the Australia Labor party, whose "precocious success stunted the Australian labour movement." Soon after the party's founding, "its socialist founders either moderated their principles or were pushed aside." Though that party and the trade-union movement liked to think of themselves as "pragmatic," their pragmatism bore heavy doses of racism and sexism. The party made promotion of a "white Australia" a key part of their policy, joining more conservative parties in extolling dispossession and cultural genocide of Aborigines. The Commonwealth Arbitration Court was guided by a "family wage" philosophy, which insured that only men's wages were set at levels that could support a family. When Labor formed a Commonwealth government on the eve of the Great Depression, the important factions within the party and the labor movement shared class-collaborationist philosophies, and like the American Federation of Labor, opposed unemployment insurance and social assistance for able-bodied males as unmanly.[21]

After Wall Street crashed, the export-dependent Australian economy collapsed in tandem with the economies of its principal markets. The Labor government considered pursuing an expansionary policy. But it relented after a Bank of England representative warned of the economic dangers of deviating from orthodoxy. As the economist Mahinda Siriwardana notes with some understatement, "This advice, however, was not popular as it tended to place the burden on the working class."[22] The party split between reformist, conservative, and ultraconservative factions. The middle group claimed the majority within the national party. At a conference with the premiers in February 1931, Prime Minister James Scullin settled on a program to reduce government expenditures by 20 percent while increasing income and sales tax and reducing public and private interest rates. The main reformist challenge came from outside the trade-union movement per se, as Jack Lang, the charismatic premier of New South Wales, attempted to invest in public infrastructure and maintain wages. He was turfed from his Labor party membership for his troubles, and his government was dismissed by the British-appointed state governor, forcing a new election that replaced the Lang regime with a conservative administration. Nationally, the fiscally conservative Labor party was defeated in a Commonwealth election in December 1931 by a coalition of even more conservative forces that called itself United Australia.[23]

The collapse in 1931 of a British Labour government, also elected in 1929, had echoes of the same ideological confusion and opportunism that marked the Australian Labor party. But the reformist element within the British parliamentary party proved stronger than within Australia. Confronted with falling revenues, Prime Minister Ramsay MacDonald wanted to cut unemployment benefits by 20 percent. But a majority of his cabinet balked. Persuaded that the country could only be saved by austerity measures, MacDonald formed a "national government" in which Labor members became a minority and had little influence relative to Conservative and Liberal ministers. The Labor party organization branded MacDonald a traitor and expelled him along with his remaining Labor ministers from the party. In opposition, the Labor party and the unions strongly defended social programs and called for more state control over the economy as an alternative to austerity and dependence on the market forces that had created the Depression to also solve it. But they continued to emphasize parliamentary action over mass actions, leaving the latter to the British Communists, who had some successes but were never able to challenge the reformist Labor movement. Labor spurned the Communist Party of Great Britain's efforts in the latter's Popular Front period to create an alliance, and, while the CPGB provided an important share of the leadership of the miners' unions, its self-admitted inability to mobilize more than a small minority of the unemployed or to make significant electoral gains demonstrated the relative conservatism of British workers compared to their continental confreres.[24]

The Communists were far more powerful in pre-Nazi Germany, where they nonetheless were weaker electorally and among organized labor than the Social Democrats (SPD). But the two parties gave almost no thought to cooperation to prevent the Nazis taking power partly because the rise of the Nazis occurred during the Comintern's Third Period, but also because the Communists were unprepared to forgive the Social Democrats' role in the murder of many Communists after World War I, including the party leader Rosa Luxemburg. The SPD, which had rejected revolution in favor of the creation of a bourgeois republic, remained theoretically a Marxist party yet in practice was absolutely wedded to parliamentary practice alone. Its chief ideologues, Karl Kautsky and Rudolf Hilferding, exemplified the view of Second International parties after World War I that socialism could be achieved piecemeal. Hilferding argued as early as 1915 that with finance capital largely in control of the capitalist system, future recessions would be shorter and less catastrophic than their predecessors. The role of socialists therefore was to defend the interests of workers in Parliament while educating them to see the importance of controlling production themselves, which winning a Social Democratic majority in the Reichstag would allow them to do. The non-Communist trade-union leadership largely accepted this strategy. While the left wing of the SPD opposed participation in any government coalition until the party had a parliamentary majority, Hilferding and the leadership majority disagreed. The SPD led the coalition in power when the Depression hit Germany and found that their economic and political analyses had been wrong. Still defending social programs and the rights of the unions, they lost their coalition partners and proved unable to adjust to either the new economic conditions or to the political dangers associated with the rise of the

National Socialists. The government, led by the Center party from 1930 to 1932, drastically cut social programs and wages. When Hitler was named chancellor, and there were calls within the party for a general strike, Hilferding stifled such pressures, claiming that they were premature and that a general strike might precipitate a civil war. The Communists, having labeled the SPD "social fascists," sought no understanding with them, failing to comprehend the reality of the Nazi menace to their own lives and their existence as a party. They had made some electoral and membership gains during the Depression, thanks to the ideological bankruptcy of the SPD, but, saddled with the Comintern policy, they overestimated their ability to battle the Nazis alone.[25]

The inability of Social Democrats in government in Germany, the United Kingdom, or Australia to defend the rights of workers to social gains acquired before the Depression might suggest that a crisis of that magnitude left workers with no options but capitulation or revolution. But the 1930s offer no such simple lesson. While France also witnessed cuts in social programs and attacks on workers' bargaining rights, a definite shift occurred during the short-lived Popular Front government of 1936 to 1938, particularly under the prime ministership of Léon Blum from June 1936 to June 1937. After the Comintern embraced united fronts of Communists with other progressive forces in 1934, the French Communists moved quickly to create a Popular Front electorally with the Socialists and the misleadingly named Radical Socialist party and to merge the CGTU and CGT. From 1935 to 1937, trade-union membership in France soared from one million to 5.3 million.[26]

When the Popular Front won the election in May 1936, regional workers' uprisings began that soon took on a national character. Workers demanded that the new government deliver immediately on promises to expand workers' rights, create a national unemployment fund, and improve old-age pensions.[27] So, rather than gradually introduce its program, the new government negotiated the Accords de Matignon of June 7, 1936, with unions, giving French workers a forty-hour week without pay reductions, paid vacations, protection of the right to organize, and higher wages. The new government also made the size of family allowances the subject of union-employer negotiations rather than an employer right and extended social insurance to rural workers. Unemployment declined over the next year, and economic growth resumed. But the Communists, while supporting Blum's government for almost a year without taking ministerial posts, demanded government aid for its Spanish Popular Front counterpart, which the right wing of the Radical Socialists opposed. Blum was forced to resign in June 1937, and his Socialist successor, Camille Chautemps, found the Radicals unwilling to concede further to the demands of working people.[28]

The Popular Front collapsed in April 1938. The new premier, Édouard Daladier, reduced social services and reneged on the forty-hour week. So, on the surface the French Popular Front experience left few long-term traces of its short-term successes. But the workers' memories of the social rights they won with their spontaneous strikes in 1936 became a touchstone for efforts by French workers to wrest wage increases and improvements in social wages in future generations.[29]

Latin American workers also fought efforts to reduce their wages and benefits, including social benefits, during the Depression, and union organizing increased in many countries. But military regimes, allied with employers, resisted expansion of state social programs as a means of dealing with increased unemployment and poverty. Some expansion of health and pension benefits occurred in Brazil, but the Depression-enlarged group of informal workers were not beneficiaries.[30] In Chile, the Communists and Socialists formed a Popular Front with the middle-class Radical party that led to Socialist and Communist participation in the Radical-led government formed after the 1938 election. But the Radicals were interested in appeasing the parliamentary right, causing the left-wing parties to leave the coalition in 1941.[31]

On the whole, then, workers in most countries discovered during the Great Depression that earlier social-wage victories could evaporate when times got tough. A partial exception to the 1930s as a decade of social-program cuts was the United States, where old-age pensions and unemployment insurance were introduced as part of the New Deal. Unemployment-insurance programs, however, were placed in the hands of state governments, which manipulated them to exclude African American workers, and the pensions were initially modest and discriminated against women who had left the labor force to marry and raise children, at a time when public policy and popular attitudes alike discouraged combining marriage and paid work.[32] Even in the early Depression years, anti-statist views within the labor movement, partly the result of experiences of state hostility to trade unionism and partly the result of American individualist ideology infecting the working class, caused the AFL to favor employee insurance won at the bargaining table over state programs. They worried that workers would not join unions if they could win state social protections and maintained their gendered opposition to social insurance. Only the persistence of mass unemployment caused the AFL to give reluctant support to unemployment insurance and social security. While the Congress of Industrial Organizations (CIO) would embrace the call for state single-payer health insurance, John L. Lewis opposed such plans, reverting to the old exclusivist AFL logic that workers could get better plans by unionizing and negotiating with employers.[33] The Canadian trade-union movement, though dominated by American "internationals," shared the perspective of its British counterparts in supporting social insurance. But the apolitical stance of Canada's Trades and Labour Congress before World War II meant that the union movement played a minor role in state considerations of social programs, which were introduced at a slower pace than in New Deal America.[34]

By contrast, Scandinavia, where the trade-union movement had achieved greater densities than almost anywhere in the world and largely controlled the Social Democratic parties, began to make social insurance the key component of its reformist politics. In Sweden the Social Democrat–led government of Per Albin Hansson, first elected in 1932 and adopting a similar fiscal policy to that proposed by John Maynard Keynes, regarded social-insurance programs as a means to smooth out the boom-and-bust cycle of capitalism. Hansson's government combined direct job-creation programs with pensions, maximum working hours, maternity benefits, and a national medical service. The Swedish Employers' Federation (SAF), faced with restive workers and a hostile and apparently unbeatable government, negotiated with the government and the Landsorganisationen i Sverige (LO), the major trade-union federation, before signing a Basic Agreement at Salsjöbaden in 1938. The SAF would cooperate with the government's full-employment policies and negotiate national labor agreements with the LO in return for acceptance by the LO and the Social Democrats of management's right to hire and fire and exercise control on the shopfloor.[35]

Similar agreements of unions and employers with state backing had already been signed in Denmark in 1933 and Norway in 1935.[36] Hansson's catchphrase for his social model was the "People's Home." It entrenched capitalist social relations along with patriarchy, the latter through an emphasis on family wages and social-insurance payouts in which the income required by a household was reduced by the free services of a child-raising, home-making, full-time housewife.[37]

The Crisis since 1975

Welfare-state philosophy became widespread in the postwar period as national governments, confronting better-organized and more demanding working classes as the war ended, agreed to a social compromise in which capital continued to control enterprises but allowed the state to provide various social guarantees for workers. Social insurance served the Bismarckian purpose of pacifying workers and turning them away from socialism and the Keynesian purpose of insuring respectable levels of consuming power across populations. In some countries, under pressure from women's movements with influence in strong labor movements, there were even gradual moves away from the former patriarchal assumptions of the welfare state.[38] In Sweden, in particular, Social Democratic policies from the early 1960s encouraged full gender equality in the economy, with a universal, free day-care policy and generous, lengthy paid maternity leaves. Care of the aged and the sick was increasingly the obligation of the state via paid staff rather than the family in social-democratic countries. While women were largely streamed into the public social-reproduction roles as they had been in the family, they now received wages for this work and generally were unionized to negotiate wages and benefits. By contrast, in countries with weak, male-dominated labor movements such as the United States, feminist successes in shaping public policy were weaker. Throughout western countries, however, in the period of neoliberalism, conservative and social-democratic governments alike weakened state commitments to daycare, homecare, and long-term institutional care. Women were increasingly expected to return to former unpaid roles of social caregivers, though feminists were more successful in defending former gains in countries with strong labor movements, such as in Scandinavia.[39]

Welfare-state gains occurred during an era of rising prosperity and considerable emphasis on the nation-state as an economic planner and protector of local jobs and businesses. By the 1980s, that model had given way to so-called economic globalization, in which national governments were supposed to encourage modernization and efficiency by opening their doors wide to foreign capital and trade with almost no restrictions. To improve their competitiveness as trading nations, governments were to cut their expenditures, particularly on social entitlements, as a means to reduce their taxation of entrepreneurs and corporations and to make their workers feel the need to accept whatever jobs and working conditions were on offer. The International Monetary Fund (IMF), the World Bank, central banks, and finance ministers, all working closely with multinational corporations, exerted coordinated pressures upon governments to move in neoliberal directions.[40] The capitalist class welcomed the new liberal rhetoric as important for their side in the class war. "Stagflation" in the 1970s, which referred simply to a combination of high inflation and limited economic growth, reduced corporate profitability. A constant theme of the bourgeois media everywhere during the post-1975 period was that allegedly high wages and overly generous social benefits were bankrupting corporations and the state. A large dose of unemployment was proposed as one solution to get a working class, allegedly too accustomed to a Keynesian world of relatively low rates of unemployment, to appreciate having any job at all at any rate of pay. Neoliberal economists spoke of the non-accelerating inflation rate of unemployment (NAIRU), or "natural rate of unemployment," and central banks welcomed the concept—it meant the level of unemployment needed to discipline the workforce to accept smaller increases in pay and allow profits as a share of the total economy to rise again. That was only possible if social benefits were low enough to scare workers with threats of cutbacks and shutdowns. So they had to be cut, and the unemployed objectively became the soldiers against inflation.[41] To what extent did working-class institutions resist efforts to reduce social benefits won prior to the beginning of the economic crisis? What factors determined the extent of their willingness to fight back, and their likelihood of preventing social losses and even making social gains?

Two extremes of the advanced capitalist world reactions to the permanent crisis that a combination of economic stagnation and globalization produced were the United States and Norway. In the United States, the arrival of neoliberalism, exemplified but not beginning with the election of Ronald Reagan as president in 1980, could not be qualified as a 180-degree ideological shift. The anti-statism of the AFL before the Depression had given way only partially to an embrace of the welfare state on the part of labor in the period that followed. Locked into a cold-war embrace of anticommunism with the state and employers, labor focused on winning social insurance at the bargaining table, assuming that Fordist mass production, lifelong employment with the same employer, and cycle-free capitalism had become an eternal norm, at least for the segments of the labor force whom they deemed worth the time to try to unionize.[42] Their membership, judging by a survey of steelworkers that indicated opposition to surrendering union-won medical coverage for a state-run universal program, often embraced similar views.[43] American labor allied with the Democratic party, well financed by big corporations and including a racist and conservative southern wing, rather than establishing a separate labor party, and worked with the Central Intelligence Agency to block efforts by workers abroad to form radical union organizations.[44] It was only mildly concerned that public social provision in the United States was feeble. Andrew Biemiller, the director of the AFL-CIO Department of Legislation, commented at hearings before the House Committee on Education and Labor in the 1970s, "[Private pension plans] have grown to the point of where they have become a form of social insurance, if you will, in the United States of America. The labor movement would have preferred . . . some other approach to these matters, but this is what has grown up in our society."[45]

While the AFL-CIO nominally favored single-payer medical insurance, by the late 1950s they argued that the workforce must rely on private-insurance employee programs with particular employers and focused their legislative efforts on simply getting medical care for seniors paid from general revenues.[46] Patriarchal in their viewpoint throughout the Fordist period, labor said little on childcare, much less public daycare.[47]

In the period of neoliberalism, labor's assumption that employer plans would gradually provide social-insurance coverage for most Americans proved hollow. Employers moved to undo the prevalence of defined-benefit pension plans, which placed the onus on employers and insurers to pay a promised rate of monthly benefit tied to prior earnings, and replace them with defined-contribution plans that made workers suffer for poor returns on investment of their pension funds and effectively tied their pensions to the boom-and-bust capitalist cycle. In 1975, three quarters of employee pension plans in the United States were defined-benefit; by 1989 almost half were defined-contribution. In recent years, almost every new pension issued has been defined-contribution.[48] Social Security, meanwhile, provides a falling replacement rate for average and low-income earners. In 1980, for those having enough years in the system to receive the top rate, Social Security replaced 51.1 percent of former earned income, but by 2000 that had fallen to 43 percent and is projected to fall to 36.7 percent by 2040. For low-income earners, the comparable numbers are 68.1, 57.8, and 49.4, respectively, or virtually assured hardcore poverty for a segment of society least likely to have supplementary sources of income for retirement.[49]

As for medical care, 170 million Americans were in private plans in the early 2000s, receiving varying degrees of coverage, while only seventy million were covered by either Medicare or Medicaid. In March 2005, 44.8 million Americans had no coverage at all, while almost 50 percent more had no coverage at some point in the year.[50] Yet 18 percent of the gross national product of the United States goes into healthcare, the highest for any country in the world, and with mediocre results as measured by life expectancy and infant-mortality rates. The power of the health-insurance industry to control the agenda options for politicians was on stark display in the Obama-initiated debate regarding compulsory medical insurance, from which the single-payer option was excised and a proposed government insurance option was eliminated.[51]

If the implicit argument for focusing on improvements at the bargaining table was to persuade individualist-minded Americans that they needed the labor movement, it failed. Trade-union density in the United States, after reaching about a third of the labor force in 1947, began a slow decline that accelerated after the mid-1970s. By 2012, only 11.3 percent of wage and salary workers in the United States were unionized, with the rate of unionization in the private sector a mere 6.6 percent.[52]

The American labor movement has been unable to find the means to combat neoliberalism ideologically or organizationally. While it has made some efforts to break with its cold-war past, and to link the labor movement with new social movements that it once denounced, it continues to support the Democratic party unconditionally and to suppress rank-and-file militancy.[53]

The timidity of the American unions has an echo in countries with stronger trade-union traditions and established social-democratic parties. While the National Union of Mineworkers fought Margaret Thatcher's efforts to destroy their union in 1984–85, they received weak support from the Trades Union Congress and were undermined by the British Labour party. The union movement had represented over half of working people when Thatcher assumed office in 1979 but was down to just over a quarter when Labour next won an election in 1997, led by Tony Blair. The unions played almost no independent political[54] role in Britain during the Blair years, during which "New Labour" followed a neoliberal agenda.

Similarly in Australia, the unions signed an accord with the Australian Labor party before the 1983 election that brought Labor back to power after eight years of conservative administration. The unions sacrificed wages to get back social guarantees, including a universal medical-care program implemented by Labor in the 1970s and then gutted by the Liberal-Country coalition. Some of the unions, such as the Metal Workers, urged the government to follow plans to restore the country's industrial base and with it male-breadwinner jobs. But the government rejected union calls for a "Keynesian and masculinist" program in favor of a neoliberal market-based strategy that protected neither traditionally male nor traditionally female jobs.[55] During the next fourteen years, while Labor governed, financial deregulation, spending cuts, greater foreign control of the economy, and wage restraint marked government policy. As Stuart Macintyre comments, "The central principle of the Australian Settlement, a strong state to protect living standards, would yield to the operation of the free market—and this at the hand of Labor."[56]

By contrast, the Norwegian labor movement developed a strong critique of neoliberalism and established a movement called Campaign for the Welfare State (CWS) in 1999. It opposed liberalization, deregulation, and the unrestricted flow of capital that capitalist globalization demanded. While only six unions founded the CWS, it soon came to embrace the entire union movement and a broad array of social groups, including public-service clients, students, pensioners, and farmers. Though started by top union officials, it created a structure that gave grassroots activists control.[57] The CWS developed a political program for preserving and extending workers' rights, as well as satisfying the demands of the environmental movement, feminists, and other groupings, and then mobilized the membership of participating groups behind the program, holding forums, rallies, and protests before asking all political parties to formally endorse the program. The CWS program received the endorsement of the Labour party, the Socialist Labour party, and the environmentally focused Centre party. While Labour and Centre had demonstrated strong neoliberal tendencies when they were in governments in the 1980s and 1990s, they felt the need to embrace the CWS to maintain their votes. The CWS was not satisfied with these endorsements. They demanded and received the written agreement that these three parties would run in the 2005 national election on a promise to work together as a coalition to implement the CWS policies. Though the right had won the previous two elections, the center-left coalition partners took 60 percent of the vote in the 2005 election and were reelected in 2009. The unions and CWS had to continually prod the new government to prevent it from falling into the neoliberal solutions that corporations and other national governments were encouraging it to follow. But privatizations stopped, as did cuts in existing social programs.[58]

Abjørn Wahl, the director of CWS, warned in July 2011 that even in Norway, complacency within the labor movement was an issue. He observed:

> The 2005 red-green government in Norway started off by carrying through a number of progressive policies. However, as time went by, and the pressure from the movement declined, the government began to slide back to old political positions. Even if great parts of the trade union movement politically had become more independent from the Labour Party, other parts were still too loyal to oppose and to keep up the pressure when welfare provisions were weakened and undermined by "their own" government. It is exactly the move to the right of the traditional Social Democratic/Socialist Parties which has made it necessary for trade unions in the current situation to become more independent politically and to take on a wider political responsibility and, not least, to keep up the pressure on the government after it has won the election and taken power.[59]

The relative success of the Norwegian labor movement occurred in a context very different from the American one. In 2004, 53 percent of Norwegian wage earners were union members, and 70 percent were covered by collective agreements. Though that represented a drop from peak unionization in the 1980s, the Norwegian labor movement had not been emaciated like the American movement. As Asbjørn Wahl wrote in 2001: "Since the Norwegian union movement has not yet been defeated in the same way as in Great Britain under Thatcher and Blair, the modernizers within Norway's Labour Party will find it much more difficult to shift the nation to the right."[60]

Apart from being more heavily unionized, Norwegians had developed a culture of dependence upon and support for a broad array of universal social programs including pensions, health insurance, and daycare. The unions had fought successfully for comprehensive public programs in the postwar welfare-state era, unlike their American counterparts, and most of the Norwegian public wanted to defend those programs. A large welfare-state workforce provided a huge base that could be mobilized against cutbacks; meanwhile, most of the public, not only the poor, regarded themselves as beneficiaries of social programs and feared the consequences of marketization of services such as healthcare, daycare, and education. As Walter Korpi and Joakim Palme observe, targeted programs do not create coalitions, whereas universal programs do. Paradoxically, "[T]he more we target benefits at the poor and the more concerned we are with creating equality via equal public transfers to all, the less likely we are to reduce poverty and inequality."[61] Norway's poverty rates were among the lowest in the advanced capitalist world, and the CWS persuaded the public that social programs were the reason for this and demonstrated that the shift of resources from the state-governed world to the private sector increased poverty.[62]

While the "modernizers" within public life, in the right-wing parties and in Labour, worked hard to wean Norwegians away from their socialist attitudes and reduced the public share of gross national product from 52 to 43 percent from 1992 to 1999, most Norwegians preferred the earlier direction in which the country had been going. So, a concerted mobilization by labor of the Norwegian population could and did have a real impact. It might appear that with its offshore oil wealth Norway could buck the trend towards neoliberalism because it had extra revenues with which to fund its social programs. But in fact all parties in the country were agreed upon setting aside oil revenues for the era when the petroleum was gone, and social programs continued to be funded from general revenues. The rest of Scandinavia, which lacks Norway's oil resources, has also continued to maintain excellent social services in the era of neoliberalism. While neoliberal ideology has certainly resulted in some cutbacks in social programs in the Scandinavian countries, they remain countries with dramatically more income equality than the North American countries or the United Kingdom, as well as very high rates of unionization.[63] The two certainly appear to be closely linked.

In Greece, relatively low union densities have limited the ability of the trade-union movement to fight international capital's determination to make Greek working people suffer for the capitalist crisis within their country. The major Greek trade-union federations, in a report in 2010, note that trade-union density in their country is only 28 percent, and that governments and employers in Greece do not involve the unions in economic decision making even to the extent that other European Union countries do. The Greek economy is dominated by small and medium-sized enterprises that are generally difficult to unionize.[64] The unions have struggled to find what strategy would work best to represent the interests of their members without alienating the rest of the working class. While they emphasized militancy in the 1970s and 1980s, they chose afterwards to focus on class collaboration so as not to alienate nonunion workers whom they hoped to recruit. But, according to one scholarly analysis in 1999, this seemed to simply cause workers without unions to see no reason to seek one.[65] The major union federations, General Confederation of Greek Workers (GSEE) in the private sector and Civil Servants' Confederation (ADEDY) in the public sector, did their best to bring the country to a halt in 2011 when their government, reduced to a puppet of the European Union, attempted to impose its latest and steepest set of austerity measures. The measures involved wiping out or weakening most social programs and the usual neoliberal prescriptions of privatizations and free trade. But they were unable at the time to prevent the Greek parliament, led by the nominally pro-labor and social-democratic Panhellenic Socialist Movement (PASOK), from passing the austerity package.[66]

By contrast, in France, where union density is less than half of Greece's but where the unions play a large role in administering social-insurance funds, the unions have been able to take advantage of a long history of worker militancy that can bring millions into the street and on work stoppages to prevent or dilute neoliberal reforms. Memories of mobilizations for the Popular Front in 1936 and the 1968 mass strike, both of which brought French workers a variety of concessions to prevent even bigger mobilizations and threats to the capitalist system itself, help to mobilize workers even now. But there are limits. In 2010, France's unions called five general strikes and massive demonstrations for months against President Sarkozy's plans to increase the retirement age from sixty to sixty-two and full pensions from sixty-five to sixty-seven. At one point they shut down the country's oil refineries. Two thirds of French voters, according to polls, supported continuing strikes against these measures, even if they were legislated back to work. But Sarkozy persisted, and the unions yielded.[67] The French case nonetheless demonstrates that union density is not the sole factor in determining the extent to which the working class can be mobilized politically, though the link between union density and the ability to resist neoliberalism in crisis conditions is an important one.

Efforts to resist neoliberalism have been sharp and sometimes successful in various Latin American countries. Globalization has generally proved detrimental to the continent's working classes. Unemployment rose from 6.6 percent in 1994 to 10.7 percent in 2000, for example, with job increases mainly occurring in the poorest-paying sectors, particularly in the informal sector, where legislated social-insurance programs largely do not apply. About 45 percent of the people of the region, or about 220 million people, were poor in 2000, with 78.7 percent of the poor being of Indigenous descent.[68]

Social progress was limited by the IMF and World Bank's ruthless insistence that as these countries got into financial trouble within the New World Order that they had to "clean house" by cutting their social expenditures. In the 1980s, the continent's health, education, and welfare expenditures dropped on average from 9.1 percent of GDP in 1982 to 8.3 percent in 1990. Workers who lost their jobs because of adjustment programs lost their pensions and health coverage.[69] The model for social programs favored by international capitalism was that of the military junta in Chile, which attempted to roll back the victories of workers during the period of the Unidad Popular government of Salvador Allende and earlier elected governments. In 1981 the Pinochet government, having brutally suppressed the trade unions, replaced government-run defined-benefit pensions, which the Allende government had extended beyond the largest workplaces, with privately run defined-contribution pensions. All workers had to put 10 percent of their earnings into a precarious private pension, much of that money paying for insurance companies' marketing, profits, and high managerial salaries. Neither employers nor the state matched the workers' forced pension investment, making this program no more than a precarious forced-investment program imposed upon workers to benefit private insurance companies.[70] Meanwhile, the single-tier public-health system gave way to a two-tier system in which those with higher incomes bought private insurance. Those unable to afford to opt out of reliance on the scaled-back public system would "receive generally inadequate treatment in dilapidated facilities and by severely underpaid personnel."[71]

Other dictatorships in Latin America, which had suppressed their union movements, including Bolivia and El Salvador, copied the Chilean model. From the point of view of a right-wing American analyst of social policy "reform," the Chilean model, "by giving up most [state] responsibility for social security . . . depoliticized an issue area that had given rise to innumerable demands from special interests."[72]

Such brazen efforts to remove state guarantees for workers in countries where a majority of the working class was in no position to meet its needs without state aid created a working-class backlash in many Latin American countries. Left-wing governments were elected in Venezuela, Bolivia, Ecuador, Nicaragua, and, in 2011, Peru.

In Venezuela, Hugo Chàvez, first elected president in 1999, focused on efforts to bring social services to the poor who had been ignored by previous regimes. His government brought thirty thousand Cuban medical personnel, including ten thousand doctors, into the country to provide services and train Venezuelans to deliver medical services. Cuba was rewarded with below-market oil prices from oil-rich Venezuela.[73] Chàvez rejected the IMF view of the world and increased social spending. His "Bolivarian socialism" stressed the need for workers' cooperatives, redistribution of wealth, and local democracy.[74] While neoliberal policy prescriptions called for growing inequalities, Venezuela recorded a significant drop in income disparities from 1998 to 2009.[75] The poverty rate dropped from 52 percent in 1998 to 31.5 percent in 2008, while extreme poverty fell from 20.1 percent of the population in 1998 to 9.5 percent a decade later.[76] Oil riches helped, but previous governments had done nothing to spread the wealth a bit more evenly during earlier oil-price booms.

Interestingly, however, the Venezuelan revolution, at least initially, owed more to Chàvez's populism than to working-class revolt, because the major working-class and peasant movements had become quite weak by the 1990s. As in Argentina and Mexico, the major trade unions in Venezuela had adopted corporatist ties to procapitalist governments over a long period and offered meager resistance to neoliberal policies of privatization.[77] The new Chàvez-led government party tried to create grassroots movements that would in turn be able to challenge and direct the central government. While this movement had a great deal of success, it faced the organized power of the Venezuelan bourgeoisie and its political parties, as well as international capital, which tried to discredit and destabilize the Chàvez government with false claims that it violated the constitution and was trying to impose a dictatorship. Indeed, as the effort to depose Chàvez in 2003 demonstrated, the right wing in Venezuela was unconcerned about democracy and happy to have a military-led government if the people were not willing to elect a government that protected all their privileges. Only mass opposition, largely spontaneous, to the coup, gave the advantage to more progressive and constitutionalist elements within the military that restored Chàvez to power.[78]

The Bolivian government of Evo Morales faced similar campaigns of destabilization. But the Morales government was more the product of popular movements than the Venezuelan regime that began in 1998 originally was, though, as in Venezuela, the formal trade-union movement had been considerably weakened by neoliberalism.[79] Bolivia was the poster child of neoliberalism in the 1980s and 1990s, with its governments agreeing to follow the "reajuste estructural" proposed by the American economist Jeffrey Sachs, whose "shock therapy" prescriptions for the former Communist states of Eastern Europe had called for massive privatizations of state industries and the destruction of most social protections built up during the Communist period. Bolivia ended protection of national industries, gutted the country's already modest social spending, and placed all its faith in the market. The result was massive unemployment; by the early 2000s, two million of the country's eleven million people had emigrated, mostly to Argentina.[80]

Among those who remained, many of the country's former miners became either coca growers or campesinos, bringing their famed trade-union militancy with them to their new occupations. Working-class consciousness, along with rising Indigenous national movements among the campesinos and cocaleros, produced militant social movements. Evo Morales was a coca grower in Chapare who had exceptional skills as an organizer and became the leading trade unionist of the federation of cocaleros. The cocaleros organized against the government's efforts, under American pressure, to exterminate the coca leaf, which was not only crucial to the economic well-being of tens of thousands of Indigenous people but crucial as well to their sacred practices.[81]

In 2000, there was a triumphal uprising against the foreign company that controlled water in Cochabamba, in which peasants, factory workers, marginal workers, and the unemployed all worked together and for a time seized power in the city.[82] That year as well, the social movements began a series of monster rallies in La Paz in which tens of thousands of demonstrators from across the country brought their demands to the country's rulers and took over the streets of the capital in the process. The Confederacíon Sindical Única de Trabajadores Campesinos de Bolivia, with about 3.5 million members, was the leading social movement, and through its membership in the Central obrera boliviana (COB), it persuaded the urban workers' movement to also join in the demonstrations that called for a socialist restructuring of Bolivia. In 2003, the social movements were united in efforts to stymie the neoliberal government's plans to sell gas to the United States and to accept a tax regime imposed by the IMF.[83]

The Movimiento Al Socialismo (MAS), which chose Morales as its leader, was the product of this social agitation. Morales was elected president in 2006 and reelected in 2010. The program of the party demonstrated a strikingly opposite view to that of neoliberalism with regard to how Bolivia should deal with its economic crisis and the grinding poverty of more than half its citizens. They viewed their country's bleak history and the way it should set upon a new path as follows:

> In the colonial era, we financed Europe's industrial revolution with the silver from the hills of Potosi, but we did not industrialize.
>
> With the Republic, we strengthened the economies of Europe and the United States via our tin, but we did not industrialize.
>
> Today that same cosmology of Western culture offers us the notion that exporting gas will usher us along the industrial route, that is to say, we will be a modern country—another big lie, because there is no hint of our traveling the industrial, modern road; on the contrary we have increased our condition of being simply exporters of raw materials.
>
> If the capitalist economy of trade and accumulation, which assumes also the power of private property, has brought us extreme poverty, we have another option, which is to revive our economic principles of reciprocity and redistribution, that is to say, to produce for the common good.[84]

Like Chàvez, Morales, in his first term of office, thumbed his nose at neoliberal nostrums about the market and the virtues of individualism. After a large and inclusive national debate, the government drew up a new constitution in which the various Indigenous nations would enjoy a great degree of self-government as well as consultation on central government matters. The new constitution received an overwhelming majority in a national referendum. The Morales government also moved quickly to take 50 percent of all revenues from foreign-owned energy companies, making the state petroleum industry the administrator. Though the government continued to seek foreign investment, the state was also largely put in charge of iron and lithium mining. It also nationalized the national telephone and telecommunications company.[85] But the communitarian powers approved in the constitution acted as a check against an overconcentration of power at the center, and unlike Soviet communism, Bolivian socialism, along with Venezuelan socialism, emphasized decentralization, popular participation, and Indigenous nationhood rather than centralized planning and a monolithic national culture.[86]

The Morales government, in its first four years of office, built 545 clinics, reduced the infant-mortality rate from fifty-four per one thousand to fifty per one thousand, implemented the country's first national retirement pension, and carried out a national adult-literacy campaign, while also hiking the monies spent on education in Bolivia.[87] In short, it tried to undo much of the damage from the 1980s neoliberal response to economic crisis. In its 2009 election platform, it promised a national universal health-insurance program and free education at all levels. There are some fears that the Morales government, in its efforts to achieve social change while containing the anger of the national bourgeoisie, which monopolizes the media, is moving too slowly. Despite the long list of reforms, Bolivians saw only minor changes in the country's extreme maldistribution of wealth.[88] But the social movements keep up a constant pressure on the government. In November 2010, for example, a protest against the rising cost of living by four hundred social organizations, led by the COB, closed down the center of La Paz and made clear the people's desire to have the energy industry entirely under government control.[89] Over time, in Bolivia, the radicalism of new social movements has reinvigorated the traditional trade unions.

Conclusion

There is no single definition of either the "welfare state" or the "social wage." They are the product of social struggles within different capitalist and postcapitalist societies, and their shape is determined by the strength of various social classes as well as their outlook on the importance of social programs versus market forces in creating a good society. In good economic times, the working class can often extract social guarantees despite opposition from much of the capitalist class, though Bismarckian programs of forced savings generally have the support of most capitalists because they make workers, as opposed to the state or employers, responsible for looking after themselves during economic downturns. Generally, the working class supports universal and permanent social programs that are recession-proofed—that is, the services and payouts can be expected to not decline when the economy tanks—and if anything, the levels of benefit payouts are raised to compensate for the loss of on-the-job wages and benefits.

But the degree to which the working class insists on holding on to what it gained in good times when recession hits depends on the extent to which, in a given jurisdiction, it regards these gains as entitlements that are fundamental to the social system or simply rewards for a high-performing economy. In the 1930s and in the postwar period, the capitalist class insisted on the latter. In the 1930s, capitalist demands for "sound money" and low taxes on potential investors dictated steep cuts in social spending. Since a return to profitability for corporations was supposed to be the goal for all of society, the workers would have to pay the price for the capitalist errors that had produced a depression. Similarly, after 1975, workers were called upon to make sacrifices so that private investors might get inspired again to invest in job creation.

In the 1930s, labor movements that had gone too far in following class-collaborationist strategies in earlier periods, for example in Australia, and/or had wasted their forces on internecine battles, as in Germany, proved unable to come up with either a socialist alternative to the labor-reducing, state-benefits-reducing strategies of the conservative forces in their countries, or a willingness to mobilize workers to fight to preserve previous gains and demand more social guarantees. In France and Spain, the Popular Front provided an alternative strategy, though the real gains were restricted, in France because of parliamentary defeat and lack of any other approach to forcing change afterwards, and in Spain because of military defeat by the international forces of fascism. Chilean workers' parties followed the same strategy but were outvoted by their middle-class allies and unable to deliver much to the workers. Scandinavia, with its powerful unions and huge Social Democrat voting bloc, likely made the most gains, following a policy, however, that was ultimately more Keynesian than socialist.

In the post-1975 period, workers in many western countries had far bigger social wages to defend than in 1930. But while the period after the Second World War had been one of growth in trade unionism and social entitlements, the extent to which either or both grew varied a great deal globally. In Scandinavia workers won important increases in social wages from states that also created favorable environments for union activity, and therefore the negotiation of better direct wages from employers. In some countries where trade union growth was slow because of state repression, other forms of worker organization arose to defend and demand extension of state social protections, as in Venezuela and Bolivia. In still other countries, where union densities were low and the rate of growth of social programs was too slow to create a sense of worker entitlement, neither the philosophical argument nor the militancy needed to demand redistribution of wealth in favor of the workers and the poor made much headway. This was particularly true in the United States. But there were outliers. France, with its low union density, retained a sense of working-class solidarity that one could trace back at least to the Popular Front, which allowed the unions to mobilize well beyond the ranks of their own members. Greece, by contrast, with a far higher union density than France but a modest representation of the entire Greek working class, proved unable to mobilize the degree of opposition necessary to stymie the plans of the entire political elite to follow IMF orders. The working class's ability to fight back and perhaps eventually to replace capitalism with worker-run socialist systems does not follow any exact prescriptions. But high rates of union density, a past history of insistence upon social-wage programs as worker entitlements that cannot be tampered with regardless of the state of the economy, and a broad sense of working-class solidarity all help in the struggle. More countries have these elements at play in the current crisis of capitalism than was the case during the 1930s, and so further efforts to make the workers pay for capital's follies will likely be met with successful resistance in an expanding number of countries.

Notes

1. Karl Marx, *Critique of the Gotha Programme* (1875), in Karl Marx and Friedrich Engels, *Selected Works* (Moscow: Progress Publishers, 1970), 13–30; accessed 11 June 2013, http://www.marxists.org/archive/marx/works/1875/gotha/ch01.htm.

2. Though Bismarck is often regarded as the father of the conservative welfare state, he gave due credit to Napoleon III for his earlier ventures. Peter Baldwin, *The Politics of Social Solidarity: Class Bases of the European Welfare State, 1875–1975* (Cambridge: Cambridge University Press 1990).

3. Ibid., 101, 105.

4. As John Saville notes, the welfare state is the result of a combination of working-class struggles, the requirements of capitalism for a more efficient industrial environment, and the recognition by capitalists that social programs are the price that needs to be paid to achieve social stability. John Saville, "The Welfare State: An Historical Approach," in *Social Welfare in Britain: An Introductory Reader*, ed. Eric Butterworth and Robert Holman (Glasgow: Fontana, 1975), 57–69.

5. In Germany, the Erfurt program, which was adopted by the German Social Democrats in 1891 as their new program to replace the Gotha program, included among ten crucial demands "free medical care, including midwifery and medicine. Free burial." The program also called for "takeover by the Reich government of the entire system of workers' insurance, with decisive participation by the workers in its administration." "The Erfurt Program, 1891," in *Protokoll des Partitages der Sozialdemokratischen Partei Deutschlands: Abgehelten Zu Erfurt vom 14, bis 20 Oktober 1891, Berlin 1891*, trans. Thomas Dunlap, accessed 11 June 2013, http://www.marxists.org/history/international/social-democracy/1891/erfurt-program.htm.

On labor's attitude generally to the welfare state, the sociologist Göran Therborn argues: "The very origin of the labour movement was a protest against, among other things, the existing distribution of income and life chances. When issues of public insurance and public social services were raised, the labour movement always insisted on a redistributive mode of finance." Göran Therborn, "Classes and States: Welfare State Developments 1881–1981," *Studies in Political Economy* 13 (Spring 1984): 23.

6. Social protections can come in a variety of forms, but for the purposes of this essay, the focus is on social-insurance programs and social provisions in the areas of housing, daycare, and social assistance for those not enrolled in formal social-insurance programs.

7. David M. Cutler and Richard Johnson, "The Birth and Growth of the Social Insurance State," *Public Choice* 120.1–2 (July 2004): 87–121.

8. Paul Weindling, "From Germ Theory to Social Medicine: Public Health, 1880–

1930," in *Medicine Transformed: Health, Disease, and Society in Europe, 1800–1930*, ed. Deborah Brunton (Manchester: Open University, 2004), 263; Dick Geary, "Labour in Western Europe from c. 1800," in *Global Labour History: A State of the Art,* ed. Jan Lucassen (Bern: Peter Lang 2006), 261.

9. Anne-Emmanuelle Birn, "No More Surprising than a Broken Pitcher? Maternal and Child Health in the Early Years of the Pan American Sanitary Bureau," in *Children's Health Issues in Historical Perspective,* ed. Cheryl Krasnick Warsh and Veronica Strong-Boag (Waterloo, Ont.: Wilfrid Laurier University Press, 2005), 75; Mary Lynn Stewart, *Women, Work, and the French State: Labour Protection and Social Patriarchy, 1879–1919* (Kingston: McGill–Queen's University Press, 1989), 13.

10. Timothy B. Smith, *France in Crisis: Welfare, Inequality and Globalization since 1880* (Cambridge: Cambridge University Press, 2004), 28–30, 224.

11. Timothy B. Smith, *Creating the Welfare State in France, 1880–1940* (Montreal: McGill–Queen's University Press, 2003), 123.

12. Paul V. Dutton, *Origins of the French Welfare State* (Cambridge: Cambridge University Press, 2002), 66, 69.

13. Alice Kessler-Harris, *Gendering Labor History* (Urbana: University of Illinois Press, 2007), 238; Edward Berkowitz and Kim McQuaid, *Creating the Welfare State: The Political Economy of Twentieth-Century Reform* (New York: Praeger, 1980), 65.

14. Derek Fraser, *The Evolution of the British Welfare State: A History of Social Policy since the Industrial Revolution* (London: Palgrave Macmillan, 2009); George R. Boyer, "The Evolution of Unemployment Relief in Great Britain," *Journal of Interdisciplinary History* 34.3 (Winter 2004): 393–433; Timothy T. Hellwig, "The Origins of Unemployment Insurance in Britain: A Cross-Class Alliance Approach," *Social Science History* 29.1 (Spring 2005): 107–36.

15. Ted Wheelwright, "World Economic Crises and the Welfare State in Australia," in *Australian Welfare: Historical Sociology,* ed. Richard Kennedy (South Melbourne: Macmillan, 1989), 20–32.

16. Ann Zulawski, *Unequal Cures: Public Health and Political Change in Bolivia, 1900–1950* (Durham, N.C.: Duke University Press, 2007), 13–25.

17. Rossana Castaglioni, "Welfare State Reform in Chile and Uruguay: Cross-Class Coalitions, Elite Ideology and Veto Players," paper presented at Latin American Studies conference, Miami, 16–18 March 2000.

18. Manuel Castells and Alejandro Portes, "World Underneath: The Origins, Dynamics, and Effects of the Internal Economy," in *The Informal Economy: Studies in Advanced and Less Developed Countries,* ed. Alejandro Portes (Baltimore: Johns Hopkins University Press, 1989). According to Castells and Portes, in 1950, the earliest year for which reliable figures exist, 46 percent of the labor force in Latin America were in informal employments. Among the urban economically active population, 30 percent were in the informal sector.

19. Fernando Claudin, *The Communist Movement: From Comintern to Cominform,* vol. 1 (New York: Monthly Review Press, 1975); E. H. Carr, *The Twilight of Comintern, 1930–1935* (London: Macmillan, 1982).

20. For example, in Canada, the Communists led a nationwide petition for non-

contributory unemployment insurance. John Manley, "'Starve, Be Damned!': Communists and Canada's Urban Unemployed, 1929-39," *Canadian Historical Review* 79.3 (September 1998): 466-91.

21. Frank Farrell, "Socialism, Internationalism and the Australian Labour Movement," *Labour/Le Travail* 15 (Spring 1985): 125-44; Stuart Macintytre, *A Concise History of Australia,* 3d ed. (Cambridge: Cambridge University Press, 2009), 128-51, 168-72 (quotation on 128).

22. Mahinda Siriwardana, "Can Policy-Makers Learn from History? A General Equilibrium Analysis of the Recovery Policies of the 1930 Great Depression in Australia," *Journal of Policy Modeling* 20.3 (June 1988): 362.

23. Ibid., 362-66.

24. John Stevenson, "Myth and Reality: Britain in the 1930s," in *Crisis and Controversy: Essays in Honour of A.J.P. Taylor,* ed. Chris Cook and Alan Sked (New York: St. Martin's Press, 1976), 90-108.

25. William Smaldone, *Rudolf Hilferding: The Tragedy of a German Social Democrat* (Chicago: Northern Illinois University Press, 1998); Fernando Claudin, *Communist Movement.*

26. Dutton, *Origins of the French Welfare State,* 137.

27. On the reasons for the strike wave of 1936, see Antoine Prost, "Les grèves de mai-juin revisitées," *Le Mouvement Social* 200 (July-September 2002): 33-54.

28. Dutton, *Origins of the French Welfare State,* 137, 146, 182; Ingo Kolbloom, *La revanche des patrons: le patronat face au front populaire* (Paris: Flammarion, 1982); Julian Jackson, *The Popular Front in France: Defending Democracy* (Cambridge: Cambridge University Press, 1990); Daniel Lefeuvre, Michèle Marguirez, and Danielle Tartakovski, eds., *Histoire du Front Populaire*(Paris: Larousse, 2006); Serge Berstein, ed., *Léon Blum* (Paris: Fayard, 2006).

29. Dutton, *Origins of the French Welfare State,* 146.

30. Stephen Haggard and Robert R. Kaufman, *Development, Democracy, and Welfare States: Latin America, East Asia, and Eastern Europe* (Princeton, N.J.: Princeton University Press, 2008), 47-49; Zulawski, *Unequal Cures,*13; Anne-Emanuelle Birn, "Historiography of Infant and Child Health in Latin America," in *Healing the World's Children: Interdisciplinary Perspectives on Child Health in the Twentieth Century,* ed. Cynthia Comacchio, Janet Golden, and George Weisz (Montreal: McGill-Queen's University Press, 2008),73-108.

31. David R. Corkill, "The Chilean Socialist Right and the Popular Front 1933-41," *Journal of Contemporary History* 11.21 (July 1976): 261-73.

32. Ann Shona Orloff, "The Political Origins of America's Belated Welfare State," in *The Politics of Social Policy in the United States,* ed. Margaret Weir, Ann Shona Orloff, and Theda Skocpol (Princeton, N.J.: Princeton University Press, 1990), 77-78; Jill Quadagno, "From Old-Age Assistance to Supplemental Security Income: The Political Economy of Relief in the South, 1935-1972," in *The Politics of Social Policy in the United States,* ed. Margaret Weir, Ann Shona Orloff, and Theda Skocpol (Princeton, N.J.: Princeton University Press, 1990), 235-63; Helen Znaniecka Lopata and Henry P. Brehm, *Widows and Dependent Wives: From Social Problem to Federal Program* (New York: Praeger, 1986).

33. Kessler-Harris, *Gendering Labor History*, 238, 247–48.

34. Alvin Finkel, "Trade Unions and the Welfare State in Canada, 1945–1990," in *Labour Gains, Labour Pains: Fifty Years of PC 1003*, ed. Cy Gonick, Paul Phillips, and Jessie Vorst (Winnipeg: Society for Socialist Studies, 1995), 59–75.

35. Larry W. Isaac, Susan M. Carlson, and Mary P. Mathis, "Quality of Quantity in Comparative Historical Analysis: Temporally Changing Wage Labor Regimes in the United States and Sweden," in *The Comparative Political Economy of the Welfare State*, ed. Thomas Janoski and Alexander M. Hicks (New York: Cambridge University Press, 1994), 93–135.

36. Geary, "Labour in Western Europe from c. 1800," 262; Mary Hilson, *Political Change and the Rise of Labour in Comparative Perspective: Britain and Sweden, 1890–1920* (Lund, Swed.: Nordic Academic Press, 2006).

37. Anne-Marie Daune-Richard and Rianne Mahon, "Sweden: Models in Crisis," in *Who Cares? Women's Work, Childcare, and Welfare State Redesign*, ed. Jane Jenson and Mariette Sineau (Toronto: University of Toronto Press, 2001), 146.

38. Jane Lewis, "Gender and the Development of Welfare Regimes," *Journal of European Social Policy* 2.3 (1992): 159–73; Linda Gordon, "The Welfare State: Towards a Socialist-Feminist Perspective," in *Socialist Register, 1990* (London: Merlin, 1990), 169–200.

39. Jane Jenson and Mariette Sineau, eds., *Who Cares? Women's Work, Childcare, and Welfare State Redesign* (Toronto: University of Toronto Press, 2001), examines a wide range of national experiences with neoliberalism from the perspective of gender. On Sweden, see Daune-Richard and Mahon, "Sweden: Models in Crisis."

40. Duane Swank, *Global Capital, Political Institutions, and Policy Change in Developed Welfare States* (Cambridge: Cambridge University Press, 2002), 26.

41. A defense of the NAIRU can be found in Laurence Ball and N. Gregory Mankiw, "The NAIRU in Theory and Practice," *Journal of Economic Perspectives* 16.4 (Fall 2002): 115–36. Pro-labor views include Andrew Jackson, "The Perverse Circularity of NAIRU-Driven Economic Policy in Canada," *Canadian Business Economics* 8.2 (July 2000): 66–81; and Jim Stanford, *Paper Boom: Why Real Prosperity Requires a New Approach to Canada's Economy* (Toronto: Lorimer, 1999).

42. Paul Buhle, *Taking Care of Business: Samuel Gompers, George Meany, Lane Kirkland, and the Tragedy of American Labor* (New York: Monthly Review Press, 1999).

43. Jacob S. Hacker, *The Divided Welfare State: The Battle over Public and Private Social Benefits in the United States* (Cambridge: Cambridge University Press, 2002), 127, 133.

44. Mike Davis, *Prisoners of the American Dream: Politics and Economy in the History of the U.S. Working Class* (London: Verso, 1986), chap. 3; Kim Scipes, *The AFL-CIO's Secret War against Developing Country Workers: Solidarity or Sabotage?* (Lanham, Md.: Lexington Books, 2010).

45. Hacker, *Divided Welfare State*, 143.

46. Ibid.

47. Sonya Michel, *Children's Interests/Mothers' Rights: The Shaping of America's Child Care Policy* (New Haven, Conn.: Yale University Press 1999), 147, 201.

48. Hacker, *Divided Welfare State*, 153.

49. Ibid., 143.

50. U.S. Census Bureau *News*, 23 March 2007; Heather Boushey and Joseph Wright, "Health Insurance Data Briefs #2: Insurance Coverage in the United States," 13 April 2004, Center for Economic and Policy Research, accessed 6 August 2013, http://www.cepr.net/documents/publications/health_insurance_2_2004_04.html.

51. Paul Street, "Health Care as a Commodity: Reflections on the Hudson Decision," MR Zine, 18 December 2010, accessed 27 June 2013, http://mrzine.monthlyreview.org/2010/street181210.html; D. Andrew Austin, *The Market Structure of the Health Insurance Industry* (Washington, D.C.: Congressional Research Service, 2009).

52. _"Union Members Summary," U.S. Department of Labor, Bureau of Labor Statistics, 23 Janary 2013, accessed 6 July 2013, http://www.bls.gov/news.release/union2.nro.htm.

53. Kim Moody, *U.S. Labor in Trouble and Transition: The Failure of Reform from Above, the Promise of Revival from Below* (London: Verso, 2007); Dan Clawson, *The Next Upsurge: Labor and the New Social Movements* (Ithaca, N.Y.: ILR Press, 2003).

54. Seamus Milne, *The Enemy Within: The Secret War against the Miners* (London: Verso, 1994); Leo Panitch and Colin Leys, *The End of Parliamentary Socialism: From New Left to New Labour*, 2d ed. (London: Verso, 2001); Bryon Sheldrick, "The British Labour Party in Search of Identity between Labour and Parliament," in *Social Democracy after the Cold War*, ed. Bryan Evans and Ingo Schmidt (Edmonton: AU Press, 2012), 149–82.

55. Peter Beilharz, "The Australian Left: Beyond Liberalism?" in *Socialist Register, 1985/86*, ed. Ralph Miliband, Marcel Liebman, John Saville, and Leo Panitch (London: Merlin, 1986), 210–32.

56. Macintyre, *Concise History of Australia*, 249–50. See also Stuart Macintyre, *Winners and Losers: The Pursuit of Social Justice in Australian History* (Sydney: Allen and Unwin, 1985).

57. Asbjørn Wahl, "In Defence of General Welfare: Norwegian Coalition against Neoliberalism," *Nordic News Network*, 4 July 2001, accessed 11 June 2013, http://www.nnn.se/n-model/wahl-1.htm.

58. Asbjørn Wahl, "Building Progressive Alliances," *Global Labour Column*, Global Labour University, 5 July 2011, accessed 6 July 2013, http://column.global-labour-university.org/2011/01/building-progressive-alliances.html.

59. Ibid.

60. Wahl, "In Defence of General Welfare."

61. Walter Korpi and Joakim Palme, "The Paradox of Redistribution and Strategies of Equality: Welfare State Institutions, Inequality, and Poverty in the Western Countries," *American Sociological Review* 63 (October 1998): 661.

62. Clare Bembra, "Health Status and the Worlds of Welfare," *Social Policy and Society* 5.1 (2006): 53–62; Lyle Scruggs and James P. Allan, "The Material Consequences of Welfare States: Benefit Generosity and Absolute Poverty in 16 OECD Countries," *Comparative Political Studies* 39.7 (September 2006): 880–904.

63. Swank, *Global Capital*, 142–52.

64. Anda Stamati, *National Report on Restructuring in Greece* (Athens: Institute of Labour GSEE/ADEDY, 2010).

65. Seraphim Seferiades, "Low Union Density amidst a Conflictive Contentious Repertoire: Flexible Labour Markets, Unemployment, and Trade Union Decline in Greece," 1999, EUI Working Paper SPS, No. 99/6, European University Institute, Florence, Department of Political and Social Sciences.

66. "Strike Protests in Athens Turn Violent," *Al Jazeera*, 28 June 2011; "Greece Passes Austerity Law," *Al Jazeera*, 29 June 2011.

67. *Globe and Mail*, 21 October 2010.

68. Rossanna Castiglioni y Daniela Vicharat, "Desarrollo social en América Latina: tendencias y desafios," *Revista Instituciones y Desarrollo* 8.9 (2001): 509–42.

69. Evelyne Huber, "Globalization and Social Policy Developments in Latin America," in *Globalization and the Future of the Welfare State*, ed. Miguel Glatzer and Dietrich Rueschemeyer (Pittsburgh: University of Pittsburgh Press, 2005), 75–105.

70. Ibid., 83–86; Stephan Haggard and Robert R. Kaufman, *Development, Democracy, and Welfare States: Latin America, East Asia, and Eastern Europe* (Princeton, N.J.: Princeton University Press, 2008), 107–9.

71. Huber, "Globalization and Social Policy," 86.

72. Kurt Weyland, *Bounded Rationality and Policy Diffusion: Social Sector Reform in Latin America* (Princeton, N.J.: Princeton University Press, 2006), 23–24. Weyland's effort to remove all class content and suggestions of imperialism from the story of the wrenching apart of welfare programs fits within neoliberal scholarship on the sundering of the welfare state, for which another notable example is Mitchell A. Orenstein, *Privatizing Pensions: The Transnational Campaign for Social Security Reform* (Princeton, N.J.: Princeton University Press, 2008).

73. Julie Feinsilver, "Cuba's Health Politics at Home and Abroad," in *Morbid Symptoms: Health under Capitalism*, ed. Leo Panitch and Colin Leys (London: Merlin, 2010), 216–39; Haggard and Kaufman, *Development, Democracy, and Welfare States*, 276.

74. Marta Harnecker, "The Bolivarian Revolution—Is It a Revolution?" in Marta Harnecker, *Rebuilding the Left* (London: Zed Books, 2007), 139–51.

75. The Gini coefficient, a measure used to demonstrate the degree to which wealth is distributed equally among members of a population (1.0 would mean that all wealth was held by one individual, while 0 would mean absolute income equality), fell from .495 to .41 in Venezuela from 1998 to 2009, a period when neoliberalism was pushing up Ginis in most countries globally. By comparison, some recent Ginis include: United States, .45 (2007), Canada, .32 (2005), European Union, .304 (2009), Norway, .25 (2008), Sweden, .23 (2005), Denmark, .23 (2005), and .25 for Norway (2005). China's Gini was .415 in 2007, and Brazil's Gini was .567 in 2005. Venezuela's neighbor, Colombia, which seemed to be the regional leader in trying to discredit the Chàvez regime's democratic credentials, had a Gini of .585, which represented a significant increase in inequality from its 1996 Gini of .538. All of these figures are interestingly supplied by the CIA, which clearly has no interest in presenting Venezuela as a country in which distributive justice is growing while Colombia becomes an even more unjust distributor of income than in the past. *CIA Factbook, 2011*, accessed 6 July 2013, https://www.cia.gov/library/publications/download/download-2011/.

76. Peter Bohmer, "Venezuela: Socialism for the 21st Century," Znet, 5 August 2009,

accessed 6 July 2013, http://www.zcommunications.org/venezuela-socialism-for-the-21st-century-by-peter-bohmer.

77. Susan Spronk, "Water Privatization and the Prospects for Trade Union Revitalization in the Public Sector: Case Studies from Bolivia and Peru," *Just Labour: A Canadian Journal of Work and Society* 14 (Autumn 2009): 165.

78. Ibid.

79. Trade-union density in Bolivia in the early 2000s was only 20 percent. Oscar Olivera in collaboration with Tom Lewis, *Cochabamba! Water War in Bolivia* (Cambridge, Mass.: South End Press, 2004), 124. Olivera and Lewis mention that the main trade-union central, the Central Obrera Boliviana (COB), had been gradually weakening at the time (129).

80. Marta Harnecker y Federico Fuentes, *MAS-IPSP de Bolivia: Instrumento Politico Que Surge de Los Movimientos Sociales* (Caracas: Centro International Miranda, 2008), 40.

81. On Evo Morales, see Sven Harten, *The Rise of Evo Morales and the MAS* (London: Zed, 2011); and Martin Sivak, *Evo Morales: The Extraordinary Rise of the First Indigenous President of Bolivia* (London: Palgrave Macmillan, 2010).

82. Olivera and Lewis, *Cochabamba!*

83. Harnecker and Fuentes, *MAS-IPSP de Bolivia,* 41–51.

84. "Nuestros Principios Ideológicos Movimiento al Socialismo," *Archivo Chile,* accessed 12 March 2013, http://www.archivochile.com/Portada/bol_elecciones05/boleleccioneso010.pdf.

85. Harten, *Rise of Evo Morales,* traces the successes and challenges of the Morales government's first term in office.

86. As evidenced in the party program (see n.84).

87. Harten, *Rise of Evo Morales*; Roger Burbach, North American Congress on Latin America, "Update: Communitarian Socialism in Bolivia," 2 April 2010, accessed 6 July 2013, https://nacla.org/news/update-communitarian-socialism-bolivia.

88. The Gini fell only from .601 to .582 during the government's first term in office. Benjamin Kohl and Rosalind Bresnahan, "Bolivia under Morales: Consolidating Power, Initiating Decolonization," *Latin American Perspectives* 37.3 (2010): 5–17.

89. Witnessed by the author during a visit to Bolivia, 22 November 2010.

7

Politics and Policies in the 1970s and Early Twenty-first Century
The Linked Recessions

JUDITH STEIN

The Great Recession had its origins in the political economy created by politicians and business leaders in the 1970s. The decisions made and patterns put in place reshaped the structure of the U.S. economy and politics, fostering the wage stagnation, indebtedness, and global imbalances that led to the Great Recession and continue to afflict workers and their unions.

There were two crises of political economy in the twentieth century, the first in the 1930s, and the second in the 1970s. People trying to understand the Great Recession often look back to the Great Depression. Especially for people on the left, the 1930s was the heroic era of working-class agency and progressive reform. But they also look back to the Great Depression because there is a robust literature on the 1930s—the causes and ending of the depression, the rise of the labor movement, and the transformation of the political system. Nevertheless, because the economy of the 1930s was self-contained, its dynamics are unlike those of the contemporary economy. Americans reformed their economy, society, and politics in the 1930s with minimal concern that imports would replace domestic production or exports could expand demand. Global connections were few and marginal to the recovery. Corporations complained about New Deal reforms, but they had no better opportunities outside of the United States.

The economies of the 1970s and the contemporary world are global. Both contained imbalances among the major trading nations that led to recession. The likeness between the crisis of the 1970s and the Great Recession has been obscured because the literature on the 1970s is slight. Histories of the 1930s are organized around the questions of the Great Depression. Except for Peter Gourevitch's *Politics in Hard Times,* an international comparison of responses to economic crises in the 1890s, the 1930s, and the 1970s, most works on the 1970s are not organized around the economic crisis.[1] That a book on the decade can have the title *Something Happened* says much about the popular notion that nothing significant happened during the decade.[2] To be sure, some scholars have noticed that profits fell sharply in the 1970s, which produced a "crisis of legitimation." Others concluded that the state could no longer fulfill its social obligations or there was a "fiscal crisis of the state." Jurgen Habermas and James O'Connor offered a Marxist version of this problem, and Daniel Bell a non-Marxist.[3] But this literature addressed the nature of capitalism, not the specifics of the 1970s. Even so, that analysis has remained on the margins of historical interpretation.

There is a growing literature on the 1970s.[4] Political historians have mapped the rise of a New Right leading to Ronald Reagan's election in 1980.[5] Labor historians have traced conflicts over race, gender, and culture, rank-and-file movements in unions, and the rise of public-sector unionism. But the works do not yield a synthetic understanding of the decade. Historians portray a Whiggish rise of the New Right but fail to ask why the right was so convincing in the late 1970s but not earlier. Labor historians scrutinize every fissure within the working class. Many conclude, in the words of Jefferson Cowie, that the working class "died of many external assaults upon it, yes, but mostly of its own internal weakness," without examining the external assaults.[6] But it is possible to find a theme that makes more sense of the decade if we examine capital as well as labor, and economic policy as well as social and cultural policy.

The most important change affecting workers in the public and private sectors in the 1970s was that the long period of postwar economic growth ended between 1973 and 1975. Productivity had slowed in the late 1960s and plummeted in the 1970s. From 1973 to 1976 it actually fell 0.54 percent.[7] (The productivity of Japan and West Germany rose 6 percent and 3 to 4 percent, respectively.[8]) Wages began stagnating in 1973. Unemployment peaked at 9 percent in May 1975, in the midst of the deepest recession since the 1930s. The recession of the 1970s was synchronized. It affected the whole developed world. It was caused everywhere by rising oil prices and glutted markets for tradables—mainly manufactured goods. It challenged previous ways of managing economies.

In the United States, as classic Keynesianism employing macroeconomic techniques and free trade faltered, the labor movement proposed microeconomic industrial policy to address the crisis. A reformed Democratic party, less responsive to labor, was uninterested. Unable to govern effectively, in 1980 Democrats yielded power to a Republican party that promised to restore prosperity. President Ronald Reagan's policies did bring back growth, but they also altered the postwar mixed economy, privileging capital and sacrificing manufacturing for the chimera of high technology, finance, and real estate. This sectoral shift profoundly changed the size and composition of the labor movement. The distortions produced by this recomposition of the economy also led in time to the Great Recession.

At the beginning of the 1970s, politicians held assumptions shaped by twenty-five years of postwar growth. The mixed economy, as it was called, was rooted in the notion that high wages and regulated capital created and sustained prosperity. From 1947–73, income and wealth were mildly redistributed, even as economic growth soared. The Keynesian idea that governments could promote employment through spending or reducing taxes was accepted by both parties. The leading Keynesian economist Paul Samuelson proclaimed, with the hubris of the age, "By the proper choice of monetary and fiscal policy we as the artists, mixing the colors of our palette, can have the capital formation and rate of current consumption that we desire."[9] In 1969, unemployment fell below 4 percent. The country, enjoying 4 percent GDP growth at the end of the 1960s, was rich enough to tackle new issues. Affluence fostered new thinking about leisure, human relations, race, consumption, environment, and a host of extra-economic concerns. The economy seemed to be on autopilot.

An early sign that the old ways were not working was the trade deficit in 1971, the first since 1893. Although not resonating in society, it did send shock waves through policy-making government agencies. The deficit was partly a function of American policy. To cement cold-war alliances, the United States aided European and Japanese export-oriented development by encouraging imports into the United States. The Bureau of the Budget announced in April 1950: "Foreign economic policies should not be formulated in terms primarily of economic objectives; they must be subordinated to our politico-security objectives and the priorities which the latter involved."[10] Three years later, the National Security Council urged the entry of Japanese goods to the United States to halt "economic deterioration and failing living standards" in Japan that "create fertile ground for communist subversion."[11] The State Department judged that "Japan's resistance to Soviet-Sino pressures will depend in large measure on whether the free world [is] willing [to] make [a] reasonable place for Japan's trade."[12] Because the Europeans were unwilling, most of Japan's exports ended up in the United States. The chair of the Council of Economic Advisers, Walter Heller, told Japanese leaders in 1964 that the U.S. tax cut of that year would produce "a strong and expanding [American] market for Japanese goods." It did.[13] This early action explains why so much Japanese steel and so many Japanese cars ended up in the United States and not Europe.

The same policy was applied in Europe. George Ball, a former lobbyist for the European Economic Community (EEC) and John F. Kennedy's undersecretary of state for economic affairs, operated on the premise that "we Americans could afford to pay some economic price for a strong Europe."[14] Ball welcomed

European imports in the United States without any thought as to their impact on American jobs.

On the export side of the ledger, U.S. trading partners aggressively pursued their own interests. The Japanese market was walled by tariffs, quotas, and state directives. In Europe, U.S. businessmen found it difficult to sell into the new European Economic Community (EEC) because of its tariffs. Instead, they supplied Europe with products from factories built within the EEC walls. In 1970, a Commerce Department official feared that these foreign subsidiaries operated as "a vacuum pump that sucks our new technology out as soon as it's created."[15] Paul Volcker, undersecretary of the treasury for monetary affairs, was surprised to find that business's "approach to foreign markets has been to put plants abroad instead of direct selling of US products."[16] Unlike the elites that led U.S. economic policy making at the outset of the Great Recession, the young Volcker did not assume that such behavior was economically efficient, necessary, or inevitable.

Duly alarmed by the trade deficit, in August 1971 President Nixon ended the gold-backed dollar to cheapen the greenback, which everyone in the government believed was too high and one of the reasons why exports were declining and imports increasing. The devaluation reduced the trade deficit, although the decline could better be attributed to the worldwide boom in 1972 and 1973 that kept Japanese and European products at home. Nevertheless, President Nixon assumed that the problem was solved and returned to the old priority of strategic goals. He said in 1972, "Trade is part of a bigger package.... That means we may have to give more than our trade interest, strictly construed, would require."[17]

The boom was short-lived. Oil prices quadrupled in the wake of the Arab-Israeli war in the fall of 1973. Throughout the developed world, rising energy prices added to the costs of production and reduced domestic demand, as more money went abroad to pay for expensive oil. The Europeans and Japanese used industrial policies to confront the new cost structure. They cartelized industries, planned shutdowns, funded new energy-efficient plants, and used non-tariff barriers to keep out foreign goods. Japan and Germany accelerated exports to pay for expensive oil. In Japan, austerity at home forced companies to export, which raised the foreign share of GDP 28 percent in 1974 and 1975.[18] Because Europe restricted Japanese imports, the goods ended up in the United States, worsening the trade deficit.[19]

Unlike its competitors, the United States did not tackle the new price structure directly, even though rising production costs and falling demand reduced productivity and corporate profits. State intervention was largely confined to the management of aggregate demand. Government relied on fiscal policy, tax rates, and spending to control growth and business cycles, and even the problems of particular industries. Democrats and Republicans stood consistently against policies that addressed particular economic sectors or systematically educated and trained the labor force. Postwar affluence made microeconomic interventions seem unnecessary.

After World War II, the U.S. GDP was three times larger than the Soviet Union's and six times larger than Great Britain's. The United States was the largest producer of steel, electricity, food, and oil. It led the world in new industries like computers and aircraft. This supremacy allowed leaders to pursue free trade and free capital movements—opening the U.S. market and subsidizing direct investment overseas—with little thought of domestic consequences. Overseas rivals in Europe and Japan were doing pretty much the opposite, protecting domestic markets and pursuing various industrial and active labor-market policies. When boom gave way to crisis, these differences became more salient.

In the United States, the new conditions set off distributional struggles between capital and labor and brought in their wake an extended period of slow growth and high unemployment. It ended the 1960s talk that the Keynesian recipe for affluence had been learned and the business cycle was a thing of the past. Nixon's successor, Gerald Ford, tried to apply classical Republican policies. To Ford, the major problem was inflation, which was caused by high wages and government spending, as much as high oil prices. Too much of the GDP was consumed, not invested. Conservatives and a mobilized business community believed that the economy faltered because of a capital shortage. Reducing corporate taxes, slowing wage growth, and cutting government spending would make more capital available for investment. From October 1974 through March 1975, the economy had experienced its steepest decline since the 1930s. Productivity plunged, profits declined, and wages fell. Initially, the president tried to ignore the rising unemployment, which peaked at 9 percent in May 1975. Chastised by GOP election losses in 1974 and the swift deterioration of the economy, he made a U-turn. Ford proposed a broad-based tax cut in early 1975, to replace his planned tax surcharge, and signed bills to create one hundred thousand public jobs proposed by the Democratic Congress. These measures worked, and during the second half of 1975 the GDP rose 7 and 8 percent after falling 5 percent during the recession months. Inflation fell from double digits to 7 percent. But unemployment was stuck at 8.5 percent. And, as the economy improved, imports grew.

Congressional Democrats demanded tax cuts, public-service jobs, and extended unemployment benefits. Although they tried to shelter their constituencies from the impact of the changes, Democrats did not recognize the new economic situation created by high oil prices and the new competition from resurrected Japan and Europe. The labor movement, too, was unprepared for the challenges posed by the new global economy. Its approach to politics and to economic policy had been premised upon the perpetuation of the long postwar boom. Its objective was to ensure that workers obtained their share of the rising productivity of postwar economic growth. A related goal was to increase the social-wage, education, health-care, and other security issues funded through progressive taxation. As a consequence, the labor movement was more syndicalist than social democratic and failed to demand forms of state intervention that addressed the changing needs of industries and the labor force in a world of ongoing technical change, open trade, and competition. The European and Japanese labor movements were much more involved in industrial policy, despite differences in the techniques each nation used. This was not the result of national DNA but the necessities of resurrecting economies after World War II.

Still, those parts of the labor movement hurt by the new trading order were the first to recognize a problem and respond. In 1969, the AFL-CIO rejected "free trade" for managed trade. Two years later, I. W. Abel of the United Steelworkers of America (USWA) and Floyd Smith of the International Association of Machinists, part of a presidential commission created to examine trade and the economy, concluded that capital movement was the cause of economic faltering. The commission had recommended that the United States extend free trade. The two labor leaders dissented, observing that American capital abroad increased 31.5 percent, compared to 7.4 percent in the United States between 1969 and 1971. This outflow was a major reason why labor productivity and growth rates had fallen absolutely and in comparison to EEC countries.

The labor federation helped write the Foreign Trade and Investment Act, or Burke-Hartke, named after Massachusetts Congressman James A. Burke and Indiana Senator Vance Hartke, who introduced it in 1971. The law would have ended the tax advantages transnationals enjoyed and empowered the president to regulate international capital transactions if he determined that they reduced domestic employment. (Presidents Kennedy and Johnson had limited capital flows for balance of payments purposes in the 1960s.) The bill also proposed to create a tripartite commission with strong powers to regulate imports and capital flows. The import-relief sections of the legislation required a rollback of imports to the quantity of goods taken in between 1965 and 1969. It would attempt to maintain a relationship between domestic production and imports. The AFL-CIO's Nathaniel Goldfinger explained the logic in the *New York Times*: "Governments now have direct and indirect barriers to imports, as well as various types of subsidies for exports. The result is that imports surge into the huge American market, the most open market to imports of all major industrial countries, while the expansion of United States exports is retarded or blocked by the practices of foreign governments."[20]

It is difficult to imagine such legislation today. But during the 1970s, when global markets were managed and industrial policies were in the saddle in most countries, such legislation, although opposed by the multinationals, was within the realm of the possible for reformers. Still, the initiative was repulsed for several reasons. First, the Nixon administration believed that trade legislation could tackle the non-tariff trade barriers of foreign nations. The Trade Act of 1974 authorized new negotiations and also increased trade adjustment assistance, liberalized the escape clause, and streamlined countervailing duties procedures. Thus, Nixon conceded that trade produced job loss. His solution was retraining workers. He admitted that asymmetrical trade treaties limited American exports but promised to eliminate foreign barriers through trade negotiations. Acknowledging the problem but resolving it through new trade treaties, Nixon, and every subsequent president, muted criticism of the new global capitalism.

A second reason that Burke-Hartke failed is that the Democratic party was not united behind it. The reform-oriented professionals, the core of the McGovern movement, ignored trade issues. The party's platform of 1972 made no mention of Burke-Hartke. This was in part because the labor movement itself was divided over the bill. The United Automobile Workers of America (UAW), which had left the AFL-CIO in 1968, did not support the legislation because it hoped to create a global automobile union and auto jobs were not then threatened, as they would be at the end of the 1970s. UAW support for trade-adjustment assistance instead of Burke-Hartke led some labor-oriented Democrats to think that compensation for lost jobs would satisfy the labor movement. Moreover, this was a new issue for liberals, who had opposed transnationals mainly because of their presumed negative impact on Third World nations, not their effects on American workers.

Most liberals were preoccupied with Watergate and Vietnam. The New Democrats, often from suburban, affluent districts, made it a badge of honor that they had jettisoned 1930s politics. Congressman James Blanchard, from Michigan, remarked, "We don't think of ourselves as New Dealers at all—or proponents of the Great Society either." Gary Hart, the new senator from Colorado, who had been George McGovern's campaign manager, snickered, "We are not a bunch of little Hubert Humphreys."[21] Coming of age during the prosperous 1960s, they believed that posteconomic issues—foreign policy, race, gender, political process, and the environment—were the important ones. They ignored or misread the new industrial competition with Europe and Japan that challenged the affluence that held the party together. Although nobody in government thought that manufacturing was disposable, notions of postindustrial society were powerful among intellectuals and environmentalists.[22] It took another crisis to challenge the complacency that underlay existing methods of managing the economy.

After the quadrupling of oil prices and the onset of the severe recession, economic critiques expanded beyond the labor movement. Now, sectoral planning, as opposed to the traditional macroeconomic planning, earned a hearing. Senators Hubert Humphrey and Jacob Javits offered the Balanced Growth and

Economic Planning Act in May 1975, when unemployment hit 9 percent. The idea behind the effort was to anticipate problems in sectors such as energy, food, and manufacturing. Keynesian activism was macroeconomic, focusing on aggregates—the effect of a budget surplus or deficit on the economy or the amount of demand produced by a tax cut. The new initiative was microeconomic, targeting particular sectors and industries. Because Keynesians had no answers to the new industrial problems, planners earned a hearing. In his presidential address to the American Economic Association in 1976, Robert Gordon, a leading Keynesian, acknowledged that "we economists pay too little attention to the changing institutional environment that conditions economic behavior." Open markets and mobile capital had altered the context of economic activity. Neither the Keynesian nor the neoclassical approach grasped the importance of institutions, of long-term relationships between capital, labor, and place in generating growth and innovation.

Knowledge of practices in other countries enhanced theoretical perspectives. American planners were aware that the United Kingdom's Labour party nationalized and merged fourteen weak firms to create British Steel in 1967. Every European nation but Germany owned steel mills (and Germany had nationalized its mines to ensure that its steel mills had cheap coal). Nationalization was not employed by the left only. In 1971, when the venerable Rolls-Royce got into trouble, the Conservative government of Edward Heath nationalized it. While nationalization was probably out of the question in the United States, other forms of regulation were not. The Ford administration, unsympathetic to the European way of managing economies, nonetheless considered cash subsidies, loan guarantees, and mergers when national champion Pan American Airways lurched toward bankruptcy in 1974. In the end, the government decided that changes in the regulatory system would be necessary in part because other airlines were also sinking.

The Humphrey-Javits planning board could presumably foresee industrial difficulties through ongoing monitoring and analysis. (The Council of Economic Advisers did not keep sectoral statistics.) Humphrey believed that the nation needed development banks, which the United States had used in housing but not in other sectors. President Gerald Ford was uninterested.[23] Alan Greenspan, the chair of the Council of Economic Advisers, told Ford that the social goals of planners would always trump economic efficiencies. "The real issues are mandatory planning of which H-J is merely a stalking horse," Greenspan concluded. The Chamber of Commerce agreed, preferring Keynesianism to the new planning: "Aggregate demand management policy is preferable to supply management policies as a countercyclical device, as it does not suggest intervention in individual economic decisions."[24]

Keynesian demand management, useful when the economy was more contained, was trumped by other government and business actions. During the recession of 1975, with markets in the developed nations glutted, banks rich with OPEC deposits began to lend money to developing countries, like South Korea, Taiwan, Mexico, and Brazil, that were eager to build up their manufacturing sectors. The only way the banks could get their money back was if these nations sold their products in the United States. Europe and Japan kept such goods out. Protection was part of their industrial policy. But the new president, former Georgia Governor Jimmy Carter, asserted in 1977 that "free access to U.S. markets is a matter of ranking importance for our allies and almost all the developing countries of the world."[25]

Humphrey had hoped that a Democratic president elected in 1976 would embrace industrial planning. But Carter, like McGovern, was nominated by the reform wing of the Democratic party. The new president had no ties to labor and positioned himself above the traditional constituencies of his party. He learned the rules of the new primary system quickly, but he won, too, because he ran in a field of many liberal candidates who divided the vote. Carter ran on the post-Watergate themes of trust and honesty. Nevertheless, despite the southern accents in the administration and the anti-Washington rhetoric, he presided over a Keynesian administration.

Carter proposed and the Congress passed a small stimulus to reduce unemployment. In the open economy, the stimulus stimulated foreign as well as domestic production. The U.S. trade deficit jumped from $9.5 billion to $34 billion in 1978, despite a cheaper dollar. If a part of the stimulus was spent on imports instead of domestic production, it might produce more budget deficits and inflation than jobs, some officials warned. But political culture determined how key actors understood the problem of imports. The president and many liberals claimed that high prices charged by oligopolies were the cause of inflation and imports; those on the right were certain that high wages won by labor unions were the cause. Together, these views monopolized a good part of the political spectrum.

Adding to the problem was that Carter's economic ideas were vague. His themes were moral, not economic. He was liberal on race, which was the dominant concern of liberalism at the time. Carter was one of a group of southern governors elected in 1970 who had pledged to implement the new civil-rights laws. But the extent of his liberalism was exaggerated after he defeated the poisonous George Wallace in the Florida primary. Carter refused to make labor reform a priority in 1978. That would have made it much easier not only to unionize the South and West but also to keep blacks and whites of the South together and in the Democratic column. Carter and most Democrats did a lot to promote black empowerment but little to promote the interracialism necessary for the party's electoral success.

This was a traditional Democratic administration, so the policies did not simply stem from Carter's personal characteristics. Yet none of Carter's Keynesian advisers recognized the international imbalances either. Typically, Council of Economic Advisers chair Charles Schultze judged business investment anemic but believed that "it is not a problem because of ample capacity abroad."[26] And, if capacity was not ample, the United States would help—abroad, not at home. The Export-Import Bank approved a $17.9 million loan to South Korea's government-owned steel company, POSCO, to finance equipment for a new mill. The policy of welcoming imports and ignoring job loss was at the heart of the problem the Carter administration had with the labor movement during its first two years.

Foreign investment abroad filled the gap opened up by the absence of an industrial policy at home. Multinational companies like Caterpillar Tractor initially bought foreign parts for domestically assembled products, while it made plans to build plants in countries where costs were lowest. The outcome was the rise of transnational production, based in international supply chains, facilitated by the growth of containerization. Electronics producers were already globalizing during the mid-1960s. But international production would fully mature only in the late 1970s and 1980s, when corporations felt intensifying pressure on costs, from rising oil prices and emerging competition from state-led newly industrializing economies in East Asia. Most European countries employed industrial policies to maintain production at home. In the United States, where foreign policy had ploughed the ground, transnational production, not industrial policies, solved the new problems. Despite home markets of similar size, European multinational reexports to the home market amounted to $260 million in 1978, compared with $4.1 billion for U.S. firms. During the 1970s, the American share of the world market for manufactured exports declined by 23 percent.[27]

The Carter administration produced incoherent policies that neither protected labor nor promoted growth. The party's comprehensive victory in 1976—Democrats controlled the presidency and the congress—misled Democratic legislators and many commentators. Both the *Wall Street Journal* and *Nation* predicted that the GOP was dead. Some believed that the Republicans would go the way of the Federalists.[28] With these sentiments expanding their appetites, Democrats imagined that they had an opportunity to complete their 1960s social-welfare agenda. If conservatives viewed the era of affluence as a triumph of free enterprise, liberals saw it as the foundation of a generous welfare state that was only half-built. The environmental and consumer movements had also emerged from the booming economy of the 1960s and early 1970s, and they, too, operated on the assumption that the economy was trouble-free. Based in a new middle class employed in education, government, and social services, these reformers had loose ties to American industries. Many decried the costs of growth, overconsumption, and the manipulation of the consumer, without acknowledging the economic difficulties facing industries and workers. They did not believe that the age of affluence had ended. Quick to believe that the economy was healed, liberals sought a consumer agency, national health care, and other reforms that could complete the 1960s agenda.

Despite the effort to construct a stronger welfare state, when it came to the economy there was a strong anti-statist streak in the reformers and their New Left cousins, who distrusted government as much as corporations. When unions forced Jimmy Carter to consider an industrial bank in 1980, it was vigorously opposed by Alfred Kahn, the father of deregulation, Charles Schultze, a high priest of postwar Keynesianism, and also by Ralph Nader, the public-interest warrior. Still, the labor legacy of the Democratic party was represented in the government. Secretary of Labor F. Ray Marshall, former Council of Economic Advisers' head Walter Heller, Secretary of the Treasury William Miller, and some of his political advisers convinced Carter to negotiate a National Accord with AFL-CIO president Lane Kirkland, George Meany's successor, in the fall of 1979. Labor agreed that the war against inflation must have a high priority and accepted seats on the Pay Advisory Committee that was to chart the course of wage restraint. In return, the president promised that the administration would not use unemployment or a recession to reduce inflation. Even though business was not a part of the National Accord, and the issues addressed were limited, it was a step toward more consensual governance.

There were other efforts to construct new institutional relationships. In the summer of 1978, Carter accepted Ray Marshall's suggestion to create the Steel Tripartite Advisory Committee (STAC) in the wake of the steel crisis in December 1977. Chaired by the Secretaries of Commerce and Labor, STAC included top union and industry leaders and the more sympathetic members of the administration. Although the president ignored the committee until faced with another steel crisis in 1980, the committee did discuss industrial policy. But only the union representatives urged a steel plan with "objectives, some goals in terms of size, market share, and everything," normal goings-on in every other major nation. Roger Altman from Treasury told the USWA president Lloyd McBride and U.S. Steel chief David Roderick that Carter would not pursue "special packages," only economy-wide policies like changing taxes and perhaps deregulation.[29] In short, macroeconomic policies remained in the saddle. The Democratic administration was closer to industry than to the union. In December 1979, the American Iron and Steel Institute had declared that "[m]any of the actions they [the Europeans] have taken—such as government takeover, subsidization, and cartelization of the industry—[are] not appropriate in the United States."[30] Carter and his Keynesian advisers agreed.

In June 1980, after the limits of Carter's policy became clear, the USWA economist Jim Smith said, "When we consider what the Japanese government has accomplished with guaranteed loan programs for steel and other target industries, ... [one wonders] if the United States government can compete in the modern world. The U.S. industry will not be able to modernize itself, with its own cash flow, and fulfill its pollution control obligations. Therefore, we see U.S. Steel and others shifting capital out of the industry as fast as possible. Either we obtain a massive program of loan guarantees to the competent steel managements that want them or worker investment in the industry." If neither took place, "we might as well prepare to lose 150,000 jobs and half our domestic capacity during the 1980s."[31] It was not a bad projection.

When government refused to act, problems did not disappear. Instead, they were transposed into the collective-bargaining process, which produced stormy conflict but zero-sum results. Much of the labor history of this era tells the story of those local turbulent clashes and working-class distress after the closure of these mills. The larger global and national story that produced the conflict is offstage, and the effort of the unions to forge a government policy in the new era of competition ignored.

Social-democratic and New Left tendencies of the party were both represented in the Carter government. In the end, however, the advocates of industrial policy needed a united party and a president who was intellectually behind the effort. Even if Carter had been committed, he had run out of time in 1980. Neither traditional Keynesianism nor the Federal Reserve Board's new monetarism improved the economy, and the failures empowered groups who proposed supply-side alternatives. Still, most who voted for Ronald Reagan were unfamiliar with the new economic theories. They had simply lost faith in Jimmy Carter. Only 11 percent of those who voted for Reagan did so because they believed he was a conservative; 38 percent because they thought it was time for a change.[32] The electorate repudiated Carter, but it was a decision based upon his performance, not ideology.

Initially, the virtues of President Reagan's program were hard to find. The keystone of his policies was the individual tax rate cuts—5 percent the first year and then 10 percent a year for the next two years. According to supply-side theory, these cuts would increase incentives for investment and work. Reagan's tax legislation also included more traditional corporate tax cuts and increased depreciation write-offs. The Federal Reserve, expecting that these measures would vastly stimulate the economy and raise inflation, kept interest rates high even after the onset of a recession in the summer of 1981. The federal fund rate was mostly in the 18 to 20 percent range. Only in the summer of 1982, one year after the recession officially began, did the Fed being to ease. The economy continued to decline until November 1982, when unemployment peaked at 10.8 percent. By then the inflation rate had fallen to 3.8 percent.[33]

During the 1982 recession, the GDP fell 2.1 percent. The recession was not only deep but blue-collar; 79 percent of the jobless were manufacturing workers. The unemployment rate for professional and technical workers was less than 4 percent; for workers in primary metals over 28 percent; for autoworkers 23 percent. Reagan had blamed the recession on Carter and then attributed the upward turn in 1983 to his supply-side and free-market policies.

GDP rose from -2.2 percent rate in the recession year 1982 to 4.5 percent in 1983 and 7.2 percent in 1984. Still, Reagan's promises of increased productivity and investment were unkept, and the trade deficit grew, now accompanied by a huge budget deficit. And every form of saving—personal, business, and public—fell during the 1980s. Investment did not rise. Spending for plant and equipment fell from 12.1 percent of GDP in 1981 to 10.3 in 1986. It averaged about 10 percent from 1986 to 1989, compared with 11.6 percent during the Carter years. Continuing the lackluster trend of the 1970s, productivity rose only 0.8 percent.[34] The budget deficit rose from 2.6 percent of GDP in 1981 to 5.4 percent in 1985. Increased consumption, resulting from the tax cuts, married to the strong dollar allowed imports to replace domestic production and made exporting impossible. The trade deficit grew to over 3 percent of GDP when it was slightly over 1 percent during the late Carter years. Most of the deficit was composed of imports of manufactured goods. In this global context, new investment inevitably went into nontradables, items that must be produced as well as consumed at home, like housing, retailing, defense, and finance.

Nevertheless, because it was a recovery, its methods—tax cuts, deregulation, and privatization—were enshrined as the new bipartisan consensus for growth, replacing the Keynesian demand management of the postwar era. Reagan's policies also transformed the structure of the economy. The United States addressed the global excess of the 1970s by exiting from many tradable industries. In the international recession of the early 1980s, U.S. steel production fell 40 percent, in contrast to drops of 12 and 21 percent in Japan and Europe, respectively. Autos, machine tools, machinery, and other high-value items reveal similar statistics.

The old jobs were replaced by new ones in real estate, retail, finance, and defense. Virtually all (97.7 percent) new jobs created from 1980 to the Great Recession were from nontradable sectors.[35] Most of the new jobs in the nontradable sectors paid less than the old ones, so inequality rose. From 1980 to 2005, which included the tech boom of the late 1990s, more than 80 percent of the total increase in Americans' income went to the top 1 percent. Economic growth was more sluggish in the first decade of the twenty-first century, but the decade saw productivity increase by about 20 percent. Yet little of the increase translated into wage growth at middle and lower incomes. The economy continued to grow and employ many. Unemployment in 2007, before the beginning of the Great Recession, was 4.6 percent.

But the stability was impermanent. The economy rooted in nontradables led to the current Great Recession. Because Americans still used manufactured goods, they imported more of them. The trade deficit peaked at 6 percent of GDP in 2006. The United States was consuming more than it was producing. Easy access to consumer credit and credit-fueled rises in home values masked wage stagnation and subsidized consumption.

That is where finance entered the picture, as its role was to fill the demand gap. Nations that accumulated dollars from their trade surplus with the United States (especially China, Japan, and Germany) bought U.S. securities, which kept interest rates low. People could borrow to maintain living standards and felt richer than they were as the prices of their housing assets rose. In short, consumption was maintained by increased national and household debt and asset inflation, instead of wages. Financial deregulation and innovation, regulatory forbearance, financial mania, and simple financial fraud kept the economy going by making ever more credit available. However, as the economy cannibalized itself by undercutting income distribution and accumulating debt, it needed ever larger speculative bubbles to grow. The house-price bubble was simply the last and biggest bubble and was effectively the only way around the stagnation that would otherwise have developed in 2001 in the wake of the high-tech collapse.

Cheap money enabled people with stagnant incomes to maintain consumption, especially home buying, which was encouraged by both parties. And for some Democrats, fostering home ownership was a politically safer alternative to supporting wage growth. In 2006, Democratic Senator Jack Reed of Rhode Island stated, "When homes are doubling in price in every six years and incomes are increasing by a mere one percent a year," extending home ownership was critical to the nation.[36] Finally, the low interest rates encouraged banks and other financial institutions to take excessive risk in order to increase earnings. The conventional wisdom was that financial institutions' risk management made regulation less necessary.

The collapse of the consumer-credit and housing-price bubbles in 2007 and 2008 ended this pattern of economic growth. Government transfer payments and tax cuts since the crash made up some of the difference in the subsequent four years. But these cannot continue indefinitely, and in any event in they tend to be saved rather than devoted to employment-inducing consumer expenditure. Consumption growth, therefore, will depend on improvements in wages and incomes. Yet these have little potential to grow in a world economy beset by a glut of labor and capital. The Federal Reserve Board's monetary easing stabilized the economy, but the cheap money did not go into investment for which there is no demand, but into tradable commodities, like oil, and currency speculation.

Republicans, believing that the crisis was caused by government spending and activism in the housing market, counsel fiscal austerity. In this climate, however, thrift seems more likely to promote a downward spiral. Democrats advocate immediate stimulus and long-term deficit reduction, which seems reasonable but does not fit the economic situation. A stimulus, like the earlier Bush and Obama efforts, will likely bring imports as well as stimulating domestic production. It is too temporary, too focused on short-term tax relief and consumer support, and too misdirected to provide the economy more than a modest and temporary boost, as opposed to the bridge to long-term restructuring and recovery that the U.S. economy requires. The theory behind such actions is that the recession was simply a market failure, caused by inadequate regulation. First, regulators allowed excessive risk-taking by banks. Second, they permitted perverse pay structures within banks that encouraged management to engage in "loan pushing" rather than "good lending." Third, regulators pushed deregulation and self-regulation too far. Together, these failures contributed to financial misallocation. Reregulate (the Dodd-Frank Wall Street and Consumer Protection Act), temporarily make up demand with the stimulus, and the economy will recover, the Democrats argued.

There was financial misallocation. But the cause was the model of globalization that produced leakage through spending on imports (the trade deficit), leakage of investment spending offshore, and leakage of manufacturing jobs offshore. The resulting deficient demand used debt and asset-price inflation to fuel growth instead of wages. Attempting to resurrect the economy of nontradables cannot produce prosperity, substantially reduce inequality, or even yield reasonable growth.

Initially, President Barack Obama seemed to understand this. Obama told CNN in September 2009, "We can't go back to the era where the Chinese or the Germans or other countries just are selling everything to us, we're taking out a bunch of credit card debt or home equity loans, but we're not selling anything to them."[37] Obama thus rejected the solution to the crisis of the 1970s, the postindustrialism that caused the current crisis. But the president's deeds did not match his words. He and his advisers acted as if this was a severe but ordinary recession. The largest item in the $787 billion stimulus was tax cuts (32 percent), which were mostly saved. The rest supported living standards, like food stamps and unemployment insurance, state and local employment, and some research and infrastructure. Money went scattershot to different energy projects and some transportation projects. This was a Keynesian stimulus that did nothing to alter the imbalances that caused the recession.

The recovery is weak. In 2012, the economy had five million fewer jobs than it did before the recession. Employment gains so far have been primarily in low-wage occupations—retail sales, office clerks, food-preparation workers, and stock clerks. These occupations grew by 3.2 percent from the first quarter of 2010 through the first quarter of 2011; mid-wage occupations grew by 1.2 percent, while higher-wage occupations declined by 1.2 percent. These numbers replicate the pattern that led to the recession. From 1999 to 2007, employment growth was concentrated in the bottom third of the skill distribution. The Bureau of Labor Standards projects that five of the six occupations with the most job growth from 2010 to 2020 will be low-wage jobs that require little or no post–high school education.[38]

The labor movement is unprepared to address these issues. The structural shift away from tradables produced new fissures and a new power structure within the labor movement. By 2012, only one of fourteen private-sector workers was in a union. The agenda of the labor movement increasingly reflected the concerns of government unions, representing 37 percent of public workers. The rise of Andrew Stern, the head of the fastest growing labor union, the Service Employees International Union (SEIU), which organized nontradable health-care, public-services, and property-services workers, reflected this shift in the economy. (Only the National Education Association, a teachers' union, is larger.) Stern, John Sweeney, who preceded Stern as president of SEIU before becoming head of the AFL-CIO in 1995, and Gerry McEntee, the head American Federation of State, County, and Municipal Employees, counseled abandoning manufacturing, which could be offshored, and concentrating on the work that could not. Tensions deepened in the labor movement as Stern and others who dealt in nontradables (James Hoffa of the Teamsters, John Wilhelm of the Hotel Employees and Restaurant Employees, and Joseph Hansen of the United Food and Commercial Workers) tried to exert their influence within, then ultimately left, the AFL-CIO in 2005 to form Change to Win. The new group's mission "is to unite the 50 million American workers who work in industries that cannot be outsourced or shipped overseas into strong unions that can win them a place in the American middle class"[39] Stern has subsequently left the labor movement, but the division within the movement lives on.

The new strategy of organizing the nontradables did not work. First, it did not halt inequality or create middle-class workers. Although the SEIU did unionize many government and service workers, its greatest success was in the arc where the AFL-CIO had succeeded—the North Atlantic and Pacific coasts. That it was not more successful in the South and Southwest than the other unions challenges the view that the SEIU possessed superior organizing strategies. Second, the alleged immunity from outsourcing has become fanciful as the boundary between tradable and nontradable became porous.

Third, the imbalance between public and private unionization is unsustainable. There were many reasons for labor's failure in June 2010 to recall Governor Scott Walker, who ended public-employee collective bargaining in Wisconsin, but the public-sector unions' cavalier ignoring of global issues important to private-sector unionism did not encourage the solidarity that public workers needed for victory. Finally, Change to Win's abdication of the producing sector of the economy not only limits the scope of the labor movement but ignores the important role of policy on the structure of the economy and thus the labor movement. It reinforces the notion that the current model of globalization is inevitable and yields the weapons of social-democratic politics and bargaining to control and shape globalization.

Moreover, there is meager possibility for the growth of the nontradable jobs. Government at all levels is the largest employer in the nontradable sector and accounted for more than 22.5 million jobs in 2008. Health care is a close second, with 16.3 million. These two combined to produce almost 40 percent of the total net incremental employment in the economy since 1990.[40] Today, as state and local government reduce employment because of budget problems, expansion of public employment in the short term is unlikely. Health care already composes 16 percent of the GDP, and it is unlikely to grow. Moreover, the federal government, which spends most on health care, is looking for ways to reduce costs, and that means reducing employment. The housing sector, usually the first industry to emerge from recession, is overbuilt. Retailing also seems an unlikely source of new jobs because its expansion was based upon debt-fueled consumption.

The obvious source for new jobs is the tradable sector. Thus the main avenue to growth must be through reduction of the eight-hundred-billion-dollar U.S. trade deficit. This can come from a combination of importing less and exporting more. America can produce more of what it consumes and export more of what it produces. Politicians like to talk about expanding exports and bringing jobs back to the United States, but to reduce the trade deficit requires reducing imports, too. Despite talk of companies returning production to the United States, the chronic U.S. trade deficit in manufactured and high-tech goods has been rising. The drivers of this deficit are Germany and China.[41] Both nations' responses to the Great Recession were export drives (like Germany and Japan in the 1970s), which succeeded. As the fortunes of these nations show, trade policy matters.

More active responses to nations that manipulate their currency and other important trade issues require American leaders to privilege economic growth over national security issues like Iran's nuclear policy or North Korea's bluster. Increasing the tradable sector will also require a better tax system, targeting of critical industries, and requiring companies that sell in the United States to also produce here. When U.S. corporate executives are in China, all they hear is the question of when they are going to put production and research and development into China. They should hear the same refrain in America.

But growth will also require the kind of labor-government-business cooperation similar to that of Germany, Scandinavia, and Japan. There is some precedent for this in the efforts that labor made in the late 1970s to collaborate with government on industrial policy. It will be difficult for a much weaker and more divided labor movement to convince government and business that this is necessary. But the labor movement cannot leave production matters to business, as they did in the affluent postwar years. Without new growth policies, the nation faces incomplete recovery, economic stagnation, and low wage employment, conditions that plant seeds for yet another crisis. Although there is no guarantee that such a program will resurrect the labor movement, it is certainly true that without new growth policies, the movement will continue to shrink.

Notes

1. Peter Gourevitch, *Politics in Hard Times: Comparative Responses to International Economic Crises* (Ithaca, N.Y.: Cornell University Press, 1986).

2. Edward Berkowitz, *Something Happened: A Political and Cultural Overview of the Seventies* (New York: Columbia University Press, 2005).

3. Daniel Bell, *The Cultural Contradictions of Capitalism* (New York: Basic Books: 1976); Jurgen Habermas, *Legitimation Crisis,* trans. Thomas McCarthy (Boston: Beacon Press, 1973); James O'Connor, *The Fiscal Crisis of the State* (New York: St. Martin's Press, 1973); Claus Offe, *Contradictions of the Welfare State* (Cambridge: Massachusetts Institute of Technology Press, 1984).

4. David Frum, *How We Got Here: The 70's—The Decade That Brought You Modern Life—For Better or Worse* (New York: Basic, 2000); Bruce J. Schulman, *The Seventies: The Great Shift in American Culture, Society, and Politics* (New York: Free Press, 2005); Andreas Killen, *1973 Nervous Breakdown: Watergate, Warhol, and the Birth of Post-Sixties America* (New York: Bloomsbury, 2006); Philip Jenkins, *Decade of Nightmares: The End of the Sixties and the Making of Eighties America* (New York: Oxford University Press, 2006); Beth Bailey and David Farber, eds., *America in the 1970s* (Lawrence: University Press of Kansas, 2004); Thomas Borstelmann, *The 1970s: A New Global History from Civil Rights to Economic Inequality* (Princeton, N.J.: Princeton University Press, 2012).

5. Bruce J. Schulman and Julian E. Zelizer, eds., *Rightward Bound: Making America Conservative in the 1970s* (Cambridge, Mass.: Harvard University Press, 2008); Kim Phillips-Fein, *Invisible Hands: The Making of the Conservative Movement from the New Deal to Reagan* (New York: W. W. Norton, 2009); Joseph Crespino, *In Search of Another Country: Mississippi and the Conservative Counterrevolution* (Princeton, N.J.: Princeton University Press, 2007); Kevin Kruse, *White Flight: Atlanta and the Making of Modern Conservatism* (Princeton, N.J.: Princeton University Press, 2007); Laura Kalman, *Right Star Rising: A New Politics, 1974–1980* (New York: W. W. Norton, 2010); Lisa McGurr, *Suburban Warriors: The Origins of the New American Right* (Princeton, N.J.: Princeton

University Press, 2001); Rich Perlstein, *Before the Storm: Barry Goldwater and the Unmaking of the American Consensus* (New York: Hill and Wang, 2001); Thomas B. Edsall and Mary E. Edsall, *Chain Reaction: The Impact of Race, Rights, and Taxes on American Politics* (New York: W. W. Norton, 1992).

6. Jefferson Cowie, *Stayin' Alive: The 1970s and the Last Days of the Working Class* (New York: New Press, 2010), 18; Nancy McClean, *Freedom Is Not Enough: The Opening of the American Work Place* (Cambridge, Mass.: Harvard University Press, 2006); Joseph A. McCartin, *Collision Course: Ronald Reagan, the Air Traffic Controllers, and the Strike that Changed America* (New York: Oxford University Press, 2011).

7. Edward F. Denison, "Explanations of Decline Productivity Growth," in *U.S. Department of Commerce, Survey of Current Business* 59 (August 1974): 4.

8. *New York Times,* 9 November 1978, D1.

9. Qtd. in Robert F. King, *Money, Time, and Politics: Investment Tax Subsidies and American Democracy* (New Haven, Conn.: Yale University Press, 1993), 147.

10. Melvyn P. Leffler, *A Preponderance of Power: National Security, the Truman Administration, and the Cold War* (Stanford, Calif.: Stanford University Press, 1992), 317.

11. *Washington Post,* 18 July 1993, H-1.

12. "Douglas MacArthur II to Department of State [Proposal for High-Level Review of U.S. Policy toward Japan]," Secret Cable, 002951, 12 March 1960, RG 59, Records of the Department of State, Central Foreign Policy Files, 1960–63, Decimal Files, 611.94/3-1260, National Archives, College Park, Md.

13. "Record of Third Meeting of Joint U.S.-Japan Committee on Trade and Economic Affairs," Tokyo, 24 January 1964 (morning), 4, file 11/63–4/64, I, box 250, Country File, Japan, National Security File, Lyndon Baines Johnson Library and Museum, Austin, Tex.

14. George W. Ball, *The Past Has Another Pattern: Memoirs* (New York: W. W. Norton, 1982), 191–92.

15. *Wall Street Journal,* 26 October 1970, 3.

16. Paul Volcker, "Memorandum of Conversation," 3–5 May 1970, Foreign Relations of the United States, 1969, III, Foreign Economic Policy, 1969–72; International Monetary Policy, 1969–72 (Washington, D.C.: Government Printing Office, 2001).

17. Qtd. in Judith Stein, *Pivotal Decade: How the United States Traded Factories for Finance in the Seventies* (New Haven, Conn.: Yale University Press, 2010), 47.

18. Robert Brenner, *The Economics of Global Turbulence: The Advanced Capitalist Economies from Long Boom to Long Downturn, 1945–2005* (London: Verso, 2006), 171.

19. United States–Japan Trade Council, "Council Report No. 58," 12 November 1976, file Tokyo, box 37, Trilateral Commission papers, Rockefeller Archive Center, Sleepy Hollow, N.Y.

20. Nathaniel Goldfinger, "What Labor Wants on Trade," *New York Times,* 4 March 1973, 157.

21. Blanchard and Hart qtd. in Julian Zelizer, *On Capital Hill: The Struggle to Reform Congress and its Consequences, 1948–2000* (Cambridge: Cambridge University Press, 2004), 157; William Schneider, "JFK's Children: The Class of '74," *Atlantic Monthly* (March 1989): 35–58.

22. Howard Brick, *Transcending Capitalism: Visions of a New Society in Modern American Thought* (Ithaca, N.Y.: Cornell University Press, 2006).

23. Doug Met for Bill Seidman and Bill Gorog, 23 March 1975, file, Humphrey-Javits Bill, box 36, Council of Economic Advisers papers, Gerald Ford Presidential Library, Grand Rapids, Mich.

24. Chamber of Commerce, Report of Task Force on National Economic Planning, 13 October 1976, Board of Directors Meeting, 11 and 12 November 1976, box 1D, Chamber of Commerce Papers, Hagley Museum and Library, Wilmington, Del.

25. Bob Ginsburg, "Memorandum for White House Staff," 22 April 1977, O/A 6237 [7], box 226, Staff Secretary Papers, Jimmy Carter Library and Museum, Atlanta.

26. Charles Schultze, Memo to President, 14 March 1978, BE-1, WHCF, box BE-16, Jimmy Carter Library and Museum, Atlanta.

27. Stein, *Pivotal Decade*, 200.

28. *Wall Street Journal*, 14 January 1977, 10; Gerald M. Pomper et al., *The Election of 1976: Reports and Interpretations* (New York: David McKay, 1977), 161.

29. Judith Stein, *Running Steel, Running America: Race, Economic Policy, and the Decline of Liberalism* (Chapel Hill: University of North Carolina Press, 1998), 265.

30. Ibid., 266.

31. Qtd. in ibid., 269–70.

32. *New York Times*, 9 November 1980, 28.

33. Brenner, *Economics of Global Turbulence*, 191–92.

34. Michael Comiskey, "Reaganomics after Two Terms," *Polity* 23 (Winter 1990): 304; Paul Krugman, *Peddling Prosperity: Economic Sense and Nonsense in the Age of Diminished Expectations* (New York: W. W. Norton, 1994), 125–27.

35. Health care added 6.3 million jobs on a base of 10 million; government added 4.1 million on a base of 18.4.

36. Qtd. in *New York Times*, 5 October 2008, 34.

37. Transcripts, State of the Union with John King, Interview with Barack Obama, September 20, 2009, accessed 3 July 2013, http://transcripts.cnn.com/TRANSCRIPTS/0909/20/sotu.01.html.

38. Eileen Appelbaum, "Low-Wage Jobs to Blame for Slow Economic Recovery," *U.S. News and World Report*, 10 April 2012, accessed 3 July 2013, http://www.usnews.com/opinion/blogs/economic-intelligence/2012/04/10/job-polarization-not-to-blame-for-slow-economic-recovery.

39. "About Us," *Change to Win*, accessed 13 June 2013, http://www.changetowin.org/about.

40. Michael Spence and Sandile Hlatshwayo, "The Evolving Structure of the American Economy and the Employment Challenge," Working Paper, Council on Foreign Relations, March 2011, 13, accessed 13 June 2013, http://www.cfr.org/industrial-policy/evolving-structure-american-economy-employment-challenge/p24366.

41. Alan Tonelson, "Resurgent March Trade Deficit Slows American Growth Even Further," American Economic Alert.Org, 10 May 2012, accessed 13 June 2013, http://americaneconomicalert.org/view_art.asp?Prod_ID=5464.

8

Neoliberalism at Work in the Antipodean Welfare State in the Late Twentieth Century

Collusion, Collaboration, and Resistance

MELANIE NOLAN

Introduction: The Neoliberal Experience

Neoliberalism is critical to understanding the experience of working people in the crises of capitalism from the 1970s to the global financial recession of 2008. Bob Jessop and others have pointed to its "ecological dominance" in the capitalist world from the late twentieth century.[1] Neoliberalism is a political project supporting competitive market forces. Under its influence, the social and moral economy shifted from a postwar commitment to maintaining full employment to one in which fighting inflation and supporting growth took precedence. Free markets and deregulation promised wealth creation and individual freedom and well-being. The promise was not completely fulfilled, as wealth created was unevenly distributed and, globally, some populations saw their standard of living worsen. The literature recognizes that neoliberalism was variously applied and developed unevenly geographically in complex ways: "[P]olitical forces, historical traditions, and existing institutional arrangements all shaped why and how the process of neoliberalism actually occurred."[2] Patterns have emerged. While research has concentrated on the advanced economies, such as the United States and United Kingdom, an antipodean model has also been teased out. New Zealand is recognized as an outstanding example of the late twentieth-century neoliberal experiment.[3] It was seen to exceed in its effects as well as its application: one of the major achievements of neoliberalism has been to redistribute wealth back to the rich after the 1980s in proportions similar to those evident in the 1920s.[4] Inequality rose everywhere in the neoliberal world since the 1980s, but it rose fastest in New Zealand.[5]

The gap between rich and poor rose in New Zealand, developing in a society with a more faltered income distribution that had less extreme income differentials between the top 1 percent and most people to begin with than in many other countries.

> New Zealand was one of the most protected and regulated economies in the Western world in 1984. New Zealand was Britain's "farm" and developed protection when it had a secure market to trade in before the latter entered the European Economic Community (EEC) in 1973. After 1984, New Zealand deregulated with market liberalization and monetarist economic polices.[6] The government relinquished considerable power over the market along the lines of neoliberal ideas about the limited role of the state. The New Zealand dollar was floated. The tariff walls and import controls were lifted, and restrictions on foreign investment were removed. The tax system was flattened; the tax on profit and the top marginal rate of income tax for high-income earners was reduced to 33 percent, while a Goods and Services Tax on all transactions was introduced. Subsidies were pared back: direct assistance to industry and agriculture that helped protect it, for instance, was abandoned. The public service was corporatized and parts were privatized.[7] New Zealand led the world in sales of state-owned assets between 1988 and 1993. New Zealand is said to have adopted the "most thoroughgoing economic reform in the OECD." *The Economist* declared its "free-market reforms more radical than any other industrial country's."[8] These measures were designed to make New Zealand more competitive internationally and more attractive to investors, which, it was expected, would help raise levels of growth.

This neoliberal structural adjustment had implications for social policy, too. There were fundamental changes to the work-welfare system that had flourished in the postwar "welfare state" period. The full-employment policy to which the government had committed itself in 1944 was abandoned as a policy aim in 1987 and was formalized with the subsequent passing of the Reserve Bank Act in 1989. The white walls of immigration, which had resulted in immigration from Britain mostly, were breached.[9] Postwar labor shortages saw the state support Maori (indigenous New Zealander) urbanization, Pacific Islander migration, and married women's paid employment. Only 7.7 percent of married women were in full-time paid employment in 1945, 20 percent by 1966, and 45.8 percent by 1991. In the process, the defense of high work standards to protect an exclusively white, male, full-time employed workforce was undermined. Since 1986, immigration has resulted in a major diversification in New Zealand's ethnic composition, too; while some immigrants were indigent refugees, most were educated and skilled. New Zealand now has one of the world's highest proportions of immigrants in its workforce. The industrial relations system, involving compulsory arbitration unique to Australasia, which had been instituted in New Zealand in 1894 (and which was extended to most workers in the postwar period), was abandoned with the 1991 Employment Contracts Act (ECA).[10] A more constrained Labour Court was instituted in place of the New Zealand Court of Arbitration. The number of unions rapidly decreased after 1991 under the ECA. The family benefit that had been instituted in 1926 and made universal in 1946 was also abandoned in 1991.[11]

Social change and neoliberal reforms unraveled a postwar system. The arbitration system had resulted in a compressed wage structure; the range of pay widened after 1991.[12] Unpaid productive work by women had received recognition under the family benefit, with its premise of an interdependence of domestic and paid work within the family economy; this was formally discounted after 1991, replaced by targeted family packages based on income. These reforms signaled the expectation that all individuals should enter the workforce, if they could, without the protection of centralized wage-fixing and without protections afforded by government intervention, which had operated for at least half a century. The market and families (and for Maori, self-determination) should sustain individuals, while the state was scaled down.[13] Unemployment and the number of welfare recipients, however, increased dramatically in the 1980s.[14] And in 1991, in the ironically named "mother of all budgets," social-welfare benefits were cut to address welfare dependency, which some interpreted as "female dependency."[15]

While neoliberal narratives are sometimes couched in conspiratorial terms—pointing to the U.S. political elite applying the theories of the Chicago economist Milton Friedman by force, coercion, and influence—most emphasize the structural imperatives of this crisis of capitalism, and also how consent was manufactured by local New Right think tanks, media, and political parties.[16] Nuanced transnational comparison reveals how New Zealand's economic and political experience differed in some key respects from countries such as the United States and United Kingdom.[17] Some have gone further to posit local varieties of liberalism and neoliberalism historically and theoretically.[18] The current challenge for scholars is not simply to reveal another variant in the global phenomenon of neoliberalism. Rather, the challenge for labor historians is to put the workers, and a defense of social justice and human agency, back into a business- and policy-elite narrative of seemingly inexorable economic and political developments that were "inevitable" and "necessary."

This essay examines antipodean responses to the post-1970s economic crisis of capitalism in the light of a longer history of the welfare state. The response to neoliberalism was complex, involving resistance as well as collusion and collaboration. New Zealand is a good example of the accommodating and the oppositional responses to neoliberalism by working people. Parties with traditional labor-party policies (New Labour) were electorally unsuccessful. Working people and their communities—which cannot be conflated with trade unions, for they cover only about 17 percent of the New Zealand workforce now—supported aspects of neoliberalism.[19] Collective opposition to radical change resulted in an electoral-system change to proportional representation to ensure that checks and balances undermined political elites' ability to bring in such change again; in 1992, 84.7 percent voted for a change in the electoral system. In 1997, the attempt to institute a neoliberal social contract between government and people was also emphatically rebuffed. Before we turn to the variety of responses, we need to explore the distinct antipodean welfare-state tradition, which is held up to explain opposition to neoliberal ideas, but which New Zealand largely shared with Australia.[20]

The Antipodean Tradition of a Strong Ethical State

The strength of the organized-labor movement in Australasian society in the twentieth century is well known.[21] Union density was the highest in the world in the early twentieth century.[22] There were high wages, although Richard White and others have questioned whether the antipodes really were "working men's paradises."[23] Australasia was conspicuous in its early democracy; elected parliaments, adult male suffrage, secret ballots, and payments of members were commonplace by Australian federation, and female suffrage—including Maori but not Aboriginal—was instituted by 1908.

Above all, the level of state intervention on behalf of the labor movement from the outset is said to have distinguished New Zealand and Australia from other colonial societies. The eight-hours movement, for instance, resulted in legislation across the region from Victoria in 1856.[24] John E. Martin has pointed to government social protectionism, particularly its control of immigration in response to the needs of the economy and unemployment, and the provision of public relief works during depressions in the late nineteenth century.[25] Stuart Macintyre and Erik Olssen noted that the labor movement recovered quickly from the employers' attacks of the 1890s to demonstrate "extremely impressive and, comparatively speaking, precocious development" in terms of trade unionism, independent labor politics, working conditions, living standards, and the establishment of a strong and predominantly class-based culture between the late 1890s and 1914.[26] Wage security for breadwinners was achieved through the regulation of income from employment through a unique compulsory-arbitration system that was introduced in New Zealand in 1894 and spread across Australia at federal and state levels by 1916.[27] Underpinning this system was a belief in the dignity of labor, around which developed a political consensus of ensuring "fair and just" wages for white male citizens. It was founded upon state intervention in the establishment of industrial tribunals for settling industrial issues and the sponsorship of trade unions.[28] Neville Kirk has argued that blue-collar and skilled workers "took the feelings and conflicts of class to the very heart of 1900s" Australasian national life and politics and the "national imprint of workers and their organizations—on state structures and patterns of national culture and consciousness—was far more profound in Australia than in both Britain and the United States."[29]

Francis G. Castles has written a detailed history of the emergence of the male wage earners' countries—that is, the Australasian wage earner's welfare state, which embraced protection for white workers in paid employment: tariffs, centralized and compulsory wage-fixing, constrained immigration, and a residual welfare system.[30] It was "residual" (as opposed to "universal") in that the unique compulsory wage-fixing system delivered social protection through a minimum living wage, a relatively egalitarian and compressed wage structure with a high degree of uniformity in wage increases, and a relatively high standard of living. Justice Henry Bournes Higgins introduced the needs-based ideal of "the family wage" as president of the Australian Commonwealth Court of Conciliation and Arbitration in 1907; his "Harvester Judgment" set the minimum wage at an amount, seven shillings per day, that he considered sufficient for a man to support a family in "frugal comfort," supplemented by a "margin of skill" where appropriate.[31] New Zealand piggybacked on this concept, which was central to its industrial-relations system. In 1919, an Australian Royal Commission on the Basic Wage estimated the cost of living of a "man with a wife and three children under fourteen years of age" to be around 50 percent higher than Higgins's Harvester standard—an amount that, if paid to workers, would have exceeded the entire national income.[32] Commission chairman A. B. Piddington began to propose the introduction of child endowment as a necessary complement to the basic wage, a suggestion that prompted the introduction of a modest scheme of child endowment for the federal Australian public service in 1921 and a family allowance in New Zealand in 1926.[33] The campaigns for family endowment for those in large families were natural corollaries of the male-breadwinner system; that is, there were important attempts to compensate for the "inequality of luck" in the class system.[34]

Despite the early architecture of a welfare state, it is important to point out that research has suggested that most unskilled laborers did not receive a basic wage sufficient to support a family of five in the following decades in Australasia.[35] Most workers were simply not included in the arbitration system until after World War II. Family size was more diverse before World War II than afterwards, but large families were not compensated for universally until the 1940s. A significant proportion of work was seasonal or dependent on the weather, and of course there was unemployment. An adequate male-breadwinner wage before the 1940s had only been aspirational. Most Indigenous people were not urbanized and not included in the developing urban occupational patterns.

That the welfare system remained partially but not fully implemented does not simply indicate that there is often a creative tension between the power of ideas and actual practices. Capitalism finds a reserve army of labor, a differentiated workforce, useful.

After arbitration, the single most important policy ensuring adequate income in the "wage earners welfare state" was full employment. Australia and New Zealand were conspicuous in their postwar international advocacy of a full-employment, male-breadwinner system—that is, a political pledge for full male employment at fair wages.[36] Australasia was not alone in having a policy of full male employment, but it also strongly advocated a male-breadwinner system. Clause 35 of the Australian–New Zealand Agreement (1944) included a resolution to cooperate in achieving full employment in Australia and New Zealand.[37] The two countries also declared that they would cooperate in propagating the policy internationally—indeed, it was their main "article of faith."[38] Full employment was embodied in the 1945 White Paper in Australia and in various postwar charters in New Zealand, both of which were inspired by John Maynard Keynes's *The General Theory of Employment, Interest, and Money* (1936).[39]

True to their word, Prime Minister Peter Fraser, his deputy Walter Nash for New Zealand, and external affairs minister Dr. H. V. Evatt for Australia advocated the full-employment policy in postwar international forums. Their advocacy was part of the reason that the objective of full (male) employment was written into the United Nations Charter, the International Labour Organization Charter, and the Monetary and Financial Conference (Bretton Woods) Agreement of 1944.[40] Fraser chaired the U.N. Economic and Social Council in 1944 and moved the full-employment clause. He declared that "for the average man the right to live depended on the right to work."[41]

The Re-establishment and Employment Act of 1944 gave preference of employment to returned servicemen in Australia. The Commonwealth Employment Service was committed to full employment. Similarly, the New Zealand government's Employment Act of 1945 established a National Employment Service "for the purpose of promoting and maintaining full employment," and this purpose carried over to the Labour Department Act of 1954.[42] New Zealand had an unemployment rate that did not exceed 0.15 percent in the 1950s; Australia's rate peaked at 2.2 percent.

Full employment and fair wages to male breadwinners were accompanied by a welfare apparatus. The Welfare State Settlement was enacted in the Social Security Act of 1938 in New Zealand and legislation in 1941–44. The welfare state grew out of the 1930s depression experience: "[T]he myth of a man-made depression where all had suffered equally . . . provided the coping-stone for the welfare state" in which social protectionism was taken a step further.[43] Arbitration was based on a male-breadwinner system and full male employment; the arbitration system awarded the average man in full-time paid employment with a dependent wife and three children a decent basic wage, although the concept of the fair wage for an average family became more notional as the government provided for family allowances universally in 1946. The 1930s depression and mass unemployment created the rationale for another significant extension of state intervention. Mass protests and urban riots were followed by the election of governments that created and sustained employment with public-works systems and the provision of welfare benefits as a last resort, if work was unavailable. The New Zealand Social Security Act of 1938 provided a substantial package of health benefits and provisions, which resulted in a half century of narrowing the gap between rich and poor.

We should avoid being romantic about the welfare-state period. Feminist historians, for instance, have pointed out that, until the late twentieth century, social policy focused on the protection of male wage earners, usually at the expense of the poor and women's status as independent citizens.[44] "Workers in the margins," including women, Maori, people from the Pacific, the unemployed, and those out of the trade-union movement's focus, were the majority of people.[45] Successive antipodean governments took to task those not "playing the game": any "shirkers" or those exhibiting "lazy" and "immoral" behavior. Politicians in the 1940s such as Bob Semple and Paddy Webb, former Australasian coal miners who were part of a contingent of Australian-born politicians in the New Zealand Labour Government from 1935 to 1949, made it quite clear what they thought the fate of "scroungers," "wasters," "harpies," "spielers," and "loafers" should be: as they repeatedly declared in various ways, "no man has any claim on the nation's production unless he pulls his weight and renders some service as an individual unit."[46]

Some go so far as to suggest that this tradition of social provision represents "social contracts" between the working classes and governments in Australasia: on one side of the Tasman, the Deakinite or Australian settlement, and on the other side, the "Populist New Zealand compact."[47] Peter Beilharz suggests a number of Australian settlements, including 1901, social welfare in the 1940s, and an accord between unions and the government in the 1980s.[48] Marian Sawer is critical of social-contract analysis, however, between the state and the working class, pointing instead to a more general social-liberal tradition in the form of "the ethical state" committed to the "substantive goal of equal opportunity for its citizens."[49] She puts the spotlight on an earlier, "foundational" policy transfer from Britain to the Australasian colonies. Sawer shows the importance of T. H. Green and his new liberal followers' calls upon the middle class to be socially responsible and to engineer the state to provide the means for equal opportunity.[50] Sawer's work resonates with Tim Rowse's earlier work on an Australian liberal tradition and its importance in national character, and with Bill Oliver's work in New Zealand, although it was never developed to the same extent.[51] Sawer argues that the Australasian system of compulsory conciliation and arbitration, family benefits, and progressive taxation institutionalized Green's new liberal, rather than socialist, ideas. This foundational culture could then develop into a path dependency, with history setting an evolutionary trajectory that resisted an easy adoption of neoliberalism. New or social liberalism and neoliberalism shared certain ideas, such as individual achievement and equality of opportunity. Socialism would have been a stronger antidote to neoliberalism, and a more differentiated pathway, but laborism and social liberalism predominated in Australasia.[52]

Neoliberalism did not sweep this history out of its way. Successive Australasian governments, while introducing many market reforms, did not deregulate banking, as occurred in the United States and Europe. Antipodean governments embellished welfare states with no-fault accident compensation and national superannuation in New Zealand from the 1970s and compulsory superannuation in Australia from the 1980s. Australasia paid back national debt and was in a position to apply Keynesian stimulus packages, thereby avoiding some of the excesses of the global economic crisis in 2008. Australia continues to have one of the strongest economies in the developed world; 2012 is the twenty-first consecutive year of economic growth. But the question remains: did working-class collective actions resist neoliberalism on the basis of a foundational political culture and history, in which working-class entitlement figured prominently, or was its reaction more complex?

Collusion: Neoliberalism Capture?

There is a strong case to argue for neoliberal "capture" in New Zealand by a political and business elite. Much literature points to a global New Right network of free-market ideologies that encompassed New Zealand think tanks, which soon gained critical purchase with New Zealand Treasury officials and politicians to "roll back" the state.[53] The promotion and circulation of neoliberal economic theory in New Zealand began within the Treasury during the late 1970s, among officials disillusioned with state intervention in the economy. The Treasury moved from being a postwar bastion of Keynesian interventionism to becoming fiercely committed to free-market doctrine and the abandonment of the collectivist state. Brian Easton argues that the crucial reason that neoliberal economics became so popular in the Treasury was that it offered an alternative and "exciting" analytical framework to the "failed" polices of the past.[54] New Zealand was in serious economic trouble and debt. The significance of this ideological capture lay in the tremendous power that Treasury wielded over other government departments in terms of its monopoly over economic advice and critical its position with the centralization of the public service. With few internal dissidents to neoliberal economics during the early 1980s, Treasury emerged as the main force behind transferring control of the economy away from interventionist politicians and into the hands of the free market and offering a coherent rationale for the abandonment of social-democratic goals of equity in favor of market liberalization and rolling back the state.

Keynesian policies and the Bretton Woods system of monetary management established in the wake of the Great Depression were widely held to be failing by the 1970s. There was high inflation, rising unemployment, and industrial discontent to varying degrees in Australia, Britain, and the United States, but the rate of increase in discontent in New Zealand was particularly high.[55] Frustrated by Prime Minister Robert Muldoon's extreme form of interventionism, Treasury officials courted Roger Douglas, the finance spokesman for the Labour party, in the hope of advancing its policy recommendations. In the lead-up to the 1984 election, Douglas and his colleagues Richard Prebble and David Caygill championed Treasury's market-liberalization strategy, dominating the economic policy agenda of the Labour party. There was a fierce debate within the Labour party before the 1984 election over economic policy that was not resolved by the time of the election, nor when the government started implementing economic reform. Although divisions emerged between those favoring the "Treasury line" in Labour, the Douglas faction eventually won the policy debate and implemented what is known as "Rogernomics." Business advocacy of the rapid and comprehensive implementation of neoliberal policies had a major impact on the fourth Labour government from 1984 to 1990.[56] Above all else, business promoted neoliberal policies because it considered that these policies would weaken the bargaining power of trade unions, placing downward pressure on wages, eventually generating a general increase in profitability and creating conditions conducive to a higher rate of economic growth. The New Right, including a transnational network of ideological entrepreneurs and think tanks, were instrumental in pushing "progressive interpretations of poverty on the defensive through a vigorous ideological campaign designed to 'roll back' the state from welfare provision."[57]

There were two major neoliberal think tanks in New Zealand in the 1980s and 1990s: the New Zealand Business Roundtable (NZBR) and the Centre for Independent Studies (CIS).[58] The NZBR was founded in 1980 as an informal group of corporate chief executives, under the directorship of Roger Kerr, a former Treasury economist and an author of *Economic Management*.[59] New Zealand's CIS was founded in 1987 with the cooperation of the Sydney-based CIS, with the Auckland businessman Alan Gibbs playing a particularly influential role. It was established for the purpose of promoting a free and liberal society based on a free-market economy, limited government, individual liberty, and choice. Brian Roper has conducted a fine-grained analysis of the think-tank and employer-group publications that cited the ideas of New Right intellectuals and shifted the terms of welfare debate.[60] Charles Murray, Lawrence Mead, and David Green all criticized the welfare state in social-democratic countries for failing to set behavioral standards for the poor and for providing the conditions to enable the growth of a subculture, or underclass of intergenerational dependents and their immoral pathologies. Roper and others have emphasized the disproportionate influence these business associations exercised over government policy-making.[61] The NZBR represented big business, and the Employers Federation represented only 9.6 percent of the 115,000 businesses. These organizations were better funded with larger staffs than trade unions and had more extensive connections with policy-making agencies.[62] They were able to fund publications and conferences.[63] They "imported overseas guests and ideas for the purpose of promoting and shaping policy debate and building coalitions to transform those ideas into action."[64] Given this concerted array of interrelated tactics, these groups were very successful.

Collaboration and Working with Neoliberalism

If we accept the influence of neoliberal capture of crucial economic-policy sectors and are reluctant to argue that most people had false consciousness, how do we explain the degree of electoral support for the Labour party in 1987 and the National party in 1993, both of which pursued market-friendly policies? Significant groups of trade unions, for instance, supported the demise of the arbitration system. Militants had never been happy with the constraints of arbitration and compressed wage structures. Pat Walsh and others have charted the "slow walk away from arbitration."[65] Amidst industrial quiescence and then disorder, strong militant unions and employers agreed upon a complex three-tier wage system. A significant proportion of unionists was frustrated within the system and sought wage-drift decompression outside first-tier arbitration and, significantly, contributed to the system's demise.

Most unionists and most New Zealanders were not neoliberals. They were fellow travelers with the ideologues over aspects of their agenda; many drew the line over supporting neoliberalism in social policy.

Clearly, Treasury and business were successful in advocating market-economic policies and anti-union industrial-relations reform. And clearly, they found political collaborators. In government, Labour's Douglas was strongly backed by Richard Prebble, Mike Moore, and Michael Bassett in support of monetarist policies, but the full Labour party cabinet endorsed the decisions in 1984 to 1990.[66] Similarly, in their turn, market liberals in the National party were led by Ruth Richardson, Simon Upton, and Jenny Shipley, but they were supported by the full National party cabinet in 1990 to 1999. And after Douglas in 1989 and Richardson in 1993 lost their roles as ministers of finance, their parties' economic policies were not radically altered.

Collaboration often involved negotiation. This open negotiation helped to counter views of "conspiracy" as well as the notion that the government had succumbed entirely to market objectives. In other words, the negotiations softened the image of government as ideologically neoliberal. The extent of debate within the cabinet needs to be considered, for instance, over the National party's attempt to introduce competition into public hospitals. It was more public over the failed attempt among Labour politicians to curb social-welfare spending in order to fund tax cuts for business and high-income earners. Bitter dissension raged within the Labour caucus and the cabinet from 1987 over the latter, between social liberals and neoliberals over the direction of social policy and the extent of state support for those in need.[67] Prime Minister David Lange blocked the incursion of New Right ideas into social policy, pledging in 1987 that his government would focus on ensuring "social justice" for the casualties of the economic reforms.[68] Douglas proposed to overhaul the welfare system at about the same time as the Royal Commission on Social Policy prematurely presented its findings to the government, which emphasized women's needs and vulnerability and the racial dimension to poverty.[69] Lange argued that it was "time for a cup of tea"—that reform be interrupted and market policies be reined in. After Douglas announced new flat-tax and guaranteed-minimum-income schemes, Lange forced Douglas to resign. When caucus reelected Douglas to the cabinet, Lange resigned.

The point that needs to be made more strongly is that, in the case of the 1980s Lange/Palmer and the 1990s Bolger governments, the hardline neoliberals failed to carry their policies through to social policy in full. Influential supporters of the Rogernomics economic policies, like Geoffrey Palmer and David Caygill, did not support radical changes to social policy. We have to take note of the debates, disagreements, and negotiations around almost every neoliberal measure.

Resistance?

Of course, some also resisted neoliberalism.[70] The Wellington Unemployed Workers Union called a national meeting in 1983, which led to the formation of Te Roopu Rawakore, the national group representing unemployed and beneficiaries, which opposed market policies from the outset.[71] While there was no general strike, there was resistance over the ECA in 1991; some estimate that a tenth of the New Zealand population took to the streets, led by trade unionists.[72] A TV1N Heylen Poll in 1991 recorded 55 percent opposed to benefit cuts in 1991, 31 percent in support, and 14 percent unsure.[73] Resistance in terms of protest, publications, and street demonstrations made little policy difference, however. There is no "myth" of passivity under neoliberalism: the period from 1984 was relatively quiescent, especially in comparison to the 1930s and the 1970s.[74] Social activism had peaked from 1968 to 1984.[75] However, when politicians attempted to apply ideas of neoliberalism to the state welfare system in the form of a neoliberal social contract, they encountered a groundswell of opposition.

The National government turned to getting tougher on beneficiaries after cutting benefits in 1991. The CIS helpfully sponsored an international social-welfare conference in 1987 to promote the American workfare proposal, whereby the state enforced greater obligations on beneficiaries for receipt of support.[76] Citing the overseas New Right intellectuals Charles Murray and Lawrence Mead, there was a great deal of criticism in the media of the welfare state for failing to set behavioral standards for welfare recipients.[77] Despite there being only a small proportion of long-term welfare recipients, there was a public discussion of the need to inculcate social obligation among an "underclass" of intergenerational dependents and their "immoral pathologies."[78] The problem lay in "generous" provision through the state welfare system.[79]

Richardson and her New Right MP allies wanted to address the growth of the "dependent underclass."[80] They wanted to rejuvenate New Zealanders' work ethic by re-creating a decent or "enterprise society." They wanted the poor to be more "self-reliant," to move off "welfare to well-being," terms that repeated the arguments of many western governments, of all political persuasions, to move people from welfare to workfare.[81] Of course, there were political-media campaigns supporting punitive welfare reforms around the western world.[82] Richardson argued that "misfits" "doped up on benefits" burdened the taxpayers of New Zealand.[83] The dole was too attractive.[84] The traditional work ethic was in decline.[85] Beneficiaries were not simply eluding their "individual responsibilities"; their attitudes remained barriers that throttled enterprise and entrepreneurial endeavor. Society needed to be remoralized. Margaret Bazley was appointed director-general of the Department of Social Welfare (DSW) and Christine Rankin general manager of income support, to further the policy process of getting people off welfare and into jobs. Under their leadership, the DSW's focus shifted from supporting beneficiaries' entitlements to applying business principles to income-support services. Staff adopted individual case-management approaches and were provided with performance-pay incentives in their contracts to have beneficiaries move into paid employment.[86] They became enamored of Wisconsin's W2 welfare program, which was based on no benefits without participation in a work or a work-related activity.

The CIS and NZBR pitched in, sponsoring and supporting a stream of American neoliberals to New Zealand. For example, Rev. Robert Sirico, an American priest and critic of state welfare programs, came to New Zealand early in 1993 to provide a theological justification for free markets and "the entrepreneurial vocation" in response to the "confused claims and ill-considered assertions" that mainstream churches had provided in their social-justice statement.[87] The NZBR invited David Green from the Institute of Economic Affairs to lecture about the need to move New Zealand from a "welfare state" to "civil society."[88] The DSW organized a Beyond Dependency Conference in April 1997 to which it invited Sister Connie Driscoll, a Catholic nun who operated a charity-based welfare program in Chicago that practiced "tough love."[89]

Andrew Gregg has examined what he describes as a mounting moral campaign against beneficiaries by business groups, media, and politicians to create a panic about the harmful "dependency-inducing" effects of the welfare system. Although common to many countries, New Zealand's efforts involved perhaps the most spectacular failure.

Jenny Shipley, the prime minister, a former minister of social welfare, minister of health, and minister of women's affairs, was a neoliberal or "market feminist" who tried to enforce reciprocal obligations in exchange for benefits by leading a campaign to develop a code of social responsibility.[90] In early 1998, the New Zealand government sent 1.4 million copies of its public-discussion document, *Towards a Code of Social and Family Responsibility,* to all households and box-holders, eliciting 94,303 responses.[91] It was intended to clarify the relationship between the state and its citizens, particularly expectations in relation to the welfare system. It emphasized the superior virtue of paid work over unpaid activities and was aimed particularly at parents whose main source of income was a social-welfare benefit.[92] The government intended that its Code of Social Responsibility would be fully debated before its principles were implemented. The attempt to codify personal obligations was complicated and controversial; it was never clear whether it was to apply to all New Zealanders or only beneficiaries. Such was the opposition that it was quietly shelved without having to face the details of its implementation or how it was going to be monitored and enforced. In 1998, "hikoi of hope," or protest marches for social and economic justice in New Zealand, met at Parliament in Wellington, having set out from both ends of the country. They were a powerful symbolic national demonstration against the Shipley government's social policies.

Human Agency and Neoliberalism: Efficiency Objectives and Equity Goals?

As John Gray noted in 1998, the "neoliberal experiment in New Zealand is the most ambitious attempt at constructing the free market as a social institution to be implemented anywhere this century." But he also noted that it was a clear example of "the costs and limits of reinventing the free market."[93] In the end, there were limits on neoliberal reform. There was collusion and collaboration as well as resistance. Douglas has described this as "unfinished business." He went on to found the Association of Consumers and Taxpayers (ACT) in 1993 with the former National MP Derek Quigley, which developed into a political party designed to implement neoliberalism.[94] While ACT has been in Parliament since 1996, it has been very much a minority and has had little influence even when in coalition in government with the National party between 2008 and 2011. The welfare state endured.[95] At the time of the fifth Labour government's election in New Zealand in 1999, government spending still accounted for more than 40 percent of GDP, higher than the OECD average and above Australia's 32 percent. As *The Economist* noted, "By international standards, New Zealand still enjoys generous state pensions.... New Zealand is hardly a test-case of the economic benefits of small government."[96] After 1999, the Labour-led coalition government started to reverse some of the previous reforms. Trade unions have been given more power in wage negotiations; the top rate of income tax was raised from 33 to 39 percent; further privatization was ruled out. Between 1999 and 2008 the Labour-led government managed some redistribution, with the bottom quintile doing much better than in the preceding two decades, while the middle three quintiles did best, with a drop in unemployment.[97] However, while the Labour government repudiated Rogernomics and economic neoliberalism, it did not return to pre-1984 policies.

We come full-circle, however, to the idea of an indigenous ethical liberalism. Gregg has argued that campaigns to fully implement neoliberalism in New Zealand were thwarted by the intervention of oppositional advocacy groups and public mobilization against the political agenda to reform welfare. He points to a social-liberal discourse about the ethical duty of the state to achieve equity, "which remained a fundamental barrier to the New Right campaign against beneficiaries," an "indigenous" response to exogenous ideas. A counterdiscourse to neoliberalism centered on the "social responsibility" of the state in achieving equity for citizens; it "remained a strong discursive element in welfare debate during the late 1990s and thwarted the New Right's reform agenda."[98]

The locus of special resistance was the social-welfare dimension of neoliberalism rather than the workplace or economic dimension. These were not entirely separate. The restructuring of the antipodean welfare state centered on an ambitious program of economic reforms that broke with labor traditions. The gender model was also restructured in the process.[99] Liberal feminists had worked toward raising the proportion of women in paid employment, but they had not called for social-welfare "reforms" to encourage this. Women's position in the family and labor market became more complex with neoliberal economic reforms. The "wage earners welfare state," enabling men to support economically dependent women and children, moved closer to a neoliberal model of dual-earner partnerships based on individual entitlement, albeit, like neoliberalism itself, developing unevenly and incompletely.[100]

That neoliberalism was not applied to the fullest possible extent was not all due to human agency, including mobilizations of the working class, although such opposition was a factor. Nor was it a case of simple pathway dependence, with New Zealanders' support for state intervention continuing to have currency. As Kathleen Thelen has suggested, rather than concentrate upon a critical juncture or even accidental or contingent development, attention should be given to how institutions are not "locked in" path dependency statically but how they are contingent, how they change and break down.[101] Neoliberal economic policies were implemented in New Zealand at the same time that public attitudes to the "social responsibility" of the state in assisting groups on the path to economic independence remained strong. Economic and social policy changes are fundamentally interconnected, but equity goals can, and did, move in a different direction to efficiency objectives, and human agency played a part.

Notes

1. Bob Jessop, "From Hegemony to Crisis? The Continuing Ecological Dominance of Neo-liberalism," in *The Rise and Fall of Neoliberalism: The Collapse of an Economic Order?* ed. Kean Birch and Vlad Mykhenko (London: Zed Books, 2010), 177–87; Bob Jessop, "Neo-Liberalism," in *The Whiley-Blackwell Encyclopedia of Globalization,* vol. 3, ed. George Ritzer (Chichester: Wiley Blackwell, 2012), 1518.

2. David Harvey, *A Brief History of Neoliberalism* (Oxford: Oxford University Press, 2005), 13.

3. Jane Kelsey, *The New Zealand Experiment* (Auckland: Auckland University Press and Bridget Williams Books, 1997); Jane Kelsey, *Rolling Back the State* (Wellington: Bridget Williams Books, 1993); Mike O'Brien and Chris Wilkes, *The Tragedy of the Market: A Social Experiment in New Zealand* (Palmerston North: Dunmore Press, 1993); Francis Castles, Rolf Gerritsen, and Jack Vowles, eds., *The Great Experiment: Labour Parties and Public Policy Transformation in Australia and New Zealand* (Sydney: Allen and Unwin, 1996); Bruce Jesson, *Only Their Purpose Is Mad* (Palmerston North: Dunmore Press, 1999).

4. Thomas B. Edsall, *The New Politics of Inequality* (New York: W. W. Norton and Co., 1984); Joseph E. Stiglitz, *The Price of Inequality: How Today's Divided Society Endangers Our Future* (New York: W. W. Norton and Co., 2012).

5. Michael Förster and Marco Mira d'Ercole, "Income Distribution and Poverty in OECD Countries in the Second Half of the 1990s," *Social, Employment, and Migration Working Papers,* No. 22 (Paris: OECD, 2005); Vasantha Krishnan and John Jensen, "Trends in Economic Well-Being: Changing Patterns in New Zealand 1989 to 2001," Working Paper 08/04 (Wellington: Ministry of Social Development, 2004); Vasantha

Krishnan, John Jensen, and Suzie Ballantyne, *New Zealand Living Standards 2000* (Ngā āhuatanga noho o Aotearoa) (Wellington: Centre for Social Research and Evaluation, Ministry of Social Development, 2002); OECD, *Society at a Glance: OECD Social Indicators* (Paris: OECD, 2005); Ruth Laugesen and Joanne Black, "All Things Being Equal," *New Zealand Listener*, 1—7 May 2010, 14–21.

6. Colin James, *New Territory: The Transformation of New Zealand, 1984–92* (Wellington: Bridget Williams Books, 1992), 145–47. New Zealand was ranked ninth highest, equal with the United States and Australia, by the Heritage Foundation/Wall Street Journal 2006 Index of Economic Freedom.

7. Jonathan Boston, John Martin, June Pallot, and Pat Walsh, eds., *Reshaping the State: New Zealand's Bureaucratic Revolution* (Auckland: Oxford University Press, 1991).

8. Qtd. in Kelsey, *New Zealand Experiment*, 8.

9. Charles A. Price, *The Great White Walls Are Built: Restrictive Immigration to North America and Australasia, 1836–1888* (Canberra: Australian Institute of International Affairs in association with Australian National University, 1974); Sean Brawley "'No White Policy in New Zealand': Fact and Fiction in New Zealand's Asian Immigration Record, 1946–1978," *New Zealand Journal of History* 27.1 (April 1993): 16–36.

10. See Joanne Burton, "Patterns of Continuity and Change: Continuing Trends in New Zealand Labour Relations and Industrial Legislation, 1968 and 1991" (M.A. thesis, Victoria University of Wellington, 1995), for a discussion of the "classic postwar era" of arbitration. Jane Margaret Scott, "Neoliberalism at Work: Media-Politics and the Employment Contracts Act" (M.A. thesis, University of Auckland, 1995).

11. Peggy G. Koopman-Boyden and Claudia D. Scott, *The Family and Government Policy in New Zealand* (Sydney: George Allen and Unwin, 1986), 134; Ian Shirley, Peggy G. Koopman-Boyden, Ian Pool, and Susan St. John, "Family Change and Family Policies: New Zealand," in *Family Change and Family Policies in Great Britain, Canada, New Zealand, and the United States,* ed. Sheila Kamerman and Alfred Kahn (Oxford: Clarendon Press, 1997), 207–451.

12. Melanie Nolan and Pat Walsh, "Labour's Leg Iron? Assessing Trade Unions and Arbitration in New Zealand," in *Trade Unions, Work, and Society: The Centenary of the Arbitration System,* ed. Pat Walsh (Palmerston North: Dunmore Press, 1994), 9–37.

13. On neoliberalism and race, see Wendy Larner, "Neo-liberalism and Tino Rangatiratanga: Welfare State Restructuring in Aotearoa/New Zealand,"in *Western Welfare in Decline: Globalization and Women's Poverty,* ed. Catherine Kingfisher (Philadelphia: University of Pennsylvania Press, 2002), 147–64.

14. The combined total of sickness, invalids, unemployed, and domestic-purposes beneficiaries more than doubled from 132,919 in 1984 to 281,783 in 1990. Ministry of Social Policy, *Statistics Report* (Wellington: Ministry of Social Policy, 1999), 19. The number of those on the unemployment benefit rose from 38,419 in 1984 to 146,812 in 1991, to reach an official rate of over 8 percent at peak. *Social Welfare Annual Reports* qtd. in *Sunday Star,* 13 September 1992.

15. Michael A. Peters, "Neoliberalism, Welfare Dependency, and the Moral Construction of Poverty in New Zealand," *New Zealand Sociology* 12.1 (May 1997): 1–34.

16. For a more general discussion about how neoliberalism became dominant, see "The Construction of Consent," in Harvey, *Brief History of Neoliberalism*, 39–63.

17. Paul Morris and Dolores Janiewski, *New Rights New Zealand: Myths, Markets, and Moralities* (Auckland: Auckland University Press, 2005).

18. Rachel S. Turner, *Neo-Liberal Ideology: History, Concepts, and Policies* (Edinburgh: Edinburgh University Press, 2008); Marian Sawer, *The Ethical State? Social Liberalism in Australia* (Carlton, Vic.: Melbourne University Press, 2003).

19. Ministry of Business, Innovation, and Employment, *Union Membership Return Report, 2011* (Wellington: Department of Labour, 2012). For an example of union-focused analysis, see Gregor Gall, Adrian Wilkinson, and Richard Hurd, eds., *The International Handbook of Labour Unions: Responses to Neo-Liberalism* (Northampton, Mass.: Edward Elgar Publishing, 2012), esp. David Peetz and Janis Bailey, "Neo-liberal Evolution and Union Responses in Australia" (62–81).

20. David Hackett Fischer, *Fairness and Freedom: A History of Two Open Societies, New Zealand and the United States* (Oxford: Oxford University Press, 2012).

21. Elim Papadakis, "Class Interests, Class Politics, and Welfare State Regime," *British Journal of Sociology* 44.2 (June 1993): 249–70.

22. Michael Quinlan and Margaret Gardner, "Researching Industrial Relations History: The Development of a Database on Australian Trade Unions, 1825–1900," *Labour History* 66 (May 1994): 106.

23. Richard White, *Inventing Australia* (St. Leonards, NSW: Allen and Unwin, 1981); James Belich, "The Pakeha Myths of Settlement" and "Getting On," in *Making Peoples: A History of New Zealanders* (Auckland: Penguin Press, 1996), 297–312 and 376–410.

24. Tony Simpson, *The Immigrants: The Great Migration from Britain to New Zealand, 1830–1890* (Auckland: Godwit Press, 1997), 212.

25. John E. Martin, "Unemployment, Government, and the Labour Market in New Zealand, 1860–1890," *New Zealand Journal of History* 29.2 (October 1995): 180–96; John E. Martin, "1890: A Turning Point for Labour," in *Pioneering New Zealand Labour History: Essays in Honour of Bert Roth*, ed. Pat Walsh (Palmerston North: Dunmore Press, 1994), 1–22.

26. Stuart Macintyre, *The Succeeding Age, 1901–1942*, vol. 4 of *The Oxford History of Australia* (Melbourne: Oxford University Press, 1997), 86–87; Erik Olssen, *Building the New World: Work, Politics, and Society in Caversham, 1880s–1920s* (Auckland: Auckland University Press, 1995).

27. Stuart Macintyre and Richard Mitchell, eds., *Foundations of Arbitration: The Origins and Effects of State Compulsory Arbitration, 1890–1914* (Melbourne: Oxford University Press, 1989).

28. Richard Mitchell, "State Systems of Conciliation and Arbitration: The Legal Origins of the Australasian Model," in *Foundations of Arbitration: The Origins and Effects of State Compulsory Arbitration, 1890–1914*, ed. Stuart Macintyre and Richard Mitchell (Melbourne: Oxford University Press, 1989), 74–103; Mary Theresa Rankin, *Arbitration and Conciliation in Australasia: The Legal Wage in Victoria and New Zealand* (London: Allen and Unwin, 1916); "Capital and Labour: Resisting Globalization," in Donald

Denoon and Philippa Mein Smith with Marivic Wyndham, *A History of Australia, New Zealand, and the Pacific* (Melbourne: Oxford University Press, 2000), 227–47.

29. Neville Kirk, *Comrades and Cousins: Globalisation, Workers, and Labour Movements in Britain, the USA, and Australia from the 1880s to 1914* (London: Merlin Press, 2003), 6.

30. Francis G. Castles, *The Working Class and Welfare: Reflections on the Political Development of the Welfare State in Australia and New Zealand, 1890–1980* (Wellington: George Allen and Unwin in association with the Port Nicholson Press, 1985), 82–88. See also W. H. Oliver, "Social Policy in the Liberal Period," *New Zealand Journal of History* 13.1 (April 1979): 32–33.

31. *Commonwealth Arbitration Reports* 2 (1907–8), pp. 3–17, Ex parte, H. V. McKay.

32. Henry Bournes Higgins, *A New Province for Law and Order* (Sydney: WEA, 1922); Meredith Atkinson, *The New Social Order: A Study of Social Reconstruction* (Sydney: WEA, 1919).

33. Jill Roe, ed., *Social Policy in Australia: Some Perspectives, 1901–1975* (Sydney: Cassell, 1976).

34. Melanie Nolan, *Breadwinning: New Zealand Women and the State* (Christchurch: Canterbury University Press, 2000).

35. P. G. McCarthy, "Justice Higgins and the Harvester Judgement," *Australian Economic History Review* 11 (1969): 16–38.

36. W. J. Waters, "Australian Labor's Full Employment Objective, 1942–45," in *Social Policy in Australia: Some Perspectives, 1901–1975*, ed. Jill Roe (Sydney: Cassell, 1976), 242; Keith Sinclair, *Walter Nash* (Auckland: Auckland University Press, 1976), 230.

37. "Australian–New Zealand Agreement between His Majesty's Government in the Commonwealth of Australia and His Majesty's Government in the Dominion of New Zealand, Made in Canberra, 21 January 1944," in *Appendices to the House of Representatives* (hereafter *AJHR*) (Wellington: Government Print, 1944), A-4.

38. Allan J. Dalziell, *Evatt the Enigma* (Melbourne: Landsdowne Press, 1967), 41–44; Sinclair, *Walter Nash*, 238–41.

39. Herbert Cole Coombs, "The Economic Aftermath of the War," in *Postwar Reconstruction in Australia*, ed. D. A. S. Campbell (Sydney: Australian Publishing, 1944), 67–99; Walter Nash, *New Zealand, a Working Democracy* (London: J. M. Dent and Sons, 1943). See also Wolfgang Rosenberg, *Full Employment: Can the New Zealand Economic Miracle Last?* (Wellington: A. H. and A. W. Reed, 1960).

40. H. V. Evatt, *Australia in World Affairs* (Sydney: Angus and Robertson, 1946), 40–41; Alan Renouf, *Let Justice Be Done: The Foreign Policy of Dr. H. V. Evatt* (St Lucia: University of Queensland Press, 1983), 118–21.

41. James Thorn, *Peter Fraser: New Zealand Wartime Prime Minister* (London: Odhams Press Ltd., 1952), 236.

42. Wolfgang Rosenberg, "Full Employment: The Fulcrum of Social Welfare," in *Social Welfare and New Zealand Society*, ed. Andrew Drago Trlin (Wellington: Methuen, 1977), 45–60.

43. Erik Olssen, "Depression and War (1931–1949)," in *The Oxford Illustrated History of New Zealand*, ed. Keith Sinclair (Auckland: Oxford University Press, 1990), 234.

44. Linda Gordon, ed., *Women, the State, and Welfare* (Madison: University of Wisconsin Press, 1990), esp. Barbara Nelson, "The Origins of the Two Channel State: Workmen's Compensation and Mother's Aid" (123–57); Theda Skocpol, *Protecting Mothers and Soldiers: The Political Origins of Social Policy in the United States* (Cambridge, Mass.: Belknap Press of Harvard University Press, 1992); Seth Koven and Sonya Michel, eds., *Mothers of a New World: Maternalist Politics and the Origins of the Welfare States* (London: Routledge, 1993).

45. Cybele Locke, *Workers in the Margins: Union Radicals in Post-War New Zealand* (Wellington: Bridget Williams Books, 2012).

46. For example, see *Wellington Evening Post*, 14 and 20 January 1936, 15 July 1936, 19 December 1936, 15 June 1937, 13 January 1939, and 21 June 1945.

47. Paul Kelly, *The End of Certainty: Power, Politics, and Business* (St. Leonards, NSW: Allen and Unwin, 1994); James Belich, *Paradise Reforged: A History of the New Zealanders from the 1880s to the Year 2000* (Auckland: Penguin, 2001), 22–23; Bruce Jesson, *Fragments of Labour: The Story behind the Labour Government* (Auckland: Penguin Books, 1989), 9; Christine Cheyne, Mike O'Brien, and Michael Belgrave, *Social Policy in Aotearoa New Zealand: A Critical Introduction* (Auckland: Oxford University Press, 2000), 18–46.

48. Peter Beilharz, "Australian Settlements," *Thesis Eleven* 95.1 (November 2008): 50–67.

49. Sawer, *Ethical State?* 116.

50. Paul Harris and John Morrow, eds., *Lectures on the Principles of Political Obligation and Other Writings* (Cambridge: Cambridge University Press, 1986); Michael Freeden, *The New Liberalism: An Ideology of Social Reform* (Oxford: Clarendon Press, 1978).

51. Tim Rowse, *Australian Liberalism and National Character* (Sydney: Kibble Books, 1978); W. H. Oliver, "Reeves, Sinclair, and the Social Pattern," in *The Feel of Truth: Essays in New Zealand and Pacific History Presented to F. L. W. Wood and J. C. Beaglehole on the Occasion of Their Retirement*, ed. Peter Munz (Wellington: A. H. and A. W. Reed for the Victoria University, 1969), 163–80.

52. Neil Massey, "A Century of Labourism, 1891–1993: An Historical Interpretation," *Labour History* 66 (1994): 45–71; Terry Irving, "Labourism: A Political Genealogy," *Labour History* 66 (1994): 1–13.

53. Diane Stone, *Capturing the Political Imagination: Think Tanks and the Policy Process* (London: Frank Cass, 1996), 167–83; James A. Smith, *The Idea Brokers: Think Tanks and the Rise of the New Policy Elite* (New York: Free Press, 1991), 190–239; Philip Mendes, *Australia's Welfare Wars: The Players, the Politics and the Ideologies* (Sydney: University of New South Wales Press, 2003), 34–37.

54. Brian Easton, "The Commercialisation of the New Zealand Economy: From Think Big to Privatisation," in *The Making of Rogernomics*, ed. Brian Easton (Auckland: Auckland University Press, 1989), 127.

55. Stephen Nickell, Luca Nunziata, and Wolfgang Ochel, "Unemployment in the OECD since the 1960s: What Do We Know?" *Economic Journal* 115 (January 2005): 1–27.

56. Brian S. Roper, *Prosperity for All? Economic, Social, and Political Change in New Zealand since 1935* (Sydney: Cengage Learning Australia, 2005).

57. Sylvia B. Bashevkin, *Welfare Hot Buttons: Women, Work, and Social Policy Reform* (Toronto: University of Toronto Press, 2002), 3–19.

58. Paul Harris and Linda J. Twiname, *First Knights: An Investigation of the New Zealand Business Roundtable* (Auckland: Howling at the Moon, 1998); Brian Roper, "Business Political Activity in New Zealand from 1990 to 2005," *Kotuitui: New Zealand Journal of Social Sciences Online* 1.2 (2006): 161–83.

59. Roger Kerr, "The New Zealand Business Roundtable: A Personal Perspective," paper presented to the Manawatu Commerce Centre, 11 June 1997, accessed 1 September 2011, http://nzinitiative.org.nz/shop/Library+by+topic/New+Zealand+Business+Roundtable.html; Anthony Hubbard, "'Crusader of the Roundtable," *New Zealand Listener*, 4 May 1992, 15–21; New Zealand Business Roundtable, *The New Zealand and Australian Social Security and Welfare Systems: A Comparative Study* (Wellington: New Zealand Business Roundtable, 1990).

60. Charles Murray, *Losing Ground: American Social Policy, 1950–1980* (New York: Basic Books, 1984); Lawrence Mead, *Beyond Entitlement: The Social Obligations of Citizenship* (New York: Free Press, 1986); David G. Green, *Social Welfare: The Changing Debate* (Sydney: Centre for Independent Studies, 1988).

61. Brian S. Roper, "A Level Playing Field? Business Political Activism and State Policy Formation," in *State and Economy in New Zealand*, ed. Brian S. Roper and Chris Rudd (Auckland: Oxford University Press, 1980), 147–71.

62. Peter Brosnan, David F. Smith, and Pat Walsh, *The Dynamics of New Zealand Industrial Relations* (Auckland: J. Wiley, 1990), 118–21.

63. Edward S. Herman and Noam Chomsky, *Manufacturing Consent: The Political Economy of the Mass Media* (London: Vintage, 1994); Alex Carey, "The Ideological Management Industry," in *Communications and the Media in Australia*, ed. Ted Wheelwright and Ken Buckley (Sydney: Allen and Unwin, 1987), 156–79.

64. Andrew Gavin Gregg, "Panic Attacks: The New Right, Media, and Welfare Reform in New Zealand, 1987–1998" (M.A. thesis, Victoria University of Wellington, 2004), 16.

65. Nolan and Walsh, "Labour's Leg Iron?" 30. See also Pat Walsh, "The Rejection of Corporatism: Trade Unions, Employers, and the State in New Zealand, 1960–1977" (Ph.D. dissertation, University of Minnesota, 1984); and Melanie Nolan and Peter Franks, *Unions in Common Cause: The New Zealand Federation of Labour, 1937–88*, ed. Peter Franks and Melanie Nolan (Wellington: Steele Roberts Aotearoa, 2011), 19–59.

66. Michael Bassett, *Working with David: Inside the Lange Cabinet* (Auckland: Hodder Moa, 2008); Richard Prebble, *Out of the Red* (Rotorua: Letter Limited, 2007).

67. Gregg, "Panic Attacks," 56.

68. Marcia Russell, *Revolution: New Zealand from Fortress to Free Market* (Auckland: Hodder Moa Beckett, 1996), 145.

69. Nikitin Sallee, "Royal Commission Pre-empts Tax Package," *New Zealand Business Review*, 17 March 1988, 1; New Zealand Royal Commission on Social Policy, *The April Report of the Royal Commission on Social Policy*, *AJHR*, H2, (Wellington: Government Printer, 1988), 11; Geoffrey Rice, *The Oxford History of New Zealand*, rev. ed. (Auckland: Oxford University Press, 1992), 488–89.

70. Wolfgang Rosenberg, *New Zealand Can Be Different and Better: Why Deregulation Does Not Work* (Christchurch: New Zealand Monthly Review Society, 1993).

71. Karen Davis, *Born of Hunger, Pain, and Strife: 150 Years of Struggle against Unemployment in New Zealand* (Auckland: People's Press, 1991); Cybele Locke, "Organising the Unemployed: The Politics of Gender, Culture, and Class in the 1980s and 1990s," in *On the Left: Essays on Socialism in New Zealand,* ed. Pat Moloney and Kerry Taylor (Dunedin: University of Otago Press, 2002), 151–68.

72. David Grant, *Man for All Seasons: The Life and Times of Ken Douglas* (Auckland: Random House, 2010), 312; Ellen J. Dannin, *Working Free: The Origins and Impact of New Zealand's Employment Contracts Act* (Auckland: Auckland University Press, 1997); 136–51; Sarah Heal, "The Struggle for and against the Employment Contracts Act, 1987–1991" (M.A. thesis, University of Otago, 1994).

73. Qtd. in Gregg, "Panic Attacks," 91.

74. Toby Boraman, *Struggles against Neoliberalism in Aotearoa/New Zealand in the 1990s* (Dunedin: Irrecuperable Distribution, 2004).

75. Brian Roper, "The Fire Last Time: The Rise of Class Struggle and Progressive Social Movements in Aotearoa/New Zealand, 1968–1977," *Marxist Interventions* 3 (2011): 7–30. For a substantive discussion of strike activity between 1968 and 1977, see Raymond Markey, "Troubled Times: 1967–88," in *Unions in Common Cause: The New Zealand Federation of Labour, 1937–88,* ed. Peter Franks and Melanie Nolan (Wellington: Steele Roberts Aotearoa, 2011), 145–82.

76. Linda Clark, "Alternatives to the Welfare State," *New Zealand Business Review,* 17 November 1987, 11. See also Michael James, ed., *The Welfare State: Foundations and Alternatives: Proceedings of CIS Conferences Held in Wellington and Sydney, November 1989* (St. Leonards, NSW: Centre for Independent Studies and New Zealand Centre for Independent Studies, 1989).

77. See Gregg, "Panic Attacks."

78. Murray, *Losing Ground*; Mead, *Beyond Entitlement*; Green, *Social Welfare.* Claims rested on a single longitudinal study conducted in 1977, which estimated that this population was 5 percent of all welfare families. Gregg, "Panic Attacks," 131.

79. James Cox, *Towards Personal Independence and Prosperity: Income Support for Persons or Working Age in New Zealand* (Wellington: New Zealand Business Review, 1998), 27–28.

80. Jenny Shipley with Simon Upton, Lockwood Smith, and John Luxton, *Social Assistance: Welfare That Works: A Statement of Government Policy on Social Assistance* (Wellington: New Zealand Government, 1991). See also Johanna Kantola and Judith Squires, "From State Feminism to Market Feminism?" *International Political Science Review* 33.4 (2012): 383–400.

81. See, for example, "For Some It's Better to Be on the Dole," *New Zealand Herald,* 20 October 1988, 12; Gareth Morgan, "Don't Work and Still Benefit," *Infometrics Memorandum* 29 (October 1988): 1–5; "New Zealand's Social Welfare Crisis," *Infometrics Memorandum* 34 (January 1990): 1–20; Anthony Hubbard, "Right by Ruth," *New Zealand Listener,* 20 August 1990, 22–26.

82. Peter Golding and Sue Middleton, *Images of Welfare: Press and Public Attitudes to Poverty* (Oxford: Martin Robertson, 1982); Bob Frankin, ed., *Social Policy, the Media, and Misrepresentations* (London: Routledge, 1999); Martin Gilens, *Why Americans Hate Welfare: Race, Media, and the Politics of Anti-Poverty Policy* (Chicago: University of Chicago Press, 1999).

83. Ruth Richardson, *Making a Difference* (Christchurch: Shoal Bay Press, 1995), 40–43.

84. A. Byrnes, "Dole Cited as Reason for Unemployment," *New Zealand Business Review,* 29 March 1990, 3.

85. T. Metcalfe, "Poor Work Ethic Blamed for Woes," *Christchurch Press,* 4 April 1991, 9.

86. Murray Petrie, *Organisational Transformation: The Income Support Experience* (Wellington: Department of Social Welfare, 1998).

87. Robert A. Sirico, "Entrepreneurial Vision," *Journal of Market and Morality* 3.1 (Spring 2000): 1–21.

88. Irving Kristol, "Forget the Money, Welfare State's Crisis Is Spiritual," *New Zealand Business Review,* 21 February 1997, 12 (first published as Irving Kristol, "The Welfare State's Spiritual Crisis," *Wall Street Journal,* Eastern ed., 3 February 1997, A14.

89. David Bedggood, "Beyond Dependency or Beyond Capitalism? A Critique of New Zealand's Drive towards Workfare," *Policy Studies* 20.2 (1999): 113; Beyond Dependency International Conference, Sheraton Hotel, Auckland, 16–19 March 1997.

90. Department of Social Welfare, *Towards a Code of Social and Family Responsibility: Public Discussion Document* (Wellington: Corporate Communications Unit, 1998); Judith Davey, *Another New Zealand Experiment: A Code of Family and Social Responsibility* (Wellington: Institute of Policy Studies, 2000); Wendy Larner, "Post-Welfare Governance: Towards a Code of Social and Family Responsibility," *Social Politics* 7.2 (Summer 2000): 244–65.

91. There was a precedent: in 1991, Bill Birch had sent a letter to every householder in New Zealand extolling the virtues of the Employment Contracts Act.

92. Barry Hindess, "A Society Governed by Contract?" in *The New Contractualism?* ed. Glyn Davis, Barbara Ann Sullivan, and Anna Yeatman (Melbourne: Macmillan, 1997), 14–26.

93. John Gray, *False Dawn: The Delusions of Global Capitalism* (London: Granta Books, 1998).

94. Roger Douglas, *Unfinished Business* (Auckland: Random House, 1993), 218.

95. Brian S. Roper, "Farewell to the Welfare State?" *New Zealand Monthly Review* 328 (March 1991): 9–11; Mike O'Brien and Chris Wilkes, *The Tragedy of the Market: A Social Experiment in New Zealand* (Palmerston North: Dunmore Press, 1993), 91–92; Francis Castles and Ian Shirley, "Labour and Social Policy: Gravediggers or Refurbishers of the Welfare State," in *The Great Experiment: Labour Parties and Public Policy Transformation in Australian and New Zealand,* ed. Francis Castles, Rolf Gerritsen, and Jack Vowles (Sydney: Allen and Unwin, 1996), 88–106.

96. "The New Zealand Economy: Can the Kiwi Economy Fly?" *The Economist* 357 (2 December 2000): 69–71.

97. Brian Easton, "Growth v. Distribution," *New Zealand Listener,* 9 August 2008, based on Ministry of Social Development, *Household Incomes in New Zealand: Trends in Indicators of Inequality and Hardship 1982 to 2007* (Wellington: Ministry of Social Development, 2008).

98. Gregg, "Panic Attacks," 167–68.

99. Melanie Nolan, "The High Tide of a Labour Market System: The Australasian Male Breadwinner Model," *Labour and Industry* 13.3 (April 2003): 73–92.

100. Sheila Shaver, "Gender Down Under: Welfare Restructuring in Australia and Aotearoa/New Zealand," *Social Policy and Administration* 33.5 (December 1999): 586–603; Hans-Peter Blossfeld and Sonja Drobninullc, eds., *Careers of Couples in Contemporary Society: From Male Breadwinner to Dual-Earner Families* (Oxford: Oxford University Press, 2001), 5–8. Jane Lewis refers to the new model as the "'adult-worker model family,' whereby it is assumed that all adults are in the labor market." Jane Lewis, "The Decline of the Male Breadwinner Model: Implications for Work and Care," *Social Politics* 8.2 (Summer 2001): 154.

101. Kathleen Thelen: "Historical Institutionalism in Comparative Politics," *Annual Review of Political Science* 2 (1999): 387; Kathleen Thelen, "How Institutions Evolve: Insights from Comparative-Historical Analysis," in *Comparative-Historical Analysis in the Social Sciences,* ed. James Mahoney and Dietrich Rueschemeyer (Cambridge: Cambridge University Press, 2003), 208–40.

PART IV

Workers and the Shakeup
of the New World Order

9

Want amidst Plenty

The Oil Boom and the Working Class in Newfoundland and Labrador, 1992–2010

SEAN CADIGAN

Newfoundland and Labrador, the easternmost province of Canada, had long been the poor cousin of Confederation.[1] By 2008 this all changed, as Newfoundland and Labrador became a "have province" within the Canadian system of calculating federal transfers of income to poorer provinces. Since 2000, average personal incomes have increased steadily, and the unemployment rate has dropped. Much of this good economic fortune has been attributed to the cyclical but steady rise in total oil production from the province's offshore oil wells since the first Hibernia project began production in 1997 (see map 9.1). The province's gross domestic product (GDP) has been rising steadily since 2000, and the province has weathered the current international recession better than any other jurisdiction in North America. The transition from "have not" to "have" status was, according to the provincial premier Danny Williams, "a momentous day for the people of this province," and his finance minister, Jerome Kennedy, stated that these people no longer had to suffer national perceptions of them as "second-rate citizens, or Canada's poor cousins."[2]

Despite the hoopla, the oil boom could not transform overnight serious environmental, economic, and social problems that have been plaguing Newfoundland and Labrador since at least the 1970s. The limits of the boom are apparent from the experience of working people. Outside of the region surrounding St. John's, the provincial capital, skilled working people have continued to leave the province due to ongoing crises in the forestry and fisheries sectors. Direct employment in the oil and mining sectors is too limited to compensate. Indirect employment has largely been in the service sector, especially in jobs dominated by underpaid and poorly represented women, who have faced significant

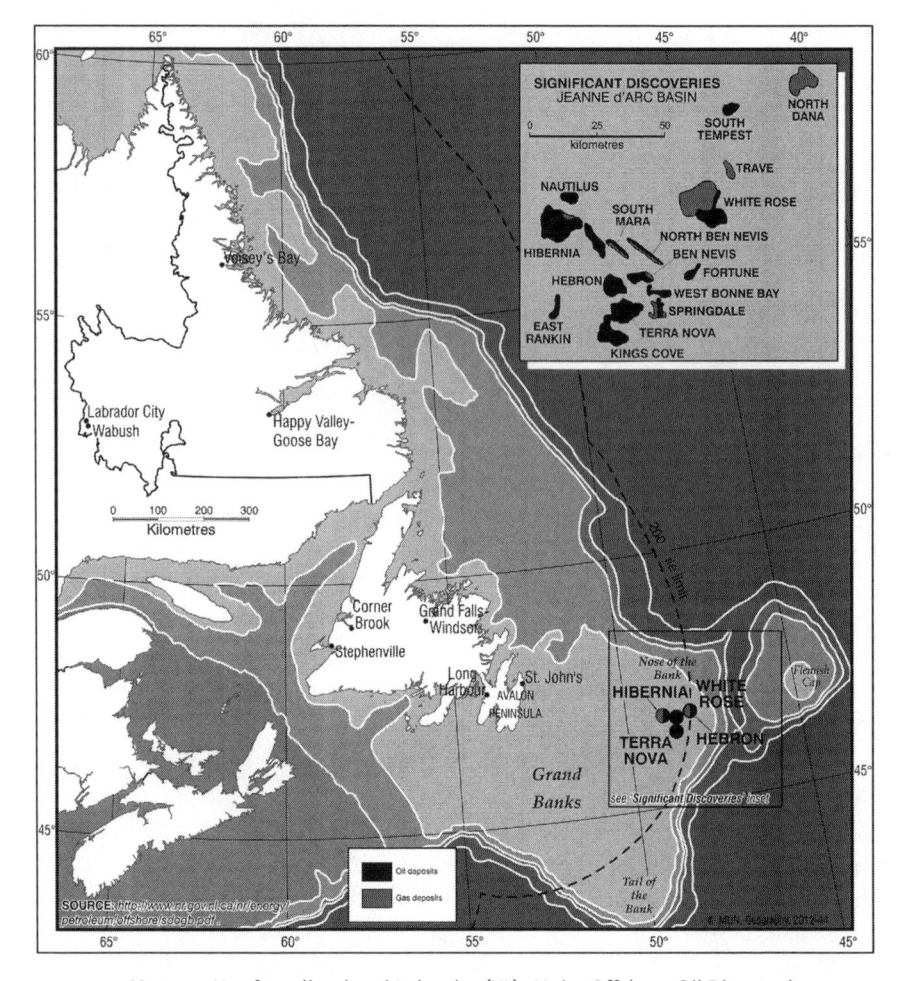

Map 9.1: Newfoundland and Labrador (NL): Major Offshore Oil Discoveries

impediments to gaining access to skilled work or representation by unions. The oil boom has further contributed to a neoliberal policy of dividing unions, especially in the public sector. Before 2005, provincial governments attacked unions largely for purposes of retrenchment. From 2005, growing oil revenue has allowed the provincial government to spend more, but by downloading the costs of some new initiatives onto public-sector unions and fostering lucrative but disruptive collective agreements in ways that appear divisive on a gendered basis. The persistence of want amidst plenty on a regional, class, and gender basis has fractured the labor movement, limiting its ability to respond to the problems of the oil boom.

The Uneven Geography of the Oil Boom

The oil boom must be understood in the context of Newfoundland and Labrador's particular political economy. A cold-ocean region of boreal forests and tundra, Newfoundland and Labrador experienced none of the agricultural settlement and related manufacturing development that, to varying degrees, fostered economic growth in the neighboring regions of North America. Early Europeans had come to Newfoundland to fish; with little prospect for import substitution or significant alternative landward economic activities, fishing people remained dependent on merchant capital and the Atlantic markets of the cod trade. Its Atlantic orientation meant that Newfoundland rejected union with Canada in the nineteenth century. Successive colonial governments attempted economic diversification through great public investments in railway development and by protecting local manufacturing. Such efforts failed to significantly diversify the economy, although they contributed to massive public debt. Governments were more successful in using subsidies, favorable royalty rates, and tax exemptions to attract foreign capital to forestry and mining. Employment in these industries was important but did not lessen overall dependence on the fishery.

By the early 1930s, Newfoundland and Labrador continued to rely on staple production amidst collapsing international prices for its exports. The limited manufacturing that had grown in the capital, St. John's, relied on fishing people as markets, but their capacity to consume waned with the depression of the period. Terrible unemployment and poverty worsened already-staggering public debt; concomitant social unrest led to political crisis and the collapse of responsible government between 1932 and 1934—government by a British-appointed commission from 1934 to 1949 and union with Canada in the latter year. From 1949, provincial governments tried to lessen dependence on the fishery with little success; Newfoundland and Labrador remained the poorest province in Canada. Resource depletion characterized the fishery and forestry, encouraging the concentration of capital and leaner forms of production by the 1980s. Such changes failed to prevent the ecological crisis of the commercial annihilation of northern cod stocks and the related shutdown of the fishery in 1992, or the downsizing and restructuring that led to the closure of two of the province's three paper mills by 2009.[3]

Little wonder, then, that Newfoundland and Labrador had been looking for economic miracles from offshore oil development since the 1970s. Federal-provincial wrangling over jurisdiction over offshore oil, but more particularly low oil prices, meant that the industry did not develop beyond the exploration stage until 1985. The Canadian and Newfoundland and Labrador governments agreed to joint management of the offshore oil sector, and the federal government provided financial support to encourage the development of the province's first commercial production at the Hibernia site. Oil production and related revenues began and grew slowly from 1997. In 2005–6, the government of Newfoundland and Labrador recorded its first budget surplus, and in 2008, the province's GDP improved dramatically, largely on the basis of a steady overall rise in total oil production and revenue (see table 9.1 and figure 9.1). Oil projects accounted for more than five billion dollars in royalties between 1997 and 2008, and by 2009 such funds accounted for roughly 28 percent of the province's revenue, supplemented by growing revenue from iron-ore and nickel mining.[4] The oil boom fueled more consumer spending on cars, houses, and retail products (table 9.2). Such a rapid, apparent turnaround in the economy, marked by higher incomes, more government spending, greater consumer spending, and inflation, is similar to the earlier oil booms of the 1970s in Alaska and Alberta.[5]

The oil boom's benefits have been regionally specific. Much of the direct skilled employment generated by the offshore industry, and most of its indirect linkages in the real estate, construction, hospitality, and retail sectors, have been in the St. John's area. The iron-ore- and nickel-mining areas of Labrador have also done well. The overall effects have been clear: while the overall population of the province decreased steadily from 580,109 in 1992 to 508,925 in 2009, the population of the northeast Avalon Peninsula, which centers on St. John's, grew slightly. Unemployment rates have remained lower in the St. John's and mining areas, and personal disposable incomes have remained higher there than in the province as a whole in 2006.[6] The lower incomes of people on the northeastern Avalon Peninsula, where employment has increased steadily while decreasing in other parts of the province, partially reflects that employment growth during the oil boom has been greater in the production of services than of goods (figure 9.2).

The oil boom has hardly helped areas that depend on primary-resource extraction and related processing, where employment has declined steadily in the past twenty years. In the fishery, disastrous modernization, overexpansion, and consequent resource depletion led to massive unemployment associated

Table 9.1. Total Oil Production (in Barrels), NL, 1997–2009

Year	Barrels	Year	Barrels
1997	1,272,219	2003	122,963,137
1998	23,799,308	2004	114,784,480
1999	66,391,556	2005	111,269,370
2000	52,798,311	2006	110,835,355
2001	54,288,400	2007	134,479,493
2002	104,333,624	2008	125,245,251
		2009	97,679,170

Source: http:/www.stats.gov.nl.ca/Statistics/Industry/PDF/Oil_Production.pdf (accessed 06/02/2010)

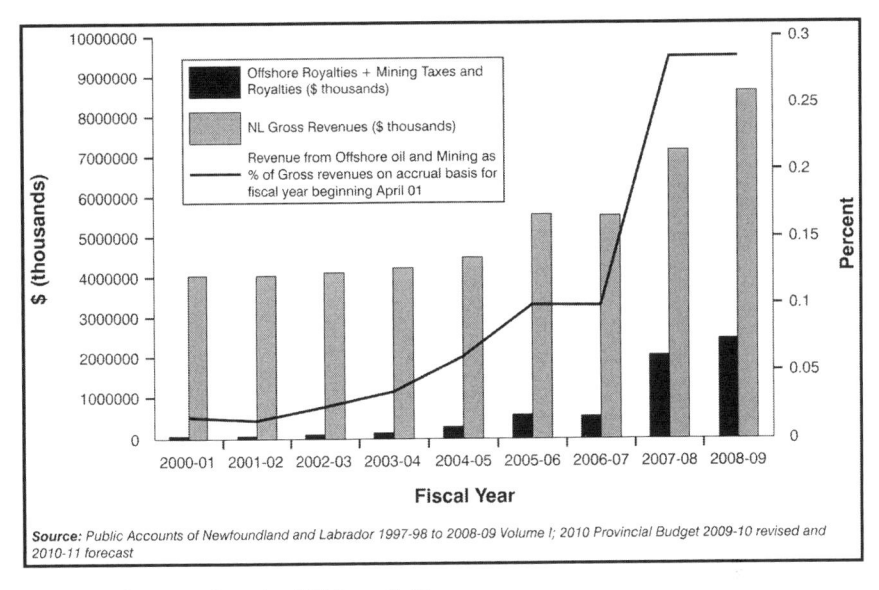

Figure 9.1: Revenue from the "Oil Boom": NL, 2000-2009

Table 9.2. Selected Economic Indicators, NL, 2000–2009

Indicators	2000	2005	2008	2009*
Per Capita GDP ($)	26,369	42,694	61,758	45,020
Personal Income ($) (millions)	11,122	13,249	15,641	16,257
Wages & Salaries $ (millions)	5,421.3	6,608.7	7,986	8,375.8
Retail Trade	4,760	5,824	7,009	7,120
Labor Force (thousands)	237.8	252.5	253.8	254.2
Employment (thousands)	198	214.1	220.3	214.9
Unemployment Rates (%)	16.7	15.2	13.2	15.5
Housing Starts	1,459	2,498	3,261	3,057

* Estimates for all rows except "Wages and Salaries."
Source: http:/www.stats.gov.nl.ca/Statistics/GDP/PDF/Labour_Income_NL. PDF (accessed 06/02/2010) except revenue figures, which are from Public Accounts of Newfoundland and Labrador 1997-98 to 2008-9 Volume 1, and 2010 Provincial Budget 2009–10 revised.

with the closure of Atlantic Canada's ground fisheries in 1992. Although the federal government provided limited compensation programs to unemployed fishers and plant workers, these were insufficient to stem the tide of significant out-migration in the almost twenty years that have followed. Newer fisheries are more capital-intensive and employ fewer people. The forestry sector, especially pulp and paper production, was the other economic mainstay of rural Newfoundland. Since the 1950s, constant mechanization of wood harvesting, corporate restructuring, and the development of lean production have characterized the industry. Overall, the industry has seen reductions in employment

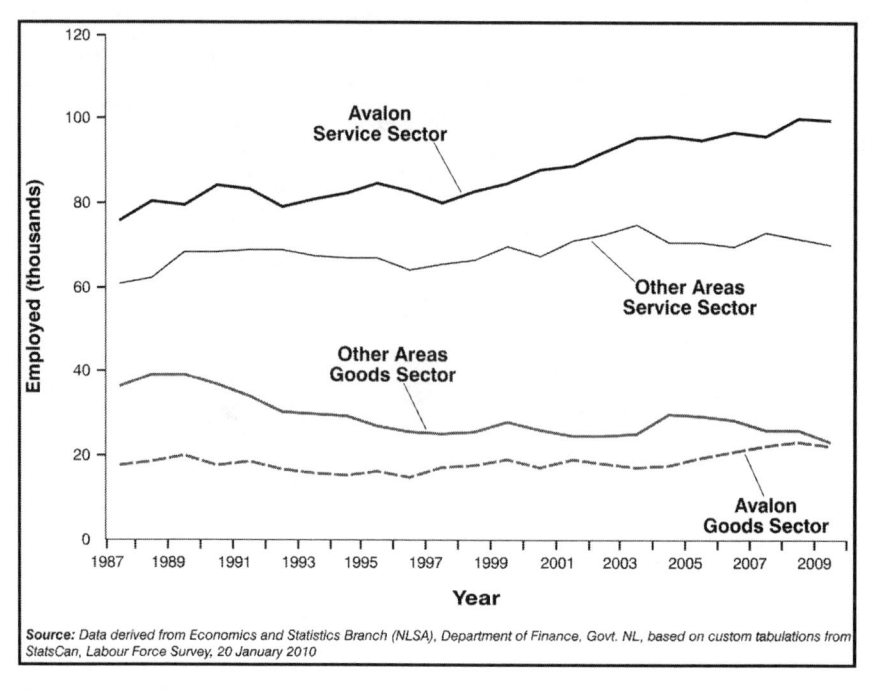

Figure 9.2: Employment by Region and Economic Sector, NL, 1987-2009

levels and benefits; more contracting out; the closure of two out of the province's three major paper mills; and a shift to unorganized workers in logging.[7]

Well-paid employment in the oil, gas, and mining sectors has yet to offset the steady decline of employment in the fisheries and forestry sectors since the late 1990s (figure 9.3). In 1992, for example, about 1,600 people worked in forestry and logging, while 9,300 people worked as fishers. By 2009, there were only 500 people working in forestry and logging, and 5,600 people remained as fishers. Over the same period, the total number of people employed in oil and gas extraction rose from 500 to 2,800 workers. While rural Newfoundland and Labrador lost 4,800 jobs in fishing and forestry, the oil sector had generated only 2,300 extra jobs. Altogether, 5,400 jobs had been lost in paper and seafood manufacture, while 1,900 jobs had been gained in the support work for the oil and gas sector. Construction work has been an important direct or indirect spinoff from mining and oil development, although it was most intensive during the startup rather than operations phase of the offshore oil industry. However, even making the overly generous assumption that all construction is oil-related, it clearly has not fully compensated for the loss of work in the fishing and forestry sectors (figure 9.4). While the oil, gas, and mining sectors

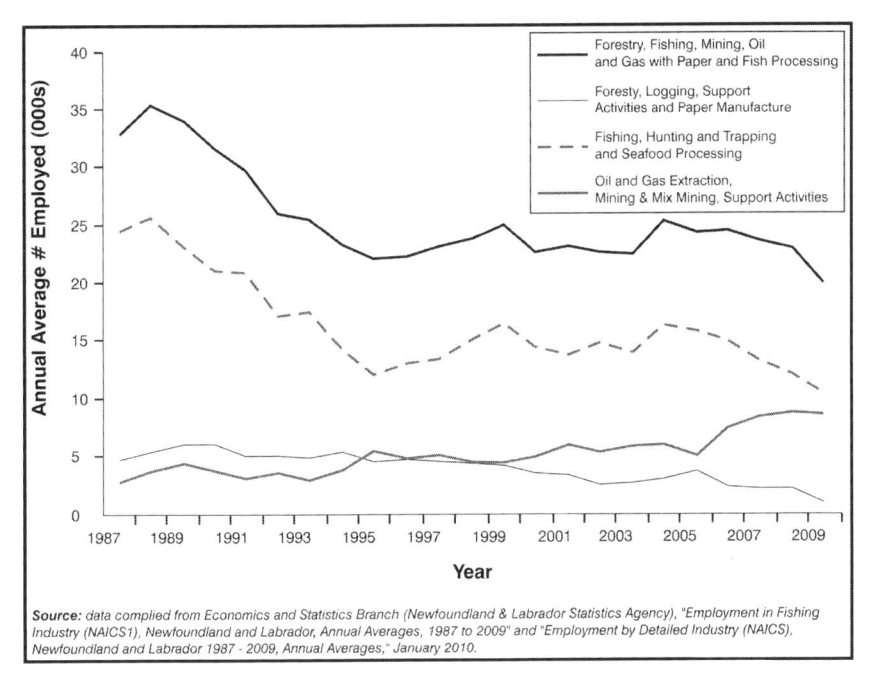

Figure 9.3: Employment by Select Primary and Related Industries, NL, 1997-2009

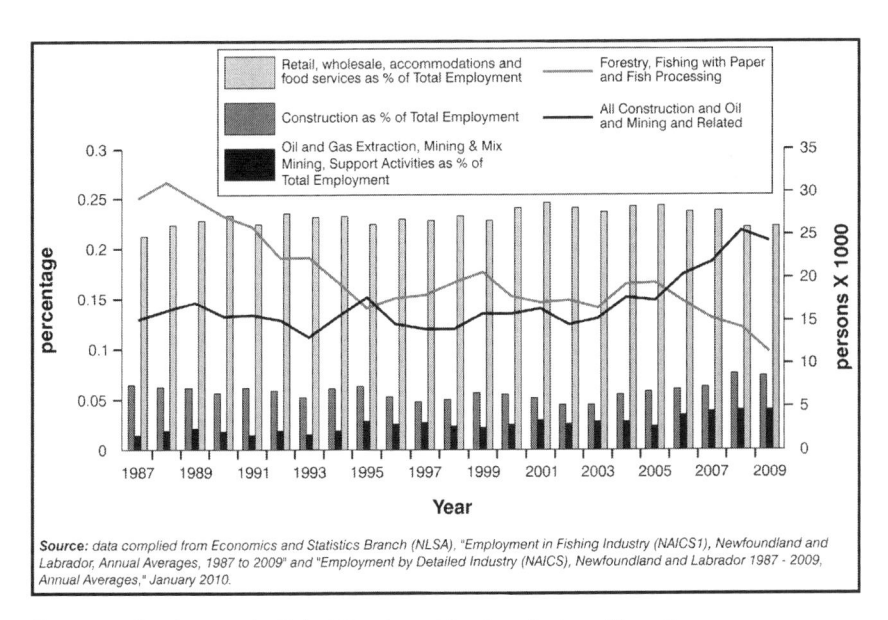

Figure 9.4: Employment by Select Goods and Services Sectors, NL, 1987-2009

have generated substantial new revenues for government, there is little evidence to show that such resources have funded significant efforts to put other core industries, particularly fishing, on a more secure footing.[8]

Class and Gender amidst the Boom

Far more people have been employed in low-paid jobs in the retail and wholesale trades, food services, and accommodations sectors than in construction or other goods production during the boom (figure 9.4). In the St. John's area, the incomes of people overall are lower than those in the mining areas of Labrador because employment has grown more in low-paid work in services production than in goods production (figure 9.5).[9] The pattern of relatively few good-paying jobs and a great many more low-paid jobs in the private-service sector is similar to the case of Alaska, where overall unemployment remains high, as does the cost of living, but where low-paid seasonal employment in tourism and fisheries is becoming relatively more important as employment lessens in the oil sector due to falling production. In Canada, Alberta has also failed to experience significant economic diversification based on oil; again, the service sector has been the most important area to expand in the age of oil.[10]

In Newfoundland and Labrador, the greater growth in low-paid service-sector work reinforced the gendered inequality of work. Women have comprised between 50 and 57 percent of all service-sector employees since 1987, but they have

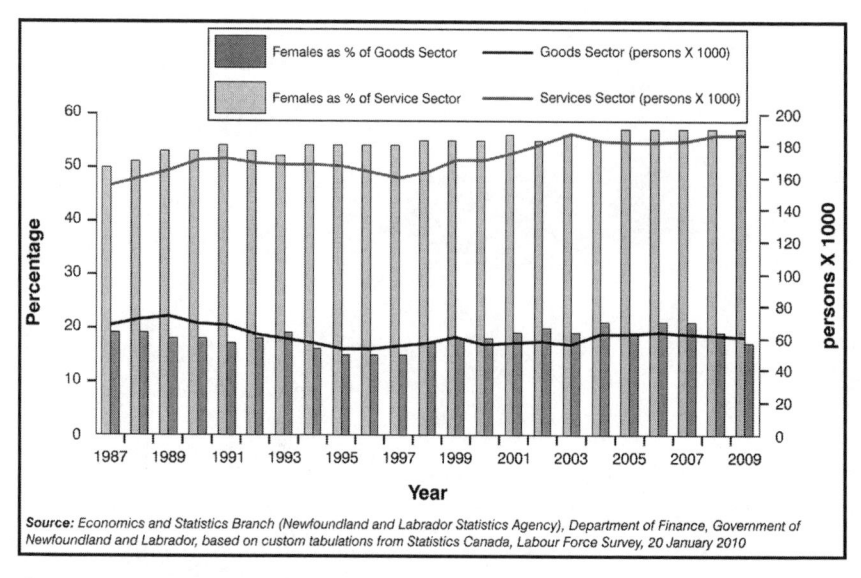

Figure 9.5: Employment by Sector and Sex, NL, 1987-2009

never held more than 21 percent of the better-paid jobs in goods production, an area dominated by male employment (figure 9.5). This demand for labor in the service sector reinforces a persistent disparity between the incomes of men and women. Since 1997, the average income derived by women from wages, salaries, and commissions has ranged from 53 percent to 60 percent of men's. Areas such as retail trade and the accommodations and food-services industries are disproportionately staffed by women and offer much lower wages.[11]

Rates of unionization are relatively high in industries that employ mostly men. Yet the private-service-sector industries that have grown most since the oil boom, and which employ far more women, remain largely unorganized. Newfoundland and Labrador has historically had much higher rates of unionization than most provinces in Canada, but working men have always fared better than women in securing collective-bargaining rights and better pay. The rate of union coverage in the construction industry has risen steadily from almost 22 percent in 2003 to 29 percent in 2008, and the rate in the mining and oil sector has ranged between 55 percent and 44 percent (see figure 9.6). Meanwhile, no more than 14 percent of workers in the accommodation and food-services industries, and just over 13 percent in the wholesale and retail trades, are covered by collective agreements. Women tend to earn much less than men because the preconceptions of male workers and employers have made it very difficult for them to enter highly skilled and better-paid areas of employment such as the oil sector. In Labrador City's iron-mining industry, for example, male workers and employers expected women to stay in traditional service-sector work and/or in unpaid domestic work rather than finding work in the mines. In 2001, women comprised less than 5 percent of all workers in the offshore oil industry in Canada, largely because its male-dominated work culture and employers' sexist suppositions limited women's recruitment. In Newfoundland and Labrador, the percentage of women working in the offshore sector reached no higher than just under 17 percent in 2007.[12] By far the poorest-paid people in the province are nonunionized women (figure 9.7).

The cyclical nature of oil-related construction has reinforced the tendency for skilled workers, mostly men, to look for more regular employment outside of the province. Consequently, local labor shortages have been a problem for the Hebron oil project, for mining-related projects such as the nickel-processing facility at Long Harbour, Placentia Bay, and for the aquaculture industry.[13] The out-migration of workers, particularly from rural areas, has been so significant that it may have contributed to lower unemployment rates in the province nearly as much as the creation of employment associated with the oil boom.[14]

The provincial government's response to the perceived labor shortage, meanwhile, has been to use federal-provincial labor-market development agreements and a provincial poverty-reduction strategy to "support" low-wage workers, reduce debts for education, and assist immigrants and disadvantaged people so

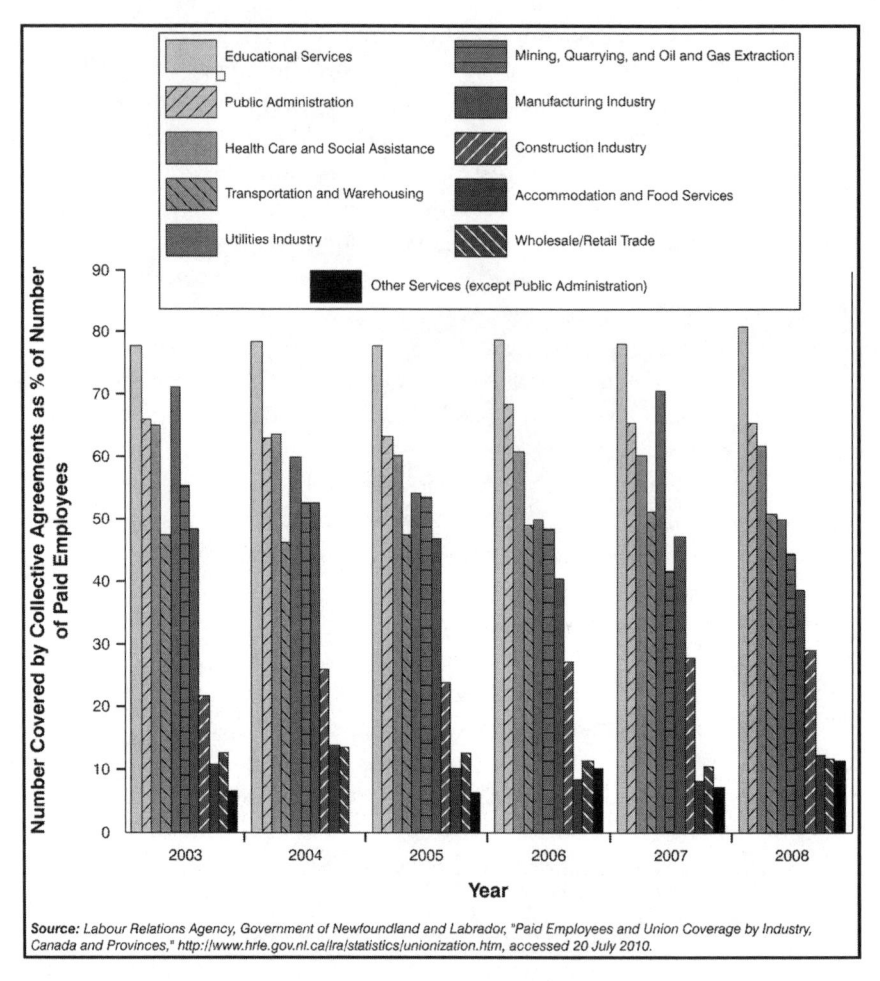

Figure 9.6: Rate of Union Coverage by Select Industries, NL, 2003-8

that they may enter the workforce.[15] These strategies indicate that, while policy makers fear the impact of skilled-labor shortages, the evidence of actual dearth appears to be mostly in the service sector. The demand for more workers in retail and wholesale, and other service areas, has continued to grow. In 2009, the Newfoundland and Labrador Employers' Council (NLEC) encouraged its members to explore recruiting temporary foreign workers and other workers from abroad to work in the province, focusing on the demand for poorly paid service-sector workers rather than better-paid skilled workers.[16]

Government and employer concerns about labor shortages have been about maintaining a reserve of cheap labor amidst the out-migration of men in skilled trades, an aging population, and the inflationary environment of the boom in the

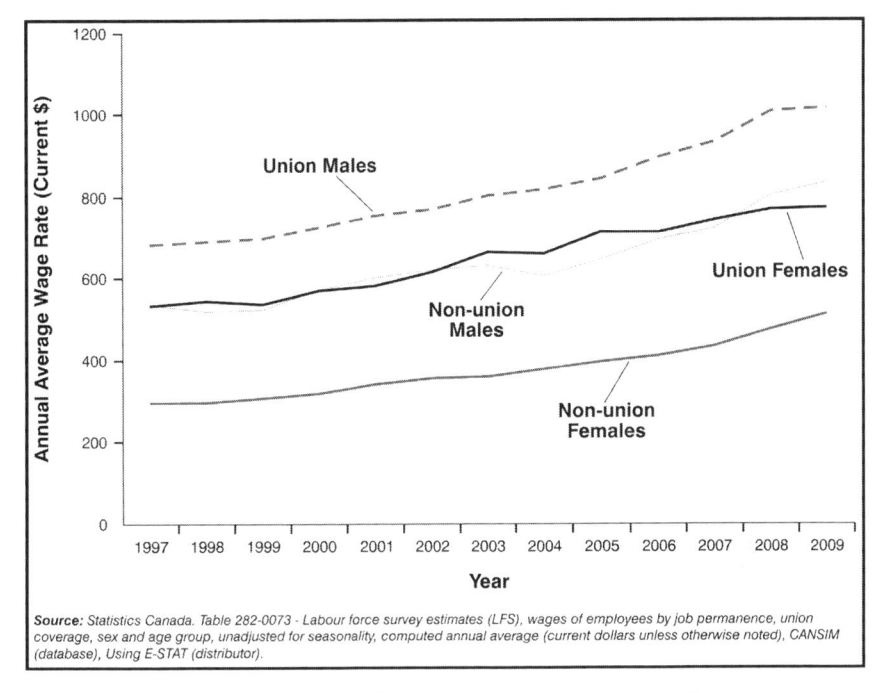

Figure 9.7: Average Weekly Wage Rate by Union Coverage, NL, 1997-2006

St. John's area and the mining centers of Labrador. Small businesses have been particularly concerned about this issue. Unlike the boom in corporate profits, which have at times escalated dramatically since 1997, small businesses have experienced very little growth in their net incomes. Needless to say, wages and other income for working people have grown slowly by comparison to corporate profits (figure 9.8). The revenue that Newfoundland and Labrador derives from the oil sector has grown substantially. This must be set against the manner in which the effective rate of taxes paid by corporations has fallen steadily by as much as two thirds during the oil boom, in large measure because of government deals with the private sector to secure resource development.[17]

The New Neoliberalism

The Newfoundland and Labrador government has aggressively pursued a climate friendly to private-sector development, although this might not be immediately apparent. Although private service-sector workers far outnumber those in public service, public-sector employment has been rising and includes more women who are disproportionately well unionized (see figure 9.9). Nevertheless, oil revenue has provided the provincial government with the means to

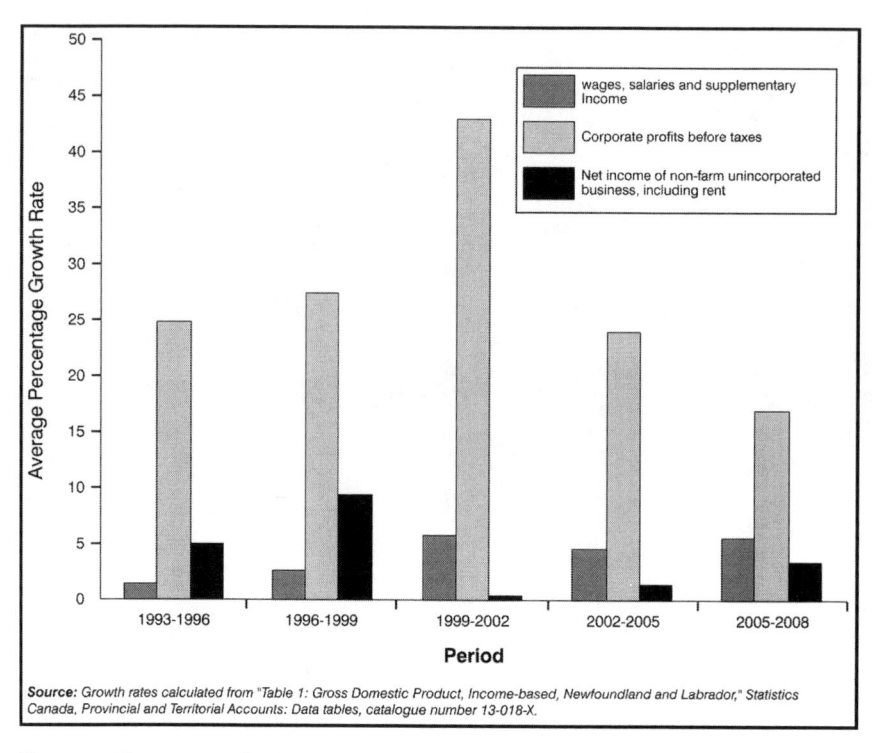

Figure 9.8: Percentage of Select Contributions to Income-Based GDP, NL, 1993-2008

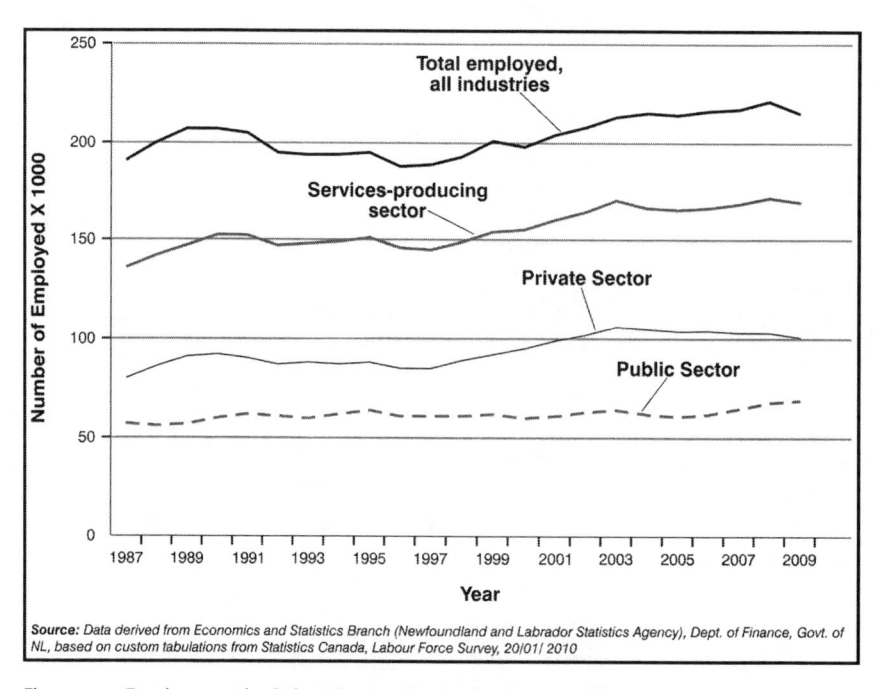

Figure 9.9: Employment by Select Service-Producing Sectors, NL, 1987-2009

add a new twist to what has been called the "assault on working people."[18] New participants in the labor market work in a climate that is hostile to organized labor. From 1979 through 2003, provincial governments engaged in a series of well-publicized battles with public-sector unions, using the declaration of more workers as providers of essential services, abrogation of existing collective agreements, back-to-work legislation, and/or imposed settlements to cut workers' benefits, worsen their working conditions, and limit their unions.[19] The assault on organized labor, in the context of a severe recession and major crisis in the province's dominant resource-sector industries, had the union movement on the ropes. There were occasional apparent victories, such as in the province's use of special orders in the Labour Relations Act (RSNL 1990, c. L-1) in 1997 to facilitate unionization of platform workers in the offshore-oil sector. However, in this case the province only accepted unions aboard the oil rigs because it felt that labor organizations were necessary to provide an orderly, safe, and stable environment for capital investment, and because interested unions accepted significant limitations on their collective-bargaining rights, particularly the right to strike in a first-contract situation, to foster industrial development. The labor movement has tried to reassert itself politically by embracing tripartism, eventually embracing a Strategic Partnership Initiative (SPI). The goal of the SPI was to promote collaboration rather than confrontation between government, business, and organized labor by focusing on strategic policy rather than collective bargaining as the way to improve society and the economy.[20]

This limited tripartism does not alter the fact that the Newfoundland and Labrador government has, since the early 1980s, embraced "lean state" tactics: retrenchment, back-to-work legislation, layoffs, wage freezes, and significant limitations on workers' right to strike. The Progressive Conservative government of Danny Williams, which came to power in 2003, continued by announcing a two-year wage freeze and job cuts early in 2004. These retrenchment measures provoked a public battle with a coalition of public-sector unions led by the Newfoundland Association of Public and Private Employees (NAPE) and the Canadian Union of Public Employees (CUPE). The unions went on strike on March 31; in April, following a series of demonstrations and bitter public exchanges, the government imposed a two-year wage freeze and then 2 and 3 percent increases per year over the next two years. The imposed settlement cut workers' sick-leave benefits by about half and promised penalties of about twenty-five thousand dollars per day for union leaders who encouraged their members to disobey the legislation and fines of $250,000 for any union that continued to strike.[21] Fred Douglas, the president of the Newfoundland and Labrador Teachers Association (NLTA), called the legislation "an affront to the generations of men and women who fought for democracy" and stated that the premier had betrayed the people of the province.[22] Earle McCurdy, the president of the Fish, Food, and Allied Workers Union, called the premier a "disgraceful dictator."[23]

At first glance, the Newfoundland and Labrador government's attack on the labor movement resembled the pervasive neoliberalism of Alberta. Since the 1980s, governments there have singlemindedly pursued a strategy for global competitiveness based on reducing social spending and state regulation of the economy and by restricting unions through amendments to labor regulations. Alberta governments have pursued retrenchment by using legislation to impose unfavorable contracts on public-sector workers. However, the difference between Alberta and Newfoundland and Labrador has been that the former's more conventional neoliberal labor policies developed during a bust in the oil sector associated with low prices in the early 1980s. In Newfoundland and Labrador, the oil sector was about to boom, and it would provide the government with the resources to pursue a different but no less neoliberal policy.[24]

At first, Williams deflected anger about his treatment of the public-sector unions by fighting with the Canadian government and oil companies. Since Newfoundland and Labrador had entered into confederation with Canada in 1949, premiers had been able to count on a good fight with Ottawa to boost their popularity.[25] In the fall of 2004, Williams had engaged in a public battle with Prime Minister Paul Martin over the federal government's clawing back of offshore oil revenue through reductions in equalization payments, which are part of a federal program for redistributing revenue from wealthier to poorer provinces. The battle was inspired; not only had Williams engaged in the classic dodge of picking a fight with Ottawa, but he also laid at the feet of Martin at least some of the responsibility for the provincial debt problems that had led to the wage freeze earlier in the year. Dave Reynolds, who had negotiated on behalf of CUPE with the provincial government during the spring, pointed out that Williams's fight with Ottawa made him unassailable at home.[26]

By 2005, the premier had transformed his image from a pugnacious opponent of public-sector unions into a scrappy little guy who was willing to take on the federal government and big oil companies.[27] The Williams government further began to court CUPE and NAPE, whose presidents had bitterly opposed the imposed settlement of 2004, by suggesting that it might loosen the public purse strings.[28] The premier extended an olive branch to the public-sector unions through inspired deviousness. Women comprised about 60 percent of the public-sector labor force in the province and therefore bore disproportionately the brunt of retrenchment. For years, public-sector unions had been fighting a 1989 decision by the provincial government to cancel a pay-equity agreement for about 5,300 women in the health-care sector to save money. In October 2004, the Supreme Court of Canada affirmed the Newfoundland and Labrador government's right to ignore such equity obligations in times of fiscal crisis. Women from the Newfoundland Labrador Federation of Labour (NLFL), NAPE, the Provincial Advisory Council on the Status of Women, and the National Action Committee on the Status of Women called on Williams to pay the approximately eighty million dollars that was due to about six thousand women in the health-care sector, arguing that equal pay for equal work is a fundamental human right for women.[29]

On March 23, 2006, Williams took many in the province by surprise through an apparently conciliatory gesture toward the labor movement when his government announced a twenty-four-million-dollar ex gratia payment to resolve the pay-equity issue.[30] The deal was a good one for the province; some estimates put the cost of making the deferred payments with compound interest much higher than eighty million dollars.[31] Although the unions were initially pleased with Williams's decision, the premier specified that the money must go to the unions to make the decisions about who got paid. This condition downloaded the cost of what Carol Furlong, the president of NAPE, called a "mammoth undertaking" onto the labor organizations. Over the next few years, NAPE and the other unions involved would have to unravel the taxation implications of the payments with the Canada Revenue Agency, establish who had a right to payments without much help from the province, sort out a formula for paying everyone fairly, and ensure that payments reflected the individual classifications of the many workers who were involved. In later commenting on the time-consuming process, Furlong remarked ruefully, "I can understand now why the premier handed it over to us."[32] Originally hoping that payments would go out in 2007, the payments did not actually take place until the end of 2008.[33] The pay-equity settlement superficially reversed a long-standing retrenchment measure, but it was fundamentally neoliberal in that the province cut much of its financial liability to working women and effectively privatized the expense of administering the settlement by downloading it onto public-sector unions.

Despite its neoliberal dimensions, the pay-equity settlement appeared to be an example of how oil-related revenue would help Newfoundlanders and Labradorians. The fight for a greater share of such revenue further helped Williams's image; his public battles with international oil companies over better royalties and an equity stake in developments such as the Hebron oil field made him a star. In January 2007, the Globe and Mail's Report on Business referred to Williams as "Danny Chavez" in an attempt to compare him to the populist-leftist Hugo Chàvez of Venezuela. Although Williams may have resented the comparison, it emphasized the premier's desire to stand up for the province's economic interests. While Prime Minister Paul Martin had agreed to a new Atlantic Accord to prevent the province from losing oil revenue to equalization clawbacks, Prime Minister Stephen Harper's decision not to honor the new provision in 2006 gave Williams another outsider to campaign against. With oil revenue and his popularity rising, the premier was able to announce in late summer 2007 that oil companies had yielded to his demands for an equity stake in the Hebron–Ben Nevis oil field and the White Rose oil field expansion. His Progressive Conservatives won the 2007 election with forty-eight out of fifty-two seats in the House of Assembly and almost 70 percent of the popular vote.[34]

The growing boom in revenue from oil and mining meant that the public-sector unions began to court the Williams government, hoping for some patronage to address their concerns. A bitter opponent of the government only three years earlier, Wayne Lucas, the president of CUPE, lauded the government's more generous 2007 budget.[35] Over the next few years, the NLFL continued to support the provincial government's labor-market-development strategies: raising the minimum wage to ten dollars per hour, the highest in the country, and investing in poverty-reduction strategies to support the entry of more people into the workforce, embracing the tripartism of the SPI.[36]

The Williams government was no less neoliberal despite spending more. For example, although his minister of fisheries, Tom Rideout, was sharply critical of Fisheries Products International's attempt to force workers at its processing plant in Marystown to accept wage rollbacks, Williams argued that workers should feel lucky to have jobs even at lower wages in such a "competitive labour market."[37] However, the premier saw the political capital in taking on a multinational corporation, particularly when it was clear that its operations in the province were likely to fold. Such was the case with the AbitibiBowater paper mill at Grand Falls–Windsor, whose forerunner, Abitibi-Consolidated Inc., had already closed a paper mill in Stephenville in 2007. In 2008, the Canadian Energy and Paperworkers Union (CEP) local that represented workers at the company's Grand Falls–Windsor mill rejected a company restructuring plan that asked for cuts in pensions and benefits in addition to layoffs. By December 2008, the company announced that it would be shutting down the plant. The province responded with legislation to take back the water, timber, and land rights that had been provided to companies since the original 1905 charter for the development of the mill.[38]

The government partially justified this expropriation by denying the legitimacy of a multinational corporation to continue to profit from provincial natural resources when it was putting so many people out of work. Appearing to be standing up for the working people of Grand Falls–Windsor and the surrounding area, the provincial government cemented a collective agreement with CUPE, one of its most vocal opponents from the 2004 public-sector strike. In 2008, the government agreed to an 8 percent wage increase for CUPE members in provincial hospitals and school boards in the first year of a four-year deal, with 4 percent raises in each of the next three years. Overall, CUPE workers would receive an approximately 20 percent wage increase over four years and a variety of other benefits. Ninety-five percent of CUPE members who voted ratified the deal. The Williams government expected it would serve as a template for other public-sector collective agreements.[39]

NAPE was unhappy with what it perceived to be concessions in the CUPE deal, especially CUPE's acceptance of the government's use of market-differential payments to recruit and/or retain workers in more remote parts of the province or in areas of skills shortages. A bitter public disagreement between the two unions saw CUPE defending the government's right to use market differentials. While NAPE maintained that the CUPE template would mean significant concessions for NAPE members, it accepted essentially the same deal in December, ratifying it in February 2009.[40] CUPE's Wayne Lucas later referred to the CUPE template as "the best collective agreement for public sector workers anywhere in the past 25 years," but it had the effect of souring the union's relations with NAPE.[41]

Premier Williams warned any other public-sector unions seeking more than the CUPE template that it might be taken off the table if the economy worsened. The NLTA had stepped into line quickly, accepting essentially the same deal as CUPE's, but the Newfoundland and Labrador Nurses Union (NLNU) did not.[42] In May 2008, the NLNU's president, Debbie Forward, had criticized the provincial budget for doing too little to encourage nursing education and recruitment in the province and recommended that the government guarantee full-time, permanent jobs to all graduating nurses.[43] The NLNU did not believe that the CUPE pay-raise template would be enough to recruit and retain nurses. Forward urged the government to negotiate on a number of issues, including a wage raise of 12 percent per year in a two-year contract that would make nursing in Newfoundland and Labrador competitive in pay with those working in the rest of Canada. However, the government would also need to provide extra funds to allow the hiring of extra support staff to fulfill the non-nursing work nurses had taken on.[44]

Angry that the NLNU was unwilling to accept the CUPE deal as a template, the new minister of finance, Jerome Kennedy, declared that the nurses had better knuckle under or face being legislated back to work under an imposed settlement. This position led one west-coast Newfoundland newspaper commentator to observe that "evidently, Premier Danny Williams wanted someone handling labour relations with the same sledgehammer approach as he does."[45] Another commentator called Kennedy's threat "a total mockery of the collective bargaining process, of pre-empting the nurses' right to strike."[46]

The cult of personality that developed around Premier Williams during the oil boom exaggerated the gendered dimensions of the boom. While the government continued to fight the NLNU—a strong union with a predominantly female membership and a forceful personality in its president, Debbie Forward—it was much more supportive of the CEP and International Brotherhood of Electrical

Workers (IBEW) locals in Grand Falls–Windsor. Both locals had predominantly male memberships made submissive and dependent by the closure of their mill. In the spring of 2009, AbitibiBowater suspended severance pay and pension benefits. With the almost adulatory praise of CUPE's Wayne Lucas, Williams stepped in, assuring the unions that his government would pay the benefits and expropriate the corporation's assets in the province as compensation. The government continued to hold out against the NLNU, forcing it to take the salary template, accept bonuses for recruitment and retention of nurses, and sacrifice an extended-losses provision that had allowed disabled nurses to receive extended disability benefits. The government had little sympathy for a strong union led by women who defied the premier, but it was prepared to be magnanimous toward the broken locals of men and their communities who supplicated for Williams's assistance against a "foreign" multinational corporation.[47]

The gendered dimensions of the Williams government's attack on collective bargaining further emerged in disputes with the Newfoundland and Labrador Medical Association (NLMA).[48] The background was a 2008 inquiry into faulty breast-cancer testing, during which a group of pathologists and oncologists threatened to resign their positions. Particularly troubling was the threat by the province's only three cervical- and ovarian-cancer specialists, all women, to resign and leave the province if something was not done.[49] The controversy was public and emotional, as many, mostly female cancer patients and their families pleaded for the premier's direct intervention on their behalf. The government moved to break the impasse by offering the pathologists and oncologists hefty pay increases, which raised their pay about 42 percent above that of other salaried specialists in the province. The premier knew that his "side deals" with the specialists would not go unnoticed by their fellow doctors, but this did not prevent him from responding personally by dispensing favors in answer to the pleas of distressed women.[50]

The NLMA rejected the "two-tier wage system that rewards oncologists and pathologists more than other salaried specialists" established by Williams in its 2009 negotiations over salaries and fees.[51] The NLMA wanted a settlement that would provide parity between provincial doctors and those in the rest of Canada and that would eliminate the disparity between those who received the side deals in 2008 and other specialists. The association also wanted resources to assist with overhead costs for specialists, allowances for rural doctors, fees for duties that were not presently covered, and shadow billing, paperwork that salaried doctors did to make their compensation comparable to fee-for-service doctors. In a vote on the government's offer during the spring of 2010, 86 percent of the 861 voting doctors rejected the government's offer of eighty-one million dollars in pay raises as insufficient, and the NLMA asked for binding arbitration.[52]

Williams was publicly unhappy that the NLMA stood up for all of its members and attempted to divide the membership by various means. The premier failed to get the NLMA to take the eighty-one million dollars and divide it among its members according to their area of specialization, a tactic much like his earlier pay-equity strategy.[53] Williams had acknowledged, in 2008, the risk of setting a precedent through his side deal with pathologists and oncologists. He began to accuse Rob Ritter, the executive director of the NLMA, of reneging on a promise in 2008 that the association would not consider the deals as precedents, a promise Ritter denied making.[54] Dismayed by the government's approach, fourteen medical specialists tendered their resignations. These specialists argued that they deserved the same pay as the oncologists and pathologists had received in 2008. On November 8, 2010, Jerome Kennedy, now health minister, released the salaries of those resigning, prompting a local newspaper to condemn the minister for his attempted public shaming of the doctors. "Perhaps the funniest part," the editorial pointed out, "is listening to Kennedy claim that the provincial government didn't cause the current fracas: apparently, it has slipped Kennedy's mind that the provincial government offered up more money for pathologists and oncologists, not once but twice, causing the differential in salaries that the specialists are now complaining about."[55]

On November 25, relations between the government and the NLMA began to thaw with Williams's announcement of his resignation. Upon hearing of the resignation, Dr. Patrick O'Shea, president of the association, suggested that Williams should go out with a settlement by providing essential-services legislation and an accompanying right to binding arbitration for doctors in exchange for their giving up the right to strike. O'Shea's offer served as the basis for a settlement in short order. The province raised its money offer by 26 percent, and the NLMA membership yielded in return their right to strike in future for binding arbitration. O'Shea noted that a key part of the deal was the ending of the "two-tier pay system" for specialists created by Williams in 2008.[56] The new premier, Kathy Dunderdale, ordered her ministers to find an end to the dispute. Thirteen of the fourteen doctors who had tendered their resignations decided to stay. A later St. John's newspaper editorial, in commenting on the better relationships between the provincial government, the NLMA, and public-sector unions, attributed previously poor relationships to Williams's personality and combative leadership style and refusal to accept the legitimacy of collective bargaining.[57] The premier was open to pleas for his paternal munificence, whether from paid-off workers or the female victims of flawed cancer testing. However, his dispensations were Williams's demonstration of his power rather than an acknowledgment of people's rights.

Conclusion

The NLMA finally got a deal, but it came out of the bargaining process bruised by the provincial government's efforts to divide its membership. While the oil boom has apparently reversed Newfoundland and Labrador's economic fortunes, revenues from offshore development have provided the government with the means to pursue a more subtle neoliberal agenda. Prior to 2005, provincial governments had engaged in a conventional assault on unions. Oil money has since allowed the government to use relatively lucrative enticements to pit unions against each other through template bargaining; to ask unions to sacrifice the entitlements of some of their members, as in the case of the NLNU; or to download the costs of administering settlements onto unions, as in the case of the pay-equity controversy.

The spleen reserved by the Williams government for the NLNU and its previous approach to pay equity suggests that gender relationships have shaped the working-class experience of the oil boom. Oil development has created a relatively small amount of direct, well-paid employment, mostly for men. Such oil-related work has been insufficient to compensate for the drastic losses in the fisheries and forestry sectors since the early 1990s. Rural Newfoundland and Labrador has benefitted little by the boom. The mining regions of Labrador have done well, as has the area around St. John's. However, most of the employment created in the latter area has been in private-sector service linkages. Jobs in such areas are generally poorly paid and nonunionized, and they are disproportionately the source of employment for women in the province. Battered by years of neoliberal attacks, lulled by the recent headiness of oil revenues, and lured by tripartism, the union movement has not confronted the limitations of the boom, which continues to be a bust for many working people.

Notes

1. This essay is a synthesis of research I have completed for two other publications: "Boom, Bust, and Bluster: Newfoundland and Labrador's 'Oil Boom' and Its Impacts on Labour," in *Boom, Bust, and Crisis: Labour, Corporate Power, and Politics in Canada*, ed. John Peters (Halifax: Fernwood Publishing, 2012), 68–83; and "Newfoundland and Labrador, 1979–2010: Contradiction, Continuity, and Oil Windfalls in the Neoliberal Assault on Labour," in *The End of Expansion? The Political Economy of Canada's Provinces and Territories in a Neoliberal Era*, ed. Bryan Evans and Charles Smith (Toronto: University of Toronto Press, forthcoming).

2. Rob Antle, "Equalization: Have Not No More," *St. John's Telegram*, 4 November 2008, A1.

3. The preceding paragraphs are based on Sean T. Cadigan, *Newfoundland and Labrador: A History* (Toronto: University of Toronto Press, 2009).

4. Tara Brautigam, "Province Braces for Prosperous Future—And Its Consequences," *Corner Brook Western Star,* 28 December 2007, 1; NL, *The Economic Review, 2009* (St. John's: Government of Newfoundland and Labrador, 2009), 7.

5. On Alberta, see Peter J. Smith, "Experiments in Governance—From Social Credit to the Klein Revolution," in *The Provincial State in Canada,* ed. Keith Brownsey and Michael Howltt (Peterborough, Ont.: Broadview, 2001), 277–308. On Alaska, see Joseph G. Jongensen, *Oil Age Eskimos* (Berkeley: University of California Press, 1990); and John Stohmeyer, *Extreme Conditions: Big Oil and the Transformation of Alaska* (New York: Simon and Schuster, 1993). The extent to which aboriginal peoples have been involved in the Alaskan oil industry suggests that caution must be used in comparing Alaska to Newfoundland. The more appropriate comparison would be to Labrador, where the Innu and Inuit peoples have played a vital role in the development of nickel mining and more recent discussions about new hydro development. However, recent analysis suggests that Labradorians have not enjoyed the same increases in living standards, no matter how otherwise flawed, that have occurred in Alaska. See Gérard Duhaime and Andrée Caron, "Economic and Social Conditions of Arctic Regions," in *The Economy of the North 2008,* ed. Solveig Glomsrød and Iulie Aslaksen (Oslo: Statistics Norway 2009), 11–23.

6. Community Resource Services Ltd., *Socio-Economic Benefits from Petroleum Industry Activity in Newfoundland and Labrador* (St. John's: Petroleum Research Atlantic Canada, 2003), 14, 20; Cadigan, "Boom, Bust and Bluster."

7. Sean T. Cadigan, "The Moral Economy of Retrenchment and Regeneration in the History of Rural Newfoundland," in *Retrenchment and Regeneration in Rural Newfoundland,* ed. Reginald Byron (Toronto: University of Toronto Press, 2002), 14–42; Barbara Neis and Rob Kean, "Why Fish Stocks Collapse: An Interdisciplinary Approach to the Problem of 'Fishing Up,'" in *Retrenchment and Regeneration in Rural Newfoundland,* ed. Reginald Byron (Toronto: University of Toronto Press, 2002), 14–42; Rosemary E. Ommer with the Coasts under Stress Research Project Team, *Coasts under Stress: Restructuring and Social-Ecological Health* (Montreal: McGill–Queen's University Press, 2007), 68–93. On recent neoliberal fisheries management, see Dean Bavington, *Managed Annihilation: An Unnatural History of the Newfoundland Cod Collapse* (Vancouver: University of British Columbia Press, 2010), 40–44, 79–80. On forestry, see Glen Norcliffe, *Global Game, Local Arena: Restructuring in Corner Brook* (St. John's: Institute of Social and Economic Research, 2005); Ommer, *Coasts under Stress,* 104–10. Peter R. Sinclair, Martha MacDonald, and Barbara Neis, "The Changing World of Andy Gibson: Restructuring Forestry on Newfoundland's Great Northern Peninsula," *Studies in Political Economy* 78 (2006): 177–99.

8. William E. Schrank, "The Newfoundland Fishery: Ten Years after the Moratorium," *Marine Policy* 29 (2005): 407–20.

9. For more specific assessments of the offshore sector's direct and indirect impacts on overall areas such as GDP and income, see Community Resource Services, *Socio-Economic Benefits*; Jacques Whitford, "Socio-Economic Benefits from Petroleum Industry Activity in Newfoundland and Labrador 2003 and 2004" (St. John's: Petroleum Research Atlantic Canada, 2005); Stantec, "Socio-Economic Benefits from Petroleum

Industry Activity in Newfoundland and Labrador, 2005-2007" (St. John's: Petroleum Research Atlantic Canada, 2009).

10. Alaska Department of Labor and Workforce Development, Division of Employment Security, "Finding Work in Alaska," accessed 10 July 2013, http://www.labor.state.ak.us/esd_alaska_jobs/ak_over.htm; Smith, "Experiments in Governance," 286-308.

11. *The Economic Review, 2008* (St. John's: Government of Newfoundland and Labrador, 2008), 3-4, 39. The provincial minimum wage in 2008 was eight dollars per hour, but it has since risen to ten dollars per hour, one of the highest in Canada.

12. Mark Shrimpton and Keith Storey, *The Effect of Offshore Employment in the Petroleum Industry: A Cross-National Perspective* (Herndon, Va.: U.S. Department of the Interior, Minerals Management Service, Environmental Studies Program, 2001), 6-7; Statistics Canada, Table 282-0008: Labour Force Survey Estimates (LFS), by North American Industry Classification System (NAICS), sex and age group, computed annual average (persons x 1,000).

13. "Hebron Offshore Deal Worth 3,500 Jobs, $20 Billion; Williams: 'Bold Steps' for N.L.," *Halifax Chronicle-Herald*, 21 August 2008, A1; Peter Walsh, "Inco Worried about Labour Crunch; Tight Labour Market Trumps Economic Crisis during Inco Update," *St. John's Telegram*, 1 November 2008, C2.

14. *The Economic Review, 2005* (St. John's: Government of Newfoundland and Labrador, 2005), 3-4; Alisha Morrissey, "Fault-Line Job Market: Province's Job Market Mediocre: Economist," *St. John's Telegram*, 12 July 2006, A1; Aaron Beswick, "Employers Hiring Intentions Up from Last Year," *St. John's Telegram*, 15 March 2006, D1; "Newfoundland Workers Help Ease Alberta Labour Crunch: Atlantic Migration Up 300 Percent," *Channel-Port Aux Basques Gulf News*, 10 July 2006, A8; *The Economic Review, 2007* (St. John's: Government of Newfoundland and Labrador, 2007), 4-5. The phenomenon of such work-related mobility is only beginning to receive serious scrutiny in Canada. See, for example, Julia Temple Newhook et al., "Employment-Related Mobility and the Health of Workers, Families, and Communities: The Canadian Context," *Labour/Le Travail* 67 (Spring 2011): 121-56.

15. "Agreements Aimed at Preparing People for Future Jobs," *St. Anthony Northern Pen*, 15 September 2008, B7; "Province Gearing Up to Enhance Labour Market," *St. Anthony Northern Pen*, 10 August 2009, B3; Nancy Kelly, "Danny Williams Hopes to Lead Country in Labour Force Participation," *Corner Brook Western Star*, 24 June 2009, 11.

16. Dave Bartlett, "Immigrants Could Help Fill Voids in Labour Market: Employers Council," *Corner Brook Western Star*, 10 March 2009, 15; Everton McLean, "Looking to Foreign Shores: Enticing Immigrant Workers Part of Dealing with Labour Shortage: NLEC," *St. John's Telegram*, 12 March 2009, D1.

17. Jim Stanford has made a similar point in "Does Growth Matter? GDP and the Well-Being of Newfoundlanders," presentation to the Newfoundland and Labrador Federation of Labour Convention, Gander, October 2003.

18. Thom Workman, *If You're in My Way, I'm Walking: The Assault on Working People since 1970* (Halifax: Fernwood, 2009), 23; see also Thom Workman, *Social Torment: Globalization in Atlantic Canada* (Halifax: Fernwood, 2003), 29-54. On Canadian trends, see Stephen McBride, "Domestic Neo-liberalism," in *Working in a Global Era: Cana-*

dian Perspectives, ed. Vivian Shalla (Toronto: Canadian Scholars' Press, 2006), 257–77. The term "assault" in this context has been most prominently used by Leo Panitch and Donald Swartz, *From Consent to Coercion: The Assault on Trade Union Freedoms,* 3d ed. (Aurora, Ont.: Garamond Press, 2003).

19. Much of the discussion for this paragraph was originally developed in Cadigan, *Newfoundland and Labrador,* 271–81.

20. The recommendations for the SPI came from a study group composed of the Newfoundland and Labrador Federation of Labour, the St. John's Board of Trade, the Newfoundland and Labrador Chamber of Commerce, the Newfoundland and Labrador Employer's Council, and the provincial Department of Industry, Trade, and Rural Development. See Strategic Partnership Study Group, *Strategic Partnership: How Business, Labour, and Government Collaborate to Produce Europe's High Performance Economies* (St. John's: Strategic Partnership Study Group, 2002), 53–54, accessed 18 April 2008, http://www.nlfl.nf.ca/Campaigns/StrategicPartnership.aspx.

21. Terry Roberts, "Back-to-Work Order Imminent: Unions: Premier Conniving to Force End to Walkout, Puddister Claims," *St. John's Telegram,* 11 April 2004, A1; "Back-to-Work Bill Tabled; Legislation Expected to Pass This Week; Stiff Penalties Await Any of 20,000 Newfoundland Civil Servants Who Defy It," *Halifax Chronicle-Herald,* 27 April 2004, A3.

22. Lydia Zajc, "Nfld. Tables Back-to-Work Bill for Thousands of Public Servants," Canadian Press, National News, 26 April 2004, 21:43 EST.

23. Barb Sweet, "Premier Dubbed 'Disgraceful Dictator' Because of Back-to-Work Legislation," *Corner Brook Western Star,* 27 April 2004, 3.

24. Smith, "Experiments in Governance," 286–308; Panitch and Swartz, *From Consent to Coercion,* 110–13, 199–200; Tom Fuller and Patricia Hughes-Fuller, "'Exceptional Measures': Public Sector Relations in Alberta," in *The Return of the Trojan Horse: Alberta and the New World (Dis)Order,* ed. Trevor W. Harrison (Montreal: Black Rose Books, 2005), 313–27.

25. Sean T. Cadigan, "Regional Politics Are Class Politics: A Newfoundland and Labrador Perspective on Regions," *Acadiensis* 35.2 (2006): 163–68.

26. Norma Greenaway, "Newfoundlanders Throw Support Behind 'Danny Millions,'" *Corner Brook Western Star,* 11 November 2004, 8.

27. CBC Television, "The National," 31 January 2005, 22:00 EST.

28. Gary Kean, "New Leadership Opens Door for Partnership: Premier," *St. John's Telegram,* 28 May 2005, A6.

29. Sheree Juneja, "Women Hit Hardest by Freeze," *St. John's Telegram,* 13 March 2004, A10; "Budgets Are Questions Best Left to Governments: Supreme Court," *Corner Brook Western Star,* 13 May 2004, 4; "Coalition Vows to Fight Pay-Equity Decision," *St. John's Telegram,* 10 December 2004, A4; Jean Edwards Stacey, "Unions Launch Petition, Urge Premier to 'Do the Right Thing' on Pay Equity," *St. John's Telegram,* 9 March 2005, A4. The considerable impediments grounded in prevailing class and gender relationships in the labor-relations system in working out pay equity are explored in Susan M. Hart, "The Pay Equity Bargaining Process in Newfoundland: Understanding Cooperation and Conflict by Incorporating Gender and Class," *Gender, Work, and Organization* 9.4

(2002): 355–71. On the broader significance of the pay-equity controversy, see Judy Fudge, "Substantive Equality, the Supreme Court of Canada, and the Limits to Redistribution," *South African Journal of Human Rights* 23.2 (2007): 235–52.

30. Jamie Baker and Tara Bradbury Mullowney, "Williams Corrects 'Black Mark' on Province with $24-Million Pay Equity Payment," *Corner Brook Western Star*, 24 March 2006, 1.

31. "Pay Equity: Co-ordinator Believes Unions Should Have Held Out for a Better Deal," *Labrador City Aurora*, 3 March 2006, 2.

32. "Health-Care Workers Face Wait for Pay-equity Funds," CBC Newfoundland and Labrador, 4 July 2006, accessed 7 July 2011, http://www.cbc.ca/news/canada/newfoundland-labrador/story/2006/07/04/pay-equity.html?ref=rss.

33. "Unions Struggle to Get Pay Equity Money," *Corner Brook Western Star*, 1 November 2006, 2; "NAPE Pay-Equity Cheques Go Out," *St. John's Telegram*, 16 December 2008, A3.

34. Alex Marland, "The 2007 Provincial Election in Newfoundland and Labrador," *Canadian Political Science Review* 1.2 (2007): 75–85; Alex Marland, "Masters of Our Own Destiny: The Nationalist Evolution of Newfoundland Premier Danny Williams," *International Journal of Canadian Studies* 42 (2010): 155–81.

35. "Things Are Looking Up, Union Leader Says," *St. John's Telegram*, 1 September 2007, A5.

36. The SPI has evolved into a full government agency and serves as a discussion group for the labor movement, employers, and the government "to discuss human resource issues." The quote is from Reg Anstey's farewell speech as the president of the NLFL in 2008. *Gander Beacon*, 13 November 2008, A5. Officially the Labour Market Sub-Committee of the Strategic Partnership Initiative (SPI), the agency's Web site is http://www.labourmarketcommittee.ca/index.htm (accessed 26 April 2011). On the long-term pattern of unions' relationships with the provincial political parties, see Larry Savage, "Contemporary Party-Union Relations in Canada," *Labor Studies Journal* 35.1 (2010): 8–26.

37. Craig Jackson, "Fish Plant Worker 'Disgusted' by Premier's Comments," *Corner Brook Western Star*, 13 September 2006, 3.

38. Terry Roberts and James McLeod, "Government Stripping AbitibiBowater: Legislation Repatriates Company's Land and Water Rights and Expropriates Hydro-generating Stations," *St. John's Telegram*, 3 December 2010, D8 (reprint of an article that originally appeared 17 December 2008).

39. "CUPE Deal Will Be Template for Other Unions: Williams," CBC Newfoundland and Labrador, 25 April 2008, accessed 6 June 2011, http://www.cbc.ca/news/canada/newfoundland-labrador/story/2008/04/25/williams-cupe.html; "CUPE Releases Details of Deal with Williams government," 22 May 2008, accessed 8 June 2011, http://cupe.ca/Newfoundland/CUPE_releases_detail.

40. "CUPE Deal Doesn't Sit Well with NAPE," CBC Web site, 4 November 2008, accessed 10 July 2013, http://www.cbc.ca/news/canada/newfoundland-labrador/story/2008/11/04/nape-cupe.html; "War of Words Erupts between NAPE, CUPE," CBC Web site, 5 November 2008, accessed 10 July 2013, http://www.cbc.ca/news/canada/newfoundland-labrador/

story/2008/11/05/nape-cupe.html; Wayne Lucas, "Here's Why CUPE Signed," *St. John's Telegram,* 20 December 2008, A22; "NAPE Reaches Tentative Agreements for 11 Units," 24 December 2008, National Union of Public and General Employees (NUPGE) Web site, accessed 8 June 2011, http://www.nupge.ca/news_2008/n24de08a.htm; "NAPE Members Vote to Accept Tentative Agreements," NUPGE Web site, accessed 8 June 2011, http://www.nupge.ca/node/2006.

41. Steve Bartlett, "Williams' Support and Success Widely Recognized," *St. John's Telegram,* 26 November 2010, A1.

42. "Newfoundland Premier Warns Unions against Asking for Too Much," Canadian Press, 19 October 2008, 19:50 EST; "Williams Issues Warning to Unions as Economy Worsens," CBC Newfoundland and Labrador, 25 November 2008, accessed 6 June 2011, http://www.cbc.ca/news/canada/newfoundland-labrador/story/2008/11/25/williams-economy.html; Nadya Bell, "NLTA Reaches Agreement with Province; Kennedy Says NAPE Discussions Going Well, Not Talking to Nurses," *St. John's Telegram,* 16 December 2008, A3.

43. Peter Walsh, "Nurses, Minister Feud: Health Minister Strikes Back at Nurses' Union," *St. John's Telegram,* 2 May 2008, A3.

44. Clayton Hunt, "Nurses Want Conciliation," *Lewisporte Pilot,* 14 May 2008, A5.

45. "Pushing for All It's Worth," *Corner Brook Western Star,* 28 January 2009, 6.

46. Bob Wakeham, "Shabby Treatment of Nurses Is Indefensible," *St. John's Telegram,* 31 January 2009, A21.

47. Moira Baird, "CUPE Asks Government to Pay Mill Workers: Says Money Can Be Taken from Abitibi Expropriation Funds," *Corner Brook Western Star,* 5 May 2009, 18; Moira Baird, "Formal Notice: Premier Says Province Will Make Sure Abitibi Workers Get Their Severance," *St. John's Telegram,* 18 April 2009, C1; Dave Bartlett, "Timing of Announcement Political: Opposition. Help for Former Abitibi Workers Announced on Eve of Nurses' Strike," *St. John's Telegram,* 20 May 2009, D1; Sue Hickey, "Province Paying Severance for Abitibi Workers: Silviculturalists, Loggers, Some Retirees Included in Plan," *Grand Falls–Windsor Advertiser,* 21 May 2009, A1. The federal government eventually agreed to pay AbitibiBowater a $130-million settlement to end a NAFTA challenge of the expropriation. See Krysta Colbourne and David Newell, "All Hands Pleased with Settlement," *St. John's Telegram,* 31 August 2010, D1; Everton Mclean, "'He Will Lose': Government's Stance 'Will Destroy Health Care,' Nurses' Union President Says," *St. John's Telegram,* 10 May 2009, A1; "Kennedy Questions Rank-and-File Nurses' Commitment to Strike," CBC Newfoundland and Labrador, 11 May 2009, accessed 6 June 2011, http://www.cbc.ca/news/health/story/2009/05/11/kennedy-nurses-vote-511.html?ref=rss; "All-Nighter Yields Last-Minute Deal in N.L. Nurses Dispute," CBC News, 20 May 2009, accessed 6 June 2011, http://www.cbc.ca/news/canada/newfoundland-labrador/story/2009/05/20/tentative-nurses-deal-520.html.

48. While unions in Newfoundland and Labrador generally bargain on behalf of their members under the legal authority of the Newfoundland and Labrador Labour Relations Act (RSNL 1990, chapter L-1), the NLMA bargains collectively for physicians under the authority of the Medical Act, 2011 (SNL 2011 chapter M-4.02, s. 5) and the Corporations Act (RSNL 1990 chapter C-36).

49. "Newfoundland Oncologists Threaten to Leave Province," CTV Canada AM, 1 August 2008, 07:12:15 ET.

50. Dave Bartlett, "Deals for Doctors a Sign of What's to Come," *Corner Brook Western Star,* 29 September 2008, 1; Sue Bailey, "Doctors vs. the Newfoundland Government: Dispute over Pay, Workload Gets Nastier," Canadian Press, 10 November 2010.

51. Sue Bailey, "Newfoundland Government Says Doctors Deal within Reach Despite Rejected Offer," Canadian Press, 15 December 2010.

52. Barb Sweet, "Doctors Go Public with Contract Proposals," *St. John's Telegram,* 24 March 2010, A1; "NLMA Waiting on Government Response for Next Move: Government Says More Doctors Working in Province Than Ever Before," *St. John's Telegram,* 30 April 2010, A2.

53. "N.L. Pitting MDs against Each Other: Doctors," CBC News, 15 November 2010, accessed 6 June 2011, http://www.cbc.ca/news/canada/newfoundland-labrador/story/2010/11/15/nl-offer-divisive-1115.html.

54. Steve Bartlett, "'Things Are Getting Out of Hand': Premier Concerned by Doctors' Rhetoric," *St. John's Telegram,* 18 November 2010, A1.

55. "Picking Battles," *St. John's Telegram,* 10 November 2010, A6.

56. "Doctors Reach Tentative N.L. Contract Deal," CBC Newfoundland and Labrador, 16 December 2010, accessed 6 June 2011, http://www.cbc.ca/news/health/story/2010/12/16/nl-doctors-deal-1216.html. See also Deana Stokes Sullivan, "Essential Service Legislation for Doctors? NLMA Head Suggests Binding Arbitration Entrenched in Law Could Resolve Dispute," *St. John's Telegram,* 27 November 2010, A1.

57. "State of the Unions," *St. John's Telegram,* 10 December 2010, A6.

10

Whose Hard Times?
Explaining Autoworkers Strike Waves in Recent-Day China

LU ZHANG

In contrast to the generally passive responses of organized labor in the West to the 2008 global economic crisis, China has witnessed a major wave of labor unrest in the forms of wildcat strikes, legal disputes, protests, and demonstrations.[1] A showcase of this autonomous worker insurgency was a wave of auto-manufacturing strikes that rocked China in the summer of 2010.[2] The historic events unfolded when a nineteen-day strike at Honda Auto Parts Manufacturing Co. Ltd. (a transmission plant that provides 80 percent of automatic transmissions for Honda's assembly plants in China) in Foshan, Guangdong Province, shut down the Japanese automaker's four assembly plants and brought Honda production in China to a dead halt. At the peak of the strike, over 1,800 striking workers, mostly young migrant workers and student intern workers, walked out, demanding not only a significant pay increase but also the ability to elect their own union officials at the factory union branch of the All-China Federation of Trade Unions (ACFTU), the only legal trade union in China.[3]

The Honda strike received extensive media coverage within and outside China.[4] Interestingly, the domestic publicity suggests a level of tacit support by the Chinese central government for the striking workers' demands for a wage increase. Indeed, against the backdrop of the central government's policy shift from an export-led growth model based on cheap labor to a more balanced one based on domestic consumption (and thereby higher wages), the success of the autoworkers strikes in winning concessions from employers inspired a strike wave across sectors and regions, pushing a rapid trend toward wage increases as more Chinese workers seek higher wages and better working conditions through concerted collective action.

There is no doubt that the Chinese automobile industry has grown dramatically over the past fifteen years: annual output increased more than twelve times, from 1.5 million to 18.3 million vehicles between 1996 and 2010, making China the number-one automobile-producing nation in the world, accounting for 23.5 percent of the total global automobile production in 2010. The startling growth in production has gone hand in hand with rapid expansion of China's domestic auto markets. By 2009, China became the world's largest auto market with over 31.6 million vehicles sold in 2009 and 2010.[5]

Why is labor unrest arising in the Chinese automobile industry at a time when the industry is burgeoning, as China becomes the new epicenter of global automobile production and consumption? How will the recent labor upheavals in the Chinese auto industry unfold? And what forces and mechanics are in play? To address these questions, this study carries out an in-depth analysis of the transformation of China's automobile industry and its labor force over the past two decades, with particular attention on how shop-floor, national, and global processes interact in complex ways to produce the specific industrial relations and dynamics of labor unrest in the Chinese automobile industry. The data for this essay draws on twenty months of field research at seven major automobile-assembly factories in six Chinese cities between 2004 and 2009.[6]

The central argument is that the massive foreign investment in China's auto sector through joint ventures and the increased scale and concentration of automobile production have created and strengthened a new generation of autoworkers with growing workplace bargaining power and grievances. However, industrial dynamics, national institutions, and socialist legacies also matter. On the one hand, China entered the global competition in the mass production of automobiles at a late stage in the "product cycle" and therefore faces a more acute profitability pressure, when profit margins have become much thinner.[7] On the other hand, I contend that the pressure for the state to maintain legitimacy with labor is particularly acute in countries with mass revolutionary and socialist legacies like China. As one of China's pillar industries with strong state intervention, the more acute contradictory pressures of simultaneously

Table 10.1 Automobile Enterprises Included in Case Study (2006)

Name	# of Formal Employees	Sales (1000 unit)	Sale Ranking	Main Product	Ownership Type	Found Year	Location (Province)
USA-1	6,569	413	1	Passenger Car	Sino-USA	1997	Shanghai
GER-1	12,531	352	2	Passenger Car	Sino-German	1985	Shanghai
GER-2	9,284	350	3	Passenger Car	Sino-German	1991	Jilin
SOE-1	13,100	300	4	Passenger Car	State-owned	1997	Anhui
SOE-2	3,049	70	N/A	Truck	State-owned	1993	Shandong
JAP-1	5,600	260	6	Passenger Car	Sino-Japanese	1998	Guangdong
USA-2	3,096	87	N/A	Passenger Car	Sino-USA	2003	Shandong

Sources: CATRC, 2006, 2007. Number of employees and sales data in 2006 were collected and compiled by the author between December 2006 and June 2007.

pursuing profitability and maintaining legitimacy with labor have driven large state-owned automakers and Sino-foreign joint ventures to follow a policy of labor force dualism, drawing boundaries between formal and temporary workers. While formal workers enjoy high wages, generous benefits, and relatively secure employment, temporary workers suffer comparatively low wages, unsecure employment, and heavier and dirtier job assignments.

Yet, the system carries notable unintended consequences. On the one hand, labor force dualism has detached formal workers from temporary workers and has kept the former relatively quiet so far, despite their serious and growing grievances. On the other hand, a new generation of temporary agency workers has been radicalized and actively protests against unequal treatment in the workplace. The managerial construction of this labor force dualism means that the main source of militancy in the Chinese auto industry resides not among formal workers who have more job security and relatively higher wages (by far) but among the temporary workers as well as auto-part workers deficient in both. I argue that the directions and outcomes of this labor force dualism, underpinned by a more acute tension between maintaining legitimacy and increasing profitability at the factory and the national level, is key to understanding the dynamics of labor unrest in the Chinese automobile industry.

Industrial Restructuring and Workforce Transformation

As one of the country's "pillar industries,"[8] the fast expansion of the automobile industry in the reform era can be characterized as a state-led "triple alliance"[9] through the establishment of centrally sanctioned joint ventures (JVs) between multinationals and large state-owned auto groups. By the early 2000s, all the world's major automakers had built JVs with one or two Chinese partners to make and sell vehicles in China. Joint ventures have had a major impact on the organization of production by importing advanced machinery and technology, global standards, as well as Taylorist and lean-production practices to maximize profits.

Meanwhile, the Chinese government's use of foreign direct investment in the auto sector was prudent: the creation of new assembly JVs must get approved by the central government, and foreign automakers are not allowed to build wholly owned assembly plants or own a majority stake in assembly JVs. Moreover, by controlling personnel decisions of senior (Chinese) management through the cadre-manager personnel system at the joint ventures, the central government makes sure that those JVs carry out the economic, political, and social agenda concordant with the goals of the party-state. Given the interventionist role of the state in the auto-assembly sector, it is no coincidence to find the resilience of some characteristics commonly associated with state-owned enterprises (SOEs) at China's leading auto JVs. Indeed, until the mid-1990s, the auto-assembly sector was still a centrally controlled monopoly sector dominated by a few preselected JVs. Those JVs were able to enjoy extremely high profits thanks to the government protection, with strict licensing requirements and heavy tariffs (ranging from 80 to 100 percent) on imported vehicles and components.[10] High-level profitability allowed large auto JVs and their state-owned Chinese partners to provide their workers with high wages, generous benefits, and guaranteed employment typically seen at large work units (*danwei*) with government protection.[11]

Since the mid-1990s, however, the broader structural change in the Chinese system—including the deepening of SOE and labor reforms in the urban areas and the government industrial-policy change to prepare the automobile industry to meet the challenge of China's World Trade Organization (WTO) accession—led to a large-scale restructuring of inefficient state-owned enterprises and layoffs in the auto-assembly sector. The 1994 automotive industrial policy called for the consolidation and rationalization of the auto-assembly sectors through mergers and reorganization (*jianbing chongzu*) with "large ones taking over smaller ones." Between 1994 and 2000, the major domestic auto groups carried out a series of enterprise restructuring and downsizing to bring labor productivity in line with the standards set by "international market rule."[12] More dramatic restructuring came along with growing competition. The loosening of entry barriers in the Chinese auto sector under the WTO agreement and the fast-growing domestic private auto markets invited another wave of foreign and domestic investment and new entrants in the auto-assembly sector. It was estimated that the average profit margin of a Chinese car maker dropped from about 12 to 14 percent in 2000 to merely 6 to 8 percent by 2007. For low-end car makers, their average profit margins were merely 2.5 to 4 percent.[13]

To cope with the tougher new environment, the major Chinese automakers quickly moved toward a leaner and meaner workplace. In organization of production, they generally combined lean production and Fordist/Taylorist mass-production techniques, while exploiting China's labor-cost advantage by employing a large number of semiskilled young workers in two or three shifts nonstop on assembly lines. In labor and employment practice, they reduced job security and sought more flexibility in hiring and firing.

The results of the industrial restructuring were impressive. The total output increased from 1.4 million vehicles in 1994 to 7.3 million vehicles in 2006. Meanwhile, the total numbers of employees declined from almost 2 million in 1994 to 1.5 million in 2001, and only slightly increased to 1.65 million in 2006 (see figure 10.1). Unlike other global examples of rapid expansion within the automobile industry accompanied by an equally rapid growth in the number of employees,[14] the full takeoff of the Chinese automobile industry was a simul-

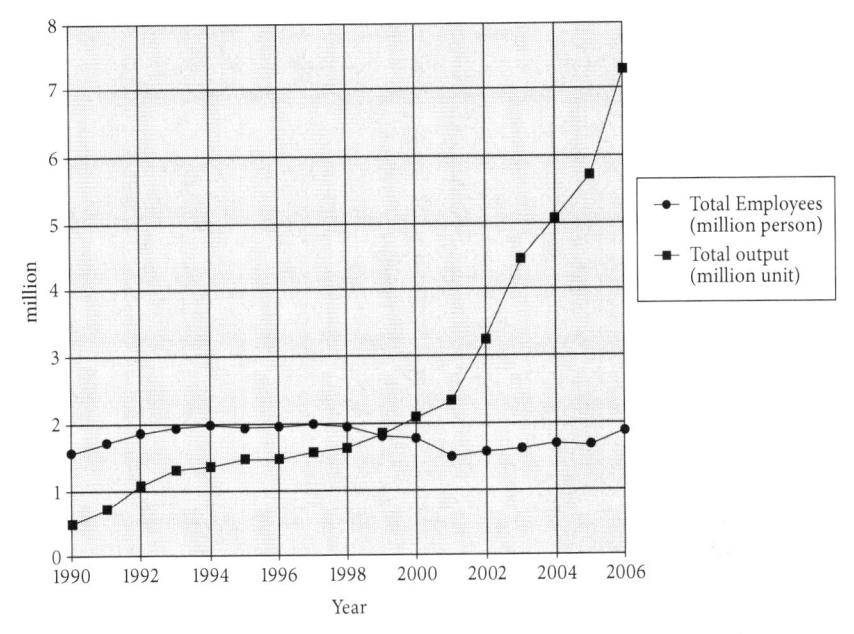

Figure 10.1: Annual Output and Number of Employees in China's Automobile Industry (1990–2006)

taneous process of weeding out inefficient SOEs and the unmaking of the old generation of state workers, along with the expansion of Sino-foreign JVs and the making of a new generation of industrial workers.[15] As a result, although the numerical change of employment in the automobile industry was not that dramatic, the composition of the workforce was almost completely transformed after the restructuring.

The Transformation of the Production Workforce and the Expansion of Labor Force Dualism

The transformation of the production workforce in the Chinese automobile industry involved two processes: the replacement of permanent, long-term state workers with "new" urban-bred, young formal contract workers under short-term (renewable) labor contracts; and the introduction of labor force dualism by tapping a large number of rural and urban youths as temporary workers through labor-hiring agencies.

The replacement of permanent state workers was carried out relatively smoothly through early retirement, reassignment, and buyouts and did not cause overt labor unrest. My fieldwork suggested that three main factors explained the relatively smooth downsizing in the auto-sector restructuring. First, most state-owned automobile assemblers had substantial financial and organizational resources accumulated in the pre-reform era, which allowed them to pay the redundant workers more generous early retirement benefits and severance compensation, or to transfer some of the redundant workers to other (less well-paid) jobs in service firms spun off from the main enterprise, thus softening the direct blow of downsizing. Second, at many state-owned enterprises, management relied on the trade union and party factory committee,[16] which in turn relied on the accumulated goodwill and political commitment of older workers, to convince those who were to become redundant that the reform was in the collective interest, and that they should therefore step aside without making a major fuss. Third, the central and local governments were more interventionist in monitoring the restructuring process at large automobile SOEs and JVs. When restructuring was proposed through setting up new JVs, there were often requirements for the new JVs to absorb redundant workers from their Chinese partners. At the same time, China's leading automakers, especially those newly built joint ventures, have kept on hiring new workers directly from technical schools with short-term renewable labor contracts. The replacement of veteran workers with young, short-term formal contract workers led to a dramatic drop in the average age and seniority of formal production workforce.

The second important aspect of workforce restructuring was the introduction of labor force dualism by using a large number of temporary workers alongside formal contract workers on production lines. Formal contract workers enjoyed high wages, generous benefits, and more secure employment under renewable labor contracts. By contrast, temporary workers were paid one half to two thirds of the wages of formal contract workers for the same or similar work, with few benefits and little job security. Among the seven major automobile factories studied, six adopted labor force dualism, with a large number of temporary workers ranging between one third and two thirds of the total production workforce.

The main reasons for using temporary workers, according to the interviewed managers, were to contain labor costs and increase labor flexibility. The human-resource managers at GER-1 and GER-2 estimated that for the cost of hiring a formal contract worker, adding all the social insurances and benefits together, they could hire at least three or four temporary workers. Management desire for increasing staff flexibility was emphasized more by the longer-established automakers who had a large number of permanent or long-term formal employees.

But unlike the conventional core-periphery model or the "flexible firm" formula, under which segmentation between the core and periphery workers corresponds to functional and numerical flexibilities, the Chinese automakers deployed both formal and temporary workers on assembly lines performing identical tasks while subjecting them to different treatment.[17] Why would automakers keep a segment of more expensive and privileged formal workers whose jobs could be done by temporary workers?

My interviews with managers indicated that another implicit motivation for adopting labor force dualism was to use temporary workers as a buffer to maintain a peaceful and committed formal workforce. As a manager at GER-1 frankly admitted, the company would rather use frequently rotated agency workers to gain flexibility than deal with the trouble of laying off their own formal contract workers. In his opinion, layoffs of the company's own formal employees could "harm the harmonious labor relations and the good publicity of the company as one of China's 'most-respected' joint ventures."[18] This could also explain why the greenfield automakers did not bother to use labor force dualism initially. Without the burden of a large number of veteran state workers, they could simply recruit young workers directly from China's abundant vocational schools with short-term renewable labor contracts. As they became "mature" and had more veteran workers, however, some of the "greenfield" factories (e.g., USA-1 and USA-2) also adopted labor force dualism.

Social Composition of the New Generation of Chinese Autoworkers

After restructuring, production workers accounted for 60 to 80 percent of the total formal contract employees. The remaining were white-collar managerial and technical staff.[19] Among the formal production workers, except for a small portion of skilled veteran workers (most in their thirties and forties) with long-term labor contracts, the majority were semiskilled/unskilled, urban-bred youths in their early twenties with one- to two-year renewable labor contracts. Newly hired formal workers were required to have a minimum of twelve years of education. More than 90 percent of the interviewed formal workers had middle-level skill certificates (equivalent to semiskilled). Despite their relatively high qualifications, about 70 to 80 percent of formal workers were doing simple repetitive line-operating work with some basic training of a week or less. Only about 20 to 30 percent of production workers were maintenance workers, technicians, and team leaders, who were defined by management as the "real" skilled core production workforce. Automation and standardization reduced the required skills for many line operators; meanwhile, the integrated "just-in-time" (JIT) production system required "disciplined and quality workers capable of working cooperatively."[20] The specific labor requirements had mixed impacts on the job security and bargaining power of autoworkers, as we will discuss below.

The social composition of temporary workers in the automobile industry changed as well. In the early 1990s, most temporary workers were peasant workers hired directly by automobile factories in relatively small numbers to cope with seasonal production change.[21] They were often recruited from the nearby countryside or townships in cooperation with local labor bureaus as a type of "rural redundant laborer export." Peasant workers earned about 50 to 70 percent of the wages of formal contract workers for doing the same work, and they were ineligible for the pensions and social-security benefits entitled to urban workers because of their rural-household registration status (*hukou*). At this stage, the boundary between formal and temporary workers was relatively easy to maintain based on the rural-urban household registration system, which has long relegated rural residents to second-class citizens and limited their access to good jobs in the urban areas.[22]

Since the mid-1990s, temporary-agency employment, known as labor dispatch (*laowu paiqian*) in China, expanded rapidly in almost every sector in China.[23] Labor dispatch is a typical triangular employment that separates the hiring from the use of labor. An agency worker is hired by (and signs a labor contract with) a labor agency and is dispatched to work at a user company. There is no employment relationship between the agency worker and the user company, and the agency worker can be "returned" (dismissed) to the labor agency without any severance compensation. Thus, agency workers are considered more flexible and worry-free for the employer than the "old" temporary (peasant) workers hired directly by the automobile factories. As of 2006, it was estimated that over 70 percent of temporary workers in China's auto-assembly sector were agency workers. Most of them were under twenty-three with an average of nine to twelve years of education.[24] The remaining were fast-growing numbers of student workers from technical/vocational schools working on assembly lines under internship.[25]

In sum, by the early and mid-2000s, the social composition of temporary workers in the automobile industry had changed from the "old temp" of peasant workers to the "new temp" of agency workers (70 percent) and student workers (30 percent), who were comprised of both rural and urban youths. About two thirds of agency workers were rural residents from the surrounding suburbs and countryside near the automobile factories. The remaining were local urban youths who were unable to find formal contract employment. The student workers consisted of rural and urban youths (about even) from all over the country. As such, the boundary between temporary and formal workers based on rural-urban hukou status became blurred. Management tended to emphasize education and skill qualifications as the new yardstick to draw a boundary between formal and temporary workers. But in many cases, temporary workers had similar education and skill levels to the formal workers. Moreover, most interviewed young rural temporary workers had strong desires to stay in the city, and they longed for economic and social advancement as well as workplace equality and dignity. But the harsh reality of being treated as second-class workers and the slim chance of becoming formal workers made them feel frustrated and resentful. As such, the recomposition of temporary workers delegitimized labor force dualism based on hukou status and contributed to the rising labor activism among the new generation of temporary workers against unequal treatment at work.

The evidence shows a clear move toward flexiblization of labor and reduced job security in the Chinese automobile factories since the mid-1990s. The fact that one to two thirds of the production workforce at China's leading automobile enterprises (key enterprises in a pillar industry with strong state intervention) were temporary workers reflected the scale and depth of flexiblization of labor in China as marketization deepened in the 1990s. It echoes the global trend toward "labor flexibility," which is a key component of the "neoliberal turn" since 1970s, as firms seek new ways of accumulating capital and states retrench from welfare provisions and social protections for their working citizens.[26] The movement toward flexiblization in the Chinese automobile industry, however, encountered resistance from formal and temporary workers. The result has been an "unsettled" process of contestation and negotiation between workers, managers/capitalists, and the state.

Autoworker Resistance and Managerial Responses

The scale and concentration of automobile production in the twentieth century has recurrently allowed autoworkers to achieve effective workplace bargaining power. This power derives from workers enmeshed in tightly integrated production processes, where a localized stoppage in one node can cause disruptions on a much wider scale than the stoppage itself.[27] The increased scale and concentration of automobile production in China over the past decade has increased the potential workplace bargaining power of Chinese autoworkers. For one thing, Chinese autoworkers are concentrated in factories of enormous size. The Volkswagen plant in the suburb of Shanghai has approximately twenty-two thousand employees. More impressive still is the concentration of around one hundred thousand autoworkers employed by the FAW Auto Group in its various factories within the "FAW auto city," a twelve-square-kilometer district in the city of Changchun, where over three hundred thousand FAW employees and their families work and live.

Moreover, the widely adopted JIT techniques in the Chinese automobile production have indeed increased the vulnerability of production to any interruptions in the flow of parts to the assembly line by eliminating the buffers built into the traditional Fordist system, and thus boosted the potential workplace bargaining power of Chinese autoworkers. For example, at one of the studied automobile assemblers, management introduced JIT production methods despite a very poor labor-management relationship, reflected among other things in the widespread acts of petty sabotage by workers. In the end, in order to keep production flowing smoothly, management felt obliged to eliminate its experiment and return to a system with greater built-in supply buffers.[28] This point was clearly illustrated in the 2010 Honda strike, as a nineteen-day strike at a transmission and engine plant could shut down the company's four assembly plants throughout China.

The increasing workplace bargaining power of Chinese autoworkers goes hand-in-hand with growing workplace grievances rooted in the grueling nature of the lean and labor-intensive mass-production paradigm, characterized by repetitive and tedious work, heavy workloads, intense production pace, long working hours, and excessive compulsory overtime. Production lines usually operate in two shifts of ten to twelve hours each. About 89 percent of interviewed workers considered the current production pace "very intense." All the interviewed workers reported strains and injuries of different degrees. Workers also complained about management's arbitrary decisions on speedups and overtimes and the lack of workers' autonomy over their own work.

To be sure, workers' wages at those large automobile factories were often double the average of other manufacturing workers in the same localities. Even temporary workers' wages, which were only one to two thirds of formal workers,' were competitive compared to the local average. It has been argued that high wages are one of the main factors accounting for the "hegemonic consent" between management and autoworkers.[29] Yet my field research found that, far from the commonly assumed "affluent workers, contented workers," more than three quarters of the interviewed formal production workers felt that they were squeezed and their work did not receive the fair reward they deserved given the fast-rising productivity and profitability accompanied by their slowly growing or stagnant wages since 2004.[30]

Workers were more indignant about the increasingly enlarged wage differences between workers and managers. As a formal worker at SOE-1 resentfully commented, "After all these years of fast growth, the paychecks and bonuses of managers and salesmen have got bigger and bigger. We workers still earn that little! But it is us frontline workers who make the cars, do the heaviest work, and generate the profits for the company! But we are the least paid and cared for here. That is not the right way to treat employees!"[31] This strong frustration of "relative deprivation" is one of the main sources of formal autoworker discontent. Thus there is no reason to assume that high wages in and of themselves can guarantee workers' consent and commitment.[32]

Temporary Workers Push Back

Temporary workers, who are often perceived as weak, docile, and vulnerable to management control due to lack of job security, took management by surprise with their feisty resistance to unequal treatment and management's arbitrary labor control. Over the course of my fieldwork, I documented various hidden and open forms of resistance among temporary workers, including sabotage, slowdowns, absenteeism, filing labor-dispute cases, quitting jobs collectively, and in the extreme case, wildcat strikes. For example, in June 2004, over three hundred student workers at the assembly shop of SOE-2 stayed in their dorms and refused to go to work to protest the delay of their monthly wages. The whole assembly line stopped for fifteen hours before workers went back to work after the problem was solved. In November 2004, around three hundred laid-off agency workers at GER-2 filed a collective labor-dispute case against the automaker and the labor agencies. Workers demanded their unpaid social-insurance premiums. In March 2005, more than five hundred agency workers at SOE-1 walked out during a morning shift to protest excessive compulsory overtime and demanded wage raises. In February 2006, right after the Chinese New Year holiday, about three hundred temporary workers (including both agency and student workers) at SOE-1 did not return to work, and management had to send its office staff to work on the shop floor temporarily before management could recruit enough new workers. In October 2006, more than two hundred student workers at SOE-2 went on strike again to protest the exclusive wage raise for formal workers and other unequal treatment between formal and temporary workers.[33]

The rising resistance by temporary workers first had to do with their changing social composition, as discussed above. More importantly, the growing numbers of temporary workers concentrated on assembly lines enabled them to shut down the entire shop by acting suddenly and collectively at the point of production. As a temporary worker at GER-2 indicated, "If we [agency workers] stop working together, the whole lines will have to stop."[34] Temporary workers also had a keener sense of injustice and resentment for being treated as second-class workers. During the interviews, temporary workers often used the words "injustice" (*bu gongzheng*), "unfair" (*bu gongping*), and the claim of "equal pay for equal work" to denounce labor force dualism and agency employment.

The concentrated and connected dormitory-residential pattern of temporary workers also facilitated their collective mobilization. Most temporary workers live in the factory-subsidized dormitory residences adjacent to the production complex, which enables temporary workers to stay connected and mobilize effectively.[35]

But when and how are temporary workers' collective actions likely to succeed? A comparison of the two wildcat strikes by temporary student workers at SOE-2 provides some insights. Both strikes broke out in a seemingly spontaneous manner among several hundred student workers staying at their dormitory rooms and refusing to go to work collectively. Both strikes were fueled by the sense of injustice with a direct goal of economic gains. The June strike was incited by the threat to workers' livelihood (the delay of their monthly pay), and it was defensive in nature. In the October strike, temporary workers proactively demanded a wage increase after the factory exclusively raised formal workers' wages. They had already targeted equal rights with formal workers, and the strike was initiated and planned in advance through workers' online social networks and organized around their closely connected dormitories. The June strike was perceived as a success because temporary workers received their delayed payment, and no one got in trouble for participating in the strike. But in the October strike, management took a tough line—striking workers were fired, and temporary workers got only a slight raise two months later.

There were several factors accounting for the different outcomes of the two strikes, including the timing of the strikes, workers' framing strategies, and management perceptions of the strikes.[36] I found that temporary workers' struggles were more likely to succeed when their grievances were shared by formal workers and when they received support from the formal workers.

In the June strike, the shared workplace grievances motivated formal workers to stand along with temporary workers. The "silent support" from formal workers played a key role in magnifying the disruptive effects of the temporary workers' strike. As a group leader recalled, "The strike by agency workers was also an outlet for formal workers to vent their discontent. Right before the strike, workers were exhausted and complained about the excessive overtime. Everyone was expecting a big bonus. But on pay day, we only found a slight raise in our monthly bonus. Folks were very disappointed and resentful. So after the night shift, agency workers went on strike, and formal workers stood aside lines, chatting and resting without working."[37]

In the October strike, however, the divisive wage policy that only raised formal workers' wages detached formal workers from supporting temporary workers. As a formal worker commented: "It is just impossible to pay everyone equally. Otherwise, why would the factory even bother to hire temporary workers? I also think it is unfair. But there are so many people not even having jobs, and I believe they are more than happy to take those temporary jobs."[38]

In spite of the divisive labor force dualism, my field research suggested that the relationship between formal and temporary workers was better characterized as detachment than antagonism. This was largely due to the fact that there hadn't been open replacement of formal workers with temporary workers, and thus there was little direct competition and confrontation between formal and agency workers over jobs. Also, the socialist egalitarian legacies were still relevant to workers and managers, especially at those early-built factories. These factors indicated the possibility of developing a more engaging and cooperative relationship between the two groups of workers.

To be sure, the relatively high wages at the major automobile factories and the perceived difficulty in finding formal employment under an oversupplied labor market inhibited many temporary workers from openly confronting management. The absence of union representation and the right to strike exacerbated the weak associational power of Chinese workers as a whole. But temporary workers' resistance allowed them to realize their collective power to struggle for change for something better. It is unlikely that the new generation of temporary workers will remain docile and quiescent in the face of unequal treatment and management arbitrary control.

Formal Workers' Growing Discontents

I found growing discontent among the formal workers as management further reduced their privileges and protection under intensified competition. Besides their stagnant or declining wages, the new formal workers were also concerned about their job security. As discussed in the previous section, most newly hired formal workers only had one- to two-year renewable labor contracts. The reduced skill levels of many line operators made it more feasible for management to staff those positions with temporary workers. There were growing feelings of insecurity among the interviewed formal production workers with short-term labor contracts. For example, during the market downturn in 2004 and 2005, GER-1 shut down several lines, cut shifts and operation hours, and laid off over two thousand agency workers. Although formal workers were able to stay in their jobs thanks to the buffer of temporary workers, their wages were cut by more than one third, and many formal workers experienced anxiety about whether they could renew their labor contracts. As a formal worker who had worked at GER-1 for three years summarized, "It is a market economy. Profitability and efficiency come first. No sentiments and feelings [*renqing wei*], no security nowadays."[39]

The interviewed managers complained about the lack of commitment and deteriorating worker morale among the young generation of formal workers. Especially when economic incentives were cut back, there were immediate withdrawals of workers' cooperation. For example, a shop manager at USA-1 mentioned that when the factory reduced its annual bonus in 2005, workers complained fervently, and there was a 30 percent higher redo rate during the first quarter. Given anticipated further cost-cutting measures in China's automobile industry, it is likely that the protection and privileges of formal workers will continue to decline. In such circumstances, one will hardly expect formal workers to remain quiescent.

Management and Union Responses and Contradictions of Labor Force Dualism

Rising resistance by temporary workers and growing discontent among formal workers caused management concerns about the limits of labor force dualism in labor control. In response, the automakers became very cautious in using temporary workers in direct production. GER-1 and GER-2 restricted the use of temporary workers to certain unskilled line positions that can be easily replaced. SOE-2 set a "15 percent limit" that restricted the percentage of agency workers to 15 percent of the total production workforce. Management also took various measures to accommodate temporary workers' demands by raising their wages and granting them more access to the companies' facilities and resources, such as free shuttle buses, meal subsidies, and company-car-purchase discounts. Temporary agency workers were also allowed to join the automobile factory unions.[40] Management and unions tried to direct temporary workers' grievances through normal channels. For example, factory-union and party-committee leaders of GER-1 set up monthly "heart-to-heart" meetings with temporary workers to hear their concerns and requests. But the temporary workers were not at all enthusiastic about those "posture" meetings. As an agency worker commented, "The real problem is this unequal system . . . and they won't change the system anyway."[41]

The interviewed managers were aware of the limits of labor force dualism. But it was hard for management to pull back completely. As a human-resources manager at GER-2 admitted,

> We want all of our workers to stay happy with the company. But let's be realistic: the company has to first make profits. For that, we need to increase productivity and flexibility and reduce labor cost. But the government wants us to help on employment and social stability; for that, we need to keep our workers quiet. That's why we brought in agency workers. But that has created some new problems. It is a dilemma. I think for now, we will just have to find a way to improve our management of temporary workers.[42]

The dilemma faced by management concerning labor force dualism reflected the ongoing tension between capital's drive toward profitability and management concerns for legitimacy (i.e. maintaining peaceful labor relations). On the one hand, workers' resistance to large-scale restructuring and downsizing of many SOEs in the 1990s pushed automobile enterprises toward protecting a core segment of the labor force to gain consensual and cooperative labor-management relations. On the other hand, China entered the global competition in the mass production of automobiles at a late stage of the product cycle, when competition was extremely high and profit margins were thin. The more acute profitability pressure drove the Chinese automakers to move toward aggressive cost-cutting measures, including the wide use of temporary workers and reduced protection for formal workers. Such measures, however, have provoked temporary workers' resistances and formal workers' discontent. What makes this labor force dualism (and labor relations in general) at China's major automobile SOEs and JVs unique is that it more directly reflects the conflicts and compromise between the multiple forces of the state, global and domestic capital, and workers, given that those enterprises are held strongly in state hands. So where is this dualism heading? To answer this question, we need to go beyond the shop floor and look into the broader national political dynamics—that is, how the Chinese party-state has responded to the rising labor unrest incited by the intensified commodification and flexiblization of labor since the mid 1990s.

State Response: The Making of Labor Contract Law and Boundary-Drawing Strategy

In 2007, three new labor laws were passed in China. The best-known of these, the Labor Contract Law (LCL), devotes one section and eleven articles to regulating agency employment and provides some legal protections for agency workers who had not been covered by previous labor laws. The LCL stipulates that a labor agency is an employer and shall sign fixed-term labor contracts of no less than two years with agency workers. The labor agency must ensure that the agency workers receive at least the minimum wage on a monthly basis, even when they are not placed at user firms. The arrangements between the labor agency and user firms must be governed by a formal contract detailing placements and payments, including arrangements with respect to social-insurance premiums for agency workers. Moreover, the LCL stipulates that agency workers shall have equal pay for equal work compared to formal workers at the user firms, and they can also join the unions at the user firms.

What has led the state to directly intervene and regulate agency employment through new labor legislation? Agency employment has expanded rapidly in almost every sector in China since late 1990s. By the end of 2010, the national total of agency workers had reached sixty million, accounting for 20 percent of the total actively employed population in China.[43] Many of the temporary-agency workers actually work in permanent posts on a long-term basis in government organizations, public-sector institutions, and state-owned enterprises, including many "strategic" sectors.[44] There is a growing class of "temporary workers in permanent jobs" in China.[45] Moreover, the ambiguous triangular employment and the lack of regulation before the enactment of LCL led to widespread social-insurance fraud, as labor agencies and user firms tried to evade their responsibilities for agency workers.[46] The ACFTU conducted several surveys and reported that agency employment complicated employment relations, increased labor-dispute cases, and made it difficult to protect agency workers' rights and interests.[47] The ACFTU called for the relevant legislative and executive departments to regulate labor dispatch.[48] Around the time that the LCL was drafted, there was extensive media coverage and public outcry about the plight of agency workers and the negative impact of agency employment on labor relations in the long run.[49] Under the general political guidelines of the Hu-Wen administration to construct a "harmonious society," criticism of agency employment that could harm stability and social harmony became dominant in official and public discourses.[50] The making of the Labor Contract Law became a highly publicized event and the showcase of the Chinese central government's determination to defend workers' rights and interests, despite the opposition and the threats of multinational and domestic business to withdraw their investment.[51]

It was within this broad political context that the Labor Contract Law took tough measures to regulate agency employment and to stabilize employment relations. To a large extent, the making of the Labor Contract Law was a politicized legislative campaign in response to the pressure of rising labor unrest and popular demand for more state protection from the vagaries of the "free" market, and to shore up the regime's legitimacy.[52]

The LCL had direct impact on management decisions regarding the use of agency workers at the company level. First, I found some improvements in wage and working conditions of agency workers under the new LCL. For instance, at the studied automobile factories, agency workers' wages were increased, and they were guaranteed with government-required social insurance. Agency workers were also granted fringe benefits that used to be limited to formal workers. However, there were still big differences in social-insurance schemes and bonuses between agency and formal workers.[53] Agency workers still lacked job security and advancement opportunities at the automobile factories where they work.[54] Moreover, I found that the studied automakers increased the numbers of temporary workers and moved toward entrenching labor force dualism.

In fact, since the implementation of the LCL, the number of agency workers had more than tripled from roughly seventeen million to sixty million by the end of 2010. How to explain the seemingly unintended consequences of the new labor law concerning agency employment? The main reason, according to the interviewed managers, was straightforward: although the Labor Contract Law has provided agency workers with some protections and made hiring agency workers more expensive by raising the entry threshold for labor agencies, it is still much cheaper and more flexible for employers to use agency workers than to hire formal contract workers, who are even more protected by the new law.[55]

The seemingly unintended consequences of the LCL, I suspect, were indeed an intended outcome of the state boundary-drawing strategy to balance the conflicting interests of employers and labor as well as "procapital" and "prolabor" forces among the lawmakers. This point can be clearly seen from the negotiations and compromises in the changes of different drafts of the LCL regarding labor dispatch. Earlier drafts of the LCL had much more strict regulations about labor dispatch, but those were removed in the final version. For instance, the second draft required that a user company signs labor contracts directly with agency employees once they have worked at the user company for more than a year. This provision was dropped in the final draft due to employers' strong objections. The main argument from the "procapital" side was that if this provision were to be put into effect, it would hurt companies' flexibility and competiveness and do more harm than good on employment. It could also drive employers to stop using agency employees once they reach the one-year term. Although representatives from the ACFTU insisted on "regulating and inhibiting" agency employment to better protect workers, the concerns about employment and the proponents for "regulating and developing" labor dispatch as a "supplementary type of employment" gained the upper hand during the debates.[56] As a result, the final draft dropped this specific provision that could have inhibited agency employment.

The above evidence reveals a state boundary-drawing strategy by legalizing agency employment and institutionalizing a dualist labor system. On the one hand, the state attempted to shore up its legitimacy with workers by providing formal contract workers with more job security. On the other hand, the state granted employers a "valve" to lower labor costs and gain flexibility by legalizing flexible agency employment outside of regular contract employment. Compared to labor force dualism at the firm level, the state boundary-drawing strategy is more systematic and institutionalized through national policy and legislation, and thus has deeper and more long-term impact on individual workers' livelihood and well-being.[57]

It is important to note that the battle over the implementation of and subsequent amendments to the Labor Contract Law continues. In 2009, the Ministry of Human Resources and Social Security (MOHRSS) began to draft the Regulations on Labor Dispatching. This was largely due to the central government's concern about the rapid expansion of labor dispatch, which might have threatened formal contract employment since the implementation of the LCL.[58] Again, there were disagreements among lawmakers. While ACFTU insisted on tightly regulating and strictly restricting labor dispatch, enterprises (especially large central SOEs) strongly opposed strict regulation.[59] The MOHRSS tended to emphasize the positive effects of labor dispatch in job creation and labor flexibility and was inclined to "regulate and develop" it.[60] Against the backdrop of the 2008 global financial crisis, Beijing's deep concern with the economy and employment might have helped the side that argued for the positive effects of the flexibility provided by agency employment for overall job growth. As a result, the attempt to include specific regulations on labor dispatch stalled. Frustrated by this outcome, in March 2011 and 2012, ACFTU submitted two comprehensive reports on the severe problems of labor dispatch to the National People's Congress (NPC) and once again proposed legislative restriction of labor dispatch.[61] The NPC Standing Committee (NPCSC) issued important directives, recasting the question of regulating labor dispatch as a political issue of "safeguarding the dominant position of the working class and consolidating the foundation of the party's rule."[62] On June 26, 2012, the twenty-seventh meeting of the Eleventh NPCSC began to review the draft Amendments to the Labor Contract Law, with a focus on revising the provisions concerning labor dispatch. The proposed major revisions took tougher measures to strictly limit the posts that can use labor dispatch and to ensure agency workers the right to equal pay for equal work as formal employees of the user company.[63] While the outcome is hard to predict at this point, it will likely depend on the CCP's ultimate assessment of the weight of maintaining stability and legitimacy (with labor) versus promoting efficiency and profitability (with capital).

The close interactions between the top-down state labor-law reforms and the bottom-up pressures of labor unrest and popular demand suggest a dynamic relationship between the party-state, labor, and capital in post-Socialist China.

Conclusion

This study has demonstrated that the massive foreign investment in China's automobile industry and the increased scale and concentration of automobile production in the past two decades have created and strengthened a new generation of Chinese autoworkers with growing workplace bargaining power and grievances. Moreover, the Honda strikers' success has shown the growing consciousness of the younger generation of Chinese autoworkers. If we look back at the previous experience of labor unrest by U.S. autoworkers in the early twentieth century and the autoworkers in Western Europe in 1950s and 1960s, we find that the first generation of migrant workers generally did not protest against the harsh conditions of work and life. The arbitrary power of management over issues such as hiring, firing, promotion, and job assignments went unchallenged in the automobile factories. But the second generation became the backbone of militant struggles that succeeded in radically transforming relationships with the factory and society.[64] The Honda strike has illustrated the willingness, determination, and capacity of the young generation of Chinese autoworkers to mobilize collectively to struggle for change.

The success of the Honda strike was coupled with the growing marketplace bargaining power of Chinese workers, derived from a labor shortage and changing demographics. The central government's policy shift from an export-led development model based on cheap labor to a more balanced one based on domestic consumption (and thereby higher wages) is certainly another crucial factor to push through major changes in the balance of power between labor and capital at the workplace.

At the same time, however, state institutions and historical legacies matter, and China's conditions are different from the previous cases of autoworkers' upsurge from Detroit to Ulsan. For one thing, the Chinese state has played a leading role in fostering a cautious restructuring and utilization of foreign direct investment in transforming the auto industry. The difficulties involved in simultaneously pursuing profitability and maintaining legitimacy with labor have driven large state-owned automakers and Sino-foreign joint ventures to follow a policy of labor force dualism, drawing boundaries between formal and temporary workers. Yet a divided labor force does not necessarily preclude robust and continuing labor activism that can lead to significant changes. I have shown that although labor force dualism has so far kept formal workers relatively quiet, it has also radicalized the new generation of temporary workers to fight back against unequal treatment and employers' violations of their rights. Moreover, by locating the case of autoworkers' resistance in the broader national political dynamics, we see how the bottom-up pressure of rising labor unrest has propelled the Chinese central government to step in to regulate and stabilize labor relations through the new labor laws, including the enactment of the Labor Contract Law, that provide more security and protection for certain segments of workers.

Contrary to the dominant position in the literature that emphasizes the structural weakness of Chinese workers vis-à-vis the party-state and vis-à-vis employers,[65] the claim in this essay is that the Chinese party-state has to strike a balance between labor and capital and that workers in China do have certain leverage and willingness to struggle for change. It has been acknowledged that the legitimacy of the CCP in the reform era is built on two pillars: sustaining fast economic growth and maintaining social stability. Yet less stressed is the centrality of maintaining stability as the fundamental political logic of the CCP.[66] That is to say, the pursuit of economic growth is not the goal but a means through which the CCP could bolster its legitimacy and achieve the ultimate goal of maintaining stability and the monopoly on political power.[67] As such, the impetus of the Chinese economic reforms and marketization in the 1990s largely came from the belief of the top CCP officials that market economic reforms are tactically necessary to create the conditions for more effective state guidance of the economy and, thus, to create a stronger and more effective developmental state, rather than their intention to pursue a capitalist economy per se.[68] Indeed, there have been clear signs of the central government reorientation in its development strategy since the mid- 2000s, when the accumulated social and environmental ills have raised the alarm of the sustainability of the single-minded unbalanced economic growth model and the regime legitimacy. Especially in the wake of the 2008 global financial crisis, the government has explicitly stated that the primary task of China's economic structure adjustment is to shift from an export-led growth model based on cheap labor to a more balanced and sustainable one based on "expanding domestic demand" and thereby higher wages for Chinese people.[69] By the end of 2010, almost every province and municipality in China had increased its monthly minimum wage by an average of 23 percent.[70]

Arguably, China's revolutionary tradition of "mass line" and the socialist legacies (such as the democratic management practices on the shop floor) have led to a unique party-masses relationship that has "endowed China's subaltern strata with a self-confidence and combativeness with few parallels elsewhere."[71] The CCP's top priority of maintaining stability and its continuing public commitment (at least in rhetoric) to "the legitimate rights and interests of workers"[72] undergird Chinese workers' legitimacy leverage derived from such revolutionary and socialist legacies as well as workers' "credible threat" of disruptive power, "on the streets as well as through strikes."[73] This legitimacy leverage, in turn, encourages Chinese workers to stand up and protest against employers' violations of their rights despite their lack of independent trade unions and other electoral-representative institutions.

Ironically, despite, indeed in large part because of the lack of electoral legitimacy, the authoritarian regime has to be more responsive and adaptive to grievances and demands from below in fear of ungovernability. Indeed, the feeble role of the ACFTU in representing the interests of rank-and-file workers and bargaining with employers have forced the central and local governments to directly intervene in workplace labor-employer conflicts, and most often to intervene in favor of labor to maintain social stability. As such, the localized and apolitical labor protests can be easily turned into political issues concerning social stability and regime legitimacy in the eyes of workers. This could explain why the widespread, localized, and apolitical labor-capital conflicts at workplaces can command direct top-down state intervention through legislation and other formal institutional changes to pacify workers. In other words, Chinese workers are indeed "bargaining without union,"[74] but they are backed up by and making use of their legitimacy leverage over the state to wring concessions from their employers. In fact, faced with mounting labor unrest in recent years, the ruling Communist Party has explicitly urged the ACFTU to "further protect workers' legitimate rights and interests," to improve "labor protection mechanism[s] to achieve decent work for the laboring masses," and to promote "harmonious labor relations and social harmony."[75] Recent studies have suggested that the ACFTU has been taking a more active role in labor organizing and collective bargaining to improve conditions for workers, under the threat that it could become totally irrelevant to workers and state bureaucrats if it cannot deliver any meaningful gains for workers and thereby mediate labor conflicts and preempt strikes.[76]

Although my case study reveals the significance of Chinese workers' bottom-up struggles and legitimacy leverage to win employers' concessions without independent unions, I am not disputing the importance of organized labor and the efforts to build a genuine worker-representative organization to struggle and collectively bargain for Chinese workers' rights and interests. Nor am I denying that an authoritarian political system remains a formidable barrier for Chinese workers' pursuit of a better workplace. The important theoretical point highlighted in this case study is that workers' constant bottom-up struggles are the genuine force in driving for meaningful change at the workplace and reforms from above. This argument is consistent with historically grounded analyses that institutional trade unionism is neither a precondition for nor a guarantee of effective working-class mobilization.[77] Rather, labor upsurge from below is the real motor for genuine labor movements, which are often a precursor to effective union involvement, not vice versa.[78] It is in this regard that I argue that we should not underestimate the impact of Chinese workers' widespread, localized, and apolitical protests. Indeed, the key theoretical insight of Frances Piven and Richard Cloward was precisely that many of the gains made by "poor peoples' movements" do not come from the establishment of formal organizations oriented toward the capture of state power but instead are the result of concessions wrung from the powerful in response to widespread, intense, spontaneous disruptions from below—in response to the threat of "ungovernability."[79] But in order to effectively exercise such "disruptive power" from below, "people must also recognize that they do have some power, that elites also depend on the masses. People have to organize, to contrive ways of acting in concert, at least insofar as concerted action is necessary to make their power effective."[80] It is important to remember that the "idea of power" itself has been an important source of workers' power.[81] Thus, there is an urgent need to confront neoliberal ideology and to raise workers' recognition of their own bargaining power. A good illustration of this point is the empowerment effects of the new Chinese labor laws in motivating ordinary Chinese workers to stand up and defend their labor rights through formal legal systems.[82] China's new labor laws, as recent evidence has indicated, are likely to serve as the catalyst for a new wave of labor activism and militancy in China—especially if employers attempt to evade the law and if the arbitration system becomes so burdened with cases that it is unable to resolve workers' grievances quickly, encouraging them to turn instead to direct action.

A fuller picture of the roles Chinese autoworkers are likely to play awaits further analysis along these and related lines.[83] It also awaits the future words and deeds of the Chinese autoworkers themselves.

Notes

1. I would like to thank Beverly Silver, Leon Fink, John French, Nelson Lichtenstein, Peter Coclanis, Joel Andreas, Ho-fung Hung, Mary Gallagher, and Sarosh Kuruvilla for their insightful comments on earlier drafts of this essay, as well as participants at the International Conference on Workers and World Crisis: Labor History and the Political Economy of Hard Times, Georgetown University, Washington, D.C., 22–24 September 2011. Portions this chapter are reprinted from Lu Zhang, "The Paradox of Labor Force Dualism and State-Labor-Capital Relations in the Chinese Automobile Industry," in *From Iron Rice Bowl to Informalization: Markets, Workers, and the State in a Changing China*, ed. Sarosh Kuruvilla, Ching Kwan Lee, and Mary E. Gallagher. Copyright © 2011 by Cornell University. Used by permission of the publisher, Cornell University Press.

2. For a useful discussion of the passive responses of European and U.S. unions in the aftermath of the 2008 crisis, see the essays in the Discussion Forum I, "Labour and the Global Financial Crisis," *Socio-Economic Review* 8 (2010): 341–76.

3. At least twelve strikes were reported to have taken place within the automobile industry in China between May and July 2010. For the detailed timeline of the 2010 auto-strike wave, see Lance Carter, "Auto Industry Strikes in China," *Insurgent Notes* 2 (30 October 2010), accessed 24 June 2013, http://libcom.org/library/auto-industry-strikes-china-lance-carter.

4. The extensive media coverage is too large to give a full citation here. Among the Chinese media reports, see, for example, Guifeng Zhang, "Bentian Bagong de laodong quanli qishi" [The Revelation of the Honda Strike for Labor Rights], *Youth Times*, 28 May 2010: A02; Meng Zheng, "Nanhai tinggong yangben" [Nanhai Strike Exampler], *Caijing Magazine*, 7 June 2010, accessed 24 June 2013, http://magazine.caijing.com.cn/2010-06-06/110453979.html; Zhenghua Zhou and Ziqian Liu, "Zhiji Nanhai Bentian 'Tinggongmeng' Shijian" [Direct Investigation of Nanhai Honda "Strike" Incident], *China Newsweek*, 2 June, 2010, accessed 12 June 2010, http://www.inewsweek.cn/cnw/news/info/society/2010-06-02/6279.shtml; Qiong Zhou, "Guangdong sheng laodong baozhang bumen guanyuan: xiwang bentian bagong shijian tuidong shouru fengpei gaige" [Guangdong Provincial Labor and Social Security Department Official: Hope Honda Strike Promote Income Distribution Reform], Caixin Online, 2 June 2010, accessed 5 June 2010, http://business.sohu.com/20100602/n272524217.shtml. Among the English coverage on the strike, see, for example, Keith Bradsher, "Strike Forces Honda to Shut Plants in China," *New York Times*, 27 May 2010; "Honda Halts Auto Produc-

tion in China amid Parts-Factory Strike," *Bloomberg*, 27 May 2010; Keith Bradsher and David Barboza, "Strike in China Highlights Gap in Workers' Pay," *New York Times*, 28 May 2010; David Barboza, "Strike Status at Honda in China Is Uncertain," *New York Times*, 1 June 2010; David Pierson, "China's Factory Workers Finding, and Flexing, Their Muscle," *Los Angeles Times*, 2 June 2010.

    5. China Automotive Technology Research Center (CATRC), *Zhongguo qiche gongye nianjian* [China Automotive Industry Yearbook] (Tianjin: China Automotive Technology Research Center Press, 2011), 1, 9.

    6. The seven case-study factories were all large-scale assembly plants with high-volume output and large numbers of employees. They held competitive market positions, and all of them receive strong government support and have substantial financial and organizational resources. The seven cases represent the two major ownership types in China's auto-assembly sector: two state-owned enterprises (SOE-1 and SOE-2) and five joint ventures (JVs) with foreign partners from America (USA-1 and USA-2), Germany (GER-1 and GER-2), and Japan (JPN-1). They are also located in distinct geographical regions, including both brownfield and greenfield production bases. I use the pseudonyms for my case-study auto-assembly factories for the purpose of confidentiality. See table 10.1 for the case information.

    7. On the original notion of the "product cycle," see Raymond Vernon, "International Investment and International Trade in the Product Cycle," *Quarterly Journal of Economics* 80.2 (1966): 190–207.

    8. The auto industry was designated as one of the country's seven "pillar industries" of strategic importance by the State Council in the seventh, eighth, and ninth Five-Year Plans (1986–90, 1991–95, 1996–2000) and has been redeclared as a "leading industry" under the tenth and eleventh Five-Year Plans (2001–5, 2006–10).

    9. The original notion of a "triple alliance" is borrowed from Peter Evans's classic work on the alliance of multinational, state, and local capital in Brazil. Eric Thun applied this term to describe the relationship between the central government and foreign and domestic capitals in the Chinese automobile industry. I use it in a similar vein but emphasizing the dominant role of the central state in forging the alliances between multinationals and China's state-owned automakers. See Peter Evans, *Dependent Development: The Alliance of Multinational, State, and Local Capital in Brazil* (Princeton, N.J.: Princeton University Press, 1979); Eric Thun, "Industrial Policy, Chinese-Style: FDI, Regulation, and Dreams of National Champions in the Auto Sector," *Journal of East Asian Studies* 4 (2004): 453–89.

    10. Hua Wang, "Policy Reforms and Foreign Direct Investment: The Case of the Chinese Automobile Industry," *Journal of Economics and Business* 6.1 (2003): 287–314.

    11. Eric Harwit, *China's Automobile Industry* (New York: M. E. Sharpe, 1995); Gregory Chin, "Building 'Capitalism with China's Characteristics': The Political Economy of Model Joint Ventures in the Automotive Industry" (Ph.D. dissertation, York University, 2003).

    12. James Treece, "China Takes Hard Road to a Market Economy," *Automotive News*, 14 July 1997, 1.

    13. Interview with a researcher at Shanghai Social Science Academy, Shanghai, 21 March 2007.

14. See, for example, John Humphrey, *Capitalist Control and Workers' Struggle in the Brazilian Auto Industry* (Princeton, N.J.: Princeton University Press, 1982); Gay Seidman, *Manufacturing Militance: Workers' Movements in Brazil and South Africa, 1970–1985* (Berkeley: University of California Press, 1994); Hagen Koo, *Korean Workers: The Culture and Politics of Class Formation* (Ithaca, N.Y.: Cornell University Press, 2001).

15. CATRC, *Zhongguo qiche gongye nianjian* [China Automotive Industry Yearbook] (Tianjin: China Automotive Technology Research Center Press, 2002–7).

16. The ACFTU (and its regional branches) is under the leadership of the Chinese Communist Party (CCP). It is both a state apparatus and a labor organization whose power of "representing" workers and "mediating and preempting" labor conflicts derives from its formal government status. The majority of funding of union operational expenses comes from a 2 percent payroll tax on employers and from the state. See Feng Chen, "Union Power in China: Source, Operation, and Constraints," *Modern China* 35.6 (2009): 662–89. At the grassroots level (i.e. the enterprise level), union branches of the ACFTU are generally incapable of representing workers due to the union's dependence on management both financially and organizationally. Unions in SOEs and Sino-foreign joint ventures are often incorporated into factory party committees. Factory party committees and unions play an important role in assisting management to mobilize workers to promote production and mediating labor-management conflicts rather than representing workers. Party secretaries are often ranked as top managers and union leaders as middle managers in SOEs and Sino-foreign joint ventures.

17. Among the early discussions of the core-periphery model, see John Atkinson, "Flexibility or Fragmentation? The United Kingdom Labour Market in the Eighties," *Labour and Society* 12.1 (1987): 87–105. For the flexible-firm formula, see Arne L. Kalleberg, "Organizing Flexibility; the Flexible Firm in a New Century," *British Journal of Industrial Relations* 39.4 (2001): 479–504; and Arne L. Kalleberg, "Flexible Firms and Labor Market Segmentation," *Work and Occupations* 30.2 (2003): 154–75.

18. Interviewee S13, GER-1, November 2006.

19. Educational credentials are the major yardstick to determine one's status as staff or worker. Most newly recruited staff have a minimum of a bachelor's degree, and they usually sign two- to five-year labor contracts initially. Staff have different pay schemes, career tracks, and statuses from blue-collar workers in the factory hierarchy. This essay focuses on the labor force dualism among production workers, but it is important to note that the sharp division between staff and workers within the formal-contract workforce is another main source of workers' discontents.

20. Interview F2, GER-2, August 2004.

21. The use of temporary workers by state-owned enterprises can be traced back to the pre-reform era, when urban enterprises hired peasants as temporaries to adjust for seasonal fluctuations of production. See Marc J. Blecher, "Peasant Labor for Urban Industry: Temporary Contract Labor, Urban-Rural Balance, and Class Relations in a Chinese County," *World Development* 11.8 (1983): 731–45.

22. See, for example, Dorothy Solinger, *Contesting Citizenship in Urban China: Peasant Migrants, the State, and the Logic of the Market* (Berkeley: University of California Press, 1999).

23. There are many different terms referring to this type of nonregular employment, such as "agency employment," "labor dispatch," "triangular employment," "labor subcontracting," and "labor leasing." The International Labour Office (ILO) uses the term "agency employment," while "labor dispatch" is more commonly used in China, Japan, and Taiwan. This essay uses "agency employment" (and "agency workers") and "labor dispatch" (and "dispatched workers") interchangeably.

24. This estimate is based on piecemeal data collected by the author from the four automobile factories currently using temporary workers. No official statistics on temporary workers in the automobile industry are available.

25. In China, vocational students are generally required to complete a minimum six-month internship during their three years of study to learn practical skills before they can graduate. This system aims to provide students the practical skills needed by the enterprises where they are expected to become formal employees upon graduation. In reality, however, with the commercialization and privatization of China's vocational education since late 1990s, many technical/vocational schools profit by sending their teenage students to work full-time at factories during the internship while charging commission fees. There is little chance for student workers to become formal employees at the user firms where they complete their "internships."

26. See David Harvey, *The Condition of Postmodernity: An Enquiry into the Origins of Cultural Change* (Cambridge: Blackwell, 1989); Beth A. Rubin, "Flexible Accumulation: The Decline of Contract and Social Transformation," *Research in Social Stratification and Mobility* 14 (1995): 297–323.

27. For a discussion of workers' workplace bargaining power, see Beverly Silver, *Forces of Labor: Workers' Movements and Globalization since 1870* (New York: Cambridge University Press, 2003), chap. 2.

28. The author's fieldwork notes, Tianjin, January 2008.

29. See Chin, "Building 'Capitalism with China's Characteristics.'"

30. The percentage was based on the interviews the author conducted in the summers of 2004 and 2005 and between September 2006 and July 2007. Workers' opinions on their wages, however, varied across the studied factories. At SOE-1, every worker I interviewed complained about their relatively low wages comparing to the wages at other leading automakers in China. At GER-2, by contrast, about half of the interviewed workers said their wages were "okay" based on the local living standard.

31. Interviewee C16, SOE-1, March 2007.

32. The strong sentiment of "relative deprivation" was also evident in the previous waves of autoworkers' struggles in Brazil and South Korea, where autoworker wages were also significantly high prior to large-scale autoworker protests. See Koo, *Korean Workers*; and Humphrey, *Capitalist Control and Workers' Struggle in the Brazilian Auto Industry*.

33. Summaries from the author's field notes, June 2004 to July 2007.

34. Interviewee F14, GER-2, October 2006.

35. Pun and Smith argue that in today's China, a "dormitory labor regime" continually reproduces a "young, transient working class" characterized as "a teenage proletariat." While the "dormitory labor regime" they found in the labor-intensive, low-tech, and

export-oriented industrial exporting zones featured teenage female migrant workers, I found that the dormitory residences of autoworkers were characterized by young male local workers aged eighteen to twenty-four with better education. See Ngai Pun and Chris Smith, "Putting Transnational Labour Process in Its Place: The Dormitory Labour Regime in Post-Socialist China," *Work, Employment, and Society* 21.1 (2007): 27–45.

36. For a detailed discussion on the two strikes, see Lu Zhang, *From Detroit to Shanghai? Globalization, Market Reform, and the Politics of Labor in the Chinese Automobile Industry* (New York: Cambridge University Press, 2014), chap. 6.

37. Interview Q 10, SOE-2, June 2004.

38. Interview Q21, SOE-2, October 2006.

39. Interview S19, GER-1, November 2006.

40. Student workers still cannot join factory unions due to their lack of de jure worker status.

41. Interview S26, GER-1, April 2007.

42. Interview F15, GER-2, October 2006.

43. Yunzhang Xiang, "Quanwei Baogao Cheng Laowu Paiqian Da Liu Qian Wan Ren, Quanzong Jianyi Xiugai Laodong Hetong Fa" [Authoritative Report Says Agency Workers have Reached Sixty Million, ACFTU Urges to Revise Labor Contract Law], *Economic Observer,* 3 March 2011, http://finance.ifeng.com/news/20110225/3503356.shtml. The total number of dispatched workers in China is still in dispute. The Ministry of Human Resources and Social Security estimated the number was around twenty-seven million as of 2010.

44. Shiyou Weng, "Laowu paiqian guiding congjin zhiding, da qiye yonggong chengben keneng shangsheng" [Labor Dispatching Regulations Will Become Tighter, Labor Cost Is Expected to Rise at Large Enterprises], *Economic Observations,* 24 October 2009.

45. Lu Zhang, "Lean Production and Labor Controls in the Chinese Automobile Industry in an Age of Globalization," *International Labor and Working-Class History* 73.1 (2008): 28.

46. Kai Chang and Kungang Li, "Bixu yange guizhi laodongzhe paiqian" [Labor Dispatch Must Be Strictly Regulated and Restrained], *China Labor* (March 2006): 9–12.

47. "Laowu paiqiangong weiquan zaoyu falv nanti" [Protections for Agency Workers' Rights Meet Legal Difficulties], *Xinhua News,* 20 June 2005, accessed 24 June 2013, http://news.xinhuanet.com/legal/2005-06/20/content_3108717.htm; Guoming Tu, "Shanghai shi qiye laowu yonggong de xianzhuang, wenti yu duice" [Agency Employment at Enterprises in Shanghai: Current Situations, Problems, and Countermeasures], in *Laowu Paiqian de Fazhan yu Falv Guizhi* [The Development and Legal Regulation of Labor Dispatch], ed. Changzheng Zhou (Beijing: China Labor and Social Security Press, 2007), 14–22.

48. "Laowu paiqiangong weiquan zaoyu falv nanti."

49. See, among others, Kai Chang and Kungang Li, "Bixu yange guizhi laodongzhe paiqian"; Bixue Wang, "Labor Dispatch Encounters Legal Difficulties, Legislation and Regulation Is in Urgent Need" ["laowu paiqian zaoyu falv nanti, lifan guifan keburonghuan"], *People's Daily,* 4 January 2006, 14; Wei Wu, "laowu paiqian chongji laodong yonggong zhidu" [Labor Dispatch Assaults Labor and Employment System], *China*

Labor and Social Security Report, 22 June 2005; Weijie Zhang, "Laowu paiqian, ruhe burang laodongzhe chikui" [How Not to Disadvantage Workers in Labor Dispatch], *Worker's Daily*, 15 March 2006, 7; Zhang Zhijin, "Laodong paiqian jigou yingdang quid" [Labor Dispatch Organizations Should Be Banned], *Economic Information Daily*, 20 August 2005.

50. For a detailed discussion on this point, see Mary E. Gallagher and Baohua Dong, "Legislating Harmony: Labor Law Reform in Contemporary China," in *From Iron Rice Bowl to Informalization: Markets, State, and Workers in a Changing China*, ed. Sarosh Kuruvilla, Ching Kwan Lee, and Mary E. Gallagher (Ithaca, N.Y.: Cornell University Press, 2011), 36–60.

51. The extensive media and scholarly discussions and debates over the Labor Contract Law are simply too large to cite in their entirety. For a quick summary of the battles over the lawmaking process between corporations and labor, see Global Labor Strategies, "The Battle for Labor Rights in China: New Developments," November 2007, accessed 24 June 2013, http://laborstrategies.blogs.com/global_labor_strategies/2007/11/the-battle-for-.html.

52. A further illustration of this politicized campaign-style lawmaking process was an unusual move by the central government—opening a public comment period on the draft Labor Contract Law in 2006. Over 190,000 comments poured in, many from ordinary Chinese workers. See Lu Zhang, "The Paradox of Labor Force Dualism and State-Labor-Capital Relations in the Chinese Automobile Industry."

53. In general, the social-insurance schemes of agency workers provided by the labor agencies were much lower than the standards of the auto enterprises. And agency workers only received 20 to 25 percent of the social insurance of formal contract workers at the studied automakers. Given that social insurance and fringe benefits constitute as much as half of the wage bills, the auto employers can save substantially by using agency workers.

54. The author's follow-up interviews with F1, F13, F17, F20, S1, S2, S13, S19, Q1, Q9, C3, C12, November 2008, May and October 2009.

55. For instance, Article 14 of the new Labor Contract Law stipulates that formal contract employees have the right to request employers to sign nonfixed-term labor contracts after two consecutive renewals of fixed-term (permanent) labor contracts.

56. The author's meeting minutes at a discussion forum organized by the Ministry of Human Resources and Social Security (MOHRSS) on revising the second draft of the Labor Contract Law, Qingdao, September 2006.

57. A classic case of this state boundary-drawing strategy is the state-enforced household registration system (hukou) between rural and urban residents. As many have noted, the hukou system has long relegated rural residents to second-class citizenship and limited their access to good jobs in the urban areas. See, for example, Solinger, *Contesting Citizenship in Urban China*.

58. Yunzhang Xiang, "Quanwei Baogao Cheng Laowu Paiqian Da Liu Qian Wan Ren, Quanzong Jianyi Xiugai Laodong Hetong Fa" [Authoritative Report Says Agency Workers Have Reached 60 Million, ACFTU Urges to Revise Labor Contract Law], *Economic Observer*, 3 March 2011.

59. Yanbing Geng and Ji Jiapeng, "Quanzong zaitui laodongfa xiugai huo she laowu paiqian xianzhi" [ACFTU Proposed to Amend the Labor Contract Law or Set Up Restrictions on Labor Dispatch Again], *21st Century Business Herald*, 9 February 2012, http://finance.qq.com/a/20120210/000164.htm.

60. "Ministry of Human Resources and Social Security Will Develop Specific Measures to Regulate the Labor Dispatch," *Xinhua News*, 27 September 2008, accessed 24 June 2013, http://news.xinhuanet.com/legal/2008-09/27/content_10121294.htm.

61. IHLO (Hong Kong Liaison Office of the International Trade Union Movement), "ACFTU Pledges to Unionise Agency Workers," March 2012, accessed 24 June 2013, http://www.ihlo.org/LRC/ACFTU/000312.html.

62. Liping Chen, "Laodong Hetong Fa Xiuzheng An Chushen: Paiqian Laodongzhe Yu Yonggong Danwei Laodongzhe Tong Gong Tong Chou" [First Review of the Draft Amendments to the Labor Contract Law: Agency Workers Entitled to Equal Pay for Equal Work], *Legal Daily*, 27 June 2012, accessed 24 June 2103, http://news.xinmin.cn/domestic/gnkb/2012/06/27/15301851.html.

63. Ibid.

64. Silver, *Forces of Labor*.

65. See, for example, Ching Kwan Lee, *Against the Law: Labor Protests in China's Rustbelt and Sunbelt* (Berkeley: University of California Press, 2007).

66. For a comprehensive and insightful discussion of the CCP's legitimacy in the reform era, see Vivienne Shue, "Legitimacy Crisis in China?" in *Chinese Politics: State, Society, and the Market*, ed. Peter Gries and Stanley Rosen (New York: Routledge, 2010), 41–68.

67. This emphasis on the centrality of building regime legitimacy in relation to promoting economic development in post-reform China parallels Castells's analysis of the development states in East Asia. See Manuel Castells, "Four Asian Tigers with a Dragon Head: A Comparative Analysis of the State, Economy, and Society in the Asian Pacific Rim," in *States and Development in the Asian Pacific Rim*, ed. Richard P. Appelbaum and Jeffrey Henderson (London: Sage Publications, 1992), 33–70.

68. On the unique relationships between the state, markets, and capitalism in China, see Giovanni Arrighi, *Adam Smith in Beijing: Lineages of the Twenty-First Century* (London: Verso, 2007), chap. 11.

69. "*Qiushi* zazhi fabiao Li Keqiang tongzhi wenzhang qiangdiao tiaozheng jingji jiegou dui cujin chixu fazhan juyou guanjianxing zuoyong" [*Qiushi* Magazine Published Li Keqiang's Article Emphasizing Adjustment of Economic Structure Is Critical to Promote Sustainable Development"], *Xinhua News*, 31 May 2010, accessed 30 June 2013, http://news.xinhuanet.com/politics/2010-05/31/c_12163253.htm.

70. China Labour Bulletin, "Unity Is Strength: The Workers' Movement in China 2009–2011," October 2011, accessed 30 June 2013, http://www.clb.org.hk/en/files/share/File/research_reports/unity_is_strength_web.pdf.

71. Arrighi, 376. Elizabeth Perry's compelling study of worker militias in modern China provides further evidence for the relative militancy of the Chinese working class emboldened by CCP's continuing mass mobilization when compared to their counter-

part in former Soviet Union. Elizabeth Perry, *Patrolling the Revolution: Worker Militias, Citizenship, and the Modern Chinese State* (Lanham, Md.: Rowman and Littlefield, 2006)

72. "Hu Jingtao: Speech at the 2005 National Model Workers and Advanced Workers Award Ceremony," *People's Daily*, 1 May 2005, A1; ACFTU, "Decisions on Strengthening the Coordination of Labor Relations, Earnestly Safeguarding the Legitimate Rights and Interests of Workers, and promoting the Construction of a Socialist Harmonious Society," Third Plenary Meeting of the ACFTU Fourteenth Executive Committee, *Workers' Daily*, 14 December 2005, A1.

73. This idea of "credible threat" of "disruptive power" is borrowed from Frances Piven and Richard Cloward, *Poor People's Movements: Why They Succeed, How They Fail* (New York: Vintage Books, 1977). As Margaret Levi succinctly summarizes, "the credible threat of disruption, on the streets as well as through strikes, is an important weapon in the labor repertoire, especially when there is such governmental and employer hostility to unions and to labor rights." Margaret Levi, "Organizing Power: The Prospects for an American Labor Movement," *Perspectives on Politics* 1.1 (March 2003): 59. For a fuller discussion on what I call "legitimacy leverage," see Lu Zhang, *From Detroit to Shanghai*.

74. Xiaodan Zhang, "Bargaining without Union: Paternalist Labor Relations in China's Reform Era" (Ph.D. dissertation, Columbia University, 2005).

75. "Hu Jintao: Attended and Addressed the 2008 Economic Globalization and Trade Unions International Forum Opening Ceremony," *Xinhua News*, 7 January 2008, accessed 30 June 2013, http://news.xinhuanet.com/newscenter/2008-01/07/content_7378124.htm; "Hu Jingtao: Speech at the 2010 National Model Workers and Advanced Workers Award Ceremony," *People's Daily*, 28 April 2010, A1.

76. See, for example, Marc Blecher, "When Wal-mart Wimped Out: Globalization and Unionization in China," *Critical Asian Studies* 40.2 (2008): 263–76; Chen Feng, "Trade Unions and the Quadripartite Interactions in Strike Settlement in China," *China Quarterly* 201 (2010): 104–24; Mingwei Liu, "Union Organizing in China: Still a Monolithic Labor Movement?" *Industrial and Labor Relations Review* 64.1 (2010): 30–52.

77. See, for example, Howard Kimeldorf, *Battling for American Labor: Wobblies, Craft Workers, and the Making of the Union Movement* (Berkeley: University of California Press, 1999); Nelson Lichtenstein, *State of the Union: A Century of American Labor* (Princeton, N.J.: Princeton University Press, 2002).

78. See Dan Clawson, *The Next Upsurge: Labor and the New Social Movements* (Ithaca, N.Y.: ILR Press, 2003); Beverly Silver, "Labor Upsurges: From Detroit to Ulsan and Beyond," *Critical Sociology* 31.3 (2005): 439–51; Levi, "Organizing Power."

79. Frances Piven and Richard Cloward, *Poor People's Movements*, qtd. in Beverly Silver and Lu Zhang, "China: Emerging Epicenter of World Labor Unrest," in *China and the Transformation of Global Capitalism*, ed. Ho-Fung Hung (Baltimore: Johns Hopkins University Press, 2009), 175.

80. Frances Piven, "Can Power from Below Change the World?" *American Sociological Review* 73 (2008): 8.

81. Frances Piven and Richard Cloward, "Power Repertoires and Globalization," *Politics and Society* 28.3 (2000): 413–14.

242 · LU ZHANG

82. According to the Ministry of Human Resources and Social Security, in 2008, 1.2 million workers filed over 693,000 labor-dispute cases with Chinese authorities, a 98 percent increase over 2007. There were twenty-two thousand collective labor-dispute cases accepted by the committees, a 71 percent increase over 2007. MOHRSS, "Laodong zhengyi tiaojie zhongcai fa shishi yi zhounian zuotanhui zhaokai" [Annual Forum Held for Labor Dispute Mediation and Arbitration Law], 9 May 2009, accessed 24 June 2013, http://www.gov.cn/gzdt/2009-05/09/content_1309305.htm. The doubling of arbitration cases and labor-related lawsuits had partly to do with the sharp increase in factory closures and wage defaults in the 2008 global economic downturn. But it also reflected workers' growing awareness of their rights and confidence in the Chinese legal systems of public redress.

83. Such related lines include autoworkers' community lives, the impacts of the new regulations on labor dispatch, regional differences in labor politics, and the expansion of automobile production into new locations, particularly West and Central China.

11

Transformative Power

Lessons from the Greek Crisis and Beyond

HILARY WAINWRIGHT

In a context of uncertainty and flux, it helps to start from the specific. My starting point is the rise of Syriza, the radical left coalition rooted in the movements resisting austerity that has become the main opposition party in the Greek Parliament. Syriza's ability to give a focused political voice to the anger and despair of millions has made a breakthrough from which we can learn. This is a matter not only of its soaring electoral support, which rose from 4 percent of the national vote in 2009 to 27 percent in June 2012 on the basis of a refusal of the policies imposed by the International Monetary Fund (IMF), the European Commission (EC), and the European Central Bank (ECB), but also of the fact that this electoral mandate is reinforced by organized movements and networks of solidarity that Syriza has been part of building. This is not to imply that Syriza's success is stable or that its momentum will necessarily be maintained. One of its seventy-one MPs, the ex-Pasok member and trade-union leader Dimtris Tsoukalas, warns that "votes can be like sand."[1] Threatening winds will blow persistently from a hostile media determined to exploit any sign of division; from national and European elites creating an atmosphere of fear towards the left; and from an aggressive fascist party exploiting xenophobic tendencies in Greek society with some success, having won 7 percent in the polls.

Syriza does not provide a template to apply elsewhere; it is a new kind of political organization in the making. Reflection on its rise, however, which has taken place alongside the collapse of support for Pasok (from around 40 percent of the vote in 2009 to no more than 13 percent in 2012), throws the present quandary of the left, especially in Europe, into relief. Such reflection also stimulates fresh thoughts on forms of political organization that could help us find ways out. The quandary is this: On the one hand, there is the inability of social-democratic parties to stand up to, or even seriously to bargain over, austerity for the masses as a solution to the financial crisis. To varying degrees these parties are demonstrating their inability to rise to the challenge of a visibly discredited neoliberal project. The decay in party democracy and culture, moreover, combined with an entrenchment of market-driven mentalities, has meant that in social-democratic parties the forces of renewal are negligible or very weak. On the other hand, most political organizations of the radical left, with the notable exception of Syriza, are in weaker positions than they were before the financial crisis of 2008. In addition, the traditional forms of labor-movement organization have been seriously weakened. There has been an impressive growth of resistance and alternatives of many kinds, many of them interconnected and many, like Occupy, besmirching the brand of an already dodgy-looking system. But through what strategic visions, forms of organization, and means of political activism they can produce lasting forces of transformation is an open question under active and widespread discussion.

In other words, while the right, in the form of neoliberalism, was ready for the collapse of the Soviet bloc in 1989, the left in the North, when faced with capitalism coming as near to collapse as it can—given its ability to call in state guarantees—has been unable to find appropriate ways of building a dynamic of change driven by its alternative values and directions for society. Syriza in its current form has been forged in the intense heat of the most ruthless turning of the screw of austerity. Syriza is going to face many problems, both within its own organization, as it changes from a coalition of parties and groups to becoming a party with its own direct membership, as well as in the face of new pressures that will come from its opponents inside and outside Greece. However, after interviewing a wide range of activists and reading interviews and reports by others, I have a grounded belief that the long and difficult process of developing a framework of rethinking political organization beyond Leninism and parliamentarism is producing qualitatively new results.

Many of the political resources that shaped Syriza's response to the present extremities and led it to a position in which it is uniquely—but still conditionally—trusted by so many people in Greek society are the outcome of considerable learning from the trial and error of other radical parties across Europe and the experience of the European Social Forum. This essay seeks to contribute toward continuing this dialectic of transnational political learning on the left. By generalizing from the distinctive features of Syriza, and also bearing in mind lessons from other experiences where parties with similar ambitions have been unable to sustain their transformative dynamic, I will suggest approaches to problems of political organization, further consideration of which might help to overcome the quandary of the left.

My discussion of these themes will focus on the problem of transforming the state. This is a major issue for Syriza as it campaigns and prepares for office in and against a notably corrupt and antidemocratic state. One of four sections of the program drawn up in 2009 by members of Synaspismos, the largest party in the Syriza coalition, is entitled "Restructuring the State." My framework for approaching this fundamental issue sees sources of democratic transformative power autonomous from the state as decisive to the possibilities of change. The economic dimension here is crucial. Political change is seriously hindered if it lacks a base in noncapitalist relations of production, including the production of services and culture, however partial and incomplete. At the same time, it must be said that a conflictual engagement in as well as against the state is a necessary condition for systemic change. Such an engagement has to be rooted in, and accountable to, forces for democratic change in society. Without a strategy of this kind to transform and, where necessary, break state power, transformative struggles will recurrently lapse into containable countercultures, and their potential for the majority of people will be unrealized.

To develop my argument, I draw particularly on the experience of the radical left of the Labour party in governing London in 1982–86 and that of the Brazilian Workers' party (PT) in opening up decisions about new municipal investment to a citywide process of popular participation in Porto Alegre from 1989 until 2004. Despite these cases being well known, their lessons for political organization have yet to be fully distilled. For my argument, what is significant is that their achievements—each of the city experiments involved a redistribution of resources and, for a period, power and capacity, from the rich and powerful to the poor and marginalized—depended on opening up to and sharing resources with autonomous sources of democratic power in the cities concerned. In other words, they combined initiatives for change from within government structures with support for developing wider, more radical sources of power outside. But it was significant that not only had such a strategic orientation failed to change the Labour party in the United Kingdom, it also turned out that neither did the PT in Brazil adopt such a dual strategy once it was elected at the national level, which partly explains the limits of the Lula government in fulfilling many expectations it had aroused for radical social change.

In the Greater London Council (GLC) and Porto Alegre experiments, political parties used their electoral mandates to move beyond the constraints imposed by the existing system and instead to strengthen and spread challenges to that system. The spirit they embodied can also be seen in widespread campaigns by public-service workers and users against privatization that involve effective strategies to change the way that public services are managed and public money administered, dragging political parties after them. All these experiences have underlined the importance of struggling to create noncapitalist social relations in the present rather than defer them to "after winning power." Lessons from these local experiences, however, can help the necessary rethinking of what political organization needs to be like in a context of plural sources of transformative power. In drawing these lessons, we need also to bear in mind that there are further distinct problems in changing state and quasi-state institutions on national and international levels.

To understand the wider significance of the way these local political experiences combine a struggle as representatives within the local state with support for democratic movements and initiatives outside, we need to distinguish between two radically distinct meanings of power. These are, on the one hand, power as transformative capacity and, on the other hand, power as domination—as involving an asymmetry between those with power and those over whom power is exercised. We could say that historically, mass social-democratic parties have been built around a benevolent version of the second understanding. Their strategies have been based around winning the power to govern and using it paternalistically to meet what they identify as the needs of the people. Both the experiences of the GLC in the early 1980s and the PT in municipal government in the 1990s were attempts to change the state from being a means of domination and exclusion to becoming a resource for transformation by campaigning for electoral office in order then to decentralize and redistribute power. I would argue that in practice Syriza is attempting the same project at a national level.

Syriza and the Dynamics of Social Change

The most distinctive feature of Syriza, in contrast with traditional parties of the left, is that it sees itself as more than simply a means of political representation *for* movements, but as being involved practically in *building* the movements. Its political instincts make responsibility for contributing to the spread and strengthening of movements for social justice a high priority. In the weeks following the election of seventy-one Syriza MPs in June 2012, its leaders stressed the importance of this as central to "changing people's idea of what they can do, developing with them a sense of their capacity for power," as Andreas Karitzis, one of its key political coordinators, put it. While the party believes that state power is necessary, it is clear that, in Karitzis's terms, "what is also decisive is what you are doing in movements and society before seizing power. Eighty percent of social change cannot come through government."[2]

This is not just talk. This view of strategies for social change influences how Syriza is allocating the considerable state resources it is receiving as a result of its high level of parliamentary representation. The party will get eight million euro (almost triple its present budget), and each MP is allocated by the Parliament five members of staff. The idea at the time of writing is that a high proportion of the new funds should go to solidarity networks in the neighborhoods—for example, to employ people to extend initiatives such as social medical centers, to spread what approaches have succeeded, to link, online and face to face, people in the cities with producers of agricultural goods. Funds will also go to strengthening the capacity of the party in Parliament, but a greater proportion will be directed towards Syriza's work in building the extraparliamentary organizations for social change. Of the five staff allocated to MPs, two will work for the MP directly. One will work for policy committees that bring together MPs and civic experts, and two will be employed by the party to work in the movements and neighborhoods. Behind these priorities is a learning process arising from the vulnerability shown by left parties in other European countries to letting parliamentary institutions, with all their resources and privileges, pull them away from the movements whose political voice they had intended to be.

From its origins in 2004, at the height of the alter-globalization movements (which had a particularly strong impact in Greece), Syriza was at least as concerned with helping to build movements for change in society as with electoral success. There was also a learning process through the European Social Forum and then the Greek Social Forum. This contributed to not only Syriza's clear strategic view of the limits of state power for social transformation but also a self-conscious insistence on norms of pluralism, mutual respect, and openness to the new ways in which people were expressing their discontent and alternatives. Providing a constant reminder of the political methodology they were trying to avoid was the KKE, one of the last orthodox Communist parties in Europe, self-confident in its self-imposed isolation and wary of contamination with "unorthodoxy." Syriza activists, by contrast, were very much part of the open, plural, curious culture of mutual learning promoted by the European Social Forum, and it was explicitly one of their goals that their new political coalition be infused with it.

The effects of this were clearly seen in how Syriza related to the youth revolt after the police shooting of Alexandros Grigoropoulos in 2008, not pushing a line or seeking to take control. And they acted in the same way when the protests gathered in Syntagma Square and beyond through 2011.

Syriza activists contributed their own principles—for example, not allowing any anti-immigrant slogans—and applied these with others, anarchists for example, to find practical solutions through the general discussions. The youth wing of Synaspismos had a workshop near the beginning of the Syntagma protests to explain and discuss this noninstrumental, principled approach.

Syriza is also shaped by the converging culture of the different generations and traditions that make up the coalition. The younger generation, now in their late twenties or early thirties, came to the left independently of any "actually existing" alternative. The older leadership had been part of the resistance to the dictatorship in the late 1960s and 1970s. Many of them became the left Eurocommunists of the

1980s. Both generations were active in the alter-globalization and social-forum movement. This meant that the collective processes of knowledge and cultural production in the movements resisting neoliberal globalization, both inside Greece and internationally in the 1990s, were central to the personal political development of Syriza activists, rather than being a sphere in which they "intervened" to promote an alternative that had already been worked out elsewhere.

Syriza activists at all levels are emphatic about going beyond protest and having alternatives that are convincing to people who are discontented with the corrupt Greek state and the "troika" of the EC, the IMF, and the ECB. This has led to an emphasis on support for initiatives that could make an immediate difference now rather than waiting for Syriza's election to government. For instance, as the cuts destroy the public-health system, doctors and nurses in Syriza are involved with others in creating medical centers to meet urgent social needs and at the same time pushing for free treatment in public hospitals and campaigning to defend health services. Syriza is also bringing together sympathetic frontline civil servants with teachers, experts, and representatives of parents' organizations to prepare changes in the organization of the Ministry of Education to make it more responsive to the people and to release the stifled capacities of state employees who genuinely want to serve the public. It is also mapping the social and cooperative economy in the country to identify how it can be supported politically now as well as to determine what kind of support it should have when the party moves into government to realize Syriza's goal of an economy geared to social needs. The party's responsiveness to the steady rise in self-organized forms of solidarity economy amidst the crisis, recognizing its potential in terms of constructing an alternative direction for society, is reminiscent of what André Gorz meant when, in outlining the strategic concept of nonreformist reforms in his *Strategy for Labor*, he stressed the importance of "enabling working people to see socialism not as something in the transcendental beyond but as the visible goal of praxis in the present."[3] When Alexis Tsipras declared that the party was ready for government, based on an unequivocal rejection of the economic-policy memorandum, it concentrated the minds and organizational discipline of Syriza activists. The movement style and culture of the organization gave way to a single-minded campaign in which loyalties to this or that group or tendency in the Syriza coalition weakened, and a new closeness emerged. But complaints also emerged about a certain opacity of when and where decisions were made and how to influence them, and fears were expressed that the large parliamentary group could reinforce this if it becomes too autonomous. And there is recognition of the danger of Tsipras becoming a celebrity symbol on which the future of the party can end up becoming dependent, weakening internal party democracy and diluting debate—shades of Lula in Brazil and of Andreas Papendreou in 1981. Although the coalition is united on the importance of its claim on government, much thought is being given to how to share leadership, maintain accountability to party and movement activists, sustain a critical politicized culture of debate, challenge, and strategic militancy—to avoid, in other words, becoming "another Pasok."

Rethinking the Franchise:
From Atomistic to Social Representation

Syriza's experience gives a practical focus to recent discussions in the alter-globalization movement about whether, in liberal democracies, to engage in, as well as struggle against, the political system—and, more specifically, whether to seek political representation for more than propaganda purposes, and if so, with what forms of organization. Syriza's self-conscious combination of organizing for government with spreading the capacity for change autonomously from the political system—through solidarity work in the community, agitating at the base of the unions, campaigning for social and political rights, as well as against racism and xenophobia and so on—raises anew the question of whether the vote is still a resource for social transformation or a perpetual source of disillusion and alienation. In other words, can representation in the existing institutions of parliamentary democracy, along with efforts to change these institutions, strengthen the wider struggle to bring somehow an end to capitalist power—the power of the financial markets, private banks, and corporations, all intertwined with and guaranteed by state institutions?

My answer is positive, albeit highly conditional. In the broadest terms, the condition is based, organizationally and culturally, on an understanding of citizenship as social and situated. In today's societies, ridden as they are with inequalities, this implies an engagement with electoral politics while at the same time strongly challenging what has become of the universal franchise: an abstract, formal political equality in a society that is fundamentally unequal.

Many propertyless men and women and their allies who struggled for the vote imagined that exposing, challenging, and overcoming unequal and exploitative relationships would be at the heart of parliamentary politics. For the Chartists and many suffragettes, the vote was the opening of a new phase in this political struggle, not a plateau on which to remain. Political representation meant for them a means of "making present" in the political system struggles over social and economic inequality.[4] The ability of the British establishment, often with the complicity, tacit and overt, of Labour's parliamentary and trade-union leaderships, to contain this potential dynamic is only a well-documented example of a phenomenon common in different forms to liberal democracies.[5] The result is a narrow form of representation in which citizens are treated as individuals in an entirely abstract way rather than as part of embedded social, and at present unequal, relationships. It is a political process that consequently tends to disguise rather than expose inequalities and protects rather than challenges private economic power.

This tendency has regularly come under challenge by later generations. They have taken up the radical democratic goals of the pioneers by seeking to break the protective membrane of parliamentary politics and open politics up to the direct impact of struggles that are shifting the balance of power in society. There is much to learn in this respect from two experiences, the radical Labour administration of the Greater London Council and the PT government of Porto Alegre. Their political leaderships in practice built their strategy for implementing a radical electoral mandate on sharing power, resources, and legitimacy with citizens organized autonomously around issues of social and economic equality. These municipal politicians started from the recognition that the inequalities they were elected to tackle—of economic power, race, gender, and more—needed sources of power and knowledge beyond those of the state alone. In both cases, the mandate was for a politics that would learn from and not repeat the compromises, national as well as local, of the past.

In the case of the GLC, the left leadership of the London Labour party, influenced by a fierce controversy in the national party, was determined to avoid the failure of the 1974–79 Labour government to implement a radical electoral mandate. This strong political will, along with a direct involvement in community, feminist, trade-union, and antiracist movements, led the would-be GLC councillors to reach out to many organizations that broadly shared their aims and involve them in drawing up a detailed manifesto. This became the mandate of the new administration after Labour won the GLC elections in 1981. It was a key reference point in conflicts with public officials in County Hall and across the river in Thatcher-led Westminster and Whitehall—a source of moral legitimacy for the radicalism of the GLC's policies. In the case of Porto Alegre, the "taken-for-granted" way of running the municipality had involved local party elites making mutually beneficial deals that reproduced a structural corruption and secrecy that ensured that the council effectively served, or at least did not upset, the economic interests of the fifteen or so families who dominated the local economy as landowners and industrialists. The PT's mission, as part of its commitment to redress the gross inequalities of the Brazilian polity and economy, was to put an end to this. Under the leadership of Olivio Dutra, it committed itself to working with neighborhood associations and other grassroots democratic organizations to open up the council's budgetary, financial, and contracting procedures.

In both cases, the strategies were effective in achieving many of their goals—so much so that in different ways the vested interests they challenged took action, equally effectively in their reactionary terms. These experiences and, in particular, the crucial relationships between autonomously organized citizens and the local state were the product of specific historical circumstances. Both the British Labour party and the Brazilian Workers' party were the product of labor and social movements and progressive intellectuals, but their divergent historical origins were based on differing understandings of democracy and hence of their strategies toward representative politics. While the PT was created to give a radically democratic lead to the struggle against dictatorship, the Labour party was founded to protect and extend workers' rights and social provision within a parliamentary democracy.

The Labour party began from an almost sacrosanct division between the industrial and the political, respectively the spheres of the unions and of the party. The rules governing the relationship have had a significant flexibility; otherwise this "contentious alliance" would not have survived. By the 1950s this division of labor had produced a profoundly institutionalized abdication of politics by the trade unions to the Labour party, which increasingly saw legitimate politics as taking place only within narrowly parliamentary confines. The unions could lobby and as part of the Labour party pass resolutions proposing what governments should do. But for them to take action directly on political issues, including broadly social ones, was out of bounds.

The London Labour party of 1981 was of a very different character. It was the product of a powerful challenge to this moderating division of labor, which came perilously close (in the eyes of the British establishment) to breaking the barriers protecting the reactionary U.K. state against the rebellious spirit of what was at that time one of the best-organized trade-union movements in Europe. The Labour party of the early 1970s was in opposition and radicalizing in reaction to the political collapse and compromise of the 1964–70 Wilson government. The Labour party at this time, especially outside the parliamentary leadership, opened its doors to the influence of social movements, including the base and some of the leadership of the trade unions. A radical manifesto was drawn up in a relatively open and participatory manner that was not only about extending public ownership but also delegating power to trade-union organizations in the workplace. In government, however, and under the pressures of the city of London, strengthened by U.S. moves toward financial deregulation, and the IMF, the doors were closed by the parliamentary leadership. The result was an unprecedented struggle throughout the labor movement that escalated into a conflict not over this or that policy but over the very nature of representation. This struggle has been well documented.[6]

By the mid-1980s, the left had lost the struggle to change the Labour party and with it the nature of working-class political representation. In the meantime, the left had not only won and kept control of the party of the capital city in 1980, with the support of most of the trade unions, but with its victory in the elections for the GLC it had gained control over a strategic authority with a budget greater than many nation-states. It had the opportunity, the will, the allies, and some of the legislative powers—before the Thatcher government started to hack away at them—to implement radical policies. Once ensconced in County Hall, Labour councillors, driven on by the struggles and organizations in which many of them were involved, and indeed had become councillors to pursue, led the GLC in ways that would transform the relationship between councillors, local government "officers," autonomous citizens' organizations (including the unions), and the majority of London citizens.[7] For a brief moment, this significant local Labour party behaved in a way comparable to the Workers' party in Brazil six thousand miles away.

The distinctiveness of the PT, at least from its foundation in 1980 to the late 1990s (and its importance for our discussion of the conditions under which representative democracy might be a resource for social transformation), is a political practice based on the belief that the formal foundations of democracy—universal franchise, rights to free speech, freedom of assembly, a free press, political pluralism, and the rule of law—had to be reinforced by effective institutions of popular, participatory democracy if the goals of democracy—political equality and popular control—were to be realized. This was the lesson the party drew from not only the experience of bringing down a dictatorship but also the extreme inequalities of Brazilian society, which made even more of a mockery of purely legal claims to political equality than in most capitalist countries. The practical character of these radically democratic forms was drawn partly from the participatory forms developed in the movements from which the PT was founded, particularly militant trade unions and the landless movement. These participatory forms were then developed through a self-conscious and collective process of trial and error in the formation of the participatory budget itself, in several major cities in addition to Porto Alegre. The culture and mentality of the party's approach to popular participation was important too. This drew on the traditions of popular education that, most explicitly in the case of Paulo Freire, were effectively a form of political consciousness-raising based on the principle of enabling people to realize their capacities. The result was a party that had committed itself to developing institutions of popular control through which it would try to share power and strengthen popular transformative capacities. There are many echoes of the PT in the character of Syriza, a reflection perhaps of their common history of struggle against a dictatorship.

Returning to the distinction between power in the sense of transformative capacity and power as domination, we can see how, in both cases, the radical political leaderships attempted to use state powers of domination—over finance and land in particular—as resources for the efficacy of popular transformative capacity. Thus, in Porto Alegre and other Brazilian cities that developed processes of participatory budgeting, after winning the mayoral elections and gaining centralized control over the budget, the party effectively delegated power over new investment and priorities to the coordinated decentralization of the participatory budget. At the same time, a group was set up to work with different neighborhood organizations to facilitate the decentralized process. This was the organization of the annual cycle of neighborhood and regional meetings at which proposals for new spending were made, evaluated according to the agreed framework of technical and substantive criteria, discussed through an elaborate but transparent and rule-governed process of horizontal decision making and negotiation, and then finalized through a committee composed of delegates from the different regions of the city and various thematic assemblies as well as representatives of the mayor. Progress on the implementation of previous decisions was also monitored through this open process, backed up by the mayor's budget office.

In the case of the GLC, there was a similar combination of council action that used its centralized power and resources to delegate power to citizens' organizations to strengthen the capacity of Londoners as workers or as citizens to determine the decisions shaping their lives. The GLC, for example, used its power to purchase land to prevent property developers from destroying an inner-city community and then delegated the management of that land to the local community alliance, which in the course of resisting the property developers had worked on its own plan for the area. It created a public enterprise board, which helped to save companies from closure on the condition that the trade unions in those companies had certain powers over how the resources were used. It set up a central office within the council with the authority to monitor other departments' implementation of the electoral mandate, including the commitment to popular participation. In other words, the centralized power to tax, to control the use of land, and so on was combined with a decentralization and delegation so the power over how state resources were allocated and managed was shared with popular groups.

As with any serious experiment, the problems must be reflected on as well as the aims and the successes. These problems shed a harsh light on the tensions between the forms of political organization developed historically within liberal representative politics to gain and sustain office *within* the state and the forms of political organization needed to build popular control *over* the state. To a significant extent, the political innovations toward the second goal were, in both cases, developed through the momentum of the process building on neighborhood, workplace, and social-movement organizations that had already formed. The pressures of the immediate often meant that difficult issues raised in the actual practice of relations between parties and autonomous initiatives and movements were not always publicly recognized and discussed.

In the case of the GLC, the emphasis on working with civic and trade-union movements was strengthened by the limited nature of its own official powers for implementing Labour's radical manifesto commitments. Much of the practical and political process of the relationship between the council and these independent organizations was dependent, however, on the GLC-appointed officers (most of whom had a movement background) and committed councillors, rather than Labour party organizations on the ground. A continuing engagement with autonomous movements, beyond the institutional relation with the unions, had not become generally built into the political habits of local Labour parties. This had begun to change in the late 1970s and early 1980s, reaching a peak with the support that local Labour parties and unions organized with others in communities and workplaces across the country, including London, for the 1984–85 miners' strike. But this social-movement struggle-oriented culture was not entrenched enough to withstand the defeats imposed by the Thatcher government, including the abolition of the GLC itself as the elected government of London.

In Porto Alegre, where relations between the PT and social movements were very close, with much overlapping membership, a major problem was the extent to which leading activists in both were drawn into government positions, weakening both the party outside government and autonomous community and social-movement organization.[8] A second problem concerned the participatory budget process itself. Although all the evidence points to a significant increase in active involvement and growth in self-confidence and organizing capacity, especially among the poor, women, and blacks, a serious limit emerged to the extent to which participatory budgeting developed popular transformative capacities beyond the point of making and prioritizing pragmatic demands. The source of this limit lay in the separation of the participatory budget process from strategic policy making, as, for example, on urban planning. As participation in budget decision making grew numerically and participants gained in confidence and political awareness, activists, including in some of the poorest areas, pressed for information and involvement in planning policy.

But this was never fully opened up. Close observer-participants suggest several explanations. One is that the PT within the municipality was not able to exert sufficient centralized control over the behavior of the different departments, to implement this desire of the participants in the participatory budget. Planning officials were particularly protective of their departmental interests. Sergio Baierle indicates that it also reflected the development of a "governmental cadre" among the PT who became distant from, and paternalistic toward, the community activists.[9]

A third problem with the participatory budget process was an absence of publicly debated and agreed-upon guidelines for agreements between City Hall and community organizations involved in the provision of services such as child care and recycling. The absence of an insistence on certain standards of equality, democracy, and public efficiency—quite a well-developed feature of the GLC's processes of grant giving—meant that the PT-led process of decentralization of resources to community organizations was vulnerable to the encroachment of the neoliberal path of community management, whose destination was usually some form of privatization.[10]

The problems encountered in London and Porto Alegre were not necessarily insurmountable. Both processes had developed a certain capacity to innovate through trial and error. But in both cases the rise of market-driven politics closed the space for further development of these experiences of democracy-driven rather than market-led reform. In the case of the GLC, its abolition took place during the period when the neoliberal right was at its most triumphant. Moreover, some sections of the left, including those whose visions of socialism had been tied to the fortunes of the Soviet Union (or, like Tony Blair, those who had no vision of socialism whatsoever), became entirely defensive, turning into naïve new converts to the capitalist market as the source of efficiency and "modernization." As a result, they only weakly defended, and sometimes attacked, the innovations of the GLC. Certainly, they worked to delete its memory rather than to learn from it. In the case of Porto Alegre, the defeat of the PT in 2004 was a result of many factors, including a loss of direction in the local PT and disappointment with the early years of the Lula government as it succumbed to the pressures of the IMF.

It is significant that the full development of both experiments was curtailed by the impact on parties of labor of the global momentum of neoliberalism, for their importance is that they illustrated in practice a direct answer to market-driven politics. This politics did so in the way it began to develop a nonmarket alternative that responded to severe democratic failings in public administration, while still recognizing the importance of the state in the redistribution of wealth and the provision of essential services and infrastructure. Whereas the conversion of social democracy to the neoliberal paradigm involved unleashing the capitalist market as if it could be the source of new energy needed to reform routinized and unresponsive state bodies, the early PT and the radical left in London (and elsewhere) looked to forms of democracy that released the creativity lying dormant among the mass of people as the source of new energy for the management of public resources for the public good.

The attempted obliteration of this option, through the pervasive ideological imposition of the dichotomy of an old statist left versus the dynamism and entrepreneurialism of the capitalist market, was in effect a continuation of cold-war mentalities into the twenty-first century. Left alternatives are underdeveloped precisely because of the successes of this obliteration. But when we look for the sources from which a transformative politics can now grow, it is important to recall that the transformative alternative did not entirely disappear. This was seen in Brazil, if not in the PT itself, through highly politicized movements and networks such as the Movemente Sans Terre. Even in the United Kingdom it survived in spirit in various campaigns, from the one that defeated Thatcher's poll tax to the more recent ones of, for example, U.K. Uncut against corporate tax evasion, combining creative forms of direct action with the research of committed academics, journalists, and trade-union whistleblowers, followed up by supportive MPs.

I want to reflect especially on the many movements and initiatives that undertook struggles against privatization since the mid-1990s. Many of these were also struggles to transform the state. There are enough examples from across the world to suggest that these indicate a significant development among public-sector unions and wider alliances, especially at a local level but with national and international support.[11] These experiences indicate a positive response to the breakdown of the division of labor characteristic of social-democratic labor movements, as noted earlier, between trade unionism as concerned with industrial relations and the employment contract and parties taking responsibility for wider political issues, including the welfare state. Here, in their refusal to accept the commodification of public services and utilities, while at the same time voicing the reassertion and renewal of the goal of maximizing public benefit rather than profit, trade unions are directly taking responsibility as citizens for what was the sphere of representative politics. In a sense, they are defending the earlier use of the state to redistribute and to decommodify; but they are also opening up a dynamic of renewal and transformation of those nonmarket relationships.

What is it that makes these struggles transformative, going beyond defending existing relationships and initiating a new dynamic that releases the creative capacities and powers of working people? The key development here is that trade-union organizations grounded in specific workplaces, and cooperating with associations of users and communities, have begun to struggle around the use values produced by their members rather than simply replicating the relations of commodity production and bargaining over the price and conditions of labor. Indeed, to win the struggle for public services they have turned their organization from being a means of representation and mobilization to also being a way of democratically socializing the knowledge that workers—and users—already have in fragmented form of the service they deliver or use, and gaining a full view of how the service could be developed and improved. They are in effect making the overcoming of the alienated nature of labor a part of their struggle to defend but also to realize the full potential of the public sphere of noncommodified provision.

Political Organization in Transition

The examples in this essay all illustrate a transition from socialist change as centered around the state to an understanding of transformative power organized in society. Government—in these cases, local government—remained important, not as the prime driver of change but as exercising specific powers of redistribution and socialization of land and finance and the defense of public services. These are powers that can support the capacities of self-organized citizens to resist and transform, in ways that they can be used against capital and in ways that can facilitate self-organization and support democratic and decentralized management of public resources, including as "commons."

What can we conclude about the implications of this transition for the nature of political organization? We have had a glimpse through these examples of the GLC, Porto Alegre, and transformative resistance to privatization, of the multiplicity of forms of political organization and initiative, in which the objective of political representation and/or government office is only one part of the process of change. The concept of the "political" has, over the past four decades or so, gained the broader meaning of concern with transforming power relations throughout society. Many of the initiatives that are, in this sense, political more often than not focus on a particular site of social relations but do so with a wider vision and cluster of values in mind. An aspect of this broader interpretation of politics is the way that these activities are increasingly creating alternatives in the present that not only illustrate the future they are working for but also seek to open up a further dynamic of change. In this respect we made a comparison with the innovative strategic thinking of André Gorz in the mid-1960s; but in thinking now about political organization, a contrast will help to identify a further feature of the present transition.

The organizational dimension of the struggle has changed considerably since Gorz's time. For many reasons, involving the political defeats of traditional organizations of labor, the socially devastating impact of neoliberal economics, and also radical changes in technology and the organization of production, we face extreme forms of fragmentation and dispersion. In effect, the problem of creating prefigurative change in the present with a dynamic toward future change is as much about ourselves creating new forms of self-organization in the present as about reforms through the state. We can see the practice of this through campaigns around resistance and alternatives to privatization. We have described how these campaigns aim to achieve changes in the present that also illustrate an alternative future, defending or recovering public provision from takeover by the market but also making them genuinely public in their organization, not merely their ownership.

These campaigns could not rely on the existing organizations of the labor movement. Considerable organizational innovation has been required involving links with communities in which the union is one actor among many, and the traditional labor parties have had only a minimum presence. Such campaigns have highlighted the need for the conversion of the union from a means of defensive bargaining to a means of gathering workers' knowledge and taking militant action to transform services in response to users' needs. This hybrid of old and new organizational forms, developed and combined for a common purpose, is a widespread pattern producing new organizational forms.[12]

Any useful mapping of distinctive features of the transition in organizational forms should include two further features of this multiplicity of political organization. The first concerns the importance of the means of communication. Organization is always in good part about communication, as well as about decision making and discipline. The new communication technologies enable a qualitatively greater variety of means of collaboration. They facilitate means of networked coordination based on common goals and shared values but recognizing a plurality of tactics and organizational forms and therefore not requiring a single center.[13] Such networked approaches to transformative politics preexisted the new technology, but there has been an escalation of possibilities that have in turn expanded our organizational imaginations, as well as producing new problems.

The second, related feature concerns knowledge. The spread of dispersed yet often connected and collaborative forms of organization also creates favorable conditions for realizing the political potential of the plural understandings of knowledge developed in practice by movements in the 1970s, especially the women's movement and radical trade-union organizations and also, from different origins, in the traditions of popular education and grassroots political organizing in many parts of the South.

The shift from a state-centered understanding of change to one focused on developing transformative power in society is associated with these radical changes in our understandings of knowledge. The movements of the 1970s asserted in their practice the creative, knowing capacity of so-called ordinary people against both the "scientific management" of the Fordist factory and the centralized, exclusively professional knowledge of the Fabian social-democratic state. Their understandings of the importance of experiential as well as theoretical knowledge, tacit as well as codified, underpinned the first phase of thinking about participatory democracy in these earlier decades of rebellion and a so-called excess of democracy. This also alters the whole context of political programs, leading to a far wider, more participatory process of the development of ideas than traditionally has taken place within political parties, emphasizing alternatives in practice as well as—indeed, often as the basis for—reforms required from the state. In many ways, the functions associated with a political party are now carried out by many autonomous actors sharing common values.

To think through the implications of this complexity for political organization, it is important to distinguish different kinds or levels of political activity. For example, the focused kind of unity required for an election campaign is not what is required for helping to build a network of social centres or alliances of community groups and trade unions, where spreading information and facilitating diversity according to local circumstances will be more appropriate. It makes sense for the question of organizational form to be related to the purpose of the activity. Moreover, there is no necessity for different activities and organizations that share common values be part of a single political framework. There is a wide variety of ways in which common values can be communicated and shared.

There remain, however, many unresolved issues. One is the problem with which we began: that of representation within the political system, to redistribute public resources and redeploy state power. This is a purpose that again requires distinctive organizational forms. To develop these, we need to return to our theoretical sketch of a critical approach to representation based on citizens not as atomistic individuals with a formal, abstract political equality, but as citizens embedded in concrete and, at present, unequal social relationships, as workers, as dispossessed in numerous different ways, as women, as ethnic minorities, as disabled people, and so on. What strategies and organizational forms best "make present" and gain political resources for the struggles to overcome these inequalities and sources of exploitation? We noted how actually existing parliamentary democracy effectively tends to occlude and reinforce inequalities of wealth and power unless directly challenged. This is a process intensified by conceding key decisions to opaque and unaccountable national and international bodies; and, as a consequence, a depoliticization of most of the central decisions affecting the future of society. This trend is often associated with neoliberal globalization, but it is only a continuation of a process endemic in liberal democracy: leaving key issues concerning the future of the poor in the hands of the capitalist market; as we saw in the past history of Porto Alegre, the future of the residents of the *favellas* in the hands of the elite of landowning families; of inner-city London communities in the hands of speculative property developers; and of public services in the hands of predatory corporations.

The common feature of the counterstrategies attempted in London and Porto Alegre was one based on municipal collaboration with those struggling directly against these inequalities: the organizations of the poor in the *favellas* through the participatory budget, the inner-city communities in London through direct involvement in formulating and implementing the council-planning process and support for their proposals against the pressures of landowners and property developers, respectively. Organizationally, they entailed a form of political representation based on an electoral mandate and accountable for its implementation to those citizens with specific sources of power, knowledge, and organization necessary—but without sufficient political support—to carry through the change. I have argued that political representation in such contexts involves a clash between two entirely different understandings and forms of organization of political power. Organizational forms are needed, therefore, for the purpose of making present in the political system struggles in society. These struggles reinforce the electoral mandate by actively claiming and elaborating the commitments made. Such forms of political representation are up against entrenched institutions that take as given and as beyond their responsibility the inequalities and problems against which these struggles and the electoral mandate are directed.

The kind of organization whose purpose it is to carry through this social, unavoidably conflictual form of representation has to be organized to serve the struggles and movements whose demands and needs it is pursuing through the political process. This is much more complex and more difficult than being "a voice." If parties are understood as those organizations seeking political representation and government office, then we are talking here about a political party. But it is a party—or parties—of a very distinctive kind (of which we have experienced so very few). For a start, it would, as should be clear from our previous evoking of the multiplicity of forms of political organizations for radical social change, be part of a constellation of organizations, outside of political institutions sharing more or less explicitly common values and goals.

Secondly, these new kinds of parties would effectively be serving within the framework of a commitment set out by the electoral mandate, developed through the participation of this wider network or constellation. Forms of accountability and transparency for the work of representatives in implementing this commitment would be central to the organizational character of the party.

Thirdly, the party organization would necessarily be double-sided, with its members, including those involved in the work of representation, involved in building these extraparliamentary organizations of transformative power. As we saw with Syriza and others, they would be involved not especially as leaders but as fellow activists, contributing to and sharing their particular sources of power and knowledge. Such a new kind of party would require specific organizational forms to counter the pressures drawing representatives into the flytrap of parliamentary politics, with all its tendencies toward a separate political class. We saw in London and the GLC and Brazil and the PT that the inability of the two parties to continue to build up the presence of social movements and open up state resources for social struggles lay in the weakness (in the case of the Labour party) or weakening (in the case of the PT) of the parties' organized links with society. There are lessons here that Syriza could well bear in mind.

Political parties are shaped in part by movements that were decisive in their origins: for the PT, the movements for democracy and equality against dictatorship and oligarchic rule; and for the London Labour party of the early 1980s, by the maturation of the movements of the late 1960s and 1970s. Parties are also constrained by the system they are working in. With Syriza, perhaps, we have one of the first parties to be shaped predominantly, though not exclusively, by the movements that have developed to resist neoliberal capitalism in the face of a political class completely disconnected from the mass of people. One of the twenty-nine women MPs that make up a third of Syriza's parliamentary group, Theano Fotiou, described the overriding purpose that the structure of the new party must fulfill: "It must be a structure for the people to always be connected to the party, even if they are not members of the party, to be criticizing the party, bringing new experience to the party."[14] They created a coalition to which nearly two million people felt connected in spite of—maybe partly because of—a determined attempt to whip up fear. Syriza arrived at this through much learning from fellow Greeks and from political experiences across Europe. It is clear that as we strengthen our continent-wide capacities to refuse austerity and organize behind the nonreformist reform of a democratic and equal Europe, we will learn a lot from them.

Notes

1. Personal interview with Dimitris Tsoukalas, Athens, 9 July 2012. My thanks to Roy Bhaskar, Vishwas Satgar, Jane Shallice, and Steve Platt for helpful discussions and suggestions on earlier drafts, to *Red Pepper* and Transnational Institute companions for their constantly stimulating collaboration, and to Marco Berlinguer for many discussions in the process of writing a joint book that includes among many themes, those of this essay.

2. Personal interview with Andreas Karitzis, Athens, 9 July 2012.

3. André Gorz, *Strategy for Labor: A Radical Proposal* (Boston: Beacon Press, 1964), 7. Gorz explains nonreformist or "structural" reforms as those conceived "not in terms of what is possible within the framework of a given system and administration, but in view of what should be made possible in terms of human needs and demands."

4. For this analysis of the radical potential of political representation as "making present," see Raymond Williams, *Resources of Hope* (London: Verso, 1989).

5. See, for example, Peter Gowan, "The Origins of the Administrative Elite," *New Left Review* 167 (March/April 1987): 4–34. On the role of Labour's leadership, see Ralph Miliband, *Parliamentary Socialism* (London: Merlin, 1961).

6. Leo Panitch and Colin Leys, *The End of Parliamentary Socialism: From New Left to New Labour* (London: Verso, 1997).

7. Public managers are known as "officers," in line with the original military model of public service.

8. In the early years of the PT government, about 10 percent of the local membership of the PT came to be employed by the municipality. The city of Porto Alegre has six

hundred government-appointed positions, a common pattern in Brazilian local government and something the PT presumably did not challenge because it strengthened their control over the state apparatus. But it does produce its own problems. See Sérgio Baierle, "The Porto Alegre Thermidor? Brazil's 'Participatory Budget' at the Crossroad," in *The Socialist Register 2003* (London: Merlin Press, 2002), 305–28.

9. Ibid. Also see Hilary Wainwright, *Reclaim the State: Experiments in Popular Democracy*, updated ed. (London: Seagull Books, 2009), 140–50.

10. See Evilina Dagnino, "Citizenship in Latin America: An Introduction," *Latin American Perspectives* 30.2 (2003): 211–25. Dagnino efers to the "perverse confluence" between, on the one hand, "the participatory project constructed around the extension of citizenship and the deepening of democracy" and, on the other hand, "the project of a minimal state, which requires the shrinking of its social responsibilities and the gradual abandonment of its role as guarantor of rights" (7).

11. See David Hall, Emanuele Lobina, and Robin de la Motte, "Public Resistance to Privatization in Water and Electricity," in *Beyond the Market: The Future of Public Services*, ed. Daniel Chavez (Amsterdam: Transnational Institute, 2005), 187–95; Mario Novelli, "Globalisations, Social Movement Unionism, and New Internationalisms: The Role of Strategic Learning in the Transformation of the Municipal Workers Union of EMCALI," *Globalisation, Societies, and Education* 2.2 (2004): 161–90; Sandra Van Niekerk, "Privatization: A Working Alternative," *South Africa Labour Bulletin* 22.5 (1998): 24–27; Hilary Wainwright, "Transformative Resistance: The Role of Labour and Trade Union Alternatives to Privatisation," in *Alternatives to Privatisation: Public Options for Essential Services*, ed. David A. Macdonald and Greg Ruiters (London: Routledge, 2012); Hilary Wainwright and Matthew Little, *Public Service Reform . . . but Not as We Know It* (Brighton: Picnic Publishers, 2009).

12. We have seen it in campaigns in the United Kingdom against tax evasion. We have also seen it with Syriza in its campaign against the troika's memorandum, as they combine work to build the movement of the squares with organizing for government. The successful campaign against water privatization in Italy was again a hybrid of local campaigners for the commons organized through autonomous groups converging for a common campaign with trade unions, especially locally, municipal political representatives, and so on. It is evident, too, in some of the most effective transnational networks such as Our World Is Not for Sale, which played a central part in the campaigns to expose and block the workings of the World Trade Organization. It is made up of a hybrid of trade unions, social movements, organizations of workers in the "informal economy," and radical research and campaigning organizations from across the world. The global, continental, and national convergences of movements and smaller organizations and initiatives through the World Social Forum processes spread and further cross-fertilized this hybrid political networking.

13. For a useful and empirically grounded analysis of recent examples, see Marianne Maeckelbergh, "Horizontal Democracy Now: From Alterglobalization to Occupation," *Interface* 4.1 (2012): 207–34.

14. Personal interview with Theano Fotiou, Athens, 3 July 2012.

12

How Workers and the Government Have Dealt with Economic Crisis and Industrial Decline

1929 and 2007

EDWARD MONTGOMERY

Introduction

The National Bureau of Economic Research, the official arbiter of recessions in the United States, lists some thirty-three business cycles since 1854. On average, every fifty-six months workers in the United States go through a period of growth and expansion and then contraction and crisis. While growth periods have been on average longer and contractions shorter in duration since World War II, the experience of boom-and-bust cycles for workers has not gone away.[1] Both 1929 and 2007 were years of widespread economic collapse that came on the heels of periods of financial innovation, rapid asset appreciation, and growing inequality. In both cases, the bursting of an asset bubble was followed by a meltdown in the financial sector, which spilled over into the rest of the economy with significant consequences for working men and women.

The Great Depression and Great Recession, which started in 1929 and 2007, respectively, are the only two U.S. recessions that have been due to a financial crisis in nearly one hundred years. While recessions due to financial crises have been rare in recent U.S. history, they are not uncommon internationally or historically. Carmen M. Reinhart and Kenneth S. Rogoff collected data on post–World War II recessions in advanced economies and found eighteen postwar banking crises. Recessions due to banking crises have been characterized by their severity and duration.[2] Reinhart and Rogoff found that, on average, output falls 9 percent and unemployment increases by 7 percentage points during these recessions.[3] While output typically recovers in two years, it takes 4.8 years for unemployment to return to pre-recession levels.

Reinhart and Rogoff also found that during financial crises, home values and stock prices fall and remain depressed for a long time, generating a sizable negative impact on household net worth. Governments also experience a rapid increase in their debt due to reductions in tax revenues collected and increases in spending to stimulate their economies. In many countries, these debt levels reached a point where growth is retarded and many governments even default on their debt.[4] The recent downgrading of government debt in Greece, Portugal, Spain, Ireland, Italy, and even the United States suggests that investors have become worried about such a possibility in numerous advanced economies.[5]

The Great Depression was perhaps the defining economic crisis in the United States and for much of the industrialized western world. The initial responses of the Federal Reserve, President Hoover, and Congress are generally viewed as either having been too tepid or actually counterproductive. With the New Deal, President Franklin D. Roosevelt took a much more activist approach by creating income-support programs for seniors, the unemployed, and farmers; insuring bank depositors and home mortgages; regulating prices and the banking and financial sectors; and creating the right to unionize. Public support for these efforts was widespread at the time, as Roosevelt captured 63 percent of the vote for his reelection in 1936, one of the biggest electoral landslides in history. The New Deal left an enduring set of institutions and programs designed to prevent future downturns from occurring and to cushion the blow of any future crisis.

The legacy of the 2007 Great Recession is yet to be fully determined. Perhaps because it is led by a scholar of the Great Depression, the Federal Reserve intervened far more aggressively than it did in 1929 to provide cheap credit and shore up a wide array of financial institutions.[6] Over the objections of many in Congress, first a Republican and then a Democratic administration went farther than President Roosevelt ever did and directly injected taxpayer dollars into private banks and mortgage loan institutions, an insurance company, and even some major manufactures by buying shares of stock in them (sometimes even against their will) to ensure their solvency. The federal government also enacted a nearly trillion-dollar economic stimulus bill, a major expansion of health insurance, and reregulated the banking industry.

Public support for President Barack Obama has been split, with his approval ratings hovering in the 45–52 percent range as he headed into his reelection bid in 2012.[7] Despite the rescue of the banks and auto industry, record corporate profitability, and a recovered stock market, business views him as hostile to its interests. Even with the passage of Dodd-Frank financial regulation and the Affordable Care Act of 2010 expanding coverage to millions, the public has not been convinced that he is looking out for their interests. While Roosevelt's party gained nine Senate and nine House seats at his first midterm election in 1934, Obama's lost six Senate and a near-record sixty-three House seats in 2010.

In a reversal of fortunes, Obama won reelection in 2012 with 51.2 percent of the vote, while Republicans lost seats in both the House and Senate. Despite this "mandate," the Republican-controlled House and the president appear to be locked in a stalemate, unable to avoid the harmful economic effects of a budget-sequestration deal that neither side liked, let alone reach agreement over the future of the New Deal and Great Society social protections for workers and the poor. With the possible exception of immigration reform, the president appears to have been reduced to urging federal agencies to use executive actions to move his agenda forward and relying upon the Federal Reserve to keep the economy growing.

In this essay, I start with a brief review of the evidence on the causes of the Great Depression and its impact on workers and their families. I examine some of the similarities and differences in the causes of the Great Recession and its impact on workers. I briefly summarize some of the different policies that Presidents Roosevelt and Obama enacted to shorten the crisis and ease the burden on workers.[8] As part of that, I will discuss in some detail President Obama's unusual step to intervene directly in the auto industry. Besides looking at what the government did for workers, I will briefly look at indicators of collective actions they took for themselves during these two major economic crises and how that shaped what followed. I will argue that while Presidents Roosevelt and Obama were both called "socialist" by critics ranging from Father Coughlin to Glenn Beck, their similarities are limited, and both the short- and long-term impacts of the policies they enacted during these crises are quite different for workers. While the near-term impact of the Great Recession was dwarfed by the Great Depression, the Great Recession exacerbated long-term structural trends that may well leave workers facing far more uncertain futures. Workers' own relative passivity in the face of these dynamics contrasts sharply with their grandparents' generation during the Great Depression. Absent a revival of their activism, we may well see the continued erosion, or even the end, of the New Deal social contract.

The Great Depression: An Overview

Some seventy years after it ended, the Great Depression remains a topic of active study, discussion, and disagreement. There is general agreement that the Great Depression started as a financial crisis that spread through the real economy, even if conservatives remain loath to credit President Roosevelt with ending or even ameliorating it.[9] Its severity and global reach forever shaped the generations who lived through the era. It led to a set of economic, social, and political institutions geared to preventing its recurrence and the creation of a social safety net that would expand significantly during the postwar period.

The events leading up to the Great Depression are strikingly similar to those before the Great Recession. Working families had managed to share in some of the prosperity of the 1920s, which brought rising wages that were used to purchase homes, automobiles, and other durable goods. Between 1918 and 1925, new-home construction increased 530 percent, and single-family home prices jumped 28 percent. Home-ownership rates rose from about 46 in 1920 to 49 percent in 1930.[10] Not surprisingly, residential mortgage debt shot up and continued to climb until 1930, when it was 241 percent higher than it had been in 1918.[11]

With the onset of the Great Depression this trend reversed itself, so that by 1940 only 44 percent of households lived in a home that they owned. The foreclosure rate surged 68 percent between 1930 and 1933, forcing many states and local areas to place moratoriums on foreclosures. David E. Wheelock analyzed mortgage-delinquency data from twenty-two cities in January 1934 and found that 44 percent of urban homes with a first mortgage were in default. For those with second or third mortgages, over 54 percent were in default. The average length of time these two groups of households had been delinquent was fifteen months and eleven months, respectively. Home prices declined 24 percent between 1929 and 1933 and did not return to pre-Depression levels until after World War II.[12]

Stock prices had climbed even faster than home prices during the 1920s, rising by nearly 500 percent. As there were no rules setting minimum margin requirements until 1933, investors could purchase shares for 25 percent down and continue to hold the shares even with zero equity.[13] Banks looking for new sources of profits moved from being trust managers for established clients to being financial-services brokers for a new class of investors and speculators.[14] The number of shareholders in the United States grew from between four to six million people in 1927 to nine to eleven million people, or about 8 percent of the population, in 1930.[15] Many of these shareholders were inexperienced, with little knowledge of the underlying value of their assets. In the words of the Securities and Exchange Commission, "little thought was given to the systemic risk that arose from widespread abuse of margin financing and unreliable information about the securities in which they were investing."[16]

"Black Thursday" in 1929, or the day the stock market crashed, is commonly taken as the marker for the beginning of what would become the Great Depression. The Dow Jones Industrial Average fell by nearly 50 percent in 1929 and, after a brief rebound in 1930, continued to slide until late in 1932, when nearly 90 percent of the value of its companies had been erased. It took until nearly the mid-1950s for the Dow to recoup its 1929 value. This asset-market collapse in turn led to banks calling in collateral and cutting lending in a desperate effort to stay afloat. There was a dramatic increase in the number of banks having to suspend operations and an increase in bank consolidations and failures. The numbers of banks in operation would fall by over 40 percent between 1929 and 1933.

Economists have emphasized that the initial credit crunch was exacerbated by bad policy decisions by the Federal Reserve, which took steps to defend the dollar's gold exchange rate, forcing them to cut the money supply, further reducing available credit.[17] No credit meant that consumers and businesses had to cut spending, which in turn led to cuts in production and worker layoffs, generating a vicious downward-spiraling economy. To stop the cascading run on the banks, President Roosevelt secured the passage of Emergency Banking Act of 1933 as soon as he was sworn in. This act imposed a bank holiday in an effort to stem the public panic and allowed the Federal Reserve to supply unlimited amounts of credit to reopening banks. While this act worked to stabilize the banking sector, the Depression was far from over.

Gross domestic product (GDP) fell by 8.6 percent in 1930, 6.5 percent in 1931, and 13.1 percent in 1932. At the trough of the Great Depression in 1933, GDP was 27 percent lower than in 1929. It is hard to comprehend the completeness of the economic collapse that occurred during the Great Depression. In terms of today's economy, such a loss in output would be equivalent to a decline of over four trillion dollars, or roughly the combined size of the current Russian, Brazilian, and Canadian economies. For workers, the massive contraction in output led to nearly ten million fewer people employed in 1932 and 1933 than in 1929 (chart 12.1). The unemployment rate nearly doubled each year, increasing from 3 percent in 1929 to 25 percent in 1933 (chart 12.2).[18] Unemployment during the Great Depression in Detroit and Chicago reached 30 percent and 40 percent, respectively, and in Colorado it reached 50 percent.[19] These numbers for Chicago and Detroit were driven in part by a 50 percent reduction in employment in the iron and steel industry and a 62 percent drop in auto-manufacturing employment.[20] Even with the 1933–37 economic turnaround, there were still over two million fewer employed workers eight years after the Depression began.

Unemployment rates in northern states were generally higher than in the more rural South. Rates also varied by skill, with occupations like plumbers, carpenters, and even engineers being hit particularly hard by the absence of any building activity. While comparable data on unemployment for racial or gender groups is not available annually, we can see in chart 12.3 that no group of workers was immune from the ravages of the Depression. Unemployment among white men more than doubled between 1930 and 1937.[21] For nonwhite men the unemployment would more than triple. For white women there would be nearly a fivefold increase in their unemployment rate, while nonwhite women's unemployment increased nearly sevenfold. Given this pattern of disproportional impact for minorities and women, it is entirely plausible that at the peak of the Great Depression between a third and a half of all women or nonwhite males were unable to find work.[22]

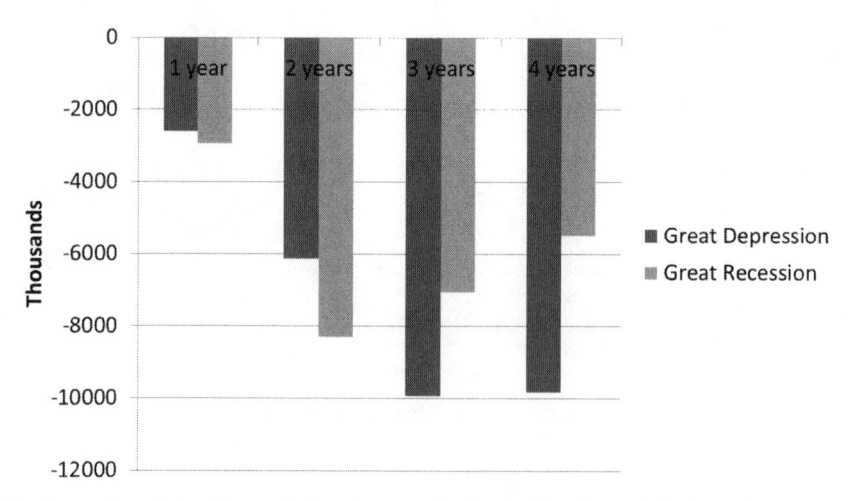

Chart 12.1. Cumulative Change in Employment during the First Years of the Great Depression and Great Recession

Source: National Bureau of Economic Research, Macro history Data Base, U.S. Non-Agricultural Employment 1900-1943, http://www.nber.org/databases/macrohistory/rectdata/08/a08171b.dat and U.S. Bureau of Labor Statistics, Current Population Survey, and Civilian Employment level.

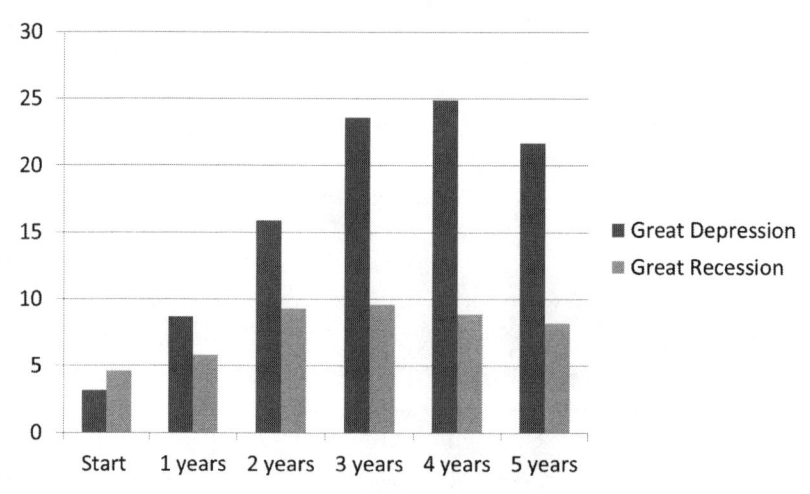

Chart 12.2. Unemployment Rates during the First Years of the Great Depression and Great Recession

Source: BLS CPS Annual unemployment rates plus average monthly rate for January to July 2012, and Stanley Lebergott unemployment series as reported in Robert Margo, "Employment and Unemployment during the 1930's," *Journal of Economic Perspectives* 7.2 (Spring 1993): 41-59.

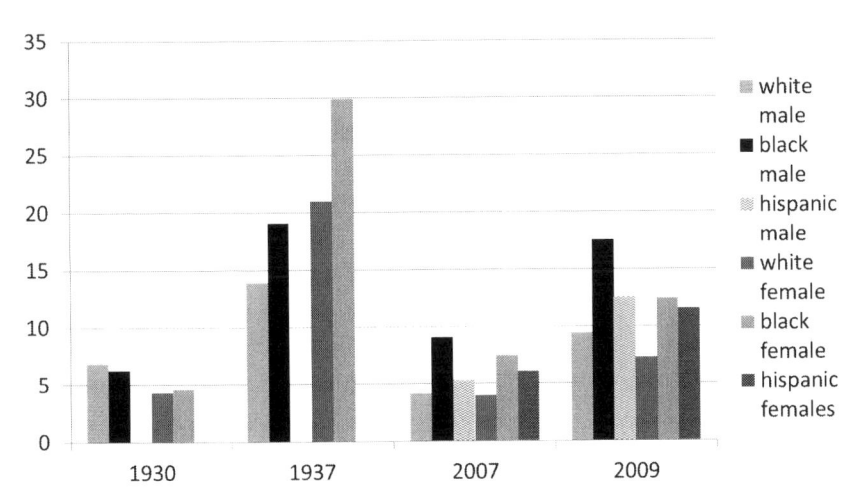

Chart 12.3. Unemployment Rates by Race and Gender during the Great Depression and Great Recession
Source: William A. Sundstrom, "Last Hired, First Fired? Unemployment and Urban Black Workers during the Great Depression," *Journal of Economic History* 52.2 (June 1992): 415-29, tables 1 and 2. Data for 1937 is the percentage of the labor force seeking jobs, not including those with government-relief jobs. Bureau of Labor Statistics annual data 2007 and 2009.

As bleak as the numbers are, the Great Depression hit workers and their families in more ways than just their ability to find a job. For those who were lucky enough to have a job, it often came with significantly reduced work hours. Employers did not hesitate to cut hours, or speed up or stretch out production, raising productivity and squeezing more from each worker.[23] By some estimates, almost half the variation in labor input in manufacturing during this period occurred through changes in hours. Squeezing labor was widely endorsed by business leaders and even the secretary of the treasury, Andrew Mellon, who said in 1930, "Liquidate labor, liquidate stocks, liquidate the farmer, liquidate real estate. People will work harder, live a more moral life. Values will be adjusted, and the enterprising people will pick up the wreck from less competent people."[24]

Millions could not find work or worked fewer hours and often earned much less each hour they could work. Pay cuts were common, as average hourly earnings fell about 2 percent in 1930 and 5.2 percent in 1931. By 1933 nominal wages were about 24 percent lower than they had been in 1929. Offsetting the squeeze on wages were cuts in the prices workers paid for rent and food, which fell by nearly a third between 1929 and 1933. Widespread deflation meant that the overall cost of living actually fell 24 percent between 1929 and 1933.

President Roosevelt believed that this deflationary spiral of falling wages and prices was hurting recovery efforts. To stabilize food prices he introduced the

Agriculture Adjustment Act of 1933 (AAA), which provided crop-price-support payments for farmers who restricted production to desired levels. He also supported the passage of the National Industrial Recovery Act of 1933 (NIRA), which exempted from antitrust regulations industry trade-association groups who banded together to control prices and production and adopt common "codes" for minimum wages and working conditions. Before the NIRA was struck down by the Supreme Court in 1935, more than five hundred industries, covering nearly 80 percent of private, nonagricultural employment, had some type of code regulating prices and setting floors under working conditions.[25] Whether these pieces of legislation were the cause is subject to debate, but wages and prices stopped falling in 1933, and real wages in manufacturing actually increased by 33 percent between 1933 and 1939.[26]

New immigrants had long represented an important source of competition for native workers to the U.S. economy. The peak for immigration to the United States occurred before World War I, when the population grew by as much as 12 percent per year because of new arrivals. In the 1920s, however, the Emergency Quota Act of 1921 and the Immigration Act of 1924 were passed primarily to limit the influx of southern and eastern Europeans, who had been arriving in large numbers since 1900, and to prohibit the immigration of Asian Indians and East Asians.[27] The onset of the Great Depression, and these changes in the nation's immigration laws, cut immigration rates in the 1930s to one sixtieth of their peak rate, and they remained low until after World War II. With the poor economy, out-migration actually exceeded in-migration in 1932 and 1933.

Onset of the Great Recession: Similarities but Differences

In 2007, the United States was rocked by the most significant financial crisis that it had experienced since the Great Depression.[28] Between 2000 and 2007, housing prices had risen 86 percent, fueled by the surge in subprime mortgages that brought a wave of new homeowners into the market. The repeal of the Depression-era Glass-Steagall Act in 1999 freed banks to enter new lines of business. The development of new financial instruments like collateralized debt obligations and credit-default swaps allowed largely self-regulated financial firms to compete for new investors and a share of the increasingly mobile global savings.

New money, new home buyers, new financial products with little knowledge of their underlying values or systemic risks, and lax regulation of underwriting and risk-management practices set the stage for an asset bubble and crash. In many ways it was eerily similar to what had occurred almost eighty years ago. Housing prices dropped 18 percent in 2008, the largest decline in a generation.

By the first quarter of 2009, housing prices were 31 percent below their peak levels in 2006, a bigger decline in housing values than during the Great Depression. Not surprisingly, mortgage-delinquency rates climbed 72 percent by 2009, while the foreclosure rate increased 130 percent. While a greater share of households with mortgages were delinquent in their payments during the Great Depression (by a factor of between three and five), the percentage going through foreclosure was more than three times higher in the Great Recession. Homeownership rates declined from 69 percent in 2006 to 65 percent in 2012, the lowest level since 1997.

The investment-banking giants Bear Stearns and then Lehman Brothers collapsed because of their exposure to housing-market losses. Lehman Brothers, with a value of about $680 billion, was the biggest bankruptcy in history, generating a cascading deleveraging in the financial-service sector and a reduction in credit. The number of problem banks tripled in 2008 and increased tenfold during 2009. The stock market, as measured by the Standard and Poor's Index, declined 40 percent in 2008. Between the stock and housing market declines, U.S. households lost some fourteen trillion dollars in net worth.

As had been the case in 1929, what started as a financial crisis soon became a real-economy problem, as a lack of credit caused investment spending to decline by 10.2 percent in 2008 and 24.8 percent in 2009. GDP dropped rapidly in the second half of 2008 and the first six months of 2009. By the trough of the Recession in June 2009, the cumulative decline in real output of 4.7 percent was more than in any other recession since the Great Depression.[29] Global market integration served to insure that this crisis also had real effects abroad.[30] GDP growth in the advanced industrialized Organization for Economic Co-operation and Development (OECD) countries fell by 3.5 percent in 2009. In countries like Ireland, Finland, Slovenia, Mexico, Japan, Hungary, and Iceland, GDP declined by more than 6 percent in 2009.[31]

Normally, changes in employment lag behind changes in output during a recession, as firms are slow to let workers go and then reluctant to hire them back even as business improves. At the end of 2008 and the beginning of 2009, however, employers dumped workers at an unprecedented rate. While 179,000 workers lost their jobs in the first three months of 2008, 1.95 million lost their jobs in the last three months of 2008, and another 2.34 million jobs disappeared in the first three months of 2009 (see chart 12.1). The rate of decline in employment was far more rapid and prolonged than was the case in any other postwar recession. By the time employment hit bottom in February 2010, more than a decade's worth of job growth had been eliminated.

The unemployment rate doubled between December 2007 and October 2009, peaking at 10.0 percent. While steep recessions are usually followed by rapid recoveries, the Great Recession's recovery looks like the Great Depression's in the slow pace of recovery for employment.[32] The unemployment rate stayed above 9 percent for twenty-eight straight months and remained above 8 percent for forty-three months. Both of these are post-Depression records. Even at this time it has been argued that measured unemployment rates do not fully reflect how bad job-market conditions are for workers. A broader measure of labor underutilization that captures those who gave up looking for work and those who took part-time jobs involuntarily topped 17 percent in 2009 and remained around 14 percent four years later.

Between December 2007 and January 2009, the number of long-term unemployed doubled, and in 2012 there were still almost four times as many people who had been unemployed for six months or longer than was the case at the end of 2007. While the incidence of long-term unemployment has declined somewhat with the recovery, in mid-2012 it was still the case that over 40 percent of the unemployed have been without work for six months or longer.[33] Historically, the long-term unemployed have had great difficulty rejoining even a reinvigorated labor market, raising the specter that many of these workers may be permanently left behind.

The economic impact of the Great Recession differed across regions and across population subgroups. Michigan, California, Rhode Island, and South Carolina suffered some the nation's highest unemployment, while Texas and North and South Dakota were among the lowest. Hispanics and Asians, regardless of gender, and white males experienced post–World War II record unemployment rates, while the unemployment rate for black males exceeded 20 percent and nearly reached 15 percent for black females. Males suffered a relatively greater increase in their unemployment rate during the downturn.[34] This was due in large part to the fact that the heavily male construction and manufacturing industries accounted for 48 percent of all job loss between December 2007 and December 2009. The recovery has also been unbalanced, but now there have been bigger employment gains for men than women in most sectors of the economy. As of mid-2012, the adult female unemployment rate has declined 0.9 percentage points, while that for adult males declined four times more.

As we noted for the Great Depression, cuts in hours compound the impact of an economic crisis on workers. While nonfarm employment declined 8.5 percent between the start of the recession in the fourth quarter of 2007 and the first quarter of 2010, average weekly hours declined another 1.4 percent. Recent work by Michael Elsby, Bart Hobjn, and Aysegul Sahin suggest that over the past six recessions, between 20 and 50 percent of the variation in labor usage by employers comes from changing worker hours.[35] Thus, the variation in total labor input that came through hours cut (15 percent) was smaller than recent experiences. Nonetheless, a loss of six hours off a typical work week was no small matter to workers.

While we saw significant deflation in wages and prices during the Great Depression, there was little of that during the Great Recession. Consumer prices fell about 4 percent in the last five months of 2008 (largely due to falling energy costs) and 0.4 percent in 2009 but rose 1.6 percent in 2010 and 3.2 percent in 2011. Median usual weekly earnings rose only 1.1 percent in 2010, compared to 3.9 percent in 2008, but they still increased. Adjusted for inflation, real earnings still rose modestly in 2008 and 2009, but they fell about 1 percent in 2010 and 2.1 percent in 2011. The recent pattern of flat or declining real wages is an unfortunate continuation of a longer, thirty-year trend of stagnating income for workers.

While one would have expected that the Great Recession would have led to a significant reduction in the flow of new immigrants, there is little evidence to support this. In the years 2004–7, the average annual flow of legal immigrants was 1.099 million, while over the period 2008–11 it averaged 1.086 million a year (about 1 percent less).[36] The Department of Homeland Security estimates that since the beginning of the recession, the total number of unauthorized immigrants living in the United States declined from 11.8 million in January 2007 to 10.8 million in 2009 but returned to 11.5 million in 2011.[37] Thus, while new immigrants ceased to be an economic factor during the Great Depression years, they continue to account for an important share of population and labor-force growth as we emerge from the Great Recession. Particularly in the low-wage segments of the labor market, native and immigrant workers will likely remain in competition for the scarce jobs that do exist.

Not a "New Deal" but a "Slightly Different Deal"

President Roosevelt was leery of direct relief and felt that the best way to support the able-bodied was through the provision of a job, preferably by the private sector, but if necessary by the government. The Civilian Conservation Corps (CCC), the Civil Works Administration (CWA), and the Works Progress Administration (WPA) were set up in 1933 to create temporary jobs. The WPA employed 3.3 million workers at its peak in November 1938 and eight million workers over its existence.[38] To prepare for future spells of unemployment, President Roosevelt also wanted employers and workers to set aside funds that would sustain job losers while helping to stabilize consumption and growth. The Social Security Act of 1935 created the federal-state partnership that is our current unemployment insurance (UI) system.[39]

Central to the government's effort to help workers and their families during the Great Recession was the 2009 American Recovery and Reinvestment Act (ARRA). ARRA tried to stimulate the economy through lower taxes; increased food-stamp, UI, and other income-support benefits; increased aid to states to support their spending on teachers, Medicaid and other critical services; and spending for highway and water infrastructure projects, job retraining, and other long-term "capacity building" projects like research and development for electric vehicles and green energy. While the Congressional Progressive Caucus and others have called for and introduced legislation with direct job-creation programs (e.g. Restore the American Dream Act), they were not part of ARRA, nor were they included in President Obama's subsequent American Jobs Act proposal.

The size and composition of the $831 billion ARRA represented a set of political compromises in an attempt to attract Republican support (more tax cuts and lower total-cost bill) while holding Democratic votes. The resultant bill was still opposed by most Republicans, who saw it as a waste of money, while Democrats worried that it was too small relative to the size of the problem. Further, many of the components were poorly designed if new job creation was the primary goal. For instance, much of the $132 billion for infrastructure went to a limited number of "shovel ready" projects to ensure that money was spent quickly. However, this often meant picking large, capital-intensive projects that tended to have fewer new jobs involved. About $116 billion went for temporary tax rebates in 2009 and 2010, the vast majority of which was saved or used to pay off debts. A similar-sized payroll-tax cut would actually have given employers an incentive to hire or keep workers.

President Obama and Congress also enacted an unprecedented series of extensions in the duration of unemployment-insurance benefits, with the federal government covering all of the cost of the extra weeks of benefits. While it has not been unusual for Congress to extend benefits during recessions, the previous record for the duration of benefits was sixty-five weeks during the 1970s. During the Great Recession workers in twenty-three states with very high unemployment were able to qualify for up to ninety-nine weeks of benefits. In February 2012, Congress voted to scale this back to seventy-three weeks, effective September 2012, and then return to the basic twenty-six weeks in December.[40] Even with ninety-nine weeks of benefits, by the end of 2011, 5.5 million workers had exhausted their benefits before finding a job.[41]

Roosevelt and Obama's efforts faced stiff opposition to steps to help workers. Their ability to overcome this opposition was quite different, in part because of differences in workers' own attitudes and mobilization. Three years after the Great Depression began, workers swept Hoover from office, demanding that the government intervene in the market and partner with them to provide economic security. They did not stop with the ballot box but took action themselves to change their economic outcomes. Even in the face of fierce employer resistance and an army of potential replacement workers among the unemployed, unionization grew dramatically in the 1930s (from 2.8 million members in 1933 to 8.9

million in 1940), especially after the passage of the pro-union National Labor Relations Act.[42] The number of days lost to strikes also increased dramatically (up 266 percent in 1934 and 431 percent higher in 1937 relative to 1929). Economic empowerment was not given to workers; they took it for themselves.

During the Great Recession, however, worker actions at the polls and their willingness to engage in collective action have been dramatically different. Two years after Great Recession began, the public voted Democrats out of office in record numbers and replaced them with a new conservative Republican majority in the House, dedicated to reducing government intervention in the market and scaling back the social safety net. Advocates for legislation that would expand unionization (the Employee Free Choice Act) have not even been able bring the bill to a vote in the Senate. The number of union members has declined by nearly a million workers since 2007, and the number of days lost to strikes in 2009 and 2010 was the lowest since data collection began in 1947.[43] While Gallup/USA Today polls show that 61 percent of the public oppose laws to take away collective-bargaining rights from public employees, only 45 percent think positively of unions, nearly an all-time low.[44]

Unlike during the Great Depression, unions or unionization does not seem to be seen by the public as the answer to workers' challenges. Only about 40 percent of white working-class (non-college) Americans voted for Democrats in the last four national elections. Eighty years after President Roosevelt ushered in a more activist paradigm, the 2012 election was set up as another test of the public's support for government economic and social action. The outcome was a disappointment to both sides, as neither progressives nor conservatives were able to wrest control, setting the stage for at least two more years of gridlock at the federal level.

Did Obama's Industry Intervention Represent a New Model?

Despite charges of a massive government takeover of everything from the banks to health care, there was nothing close to the New Deal's scale of activity in response to the Great Recession. That said, there were significant instances of direct market intervention during the Great Recession. From the time of the rescue of Bear Sterns in early 2008, the Federal Reserve and Treasury Department were actively intervening in the affairs of individual companies and financial markets generally. The scale and scope of intervention grew as the crisis deepened. In July 2008, the Housing and Economic Recovery Act sought to support the housing market by acquiring 80 percent of the government-created, but privately owned, Enterprises (Fannie Mae and Freddie Mac) and placing them in conservatorship to prevent them defaulting on trillions in outstanding mortgage obligations. Then, in October 2008, the Emergency Economic Stabilization Act passed, giving the Treasury Department authority to use up to seven hundred billion dollars to buy distressed mortgage-backed securities or provide other support to financial institutions through the Troubled Asset Relief Program (TARP). In part because of the need to provide support quickly (and the difficulty of determining the value of the toxic mortgages), Treasury ended up using about $205 billion to buy preferred stock and warrants in over seven hundred domestic and foreign financial companies.[45]

Camden Fine, the CEO of the Independent Community Bankers of America, said in response that "the entire notion of the government becoming a common shareholder in any bank—let alone the 19 largest banks—is chilling."[46] Judging by this reaction and charges of "socialism" leveled at President Obama, one would think that the idea of the federal government helping, let alone owning stock in, individual banks or companies was unprecedented, and that these businesses were being used to achieve some nefarious social policy goals.[47] While not exactly routine, federal interventions have not been rare and have generally been justified by the need to prevent some type of "systemic" failure resulting from linkages between a particular business or sector and the rest of the economy.[48] In 1918 President Wilson seized control and operated the nation's railroads for two years, while during World War II the federal Office of Alien Property Custodian took over (and managed) the U.S. subsidiaries of German and Japanese firms on average for seven years before auctioning them off.[49] Under Presidents Nixon, Ford, and Carter, the federal government extended loans to Lockheed in exchange for stock warrants; took over Penn Central railroad in 1976 and operated it as Conrail until 1987, when it was privatized; and extended loan guarantees to Chrysler again in exchange for stock warrants.[50] President George W. Bush gave ten billion dollars in loan guarantees to the airlines after September 11, 2001, also in exchange for stock warrants. It is of interest to note that in each of these cases the taxpayer ultimately made a profit on their investment.

In the vast majority of the more than seven hundred banking interventions under TARP, the federal government's ownership share was quite limited, and it held only nonvoting shares. In only a handful of cases did it come close to taking a controlling interest in a financial institution—Citigroup (21 percent share), Bank of America (35 percent share), GMAC (56 percent share), and AIG (80 percent share)—and only in the two instances when it became a majority owner did the federal government appoint any members to the Board of Directors. Despite the hue and cry, the financial-sector rescue effort was quite business-friendly, as the taxpayer provided broad-based financial supports yet gained little or no say in how its resources would be used.[51] This lack of control was easy to see in the financial industries' fierce resistance to the administration's efforts at re-regulation and, despite dramatic increases in their profits in

2009–10, their reluctance to actively participate in various Treasury programs to help underwater homeowners or expand credit.

The two largest purchases a typical person makes in their lifetime are a house and a car. Both of these purchases are highly sensitive to the availability of credit. The bursting of the housing bubble caused a seizure in the credit markets, with significant consequences for the banks and the auto industry. While the notion of "too big to fail" was controversial when it came to banks, it was doubly so when it came to the auto industry. It should be noted that conditions at General Motors (GM) and Chrysler were not solely due to the credit crunch: high gas prices (topping four dollars per gallon in June 2008), increased competition from imports, foreign transplant operations with cheaper nonunion labor, the companies' legacy health-care costs, management missteps, overcapacity in production and sales structure, and poor product quality all played major roles in their condition. Nonetheless, more was at stake than just the future of GM or Chrysler. Their closure would affect not only their own employees and investors but the thousands of companies in their supply chains. . Restaurants, grocery stores, real estate agents, and a myriad of other businesses near affected plants would lose revenue from the purchases of laid off workers, while local governments stood to lose sales-, property-, and income-tax revenues. Randall W. Eberts and Joe A. Stone estimated that it typically takes cities about eight years to recover from a structural shock like a major plant closure.[52]

These ripple effects were already being felt in the economy by the end of 2008. Overall auto sales fell 34 percent during the year, and even Toyota, Honda, and Nissan experienced sales declines in excess of 30 percent. With sales down, 1.7 million motor-vehicle and parts workers were laid off in 2008. These displaced workers were heavily concentrated in Michigan, Indiana, and Ohio, but the effects were also felt in the southern auto states of Kentucky, Tennessee, and the Carolinas. Unemployment rates in auto communities like Pontiac, Flint, and Detroit, Michigan, reached Depression-era levels of 25 percent or more.

Many of the bigger auto-parts suppliers, and even the bigger dealerships, had come to serve multiple auto companies, so the failure of any one of these companies could send shock waves through the whole auto-supply chain. Indeed, Toyota, Honda, and others endorsed aid for Chrysler and GM in part because of the fear of a cascading impact on their own viability from the potential bankruptcy of major suppliers, who were already under considerable strain because of sagging sales and tight credit. Studies by the Government Accountability Office estimated that 1.1 million jobs throughout the economy would be lost with the liquidation of these auto companies.[53] Some private-sector forecasters produced even greater impacts, ranging from 2.5 million to 3.3 million jobs at risk.[54]

Conservative commentators and politicians from southern states that were home to nonunion transplant companies rejected these "systemic risks." They argued for a "liquidationist" approach to the unionized Detroit Three. Despite the fact that labor costs are only 10 percent of the cost of making a car, they tended to focus exclusively on the United Auto Workers (UAW) as the source of the Detroit Three's troubles. Even though liquidity in the consumer and corporate credit markets was dropping precipitously, they argued that private investors would step in and provide the billions needed to reorganize.[55] While it is certainly true that GM and Chrysler could have gone into Chapter 7 bankruptcy and liquidated their assets, counting on a Chapter 11 reorganization (which would have been necessary for them to stay in business), without the government standing in as a lender of last resort, was pure fantasy. A private investor would have had to come up with an amount equivalent to half of all outstanding nonfinancial commercial debt at the time (sixty-three billion dollars) to finance the reorganizations. There were simply no white knights with this amount of money in their pocket.

Presidents Bush and Obama had both reluctantly agreed to use TARP funds to rescue GM and Chrysler.[56] President Bush provided seventeen billion dollars in loans and ordered the companies to present reorganization plans to President Obama if they wanted continued support. Obama set up an Auto Task Force to examine their reorganization efforts and to help decide whether to provide additional support.[57] He instructed his auto team to take a "commercial approach" to decisions around the companies; to not get involved in day-to-day operations; and to not pursue other policy objectives through the reorganization.[58] Some on the Auto Task Force felt strongly that Chrysler would never be viable and that the government should not invest more money in what could ultimately prove to be a futile effort to save it. The path to long-term viability for GM seemed clearer, generating broad support for further investments. Aggressive timelines for restructuring were set for each company, requiring them to reach new agreements with their workers and retirees, dealers, creditors, bond holders, and other affected parties, which would substantially reduce their claims against the company, in exchange for support.

For auto workers, the reorganization at GM meant that the Hummer, Saturn, and Pontiac brands would be abandoned and their production facilities shuttered. In all, GM closed thirteen plants, and Chrysler closed four more. On top of this, retirees' dental benefits were eliminated; health-care co-pays increased; the risks of future health-care inflation were shifted onto the workers; and pay for a new worker was slashed, among other concessions (see chart 12.4). The Center for Automotive Research found that UAW concessions since 2007 have reduced average hourly labor costs by 20 to 35 percent (from seventy-two to seventy-eight dollars per hour to fifty to fifty-eight dollars per hour).[59] Labor costs at GM now average about fifty-six dollars per hour and fifty-two dollars per hour at Chrysler, while the nonunion Toyota and Honda have labor costs of fifty-five dollars and fifty dollars per hour, respectively.

- GM cut white collar workforce by 10,000 and blue collar workforce by 32,000 closing 13 plants and idled 3 more
- Chrysler cut workforce by 24,000 and closes 4 plants
- Retiree health and dental benefits scaled back and future benefits to come from VEBA funded largely by company stock
- Two tier wage scale adopted for new hires with a starting wage of $14 per hour
- Job Bank eliminated
- Cost of living raise dropped
- Performance bonuses dropped
- Holidays reduced
- Tuition benefits dropped
- Skilled Trade differentials reduced
- **Overall average hourly labor cost cut from $72–78/hour to $50–58/hour or 26-31 percent since 2007**

Chart 12.4. Impact on Auto Workers and Retirees
Source: "2011 Detroit 3-UAW Labor Contracts" by Kristin Dziczek, at www.chicagofed.org/digital . . . /Dziczek_DABE_January_2012.pdf and U.S. Government Accountability Office Report, "TARP: Treasury's Exit from GM and Chrysler Highlights Its Competing Goals, and Results of Support to Auto Communities Are Unclear," May 2011, GAO-11-471.

Knowing that the restructuring would have a profound impact on workers and the thousands of communities with auto facilities, President Obama created the White House Council for Auto Communities and Workers. Its job was to coordinate the federal response to this economic storm, much like FEMA's role following natural disasters.[60] The council had representatives from every domestic agency and collectively sought to stabilize the companies, suppliers, and dealers; to make the domestic industry more competitive in the future by facilitating investments in new technologies; and to begin rebuilding and diversifying auto communities by investing in worker retraining, local business infrastructure, and economic development. Mayors from auto communities had consistently stressed the negative consequences of having abandoned production plants in their communities, as so often happens following a bankruptcy. The council's efforts yielded a $773 million environmental trust (the largest in U.S. history) to clean up and repurpose some eighty-nine abandoned properties across thirteen states.

Were these efforts successful? The companies have not resolved all of their problems, yet they both report making a profit for the first time in years. For workers, rather than losing one to three million jobs as forecasted, direct employment in motor-vehicle and parts manufacturing and dealers is up about 325,000 jobs since the reorganizations occurred in June 2009. In the three biggest auto states (Michigan, Ohio, and Indiana), unemployment is down between 2.5 and 5.5 percentage points, while the national unemployment rate has only declined 1.9 percentage points. For the taxpayer, about 52 percent of the TARP money invested in the auto effort has been repaid, and the Congressional Budget Office expects that ultimately all but about seventeen billion dollars will be repaid.[61] Robert Scott has estimated that there was actually a net savings to the federal government from doing the bailout of between $70 and $389 billion.[62] These savings come from not having to incur the expense of supporting more laid-off workers or the loss of tax revenues from affected companies and their workers. When the budgetary savings for states and local governments are added to this, taxpayers at all levels will get up to a twenty-sevenfold return on their investment. While Obama's critics still insist it was a waste, the voters of Michigan and Ohio thought otherwise in 2012.

Looking Ahead

The New Deal in the 1930s led to a reshaping of our economic and social institutions. As a result, since World War II economic downturns have generally been shorter and milder. The 1950s brought increasing numbers of union jobs, which offered a ticket into the middle class. At the same time, veterans programs opened up opportunities to attend college and buy a home to millions. The civil-rights and women's movements in the 1960s and 1970s helped more people share in the economy's gains and exercise their voice in the political process.[63] Will the Great Recession usher in a similar period of positive change and transformation for workers? While one must be humble about future predictions, differences in economic and political conditions leave me pessimistic about the near-term prospects for workers. Rather than the start of a new upsurge for workers, I fear that the Great Recession is a harbinger of stagnation, or even decline, to come.

One major difference between the Great Depression and Great Recession eras is the changing nature of jobs. While about ten million jobs were lost between 1929 and 1933, employment grew on average 4.8 percent each year from 1933 to 1937, or nearly four times faster than during the current recovery. For workers who made it through the Great Depression, the basic structure of employment in the economy in 1940 and even 1950 was not very different from that of 1929 (see charts 12.5 and 12.6). Manufacturing, construction, and mining were 40 to 45 percent of the economy, and the service sector was a relatively modest component. Once jobs came back, workers were able to fit back into them with only modest changes. I want to emphasize that this is in no way to dispute the severity of the impact of the Great Depression and its lasting impact on the generation who lived through it. It is simply to say that the jobs they went back to as the economy recovered were fairly similar to those that they had lost.

ECONOMIC CRISIS AND INDUSTRIAL DECLINE · 281

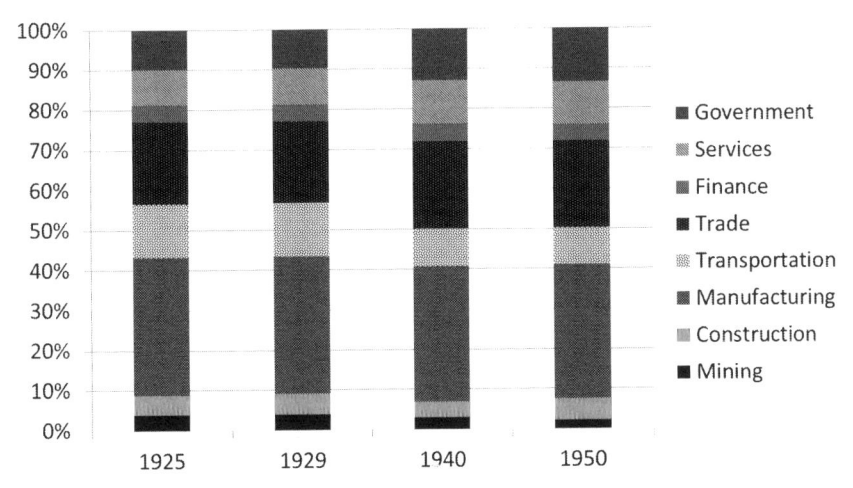

Chart 12.5. From 1925 to 1950, 34 Percent of Nonfarm Jobs Were in Manufacturing
Source: Bureau of Labor Statistics employment data

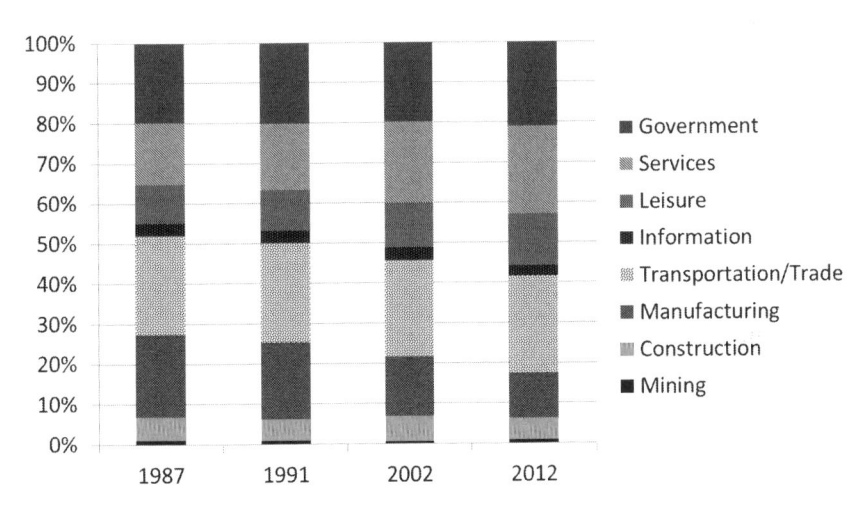

Chart 12.6. From 1987 to 2012, Manufacturing's Share of Nonfarm Jobs Fell from 21 to 11 Percent
Source: Bureau of Labor Statistics employment data

Unfortunately, not only is current job growth weak, but for much of the past twenty years the economy seems only able to create significant employment growth during either a dot-com boom or housing "bubble." Those jobs that do appear often have different skill requirements, in different sectors of the economy, and at newer, smaller firms than those jobs that were lost. Manufacturing's share of employment has been on a fifty-year path of decline, and service-producing industries employ five times more workers than goods-producing industries. Work by Claire Liang, David McLean, and Mengxin Zhao document that over the past fifty years, the pace of creative destruction has increased, with smaller and younger firms, who are reliant on external financing, increasingly creating our growth rather than the older or larger firms that were historically dominant.[64]

Chart 12.7 contrasts the largest employers in 1955 and 2010. The biggest employer in 1955 was General Motors, which offered union jobs with high wages and good benefits to over a half-million employees. Indeed, eight of the ten biggest employers were manufactures or oil companies. By 2010 the biggest company was almost four times larger than GM was in its heyday, with over two million employees, but it is a retailer with relatively low wages and benefits—Wal-Mart. Retailers and banks make up six of the top ten biggest employers, while only three manufacturers make the list. General Electric is the only company that managed to be on both lists, but today only one in seven GE workers is unionized.

Globalization has fundamentally changed where and how goods and services are being made. U.S. trade has doubled every decade since 1960, so what happens internationally matters significantly more today than it ever did. During the Depression, the passage of the Smoot-Hawley Tariff Act led to a draconian 233 percent reduction in net exports. This huge reduction in trade translated into only a 0.3 percent decline in GDP between 1929 and 1933.[65] Today such a decline in net exports would reduce GDP by over 7 percent (or twenty-three times as much). While trade can lead to better, cheaper, or more varied products for consumers, it brings with it new competitors for domestic firms and

1955	2010
• General Motors – 577,667	• Wal-Mart – 2,100,000
• US Steel – 268,142	• UPS – 408,000
• General Electric – 210,551	• IBM – 399,409
• Chrysler – 167,813	• McDonalds – 385,000
• Exxon – 155,000	• Target – 351,000
• AMOCO – 135,784	• Kroger – 334,000
• CBS – 117,143	• Sears – 322,000
• AT&T – 98,141	• Hewlett Packard – 304,000
• Goodyear – 95,727	• General Electric – 304,000
• Firestone – 90,000	• Bank of America – 283,717

Chart 12.7. The Biggest Employers Are No Longer in Manufacturing
Source: "America's Biggest Companies, Then and Now (1955 to 2010)," 24/7 Wall St., accessed 25 June 2013, http://247wallst.com/2010/09/21/americas-biggest-companies-then-and-now-1955-to-2010.

workers. Just our fifteen largest trading partners have thousands of companies and 1.6 billion workers, representing ten new potential competitors for every U.S. worker. For less-educated workers, this has contributed to declining wages and increased employment instability.

Of course, globalization is not the only factor at work changing the landscape under the feet of workers. Technological change has increased the demand for skilled workers. Unionization has declined steadily, so only one in ten workers is a union member today. The loss of worker bargaining power has contributed to stagnant real wages and rising inequality. The top 1 percent of individuals has a share of income not seen since the beginning of the Great Depression, and the gap between CEO pay and that of the average worker is unprecedented.

In the face of these challenges, workers have been largely silent. The Occupy Wall Street movement's efforts have largely dissipated. Public-sector workers' pay and benefits (and even their right to collectively bargain) are under sustained attack, but the public seems to view these less as an attack on them than one on a "special interest" group. The federal government is sidelined in its efforts to help workers by political gridlock. While the Great Recession did not match up to the Great Depression in intensity or duration, it remains unclear as to whether today's generation of workers will be able to forge the kind of successful strategies for collective action on the job site or through their government representative that their parents and grandparents did. Absent this, the rapidly changing structure of the economy will make it harder and harder for many to grab onto the economic ladder of success.

Notes

1. For the period 1919–45, the average expansion lasted thirty-five months, and average contraction lasted eighteen months. For the period 1945–2009, the average expansion lasted fifty-nine months, and the average contraction lasted eleven months. See National Bureau of Economic Research, "U.S. Business Cycle Expansions and Contractions," accessed 25 June 2013, http://www.nber.org/cycles.html.

2. Carmen M. Reinhart and Kenneth S. Rogoff, *This Time Is Different: Eight Centuries of Financial Follies* (Princeton, N.J.: Princeton University Press, 2009). See also Robert Hall, "Why Does the Economy Fall to Pieces after a Financial Crisis?" *Journal of Economic Perspectives* 24.4 (Fall 2010): 3–20.

3. Reinhart and Rogoff, *This Time Is Different*; see also Carmen M. Reinhart and Kenneth S. Rogoff, "The Aftermath of Financial Crises," *American Economic Review: Papers and Proceedings* 99.2 (2009): 466–72.

4. Reinhart and Rogoff, "Aftermath of Financial Crises"; Reinhart and Rogoff, *This Time Is Different*.

5. "United States of America Long-Term Rating Lowered to 'A++' Due to Political Risks, Rising Debt Burden," Standard and Poor's, 5 August 2011, accessed 25 June 2013, http://www.standardandpoors.com/ratings/articles/en/us/?assetID=1245316529563.

6. See, for example, Ben S. Bernanke, "The Macroeconomics of the Great Depression: A Comparative Approach," *Journal of Money Credit and Banking* 27.1 (February 1995): 1–28.

7. Based on Gallup poll data, accessed 25 June 2013, http://www.gallup.com/poll/116479/barack-obama-presidential-job-approval.aspx.

8. Marc Labonte, "The 2007–09 Recession: Similarities to and Differences from the Past," Congressional Research Service, Report R40198, 6 October 2010.

9. Harold Cole and Lee Ohanian, "How Government Prolonged the Depression," *Wall Street Journal*, 2 February 2009; and Greg Hannsgen and Dimitri B. Papadimitriou, "Lessons from the New Deal: Did the New Deal Prolong or Worsen the Great Depression?" Working Paper No. 581, Levy Economics Institute of Bard College, October 2009.

10. U.S. Census Bureau, Census of Population and Housing, decennial volumes.

11. David E. Wheelock, "The Federal Response to Home Mortgage Distress: Lessons from the Great Depression," *Federal Reserve Bank of St. Louis Review* 90.3 (May/June 2008): part 1, 133–48.

12. Based on nominal home price data data from Robert J. Shiller, accessed 8 July 2013, http://www.econ.yale.edu/~schiller/data.htm.

13. Peter Rappoport and Eugene N. White, "Was the Crash of 1929 Expected?" *American Economic Review* 84.1 (March 1994): 271–81.

14. Eugene N. White, "The Stock Market Boom and Crash of 1929 Revisited," *Journal of Economic Perspectives* 4.2 (Spring 1990): 67–83.

15. Victor Perlo, "People's Capitalism and Stock-Ownership," *American Economic Review* 48.3 (June 1958): 333–47 (esp. table 1, p. 333).

16. U.S. Securities and Exchange Commission, "The Investor's Advocate: How the SEC Protects Investors, Maintains Market Integrity, and Facilitates Capital Formation," accessed 25 June 2013, http://www.sec.gov/about/whatwedo.shtml.

17. Ben S. Bernanke, *Essays on the Great Depression* (Princeton, N.J.: Princeton University Press, 2000); Christina Romer, "The Great Crash and the Onset of the Great Depression," *Quarterly Journal of Economics* 105 (August 1990): 597–624.

18. Robert Margo, "Employment and Unemployment during the 1930's," *Journal of Economic Perspectives* 7.2 (Spring 1993): 41–59.

19. Nick Taylor, *American-Made, the Enduring Legacy of the WPA: When FDR Put the Nation to Work* (New York: Bantam Books, 2008), 9

20. Calculations based on the U.S. Index of Factory Employment data available from the National Bureau of Economic Research.

21. William A. Sundstrom, "Last Hired, First Fired? Unemployment and Urban Black Workers during the Great Depression," *Journal of Economic History* 52.2 (June 1992): 415–29.

22. If these 1937 unemployment rates are scaled up by the ratio of overall unemployment in 1933 to its level in 1937 (1.74), unemployment rates for white males would be estimated at 24.2 percent, 33.2 percent for black males, 36.5 percent for white females, and 52 percent for black females at the depth of the Great Depression.

23. Michael Bordo and Charles Evans, "Labor Productivity during the Great Depres-

sion," *Economic Letters* 47.1 (January 1995): 41–45, for evidence that manufacturing productivity rose substantially between 1929 and 1933.

24. Qtd. in Taylor, *American-Made*, 36.

25. For a discussion of the NIRA, see ibid.; Cole and Ohanian, "How Government Prolonged the Depression"; and Harold Cole and Lee Ohanian, "New Deal Policies and the Persistence of the Great Depression: A General Equilibrium Analysis," *Journal of Political Economy* 112.4 (2004): 779–816. The AAA was also struck down by the Supreme Court, but a revised AAA of 1938 survived.

26. The increase in real wages despite massive unemployment in the mid-1930s has been attributed to either market imperfections or government policy by Keynesian and new classical economists.

27. The Native Origins Act and Asian Exclusion Act were part of the Immigration Act of 1924.

28. James Stock and Mark Watson, "Disentangling the Channels of the 2007–2009 Recession," memo prepared for Brookings Panel on Economic Activity, 22–23 March 2012. Stock and Watson argue that the Great Recession was primarily caused by an energy shock. This has not been the consensus view.

29. The Great Depression cumulative decline in output was 26.7 percent, or nearly seven times greater.

30. Joseph E. Stiglitz, *Free Fall: America, Free Markets, and the Sinking of the Global Economy* (New York: Norton, 2010).

31. OECD Economic Outlook No. 89, Annex Table 1, data on Real GDP, accessed 8 July 2013, http://www.oecd.org/eco/outlook/economicoutlookannextables.htm.

32. Michael Bordo and Joseph Haubrich, "Deep Recessions, Fast Recoveries, and Financial Crises: Evidence from the American Record," unpublished memo, 13 September 2011.

33. U.S. Department of Labor, Bureau of Labor Statistics, October 2010, accessed 25 June 2013, http://www.bls.gov/opub/ils/summary_10_10/ranks_unemployed_year.htm#chart1. During the Great Depression, 60 percent or more of the unemployed had been out for six months or longer. See Robert Margo, "The Microeconomics of Depression Unemployment," *Journal of Economic History* 51.2 (June 1991): 333–41.

34. Adult male unemployment would go from 4.4 to 10.2 percent before declining to 7.7 percent in July 2012, while the rate for adult women would go from 4.4 to 8.2 percent before declining to 7.5 percent.

35. Michael Elsby, Bart Hobjn, and Aysegul Sahin, "The Labor Market in the Great Recession," National Bureau of Economic Research Working Paper No. 15979, May 2010.

36. This data reflects Department of Homeland Security counts of new legal permanent residents and does not capture the flow of unauthorized immigrants.

37. Michael Hoefer, Nancy Rytina, and Bryan Baker, "Estimates of the Unauthorized Immigrant Population Residing in the United States: January 2011," *Population Estimates*, Office of Immigration Statistics, March 2012, accessed 8 July 2013, http://www.dhs.gov/xlibrary/assets/statistics/publications/ois_ill_pe_2011.pdf.

38. Linda Levine, "Job Creation Programs of the Great Depression: The WPA and CCC," Congressional Research Service, 14 January 2010, R41017; and Work(s) Progress Administration Photograph Collection at the Colorado State Archives, accessed 25 June 2013, http://www.colorado.gov/dpa/doit/archives/wpa/home.htm.

39. Wisconsin was the first state to have a UI program, but it did not issue its first benefit check until 1936. The other forty-eight states did not even pass legislation setting up their programs until August 1937.

40. National Employment Law Project, Fact Sheet, Phase Out of Federal Unemployment Insurance, June 2012, accessed 25 June 2013, http://www.nelp.org/page/-/UI/2012/FactSheet_UI_Phase-Out.pdf?nocdn=1.

41. Government Accountability Office, "Unemployment Insurance: Economic Circumstance of Individuals Who Exhausted Benefits," February 2012, GAO-12, accessed 8, July 2013, http://www.gao.gov/assets/590/588680.pdf.

42. Data on unionism and strikes are from the U.S. Census Bureau, *Historical Statistics of the United States: Colonial Times to 1970*, Series D946–951 and D970–985, 1 (Washington, D.C.: U.S. Government Printing Office, 1975).

43. Bureau of Labor Statistics data on work stoppages and members of unions, accessed 8 July 2013, http://www.bls.gov/news.release/wkstp.to1.htm and http://www.bls.gov/cps/cpslutabs.htm.

44. Akito Yoshikane, "Polls: Union Popularity Still Low, but Public (Mostly) Supports Bargaining Rights," *In These Times,* 23 February 2011.

45. Government Accountability Office, "Financial Assistance: Ongoing Challenges and Guiding Principles Related to Government Assistance for Private Sector Companies," August 2010, GAO 10-719, accessed 8 July 2013, http://www.gao.gov/assets/310/308457.pdf.

46. Eamon Javers, "Federal Ownership May Raise Conflict," *Politico,* 29 April 2009.

47. J. W. Verret, "Treasury Inc.: How the Bailout Reshapes Corporate Theory and Practice," *Yale Journal on Regulation* 27.2 (Summer 2010): 283–350, holds the view that the federal government never before intervened in state-chartered corporations.

48. The FDIC and other banking regulators do routinely take over failing banks as part of the liquidation process. State and federal government workers also routinely hold equity positions in private firms through their pension funds.

49. Stacey R. Kole and J. Harold Mulherin, "The Government as a Shareholder: A Case from the United States," *Journal of Law and Economics* 40.1 (April 1997): 1–22.

50. Phillip Longman, "Washington's Turnaround Artists," *Washington Monthly,* 3 September 2009.

51. TARP funds did come with limits on executive compensation and the payment of stock dividends and the need to pass "stress tests," but given the conditions private-sector lenders routinely impose, it's hard to find these limits particularly onerous.

52. Randall W. Eberts and Joe A. Stone, *Wage and Employment Adjustment in Local Labor Markets* (Kalamazoo, Mich.: W. E. Upjohn Institute for Employment Research, 1992).

53. See also the Center for Automotive Research, "CAR Research Memorandum: The Impact on the U.S. Economy of a Major Contraction of the Detroit Three Automak-

ers," November 2008, accessed 8 July 2013, http://graphics8.nytimes.com/packages/pdf/autorecess.pdf; and Howard Wial, "How a Metro Nation Would Feel the Loss of the Detroit Three Automakers," Metropolitan Policy Program, Brookings Institution, unpublished paper, 2008.

54. Mark Zandi, Testimony before the U.S. Senate Banking Committee, "The State of the Domestic Auto Industry: Part II," 4 December 2008, estimated losses of 2.5 million. Robert Scott, "When Giants Fall: Shutdown of One or More U.S. Automakers Could Eliminate 3.3 Million Jobs," Employment Policy Institute Briefing Paper No. 227, 3 December 2008, reports losses of 3.3 million.

55. For instance, the volume of nonfinancial commercial paper declined from $223.8 billion in January 2009 to $107.3 billion in July 2009, or by 52 percent.

56. Bill Canis, James M. Bickley, Hinda Chaikind, Carol A. Pettit, Patrick Purcell, Carol Rapaport, and Gary Shorter, "U.S. Motor Vehicle Industry: Federal Financial Assistance and Restructuring," Congressional Research Service report R40003, 29 May 2009. About $12.5 billion went Chrysler, $51 billion to GM, and the remaining $16 billion to recapitalize GMAC (now Ally Financial).

57. I was a member of President Obama's Auto Task Force and served as the director of recovery for auto communities and workers.

58. Ron Bloom, Testimony before Senate Banking, Housing, and Urban Affairs Committee, 10 June 2009, accessed 8, July 2013, http://www.banking.senate.gov/public/index.cfm?FuseAction=Hearings.Testimony&Hearing_ID=e4434686-9de0-4d73-99eb-b49b0ac31ee5&Witness_ID=9a2a802d-db2e-40c4-a97d-031375049b31; and Steven Rattner, "Reflections on Auto Restructurings," paper presented at Brookings Institution, 21 October 2009.

59. Kristen Dziczek, "2011 Detroit 3–UAW Labor Contracts," accessed 8 July 2013, http://www.chicagofed.org/digital_assets/others/region/midwest_economy/Dziczek_DABE_January_2012.pdf.

60. *Annual Report of the White House Council on Automotive Communities and Workers*, May 2010, accessed 8 July 2013, http://www.dol.gov/autocommunities/pdf/2010AnnualReport.pdf.

61. Congressional Budget Office, "Report on the Troubled Asset Relief Program—March 2012," 28 March 2012, accessed 25 June 2013, http://www.cbo.gov/sites/default/files/cbofiles/attachments/03-28-2012TARP.pdf.

62. Robert Scott, "Huge Return on Taxpayer Investment," *Employment Policy Institute Briefing Paper* No. 290, 18 November 2010.

63. The share of the eligible population voting went from 43 percent in 1920 to 63 percent in 1960.

64. Claire Liang, David McLean, and Mengxin Zhao, "Creative Destruction and Finance: Evidence from the Last Half Century," unpublished memo, June 2011, accessed 8 July 2013, http://sites.kauffman.org/efic/resources/Creative-Destruction-and-Finance.pdf.

65. Christina Romer, "The Nation in Depression," *Journal of Economic Perspectives* 7.2 (Spring 1993): 19–39.

Contributors

SVEN BECKERT, the Laird Bell Professor of American History at Harvard University, specializes in the history of the United States in the nineteenth century, with a particular emphasis on the history of capitalism, including its economic, social, political, and transnational dimensions. He has published *The Monied Metropolis: New York City and the Consolidation of the American Bourgeoisie* and coedited, with Julia Rosenblaum, *The American Bourgeoisie: Distinction and Identity in the Nineteenth Century*. His *The Empire of Cotton: A Global History* will be published by Alfred A. Knopf in 2014.

SEAN CADIGAN is a professor of history at Memorial University who publishes on labor, settler relations, and Maritime history. His first book was *Hope and Deception in Conception Bay: Merchant-Settler Relations in Newfoundland, 1785–1855*, and his more recent publication is a definitive regional history, *Newfoundland and Labrador: A History*.

LEON FINK is Distinguished Professor of History at the University of Illinois at Chicago. He is the author or editor of eight books, most recently *Sweatshops at Sea: Merchant Seamen in the World's First Globalized Industry, from 1812 to 2000*; *Upheaval in the Quiet Zone: 1199SEIU and the Politics of Health Care Unionism*, coauthored with Brian Greenberg; and (as editor) *Workers across the Americas: The Transnational Turn in Labor History*.

ALVIN FINKEL is a professor of history at Athabasca University. He has edited and authored books on Canadian history, the West, labor history, and the history of social policy. His early books include *Business and Social Reform in the*

Thirties and *The Social Credit Phenomenon in Alberta,* and his most recent book is *Social Policy and Practice in Canada: A History.*

WENDY GOLDMAN, a professor of history at Carnegie Mellon University, is a political and social historian of Russia and the Soviet Union. She is the author of two recent books on Stalinist terror, *Inventing the Enemy: Denunciation and Terror in Stalin's Russia* and *Terror and Democracy in the Age of Stalin: The Social Dynamics of Repression,* as well as numerous articles on Soviet social history and an award-winning book, *Women at the Gates: Gender and Industry in Stalin's Russia.*

GAETEN HEROUX is an independent researcher and activist with the Ontario Coalition against Poverty.

JOSEPH A. MCCARTIN is a professor of history at Georgetown University, where he also directs the Kalmanovitz Initiative for Labor and the Working Poor. His books include *Collision Course: Ronald Reagan, the Air Traffic Controllers, and the Strike That Changed America* and *Labor's Great War: The Struggle for Industrial Democracy and the Origins of Modern American Labor Relations, 1912–21.*

DAVID MONTGOMERY, the Farnam Professor Emeritus of History at Yale University, was one of the foremost historians of labor in the United States over the past three decades, known internationally as an architect of the field of New Labor History that emerged after the 1970s. His books include *The Fall of the House of Labor: The Workplace, the State, and American Labor Activism, 1865–1925,* and *Citizen Worker: The Experience of Workers in the United States with Democracy and the Free Market during the Nineteenth Century.* The essay for this book was the last before his death in 2011.

EDWARD MONTGOMERY is the dean of the Georgetown University Public Policy Institute and an economist who has researched and published in the areas of wage and pension determination, social insurance, productivity, and unions. He recently served on the President's Auto Task Force.

SCOTT REYNOLDS NELSON is Legum Professor of History at the College of William and Mary. He is the author of *Iron Confederacies: Southern Railways, Klan Violence, and Reconstruction* and *Steel Drivin' Man: John Henry, the Untold Story of an American Legend,* which won several awards, including the Merle Curti Prize for the best book in U.S. social and cultural history. He is coauthor, with Carol Sheriff, of *A People at War: Civilians and Soldiers in America's Civil War.*

CONTRIBUTORS

MELANIE NOLAN is a professor and director of the National Centre of Biography at Australian National University. She the author of two monographs, six edited volumes, and many articles on New Zealand, Australian, and comparative history, in particular labor and social history. Her monographs include *Kin: The Collective Biography of a Working-Class New Zealand Family* and *Breadwinning: New Zealand Women and the State*.

BRYAN D. PALMER is a professor of Canadian studies and history and Tier I Canada Research Chair at Trent University. He has published numerous books and articles dealing with Canadian and transnational labor and social history, as well as the history of the international left. Coauthored with Greg Kealey, his book on the Knights of Labor, *Dreaming of What Might Be: The Knights of Labor in Ontario, 1880–1900*, won the AHA/CHA Corey prize. His most recent books include *Cultures of Darkness: Night Travels in the Histories of Transgression* and *James P. Cannon and the Origins of the American Revolutionary Left, 1890–1928*.

JOAN SANGSTER is a professor of history at Trent University, Ontario. She is the author of five books, including *Dreams of Equality: Women on the Canadian Left, 1920–60*, *Regulating Girls and Women: Sexuality, Family, and in the Law, Ontario 1920–60*, and *Earning Respect: The Lives of Working Women in Small-Town Ontario, 1920–1960*.

JUDITH STEIN is Distinguished Professor of History at the City College and Graduate Center of the City University of New York Graduate Center. She specializes in African American history and twentieth-century political and economic U.S. history. As well as many articles, she is the author of *The World of Marcus Garvey: Race and Class in Modern Society*, *Running Steel, Running America: Race, Economic Policy, and the Decline of Liberalism*, and most recently *Pivotal Decade: How the United States Traded Factories for Finance in the Seventies*.

HILARY WAINWRIGHT is co-editor of *Red Pepper* and a senior research associate in the International Centre for Participation Studies at the Department of Peace Studies, University of Bradford, UK.

LU ZHANG, assistant professor of sociology at Temple University, is a historical sociologist specializing in globalization, labor movements, and the political economy of development in China. Her most recent publication is a chapter on workers in the auto industry in China in the collection *From Iron Rice Bowl to Informalization: Markets, Workers, and the State in a Changing China*.

Index

Abel, I. W., 146
Abolin, A., 66–67
Aborigines, 117, 164
Accords de Matignon, 119
Addams, Jane, 106
Affordable Care Act, 264
agriculture: and the Agricultural Adjustment Act (AAA), 269–270; campesinos, 115, 130; coca growing, 130; in Egypt, 84, 90–94; in India, 84, 89–92; plantation farming, 49–50, 86–94; sharecropping, 83–84, 88, 92–94; subsistence farming, 89, 94; sugar production 100–101, 104; tenant farming, 94; in the USSR, 61–66, 68, 75–76
AIG, 276
Algeria, 92
All-China Federation of Trade Unions (ACFTU), 213, 228–230, 232–233
Allegheny City, 51
Allende, Salvador, 128
Altman, Roger, 151
American Civil War, 46, 49, 52, 85, 90–91, 99–101
American Economic Association, 148
"American Exceptionalism," 54
American Federation of Labor (AFL), 3, 28, 106–107, 115, 117, 120
American Federation of Labor-Congress of Industrial Organizations (AFL-CIO), 123, 146–147, 151, 156
American Federation of State, County, and Municipal Employees, 156
American Iron and Steel Institute, 151

American Jobs Act, 274
American Railway Union (ARU), 99, 104–106
American Recovery and Reinvestment Act (ARRA), 273–274
American South: and cotton, 85–94; and plantation agriculture, 49–50, 85–86, 91–94
Amin, Samir, 10
anarchists, 115, 247
Anatolia, 93
Arab-Israeli War, 144
arbitration, 116
Armour & Company, 53
Associated Charities of Toronto, 31
Association for Improving the Condition of the Poor, 48
Association of Consumers and Taxpayers (ACT), 174
Atkinson, Edward, 89
austerity measures: Greece, 1, 12, 127, 130, 243–248; Spain, 1, 12
Australia, 92, 115–117, 125, 133, 164–169, 174
Australian Commonwealth Court of Conciliation and Arbitration, 165
Australian-New Zealand Agreement (1944), 166
Australian Royal Commission on the Basic Wage, 165
Australian Settlement, 125
automobile industry, 143, 147, 153, 213–234, 264, 267, 276–277

Auto Task Force, 278
Avalon Peninsula, 190–192

Baierle, Sergio, 254
Balanced Growth and Economic Planning Act (1975), 148
Baldwin, Rev. Arthur H. (All Saints Church, Toronto), 23
Ball, George, 143–144
Bank of America, 276
banks: Bank of England, 117; banks in the United States, 50, 52–53, 108, 148, 154–155, 264, 266–267, 276; loans from European banks, 49, 52. *See also* European Central Bank
Barbera, Robert, 6–7
Baring Brothers, 52, 88
Bassett, Michael, 170
Bazley, Margaret, 172
Bear Stearns, 271, 275
Beck, Glenn, 265
Beijing, 230
Beilharz, Pater, 167
Belgian Congo, 94
Belgium, 54
Bell, Daniel, 142
beprizorniki, 75
Beyond Dependency Conference, 173
Biemiller, Andrew, 123
Bishop, Joel, 50
"Black Thursday," 266
black workers: and dock work, 49, 52; and plantation labor, 49–50, 84–92; and racial restrictions, 104–105, 120, 267; and the Republican Party, 99–100. *See also* civil rights
Blair, Tony, 125–126, 255
Blanchard, James, 147
Blum, Léon, 119
Bolger, Jim, 171
"Bolivarian socialism, 129–130
Bolivia, 130
Bolshevik Party, 61–64, 67–71, 73, 75–76
Borden, Sir Robert, 34
Braudel, Fernand, 10
Brazil, 87–90, 149, 245–246, 248, 250–260
Brazilian Workers' party (PT), 245–246, 250–256, 260–261
Brenner, Robert, 9
Bretton Woods. *See* Monetary and Financial Conference (Bretton Woods) Agreement
Briansk, 70
British Fabians, 27, 258
British Guyana, 89

British Locomotive and Engineers Brotherhood, 103
British Steel, 148
Brody, David, 11
Brosius, Marriott, 106–107
Brotherhood of Locomotive Engineers, 102–103
Brotherhood of Locomotive Firemen (BLF), 101, 103–105
Buck, Tim, 38
Bukharin, N. I., 71
Bureau of Industries (Canada), 25
Bureau of Labor Standards, 156
Burke, James A, 146
Bush, George W., 276, 278
business unionism, 3, 38
Bust, George, 33
byvshie liudi, 65–66

Callinicos, Alexander, 7
Campaign for the Welfare State (CWS), 125–126
Canada, 187–206
Canada Revenue Agency, 201
Canadian Energy and Paperworkers Union (CEP), 202
Canadian Expeditionary Force, 33
Canadian Labour Union, 21
Canadian Patriotic Fund, 33
Canadian Post, 22
Canadian Socialist League, 27
Canadian Union of Public Employees (CUPE), 199–200, 202–204
capital accumulation, 113
capital investment: in Canada, 199; from Europe, 86–95; in the USSR, 60, 70, 76
Capital: Volume 1, 4, 61
Capital: Volume 2, 19
Carter, Jimmy, 149–153, 276
Castles, Francis G., 165
Caterpillar Tractor, 150
Caygill, David, 169, 171
Center for Automotive Research, 278
Center party (Germany), 119
Center party (Norway), 125
Central Asia, 90, 92–94
Central Committee Plenum, 71, 74–75
Central Council of Trade Unions (VTsSPS), 66, 68
Central Intelligence Agency (CIA), 123
Central obrera boliviana (COB), 130–132
Centre for Independent Studies (CIS), 169, 172

Chamber of Commerce, 148
Change to Win, 156–157
charities: and unemployment relief, 31, 47–49, 113
Chartists, 249
Chautemps, Camille, 119
Chávez, Hugo, 129, 131, 201
Cheap Cotton by Free Labor, 89
Chicago, Burlington, and Quincy strike, 103
Chicago Civic Federation, 105
Chicago Daily News, 105
Chicago Exposition, 106
child health programs, 114–115
China, 92, 154, 157–158, 213–234
Chinese Communist party (CCP), 231–233
Chinese labor, 25, 92, 155
Christian socialists, 27
Chrysler, 276–278
Citigroup, 276
Civic Employment Bureau (Toronto), 28, 32
Civilian Conservation Corps (CCC), 273
civil rights, 72, 149–150, 280
Civil Servants' Confederation (ADEDY), 127
Clarke, Edmund Frederick (mayor), 26
clerical work, 55
Cleveland, Grover, 52–53, 105, 107
Cloward, Richard, 233
Cochabamba, 130
Code of Social Responsibility (New Zealand), 173
Cold War, 123, 143–144, 255
collective bargaining, 152, 233, 275, 283
collective farms, 60, 63, 65, 67–68, 75
collectivization, 60–61, 65, 68, 70–73, 75–76
College Street People's Church (Toronto), 30
Comintern, 73, 116, 118–120
Commerce Department (U.S.), 144
Commissariat of Labor, 65
Commission on Unemployment (Ontario), 32
Commons, John R., 11
Commonwealth Arbitration Court, 117
Commonwealth Employment Service, 166
Communist party of Greece (KKE), 247
communists: in Canada, 27, 37; in Chile, 120; in France, 114–115, 119; in Germany, 73, 118–119; in Great Britain, 118; Trotskyism, 55. *See also* Bolshevik Party
compulsory overtime, 222–223
Confederacíon Sindical Única de Trabajadores Campesinos de Bolivia, 130–131
Confédération générale du travail (CGT), 114–115, 119

Confédération générale du travail unitaire (CGTU), 114–115, 119
Congress (US), 51–52, 55, 99–100, 106–108, 145–146, 149, 264–265, 275, 287
Congressional Budget Office, 280
Congressional Progressive Caucus, 274
Congress of Industrial Organizations (CIO), 55, 120
Conrail, 276
Conservative party (Canada), 54
Conservative party (U.K.), 118, 148
consumer movement, 150–151
Cooke, Jay, 46
Cost of Capitalism, The, 6
cotton, 85–94. *See also* American South
Cotton Supply Reporter, 92
Coughlin, Father, 265
Council of Economic Advisers, 143, 148, 150–151
Council of People's Commissars (Sovnarkom), 71
Cowie, Jefferson, 142
Coxey's Army, 50–51, 53
craft unions, 28, 47, 55, 99–106, 116–117, 120
Crane, William, 105
currency (U.S. dollar), 50–53, 99, 101, 104, 108, 144, 153–155, 267. *See also* Federal Reserve, monetarism
Curry, John, 23

Daladier, Édouard, 119
Danson, J. T., 88
danwei, 216
Debs, Eugene, 99–108
decentralization, 252–255
defined-benefit pension plans, 123–124, 128
defined-contribution pension plans, 123–124, 128
deindustrialization, 142, 151–152, 191–192, 277–278
Democratic Party: during the Cold War, 123; in the Gilded Age, 52, 99–100, 104–108; and the Great Recession, 124, 154–156, 264–265, 273–275; and neoliberal economics, 142, 144–145, 149–150
Denmark, 121
Denning, Michael, 20
Department of Homeland Security, 273
Department of Social Welfare (New Zealand), 172–173
depression: of 1873–79, 45–48, 101; of 1893, 45, 52–54, 99–101, 104, 108. *See also* Great Depression; Great Recession

de Sismondi, J. C. L. Simonde, 20
Dnepropetrovsk, 66–67
Dodd-Frank Wall Street and Consumer Protection Act, 155, 264
domestic work, 47
Donbas, 69
dot-com boom, 281
Douglas, Fred, 199–200
Douglas, Robert, 169–171, 174
Dow Jones Industrial Average, 266
downsizing, 189, 216–218, 226
Driscoll, Connie, 173
Drury, Ernest, 29–30
Dubofsky, Melvyn, 11
Dunderdale, Kathy, 205
Dupriez, Leon, 53
Dutra, Olivio, 250

Easton, Brian, 168
Eberts, Randall W., 277
Eby, Rev. G. S., 30
Economic Management, 169
Economist, The, 90–93, 162, 174
Edwards, Richard, 8
Egypt, 84, 90–94
eight-hour day, 50–51, 108, 164
Eikhe, R. I., 75
Elsby, Michael, 272
Emergency Banking Act, 267
Emergency Economic Stabilization Act, 276
Emergency Quota Act, 270
Employee Free Choice Act, 275
Employers Federation (New Zealand), 170
Employment Contracts Act (New Zealand), 163
Employment Service of Canada, 34
enclosure (England), 60, 63–64
energy prices, 143–144, 147, 150
environmentalism, 147, 150
Ethiopia, 52
European Central Bank (ECB), 243, 248
European Commission (EC), 243, 248
European Economic Community (EEC), 143–144, 146, 162
European Social Forum, 244
European Union, 127
Evatt, H. V., 166
exported goods: agricultural commodities, 52, 85–94; manufactured goods, 61; from the United States, 52, 85–90, 141, 143–144, 146–147
extra judicial trials, 72

famine, 65–67, 76
Fannie Mae, 275–276
Farmers' Alliance, 50
fascism, 72, 243
favelas, 259
FAW Auto Group, 221
Federalists, 150
Federal Reserve, 6, 152–154, 264–265, 267, 275. *See also* currency (U.S. dollar)
feudalism, 61
financial crisis (2008), 1–2
financial deregulation, 125, 143, 154–155, 162, 168, 251, 264, 270
Fine, Camden, 276
Finland, 75, 271
Fish, Food, and Allied Workers Union, 200
fisheries, 187–194, 202, 206
Five-Year Plan (1929), 60, 67–68, 70–71, 73
Five-Year Plan (1933), 65, 71
Fleming, Frank, 37
food prices, 63, 66, 269–270
food shortages, 62–68, 70, 76
Ford, Gerald, 145, 148, 276
Fordism, 84, 123, 216, 221–222, 258
Ford Motor Company, 54
Foreign Trade and Investment Act, 146–147
forty-hour week, 108, 119
Fotiou, Theano, 261
France, 53–54, 85, 114–120, 128, 133
Fraser, Peter, 166
Freddie Mac, 275–276
Frederick, Maryland, 51
Free Cotton: How and Where to Grow It, 89
Free Employment Bureau (Toronto), 29
"free market," 52–53, 63, 85, 93, 132, 145, 150, 153, 161, 168–169, 172–174, 225, 228, 255
free trade, 93, 122, 127, 142, 145–146
French Revolution, 106
Friedman, Milton, 6, 163
Friere, Paulo, 252
Frontier College, 35
Furlong, Carol, 201

Galbraith, John Kenneth, 6
Gems of Socialism, 27
gender equality, 121–122
General Confederation of Greek Workers (GSEE), 127
General Electric, 53, 282
General Managers' Association (GMA), 103–104, 108
General Motors, 53, 277–278, 282

General Theory of Employment, Interest, and Money, The, 166
George, Henry, 103
German Togo, 94
Germany, 53, 72, 75, 85, 113–114, 118–119, 133, 142, 148, 154, 157–158, 276
Gestapo, 73
Gibbs, Alan, 169
Gilded Age, 99–108
Gindin, Sam, 9
global commodity markets, 86–90
globalization, 11, 83–88, 94, 122–123, 125, 128, 141, 147, 150, 155–156, 161, 214–215, 247–249, 259, 281–283
Globe (Toronto), 21–22
Globe and Mail's Report on Business, 201
GMAC, 276
Goldfinger, Nathaniel, 146
Gompers, Samuel, 107
Goods and Service Tax (New Zealand), 162
Gordon, David M., 8
Gordon, Robert, 148
Gorz, André, 248, 257
Gourevitch, Peter, 141–142
grain production, 61–63, 68, 71
Grand Masters of the Railway Firemen, Conductors, and Carmen, 104
Grand Rapids, 51
Grant, Ulysses S., 50
grassroots activism, 125, 129, 243–244, 256, 258
Gray, John, 173
Great Britain: capitalist expansion, 10, 53; and the Great Depression, 54, 113. *See also* Greater London Council (GLC)
Great Depression, 3, 6, 38, 54, 113–114, 116–120, 123, 141–142, 167, 169, 263–283
Greater London Council (GLC), 245–246, 250–257, 260
Great Lakes, 104
Great Northern Railway, 104
Great Recession, 1, 12, 127, 141–144, 154, 157–158, 161, 213, 230, 232, 243–244, 263–268, 270–283
Great Society, 265
"Great Terror," 60–61, 72–76
Great White Fleet, 52
Greece, 127, 133, 243–244
Greek parliament, 243
Greek Social Forum, 247
Green, David, 170, 173
Green, T. H., 167–168

Greenspan, Alan, 148
Gregg, Andrew, 173–174
Gribble, Wilfred, 29
Grundrisse, 19
"gunboat diplomacy," 53
Gunder Frank, Andre, 10
Gutman, Herbert, 11

Habermas, Jurgen, 142
Hamilton, George, 37
Hansen, Joseph, 156
Hansson, Per Albin, 121
Harper, Stephen, 201–202
Harrison, Carter, 49
Hart, Gary, 147
Hartke, Vance, 146
Harvey, David, 8
Hastings, Charles, 37
Hayes, Rutherford B., 46
healthcare, 114–115, 120, 123–126, 128–129, 132, 146, 151, 157, 167, 171, 200, 248, 264, 278
Heath, Edward, 148
Heller, Walter, 143, 151
Hevey, W. J., 38
Higgins, Henry Bournes, 165
Hilferding, Rudolf, 118–119
Hill, Albert, 29
Hill, James J., 104
Hitler, Adolf, 71, 118
Hobjn, Bart, 272
Hoffa, James, 156
Holland: capitalist expansion, 10
Holmes, W. H., 89
homelessness: in Canada, 21–23, 29–30, 36–37; in the USSR, 65, 67, 75. *See also* vagrancy
Homestead Act, 50
Homestead Strike, 51
Honda, 213, 222, 230–231, 277–278
Hoover, Herbert, 264, 274
Hotel Employees and Restaurant Employees Union, 156
households, 60, 63, 65, 69, 113, 117, 119, 121, 165–166, 266, 269, 277
House of Industry (Toronto), 21–23, 25–26, 29–33, 36–37
housing, 64, 66, 74, 134, 148, 153–155, 157, 281
Housing and Economic Recovery Act, 275
Hugo, Victor, 101
hukou, 220

Hummer, 278
Humphrey, Hubert, 147–148

immigration: from Africa to the United States 85–92; from Asia to the United States, 52, 270, 272; from China to Algeria, 92; from Europe to the United States, 45–48, 52, 100; Immigration Act (1924), 270
imperialism, 87–94, 164
imported goods (U.S.), 100–101, 141, 143, 146, 150, 153, 155
indentured servitude, 52, 84, 92
Independent Community Bankers of America, 276
India, 84, 89–90, 93
Industrial Banner, 33
Industrial Congress, 50
industrialization: of Bolivia, 131; of Toronto, 28; of the USSR, 61–72, 75–76
industrial revolution, 85, 88, 131
industrial unionism, 54, 67–68, 70
Industrial Workers of the World (IWW), 32, 54
inflation, 65–66, 122, 145–146, 149, 152–153, 161, 169, 196
informal sector, 116, 120, 128
Institute of Economic Affairs, 173
International Association of Machinists, 146
International Brotherhood of Electrical Workers (IBEW), 203–204
International Brotherhood of Teamsters (IBT), 55, 156
International Harvester, 53
International Labour Organization Charter, 166
International Monetary Fund (IMF), 122, 128–129, 131, 133, 243, 248, 251, 255
Iran, 157
Ireland, 264, 271
Iron Age, 53
Italy, 264
Ivanovo, 66, 69

Japan, 72, 85, 142–146, 149, 152, 154, 157, 271, 276
Javits, Jacob, 147–148
Jessop, Bob, 161
jianbing chongzu, 216
Johnson, Lyndon, 146
joint ventures (JVs), 215–218, 227
"just-in-time" (JIT) production, 219, 221–222

Kabakov, I. D., 75
Kahn, Alfred, 151
Kamenev, L. B., 71
Karitzis, Andreas, 246
Kautsky, Karl, 118
Kennedy, Jerome, 187, 203, 205
Kennedy, John F., 143, 146
Kentucky, 277
Kerr, Roger, 169
Keynes, John Maynard, 6, 121, 166
Keynesian economics, 4, 8, 121–122, 125, 142–143, 145, 148–155, 168–169
Keyssar, Alexander, 47
Kirk, Neville, 164–165
Kirkland, Lane, 151
Kirov, S. M., 72, 76
Knights of Labor, 21, 25, 48–51, 103–104
Know-Nothing Party, 48
Knoxville, 103
Kondratieff, Nikolai, 5
Korpi, Walter, 126
Krugman, Paul, 5–6
kulaks, 62–64, 67–68, 72, 74–75

Labor Contract Law (China), 227–229, 231, 233–234
labor force dualism, 215, 218–219, 224–225, 228–229
Labor Leader, 38
Labor party (Australia), 117, 125
Labour Court (New Zealand), 163
Labour Department Act (New Zealand), 166
Labour Gazette, 33
Labour party (New Zealand), 169–171
Labour party (Norway), 125–127
Labour party (U.K.), 115, 117–118, 124, 148, 245, 249–254, 261
Labour Relations Act (Canada), 199
Landorganisation i Sverige (LO), 121
Lang, Jack, 117
Lange, David, 171
laowu paiqian, 220
Latin America: Argentina, 130; Bolivia, 115, 129–133; Chile, 115, 120, 128–129; Cuba, 129; Ecuador, 129; El Salvador, 129; Nicaragua, 129; Peru, 129; Uruguay, 115; Venezuela, 129–130, 133. *See also* Brazil
Latvia, 75
Laughlan, Arthur, 26
Lawrence, Colorado, 52
lean-production, 215
"left opposition" (USSR), 63, 71
Lehman Brothers, 271

Leninism, 244
Les Blancs et les Noirs en Amérique et le Coton dans les deux Mondes, 89
Lewis, John L., 120
Liang, Claire, 282
Liberal-Country coalition, 125
liberalism, 93
Liberal party (U.K.), 115, 118
Libya, 52
life-insurance, 101–102
lishentsy, 65, 74
Liverpool Mercury, 89
livestock, 63, 65, 68
Lockheed, 276
Locomotive Firemen's Magazine, 101–102
Lucas, Wayne, 202–204
Lula, 245, 248, 255
Luxemburg, Rosa, 118
lynching, 108

MacDonald, "Moscow Jack," 37
MacDonald, Ramsay, 117–118
Macintyre, Stuart, 125, 164
Maguire, Charles A., 36
Manchester Cotton Supply Association, 90, 92
Mandel, Ernest, 7–9
manufacturing: and capital investment, 28, 149–150; and productivity, 53–54, 142; and relocation, 56, 142, 153–154, 272, 281–282
Maori, 162–164, 167
Marks, Joseph T., 33
Marshall, Ray, 151
Martin, Paul, 200–201
Marx, Karl: on contradictions of capitalism, 4–5, 7, 19–20, 113; on primitive accumulation, 61
Marxists: on capitalist development, 5, 10; on economic crises, 5–10, 142
Mathieu, M. J., 91
McBride, Lloyd, 151
McCurdy, Earle, 199–200
McEntee, Gerry, 156
McLean, David, 282
McGovern, George, 147, 149
Mead, Lawrence, 170, 172
Meany, George, 151
Medicaid, 124, 274
Medicare, 124
Melasel, Nick, 33
Mellon, Andrew, 269
Menshiviks, 70

Merivale, Harman, 89
Metal Workers union (Australia), 125
Mexico, 46, 93–94, 271
Mikoian, A. I., 75
military regimes, 120
militia, 65–67
Mill, John Stuart, 5
Miller, William, 151
mill towns, 45, 49
mining: in Australia, 167; in Bolivia, 130–131; in Canada, 189–192, 195–197, 202, 206; in Chile, 115; in France, 84; in Great Britain, 118, 124, 254; in the United States, 46, 49–52; in the USSR, 73–74
Ministry of Human Resources and Social Security (MOHRSS), 229–230
Minnesota, 55
Minsky, Harold, 5, 7
mir, 62
Mississippi River, 104
Mitchell, Timothy, 91
Molotov, V. I., 62
monetarism, 4, 6, 8, 162
Monetary and Financial Conference (Bretton Woods) Agreement, 166, 169
Monongahela Valley, 51
Monthly Journal, 103
Moore, Mike, 170
Morales, Evo, 130–131
Morgan, J. P., 53
Morris, William, 27
Movemente Sans Terre, 256
Movimiento Al Socialismo (MAS), 131
Muldoon, Robert, 169
Murray, Charles, 170, 172

Nader, Ralph, 151
Napoleon III, 92, 113
Nash, Walter, 166
Nation, The, 150
National Bureau of Economic Research, 263
National Education Association, 156
National Employment Service (New Zealand), 166
National Guard, 51
National Industrial Recovery Act (NIRA), 270
National Insurance Act, 115
nationalization, 60, 131, 148, 276
National Labor Relations Act, 275
National Labor Union, 50
National party (New Zealand), 170–172, 174
National People's Congress (NPC), 230

National People's Congress Standing Committee (NPCSC), 230
National Socialism, 118–119
neoliberalism, 12, 122–131, 145, 151–153, 161–175, 188, 197, 199–200, 206, 221, 233–234, 244, 255, 257–258, 261
New Deal, 54, 108, 120–121, 141–142, 147, 264–265, 275, 280
"New Democrats," 147, 149
New Economic Policy (NEP), 62, 65
New England, 46
Newfoundland, 187–206
Newfoundland and Labrador Employers' Council (NLEC), 196
Newfoundland and Labrador Medical Association (NLMA), 204–206
Newfoundland and Labrador Nurses Union (NLNU), 203, 206
Newfoundland and Labrador Teachers Association (NLTA), 199
Newfoundland Association of Public and Private Employees (NAPE), 199–201, 203
Newfoundland Labrador Federation of Labour (NLFL), 201–202
New Haven, 49
New Labor History, 11, 84
"New Labour," 125
New Left, 3, 151–152
New Right, 142, 163, 169–174
New York, 45, 48, 100, 107
New York State Board of Charities, 47
New York Stock Exchange, 52, 117, 266
New York Times, 146
New York World, 50
New Zealand, 54, 115, 161–175
New Zealand Business Roundtable (NZBR), 169–170, 172–173
Nikolaev, L. V., 72
Nine-Hour League, 21
Nissan, 277
Nixon, Richard, 144–145, 147, 276
nonunion workers, 53
North Korea, 157
Norway, 121, 123, 125–127

Obama, Barack, 124, 155, 264–265, 274, 276, 278–280
Occupy Wall Street, 1, 12, 244, 283
O'Connor, James, 142
Office of Alien Property Custodian, 276
oil production, 53, 127–128, 129, 142, 144–145, 187–206
O'Leary, Arthur, 38

Oliver, Bill, 167–168
Oliver, Joseph (mayor), 30–31
Olney, Richard (attorney general), 51, 105–106
Olssen, Erik, 164
Ontario Workman, 21
Organization for Economic Co-operation and Development (OECD), 174, 271
Organization of the Petroleum Exporting Countries (OPEC), 150
O'Shea, Patrick, 205
Ottoman Empire, 87

Palladium of Labor, 21
Palme, Joakim, 126
Palmer, Geoffrey, 171
Panhellenic Socialist Movement (PASOK), 127
Panitch, Leo, 9
Papandreou, Andreas, 248
Pasok, 243, 249
passportization, 60, 64–65
Pay Advisory Committee, 151
peasantry: in Latin America, 115, 129–130; under colonial governments, 92; in the USSR, 62–68, 71, 73–75
Peffer, William A., 51
Penn Central, 276
pensions: Civil War pensions, 52; national pension plans, 108, 113–115, 120, 128, 132, 174; union pensions, 277–279
People's Commissariat of Internal Affairs (NKVD), 72–75
Perlman, Selig, 11
Peterson, William, 4
Peter the Great, 64
Phelan, J. E., 103
Philadelphia, 45–46
Piddinton, A. B., 165
Pillsbury, George, 104
Pinochet, Augusto, 128
Pitsula, James, 23
Pittsburgh, 51, 55
Piven, Frances, 233
Placentia Bay, 195
Politburo, 62, 75–76
Politics in Hard Times, 141–142
Politics of Labor, The, 25
Popular Front, 54, 116, 118–120, 128, 133
Populist party, 106, 108
Porto Alegre, 245, 250, 252–255, 257, 259
Portugal, 264
POSCO, 150

Prebble, Richard, 169–170
Preobrazhensky, Evgeny, 61
priests, 72, 74
primitive accumulation, 61
privatization, 127–130, 153, 162, 174, 201, 245, 255–257
Progressive-Conservatives, 199–201
Progressive Era, 99–108
Provincial Publicity Campaign on Unemployment, 33
public employment, 50, 55, 125, 127–128, 145–146, 151, 156–157, 188, 199–201, 227, 248, 283
public sector unions, 127, 142, 156–157, 188, 199–203, 205–206, 213, 227, 256, 283
Pullman, George, 105
Pullman Palace Car Company, 99, 105
Pullman Strike, 51, 53, 99, 105–106

Quigley, Derek, 174

Radical Party (Chile), 120
Radical Socialist party, 119
railroads: construction of, 46, 85, 93, 100–101, 189; and the export market, 52, 104; government control of, 276; railroad engineers, 101–103; railroad firemen, 101–102, 104–105, 108
Rankin, Christine, 172
Reagan, Ronald, 6, 123, 142, 152–153
real estate, 142, 153–154, 253, 259–260, 269
"real wages," 65–66, 76, 273
Reconstruction (U.S.), 88–90, 99–100
red-baiting, 35, 37–38
Reed, Jack, 154
Reed, Thomas, 100
Re-establishment and Employment Act (Australia), 166
regulation, 6, 108, 143, 151
Reich, Michael, 9
Reichstag, 118
Reinhart, Carmen M., 263–264
Republican Party: during the Cold War, 142, 144–145, 150; in the Gilded Age, 52, 99, 106–108; and the Great Recession, 155, 264–265, 275; and the New Deal, 264
Reserve Bank Act (New Zealand), 162
Restore the American Dream Act, 274
retail work, 66, 153, 156–157, 190–191, 194–196, 282
Revue des Deux Mondes, 90
Reynolds, Dave, 200
Rhineland, 48

Richardson, Ruth, 170–172
Richmond, 50
Richmond League, 50
Rideout, Tom, 202
"right opposition" (USSR), 63, 71–72, 74
riots: in the USSR, 63, 67
Ritter, Rob, 205
Riutin, M. N., 71
"Riutin Group," 71
Roderick, David, 151
Rodgers, Daniel, 54
"Rogernomics," 169, 171, 174
Rogoff, Kenneth S., 263–264
Rolls-Royce, 148
Romania, 75
Roosevelt, Franklin D., 264, 267, 269–270, 273–274
Roosevelt, Theodore, 52–53
Roper, Brian, 170
Rosenthal, Anton, 102
Rothschilds, 88
Roussel Law, 114
Rowse, Tim, 167
Royal Commission on Social Policy, 171
Royal Commission on the Relations of Labor and Capital, 25
Ruskin, John, 27
Russian Civil War, 62
Russian Revolution (1905), 70
Russian Revolution (1917), 70
Russo-Japanese War, 52
Rykov, A. I., 71

Sachs, Jeffrey, 130
Sahin, Aysegul, 272
Salsjöbaden, 121
Samuelson, Paul, 10, 143
Sarkozy, Nicholas, 128
Saturn, 278
Sawer, Marian, 167
Scandinavia, 121–122, 126–127, 133, 157
Schultze, Charles, 150–151
Scott, Robert, 280
Scullin, James, 117
seasonal work, 47, 93–94
Second International, 118
Securities and Exchange Commission, 266
Semple, Bob, 167
seniority principle, 55
seredniaki, 62
Service Employees International Union (SEIU), 156
service sector work, 55, 151, 187, 194–197

sharecropping, 83–84, 88, 92
Shelton, William (mayor), 49
Shipley, Jenny, 170–171, 173
show trials, 73
Sirico, Rev. Robert, 172–173
Siriwardana, Mahinda, 117
Skocpol, Theda, 11
slavery: in the American South, 45, 85, 94; and the Atlantic world, 87–94
slave trade, 83–88
slow-downs, 67
Smith, Adam, 85
Smith, Floyd, 146
Smith, Goldwin, 27
Smith, Jim, 152
Smoot-Hawley Tariff Act, 282
Social Democratic Party: in Canada, 32; in Germany, 113–114, 118–119; in Norway, 126; in Sweden, 121
social insurance, 113–116, 121, 123, 128, 130, 132
Socialist International, 52
Socialist Labour party (Norway), 125
Socialist party (Canada), 27, 29
Socialist party (France), 119
Socialist party (U.S.), 106–108
Socialist Revolutionaries, 70
Social Problems Conferences, 27
Social Security (U.S.), 124, 273
Social Security Act (New Zealand), 167
Something Happened, 142
South Dakota, 100, 272
South Korea, 149–150
Soviet Constitution, 74–75
Spain, 54, 119, 133, 264
Spanish Civil War, 119, 133
Spanish Empire, 52
special settlements (USSR), 63, 75
speedups, 222, 269
"stagflation," 122
Stalin, Joseph: and economic development, 5, 62–63; and political opposition, 71–76
Standard Oil, 53
State Department (U.S.), 143
state education, 60, 126, 132, 146
state government, 49–50, 120, 155–157, 277–278
state-owned enterprise (SOE), 215–218, 226–227
Steel Tripartite Advisory Committee (STAC), 151
Steel Workers Organizing Committee (SWOC), 55

Stern, Andrew, 156
Stewart, Bryce, 36
stimulus (economic), 55, 149, 264, 273–274
St. John's, 189–190, 194, 196–197, 205–206
Stone, Joe A., 277
St. Paul Chamber of Commerce, 104
Strategic Partnership Initiative (SPI), 199
Strategy for Labor, 248
strikes: in Australia, 116; in Canada, 21, 202–203, 205; in China, 213, 223–224, 230–232; in France, 120, 128; in Great Britain, 124–125, 254; and replacement workers, 104; in the USSR, 67, 69–70; in the United States, 45–46, 49, 51–54, 91, 99, 103–106, 275. *See also* Pullman Strike; work stoppages
subsidization, 56, 100, 145, 151–152, 162, 190
Sue, Eugene, 101
suffragettes, 249
Supreme Court (U.S.), 60
Sweden: fiscal policy, 121; and social insurance, 121; and unemployment, 54
Swedish Employers' Association (SAF), 121
Sweeney, John, 156
Synaspismos, 245, 247
Syriza, 243–248, 260–261

Taiwan, 149
Tarentum, Pennsylvania, 55
tariff barriers, 52, 100–101, 143–144, 165, 282
Taylorism, 215–216
temporary workers, 215–218, 222–224
ten-hour day, 46
Te Roopu Rawakore, 171
textile industry, 49, 52, 66, 69, 85
Thatcher, Margaret, 6, 124, 126, 250, 254, 256
Thelen, Kathleen, 175
Third Period thesis, 116, 118. *See also* Comintern
Thompson, E. P., 11
Thompson, Phillips, 25
Tillman, Ben, 108
tobacco plantations, 87
Tomskii, M. P., 71
Toronto District Labor Council, 34, 38
Toronto Great War Veterans' Association, 35
Toronto Labour Council, 27
Toronto Star, 31
Toronto Trades and Labour Council, 32, 38
Towards a Code of Social and Family Responsibility, 173

Toyota, 277–278
Trade Act (1974), 147
trade deficit, 143–144, 149, 153–155, 157, 160
Trades and Labor Assembly (Denver), 49
Trades and Labor Congress of Canada, 21, 28
Trades and Labour Congress (Canada), 120
Trades Industrial Toy Association, 32
Trades' Union, 45
Trades Union Congress (TUC), 124
transnational labor history, 83
Treasury (U.S.), 51–52, 151, 275–277
Trotsky, Leon, 63, 71, 73
Trotskyists, 55, 71–74
Troubled Asset Relief Program (TARP), 276, 278, 280
Tsipras, Alexis, 248
Tsoukalas, Dimitris, 243
Tweed, "Boss" William M., 49

U.K. Uncut, 256
underemployment, 25–26, 35–36, 55
"undeserving poor," 21, 37, 48, 113
unemployment: and economic growth, 142–143, 187–206; insurance against, 34, 54–55, 113, 117, 120, 155, 264; non-accelerating inflation rate of unemployment (NAIRU) 122; and protests, 24–27, 29–30, 35–37, 50, 127–128, 171–172; and rural populations, 20; and seasonal work, 47; and work relief, 28–29, 31–32, 48, 50, 55, 162–164, 167, 273–274; in Toronto, 21–38
Unidad Popular, 128
Union League, 49–50
Union of Soviet Socialist Republics (USSR): economic development of, 5, 60–68, 75–76, 145; foreign policy, 116, 255; newspapers in the USSR, 67, 73–74; political opposition, 71–74
Union Pacific, 104
United Australia, 117
United Automobile Workers of America (UAW), 147, 278
United Food and Commercial Workers, 156
United Electrical Workers (UEW), 55–56
United Nations (U.N.), 56
United Nations Charter, 166
United Nations Economic and Social Council, 166
United Steel Workers of America (USWA), 146, 151–152
Upton, Simon, 170–171

urbanization, 60, 64, 67, 70–71, 73–76, 94, 162, 217–220
U.S. Steel, 53, 151–152

vagabondage, 64, 76
vagrancy, 22–24, 29, 31–32, 93, 167
van der Linden, Marcel, 84
Victoria, Queen, 164
Volcker, Paul, 144
Volkswagen, 221
von Bismarck, Otto, 113–114
Vyshinskii, A. Ia., 73

wage labor: in a capitalist society, 61; in the creation of a proletariat, 20, 94–95; and industrialization, 46–47, 64, 145–146. *See also* globalization
Wahl, Abjørn, 126
Walker, Scott, 157
Wallace, George, 149
Wallerstein, Immanuel, 10
Wall Street, 117. *See also* New York Stock Exchange
Wall Street Journal, 150
Wal-Mart, 282
Walsh, Pat, 170
wartime production, 33–35
Webb, Paddy, 167
Weber, Max, 20
welfare state, 115, 121, 126–127, 132, 163–166, 171–174
Welfare State Settlement (New Zealand), 166
Wellington, 173
Wellington Unemployed Workers Union, 171
West Africa, 90, 94
West Indies, 87
Westinghouse, 53, 55–56
What Congress Has Done, 106
Wheelock, David E., 266
White, Richard, 164
white-collar work, 28, 75, 85, 219
White House Council for Auto Communities and Workers, 279
Wilhelm, John, 156
Williams, Danny, 187, 199–205
Wilson, Harold, 251
Wilson, Thomas, 23
Wilson, Woodrow, 276
Wisconsin, 49, 157, 172
women: and gendered labor markets, 187–188, 194–195, 200, 267; maternal pensions 114, 120–122, 174; as widows, 48; work opportunities in industry, 28, 47, 49, 65

Wood, Fernando (mayor), 48
Workers' Opposition, 62–63
Workers Party of Canada, 37
Works Progress Administration (WPA), 55, 273
work stoppages, 65, 67
work-welfare, 162–163, 172–173
World Bank, 122, 128
World Trade Organization (WTO), 216
World War I, 33–34, 88, 114, 118, 270
World War II, 120, 145, 165, 263, 266, 270, 276, 280

Zhao, Mengxin, 282
Zinoviev, G. E., 71, 73
Zinovievites, 72

THE WORKING CLASS
IN AMERICAN HISTORY

Worker City, Company Town: Iron and Cotton-Worker Protest in Troy
    and Cohoes, New York, 1855–84   *Daniel J. Walkowitz*
Life, Work, and Rebellion in the Coal Fields: The Southern West Virginia Miners,
    1880–1922   *David Alan Corbin*
Women and American Socialism, 1870–1920   *Mari Jo Buhle*
Lives of Their Own: Blacks, Italians, and Poles in Pittsburgh, 1900–1960   *John Bodnar,
    Roger Simon, and Michael P. Weber*
Working-Class America: Essays on Labor, Community, and American Society
    Edited by Michael H. Frisch and Daniel J. Walkowitz
Eugene V. Debs: Citizen and Socialist   *Nick Salvatore*
American Labor and Immigration History, 1877–1920s:
    Recent European Research   *Edited by Dirk Hoerder*
Workingmen's Democracy: The Knights of Labor and American Politics   *Leon Fink*
The Electrical Workers: A History of Labor at General Electric and Westinghouse,
    1923–60   *Ronald W. Schatz*
The Mechanics of Baltimore: Workers and Politics in the Age of Revolution,
    1763–1812   *Charles G. Steffen*
The Practice of Solidarity: American Hat Finishers in the Nineteenth Century
    David Bensman
The Labor History Reader   *Edited by Daniel J. Leab*
Solidarity and Fragmentation: Working People and Class Consciousness
    in Detroit, 1875–1900   *Richard Oestreicher*
Counter Cultures: Saleswomen, Managers, and Customers
    in American Department Stores, 1890–1940   *Susan Porter Benson*
The New England Working Class and the New Labor History   *Edited by
    Herbert G. Gutman and Donald H. Bell*
Labor Leaders in America   *Edited by Melvyn Dubofsky and Warren Van Tine*
Barons of Labor: The San Francisco Building Trades and Union Power
    in the Progressive Era   *Michael Kazin*
Gender at Work: The Dynamics of Job Segregation by Sex during World War II
    Ruth Milkman
Once a Cigar Maker: Men, Women, and Work Culture in American Cigar Factories,
    1900–1919   *Patricia A. Cooper*
A Generation of Boomers: The Pattern of Railroad Labor Conflict
    in Nineteenth-Century America   *Shelton Stromquist*
Work and Community in the Jungle: Chicago's Packinghouse Workers, 1894–1922
    James R. Barrett
Workers, Managers, and Welfare Capitalism: The Shoeworkers and Tanners
    of Endicott Johnson, 1890–1950   *Gerald Zahavi*
Men, Women, and Work: Class, Gender, and Protest in the New England
    Shoe Industry, 1780–1910   *Mary Blewett*

Workers on the Waterfront: Seamen, Longshoremen, and Unionism
   in the 1930s   *Bruce Nelson*
German Workers in Chicago: A Documentary History of Working-Class Culture
   from 1850 to World War I   *Edited by Hartmut Keil and John B. Jentz*
On the Line: Essays in the History of Auto Work   *Edited by Nelson Lichtenstein
   and Stephen Meyer III*
Labor's Flaming Youth: Telephone Operators and Worker Militancy, 1878–1923
   Stephen H. Norwood
Another Civil War: Labor, Capital, and the State in the Anthracite Regions
   of Pennsylvania, 1840–68   *Grace Palladino*
Coal, Class, and Color: Blacks in Southern West Virginia, 1915–32   *Joe William Trotter Jr.*
For Democracy, Workers, and God: Labor Song-Poems and Labor Protest,
   1865–95   *Clark D. Halker*
Dishing It Out: Waitresses and Their Unions in the Twentieth Century
   Dorothy Sue Cobble
The Spirit of 1848: German Immigrants, Labor Conflict, and the Coming
   of the Civil War   *Bruce Levine*
Working Women of Collar City: Gender, Class, and Community in Troy,
   New York, 1864–86   *Carole Turbin*
Southern Labor and Black Civil Rights: Organizing Memphis Workers   *Michael K. Honey*
Radicals of the Worst Sort: Laboring Women in Lawrence, Massachusetts,
   1860–1912   *Ardis Cameron*
Producers, Proletarians, and Politicians: Workers and Party Politics in Evansville
   and New Albany, Indiana, 1850–87   *Lawrence M. Lipin*
The New Left and Labor in the 1960s   *Peter B. Levy*
The Making of Western Labor Radicalism: Denver's Organized Workers,
   1878–1905   *David Brundage*
In Search of the Working Class: Essays in American Labor History
   and Political Culture   *Leon Fink*
Lawyers against Labor: From Individual Rights to Corporate Liberalism   *Daniel R. Ernst*
"We Are All Leaders": The Alternative Unionism of the Early 1930s   *Edited by
   Staughton Lynd*
The Female Economy: The Millinery and Dressmaking Trades, 1860–1930
   Wendy Gamber
"Negro and White, Unite and Fight!": A Social History of Industrial Unionism in
   Meatpacking, 1930–90   *Roger Horowitz*
Power at Odds: The 1922 National Railroad Shopmen's Strike   *Colin J. Davis*
The Common Ground of Womanhood: Class, Gender, and Working Girls' Clubs,
   1884–1928   *Priscilla Murolo*
Marching Together: Women of the Brotherhood of Sleeping Car Porters
   Melinda Chateauvert
Down on the Killing Floor: Black and White Workers in Chicago's Packinghouses,
   1904–54   *Rick Halpern*
Labor and Urban Politics: Class Conflict and the Origins of Modern Liberalism
   in Chicago, 1864–97   *Richard Schneirov*

All That Glitters: Class, Conflict, and Community in Cripple Creek   *Elizabeth Jameson*
Waterfront Workers: New Perspectives on Race and Class   *Edited by Calvin Winslow*
Labor Histories: Class, Politics, and the Working-Class Experience   *Edited by
    Eric Arnesen, Julie Greene, and Bruce Laurie*
The Pullman Strike and the Crisis of the 1890s: Essays on Labor and Politics   *Edited by
    Richard Schneirov, Shelton Stromquist, and Nick Salvatore*
AlabamaNorth: African-American Migrants, Community, and Working-Class Activism
    in Cleveland, 1914–45   *Kimberley L. Phillips*
Imagining Internationalism in American and British Labor, 1939–49   *Victor Silverman*
William Z. Foster and the Tragedy of American Radicalism   *James R. Barrett*
Colliers across the Sea: A Comparative Study of Class Formation in Scotland
    and the American Midwest, 1830–1924   *John H. M. Laslett*
"Rights, Not Roses": Unions and the Rise of Working-Class Feminism, 1945–80
    Dennis A. Deslippe
Testing the New Deal: The General Textile Strike of 1934 in the American South
    Janet Irons
Hard Work: The Making of Labor History   *Melvyn Dubofsky*
Southern Workers and the Search for Community: Spartanburg County,
    South Carolina   *G. C. Waldrep III*
We Shall Be All: A History of the Industrial Workers of the World (abridged
    edition)   *Melvyn Dubofsky, ed. Joseph A. McCartin*
Race, Class, and Power in the Alabama Coalfields, 1908–21   *Brian Kelly*
Duquesne and the Rise of Steel Unionism   *James D. Rose*
Anaconda: Labor, Community, and Culture in Montana's Smelter City   *Laurie Mercier*
Bridgeport's Socialist New Deal, 1915–36   *Cecelia Bucki*
Indispensable Outcasts: Hobo Workers and Community in the American Midwest,
    1880–1930   *Frank Tobias Higbie*
After the Strike: A Century of Labor Struggle at Pullman   *Susan Eleanor Hirsch*
Corruption and Reform in the Teamsters Union   *David Witwer*
Waterfront Revolts: New York and London Dockworkers, 1946–61   *Colin J. Davis*
Black Workers' Struggle for Equality in Birmingham   *Horace Huntley
    and David Montgomery*
The Tribe of Black Ulysses: African American Men in the Industrial South
    William P. Jones
City of Clerks: Office and Sales Workers in Philadelphia, 1870–1920   *Jerome P. Bjelopera*
Reinventing "The People": The Progressive Movement, the Class Problem,
    and the Origins of Modern Liberalism   *Shelton Stromquist*
Radical Unionism in the Midwest, 1900–1950   *Rosemary Feurer*
Gendering Labor History   *Alice Kessler-Harris*
James P. Cannon and the Origins of the American Revolutionary Left, 1890–1928
    Bryan D. Palmer
Glass Towns: Industry, Labor, and Political Economy in Appalachia, 1890–1930s
    Ken Fones-Wolf
Workers and the Wild: Conservation, Consumerism, and Labor in Oregon,
    1910–30   *Lawrence M. Lipin*

Wobblies on the Waterfront: Interracial Unionism in Progressive-Era Philadelphia
   Peter Cole
Red Chicago: American Communism at Its Grassroots, 1928–35   *Randi Storch*
Labor's Cold War: Local Politics in a Global Context   *Edited by Shelton Stromquist*
Bessie Abramowitz Hillman and the Making of the Amalgamated Clothing Workers
   of America   *Karen Pastorello*
The Great Strikes of 1877   *Edited by David O. Stowell*
Union-Free America: Workers and Antiunion Culture   *Lawrence Richards*
Race against Liberalism: Black Workers and the UAW in Detroit
   David M. Lewis-Colman
Teachers and Reform: Chicago Public Education, 1929–70   *John F. Lyons*
Upheaval in the Quiet Zone: 1199/SEIU and the Politics of Healthcare Unionism
   Leon Fink and Brian Greenberg
Shadow of the Racketeer: Scandal in Organized Labor   *David Witwer*
Sweet Tyranny: Migrant Labor, Industrial Agriculture, and Imperial Politics
   Kathleen Mapes
Staley: The Fight for a New American Labor Movement   *Steven K. Ashby
   and C. J. Hawking*
On the Ground: Labor Struggles in the American Airline Industry   *Liesl Miller Orenic*
NAFTA and Labor in North America   *Norman Caulfield*
Making Capitalism Safe: Work Safety and Health Regulation in America,
   1880–1940   *Donald W. Rogers*
Good, Reliable, White Men: Railroad Brotherhoods, 1877–1917   *Paul Michel Taillon*
Spirit of Rebellion: Labor and Religion in the New Cotton South   *Jarod Roll*
The Labor Question in America: Economic Democracy in the Gilded Age
   Rosanne Currarino
Banded Together: Economic Democratization in the Brass Valley   *Jeremy Brecher*
The Gospel of the Working Class: Labor's Southern Prophets in New Deal America
   Erik Gellman and Jarod Roll
Guest Workers and Resistance to U.S. Corporate Despotism   *Immanuel Ness*
Gleanings of Freedom: Free and Slave Labor along the Mason-Dixon Line,
   1790–1860   *Max Grivno*
Chicago in the Age of Capital: Class, Politics, and Democracy during the Civil War
   and Reconstruction   *John B. Jentz and Richard Schneirov*
Child Care in Black and White: Working Parents and the History of Orphanages
   Jessie B. Ramey
The Haymarket Conspiracy: Transatlantic Anarchist Networks   *Timothy Messer-Kruse*
Detroit's Cold War: The Origins of Postwar Conservatism   *Colleen Doody*
A Renegade Union: Interracial Organizing and Labor Radicalism   *Lisa Phillips*
Palomino: Clinton Jencks and Mexican-American Unionism
   in the American Southwest   *James J. Lorence*
Latin American Migrations to the U.S. Heartland: Changing Cultural Landscapes
   in Middle America   *Edited by Linda Allegro and Andrew Grant Wood*
Man of Fire: Selected Writings   *Ernesto Galarza, ed. Armando Ibarra
   and Rodolfo D. Torres*

A Contest of Ideas: Capital, Politics, and Labor   *Nelson Lichtenstein*
Making the World Safe for Workers: Labor, the Left, and Wilsonian
    Internationalism   *Elizabeth McKillen*
The Rise of the Chicago Police Department: Class and Conflict, 1850–1894   *Sam Mitrani*
Workers in Hard Times: A Long View of Economic Crises   *Edited by Leon Fink,
    Joseph A. McCartin, and Joan Sangster*

The University of Illinois Press
is a founding member of the
Association of American University Presses.

University of Illinois Press
1325 South Oak Street
Champaign, IL 61820-6903
www.press.uillinois.edu